JOHN RUSKIN
AND VICTORIAN
ARCHITECTURE

———

MICHAEL W. BROOKS

RUTGERS UNIVERSITY PRESS

NEW BRUNSWICK AND LONDON

Library of Congress Cataloging-in-Publication Data

Brooks, Michael, 1936–
John Ruskin and Victorian architecture.
Includes bibliographical references and index.
1. Ruskin, John, 1819–1900—Contributions in architecture.   2. Architecture, Victorian—Great Britain.   3. Architecture—Great Britain.   I. Title.
NA967.5.V53B76   1987   720   86–15452
ISBN 0–8135–1205–0

British Cataloging-in-Publication Information Available.

John Ruskin and Victorian Architecture

For My Mother

Rose Smolin

CONTENTS

ILLUSTRATIONS

PREFACE

John Ruskin's *The Seven Lamps of Architecture* was published in 1849. The first volume of *The Stones of Venice* appeared in 1851, and the next two followed in 1853. No books on architecture, before or since, have commanded such immediate attention. They were widely reviewed, and, since many reviewers gave long summaries and generous quotations, they must have reached a far greater audience than sales figures alone would indicate. There were many who hoped that Ruskin's popularity would be as brief as it was unexpected. In 1854 a writer for the *Civil Engineer and Architect's Journal* assured his readers that "the tide is beginning to turn against Ruskin; his popularity is now ebbing away very fast."[1] In 1858 the *Building News* declared that "each year Mr. Ruskin has found himself with less real power, and with a stronger conviction on the part of the public that he is crotchety and unsound."[2] Twelve years later the *Architect* announced confidently that "the days of Ruskinism are ended."[3] Four years after that, however, on October 16, 1874, the *British Architect* acknowledged that Ruskin was "the Foster-father of one half of our younger architects."[4] Ruskin's influence became broader and perhaps more amorphous in the following decades, but it did not really diminish until the first years of the twentieth century. When Ruskin died in 1900, the architect John Brydon, occupying the chair at the regular fortnightly meeting of the Royal Institute of British Architects, hoped that "the Literature Committee of the Institute might prepare a paper on the influence of Ruskin in relation to architecture in this country—his great influence on architecture."[5]

My study of that influence is indebted to a great many people whom I cannot acknowledge by name. I owe an immense debt to librarians and archivists. I would especially like to thank those who have assisted me at the Avery Library of Columbia University, the Research Collections of the New York Public Library, the Library of Congress, and at the Library and the Drawings Collection of the Royal Institute of British Architects. James Dearden was extremely generous in making available the collection at the Ruskin Galleries, Bembridge School, Isle of Wight. The staff at the Fine Arts Library of the University of Pennsylvania has been unfailingly helpful over a period of several years.

Kristine Ottesen Garrigan and Douglas Hickman commented on Chapter Eleven. Jane Hughes assisted with the illustrations. Robin Ross of Morgan Wells Associates photographed the stained-glass windows at Saint Giles's church on very short notice.

Much of my research was done with the aid of a Summer Stipend from the National Endowment for the Humanities. I received a grant toward the expenses of preparing the manuscript from West Chester University. Three successive department chairmen—David McKenty, Joseph Browne, and Kostas Myrsiades—were patient and helpful.

Most of chapter 2 appeared in *Victorian Newsletter* and most of chapter 3 in *Prose Studies.* I am grateful for permission to reprint this material. Sir Ralph Millais gave permission to quote letters by John Everett Millais and previously unpublished writing by John Ruskin is reprinted here with the permission of the Ruskin Literary Trustees, c/o George Allen & Unwin.

Illustrations from the *Annales archéologiques,* the *Architect,* the *Architectural Magazine,* the *Building News,* the *Hobby Horse,* and the *Illustrated London News* are reprinted with permission from the Art, Prints, and Photographs Division of the New York Public Library, Astor, Lenox, and Tilden Foundations. Material from the *Builder* and the *British Architect* was made available by the photo-duplication department of the Library of Congress. The Avery Library of Columbia University made it possible to reproduce plates from *Examples of the Architecture of the Victorian Age* and *The National Academy of Design: Photographs of the New Building.*

I have tried to acknowledge my direct debts in footnotes, but many of the most important are indirect. I first studied Ruskin with Malcolm Ross in a graduate seminar at the University of Toronto. We discussed every aspect of Ruskin except his views on architecture, but the questions raised then have continued to reverberate in my mind. I would also like to thank three friends whose conversation has increased my understanding of Victorian buildings: Trina Vaux, Hugh McCauley, and Margot Gayle. I owe a similar debt to members of The Friends of Cast-Iron Architecture and the Delaware Valley chapter of the Society of Architectural Historians.

I am grateful to Kathryn Gohl for her care with the manuscript and to Leslie Mitchner for her crucial editorial enthusiasm.

My wife Lois shares my interest in both John Ruskin and Victorian architecture. She participated in this study from the beginning, sharing knowledge from her first career in English history and her second in construction management. She has tested my ideas, advised further research on dubious points, and insisted throughout on organization and clarity.

John Ruskin and Victorian Architecture

I

AN ARCHITECTURAL
EDUCATION

It was far from inevitable that John Ruskin would write on architecture. As a young man he sketched, analyzed the geological structure of the Alps, studied the theology of Hooker, read the poems of Wordsworth, and dreamed of becoming either a great poet or an eloquent clergyman or perhaps both simultaneously. Architecture was a secondary interest. If he cared about it, as indeed he did, it was because Sir Walter Scott had shown how poetic associations might cling to a crumbling ruin and because his drawing masters had taught him how a castle might bring a composition in watercolors to perfection. That Ruskin came to architecture from the outside was the source of some of his weaknesses, but many of his strengths. Had he begun his education by reading Vitruvius and drawing the five orders, he would never have served as a catalyst in an architectural revolution.

English architecture in the 1830s and 1840s suffered from a cultural lag. It was a step behind the rest of English culture. Ruskin's education cut him off from the Profession, as it was beginning to call itself, but ensured his kinship with the public. His training in literature kept him aware that a building is an act of expression, not merely a utilitarian artifact. His training in watercolor made him sensitive to qualities of color and texture which were undervalued in early Victorian churches and public buildings. The fact that Ruskin first experienced buildings as parts of sublime or picturesque scenes had a determining influence on his theories. His architectural education proceeded in fits and starts, but always in one direction: from a watercolorist's interest in architecture as a subordinate part of a landscape to his eventual advocacy of buildings that would capture the qualities of nature in the curve of their arches and the mass of their walls.

I

It is not easy to locate the first step in this process, but a convenient starting point is provided in that most beloved of all books of Ruskin's childhood, Maria Edgeworth's *Harry and Lucy*:

> "Now for the first sight of the castle," cried Lucy; "and there it is, look, Harry, with its towers and turrets, and spires, and pointed pinnacles. It is a Gothic castle, I know; I have seen a print like it in Britton's *Beauties of England*. Look out of my window, Harry, and you will see much better."
>
> While they slowly ascended the hill, they had leisure to examine the front of the castle, though it was now and then intercepted from their view by the long-extended arms of the trees.
>
> "I like that great deep dark archway between those two projecting towers," said Lucy. "So do I," said Harry.
>
> "I like it because of the light and shade," said Lucy, "and because it is like a picture; it is picturesque, is it not, mamma?" [1]

Two things strike us in this passage: the speakers are tourists and they have already begun to think in terms of the sublime and the picturesque.

It was in the late eighteenth and early nineteenth centuries that tourism first became a cultural experience for the middle classes. Tours—first to the Lake Country, then to Europe—were the well-merited reward that John James and Margaret Ruskin gave themselves after years of privation. There was nothing frivolous about these journeys. The Ruskins visited the Lake Country for its views much as we might today visit the Uffizi for its Botticellis. Tours were an essential part of young John's education, and he first took drawing lessons so that he could memorialize them properly. A typical result is shown in figure 1. A work of architecture is seen from a distance, its forms assimilated to those of the hillside. There is careful attention to the kind of broad masses of light and shade that Maria Edgeworth's Lucy admired, and there is even a deep, dark archway between the two projecting towers.

Much of Ruskin's introduction to the sublime and the picturesque came from William Wordsworth's *Guide through the District of the Lakes* (1823)

Fig. 1.   Dover Castle. John Ruskin, c. 1832. Pencil drawing, 7" × 10¼". The Ruskin Galleries, Bembridge School, Isle of Wight.

and from Samuel Prout's volumes of picturesque sketches of scenes in France, Flanders, and Italy.[2] Both Wordsworth and Prout offered important lessons to a young student of architecture.

Two types of buildings figure in Wordsworth's *Guide*—the cottages native to the Lake District and the villas that were being built as an ironic outcome of the region's new popularity. Both are evaluated by a single standard: Does the structure harmonize with its surrounding landscape? The cottages meet the test. Built of local stone, with mosses, ferns, and flowers growing from the rough surfaces of their slate roofs, they "remind the contemplative spectator of a production of Nature, and may (using a strong expression) rather be said to have grown than to have been erected."[3] The villas, by contrast, nearly always jar with their setting, and Wordsworth offers practical advice to the prospective builder—advice that Ruskin must have studied carefully.

First, setting should be carefully considered. A villa in the Lake District proper should always be set well back from the peak of a mountain, partly because no work of architecture can compete with the dramatic features of a landscape and partly because an exposed building prompts thoughts of cold and discomfort in a land where the winter weather is so harsh. In the hilly country on the edge of the district, on the other hand, where the features of nature are less commanding, a mansion can properly be made the principle feature of a view.

Second, the color of a building should always be keyed to the overall harmony of its surroundings. The predominant color of the district is a bluish gray derived from both the stones and the lichen that cover them. This is often modified by a red tinge added by the iron content of the soil. If a gentleman builds where the iron content is rich, he need only hew his stone from the nearest quarry and harmony will be assured. If the iron content is low, however, the landscape will suffer from what Wordsworth calls the chief defect of the area—an excessive prevalence of a bluish tint. In this case, the villa builder should choose a warm color capable of enlivening but not disturbing the countryside. White should be avoided, for its glare disturbs the repose of a landscape.

Finally, the prospective builder should learn the lessons taught by the cottages: it is possible to build in shapes that echo those of nature and to incorporate features—hospitable porches or chimneys with warm curls of smoke—that arouse pleasant associations in the distant spectator.

This distance is assumed in all of Wordsworth's comments. We never enter a building or even approach it. We are always standing well back, integrating architecture and nature in a single view. Wordsworth writes much of his *Guide* from a landscape artist's point of view, and this must have been impressive to a young boy who traveled with pencil and brushes in hand. Not surprisingly, Wordsworth's influence merges with that of Ruskin's instructors in watercolor.

Samuel Prout was not an instructor in a technical sense.[4] Unlike Charles Runciman, Copley Fielding, and J. D. Harding, he did not actually give Ruskin lessons. He was a friend of the family who admired and encouraged Ruskin's talent, and there was a period in Ruskin's late teens when his style was so close to Prout's that it could fairly be called imitative.

The other artists Ruskin admired emphasized nature. Prout sketched in cities and found architecture fascinating quite apart from any natural setting. He represents, therefore, a significant departure in the tradition of watercolor that nurtured Ruskin's imagination. "Before Prout," Ruskin said in the *Art Journal* in 1854, "to seek [the picturesque] in a city would have been deemed an extravagance, to raise it to the height of a cathedral, an heresy."[5]

Prout's techniques can be seen in his drawing of the Hôtel de Ville in Brussels (fig. 2). It is a town subject, one in which citizens of Brussels provide scale, visual interest, and a certain sense of clutter that contrasts with the more compact organization of the building. The time is vague, and no blatant touch of modernity is allowed to jar against the historical associations. The interest is in the architecture, yet Prout gives far less informa-

Fig. 2.   Hôtel de Ville,
Brussels. Samuel Prout.
Sketches by Samuel
Prout (1895), ed.
Charles Holme.

Fig. 3.   Tom Tower,
Christ Church, Oxford.
John Ruskin, 1838.
Graphite and white
gouache on blue-gray
paper, 312 mm. × 261
mm. Courtesy of the
Harvard University Art
Museums (the Fogg Art
Museum). Gift: Den-
man W. Ross.

tion about the details of the building than one might at first expect. He reproduces a sense of surface and decorative detail by a symbolic shorthand of little lines, squiggles, and dots. This conveys the impression of rich ornament and texture but very little specific information. This aspect of Prout's style was one that Ruskin was to outgrow; but for many years, as we can see by comparing the *Hôtel de Ville* with Ruskin's drawing of Tom Tower (fig. 3), the disciple was content to see with his master's eyes.

Prout contributed to Ruskin's architectural education in three ways. First, he encouraged Ruskin to relish the visible effects of time on surfaces. He "taught me generally to like ruggedness," Ruskin wrote in 1879, "and the conditions of joint in moulding, and the fitting of stones in walls which were most weatherworn, and like the grey dykes of a Cumberland hill-side (14.385).

Second, he encouraged his young admirer to revolt against all that was neat and tidy in Georgian architecture. In 1844 Ruskin wrote to Prout of the trim little eighteenth-century town of Saint Leonards:

> I never saw a place I thought so in every way unfit for human domicile, a white-washed brickfield, a symmetrical desolation, a Babylonish abortion of rectilinear solitude, the melancholy of the wilderness without its liberty. I have lived in many horrible places, in Leamington, Bath, and Cheltenham, not to speak of sundry weeks of headache and gaslight in London. But I think I could *not* live in St. Leonards. (38.338)

Finally, Prout showed Ruskin that he could escape the ugliness of modern cities not only in the countryside but in the older towns of Europe as well. In 1854 Ruskin described the impression that Rouen had made on Prout and, through him, on the young Ruskin as well:

> the city lay under its guarding hills, one labyrinth of delight, its grey and fretted towers, misty in their magnificence of height, letting the sky like blue enamel through the foiled spaces of their crowns of open work; the walls and gates of its countless churches wardered by saintly groups of solemn statuary, clasped about by wandering stems of sculptured leafage, and crowned by fretted niche and fairy pediment—meshed like gossamer with inextricable tracery. (12.311)

It is the delight in profusion—almost in confusion—that is most striking in this passage. Many early-nineteenth-century architects had difficulty responding to medieval ornament with this unmixed pleasure. The Greek Revival had taught them to admire "chastity" in decoration, and the fretted niches and wandering stems of Gothic foliage were so abundant as to seem unarchitectural. Ruskin was never troubled by such worries.

II

It was John Claudius Loudon who presided over the next stage in Ruskin's architectural education.[6] Loudon was very nearly the archetypal Victorian Scotsman: ambitious, inventive, opinionated, and preternaturally industrious. A landscape architect by training, he wrote pamphlets on topics ranging from furniture design to the layout of cemeteries. He compiled the large and influential Encyclopedia of Cottage, Farm and Villa Architecture (1833) and, in 1837 and 1838, published Ruskin's papers titled "The Poetry of Architecture" in his Architectural Magazine.

Contact with Loudon gave Ruskin a more practical acquaintance with architecture than he had experienced previously. In the Architectural Magazine he found utilitarian discussions on ventilation as well as articles on the new theories of A. W. N. Pugin. There were stimulating analyses of the National Gallery, the new Houses of Parliament, and the proposed Royal Exchange. It was through Loudon that Ruskin came to spend two fascinating hours comparing sketches and discussing Gothic architecture with Edward Buckton Lamb, then one of Loudon's protégés and later an extravagantly original Gothic Revival architect. His Villa in the Style of the Thirteenth Century illustrates the stage that the revival had reached in the 1830s (figs. 4 and 5).

Contact with Loudon's circle surely strengthened Ruskin's incipient antagonism toward the kind of architectural classicism that rested on the authority of Vitruvius. In the Architectural Magazine Ruskin found the Roman author not only denounced but actually found wanting in comparison with his own essays. In December 1838, Loudon said of Ruskin's contributions:

> These essays will afford little pleasure to the mere builder, or to the architect who has no principle of guidance but precedent; but for such readers they were never intended. They are addressed to the young and unprejudiced artist; and their great object is to induce him to think and to exercise his reason. The great bane of modern architecture is the tendency of all architects to be ruled by precedent.[7]

Loudon also reinforced Ruskin's tendency to value architecture as an embodiment of human emotion. Loudon believed that an owner's personality—his cheerfulness or his melancholy as the case might be—should find expression in his villa. When we find Ruskin praising a simple building because it expresses humility and recommending one window design for an imaginative man but a quite different one for a rational man, we know that he is under Loudon's spell.

Fig. 4. Villa in the style of the thirteenth century. E. B. Lamb. Architectural Magazine, *1835.*

Fig. 5. Villa in the style of the thirteenth century (interior). E. B. Lamb. Architectural Magazine, *1835.*

Nevertheless, the reader who studies Ruskin's papers in their original context will be struck by the degree to which Ruskin differs from both Loudon and the other contributors. The most obvious difference is that they are fascinated by practical matters, while Ruskin entirely neglects them. We would not expect papers titled "The Poetry of Architecture" to overlap extensively with an article titled "The Corrugated Cast-Iron Roof of the Coal Depot of the London Gas-Works, Vauxhall," but there ought to be some shared assumptions about the relation between the utilitarian functions of a building and its appearance. But Ruskin consistently discusses a building as something to be seen rather than to be used.

Another significant contrast between Ruskin and the other contributors is that they have significantly different approaches to the picturesque. When one of Loudon's writers asserted that the much-despised Ducal Palace in Venice could not be so absurd as most architects supposed because it had proven so popular with painters, another promptly replied: "'That it has no little fascination for painters,' is no proof of its fine architectural character. That proves either too much or too little; since the same line of argument would establish, that every crazy tottering old cottage or gable, in short, anything that is picturesque in the eye of a painter, is really a fine piece of architecture."[8] Ruskin's approach is quite obviously the painter's, and both Wordsworth and Prout had taught him to admire crazy, tottering old cottages.

Finally, Ruskin dissents from Loudon's treatment of architectural style. The reader of the *Encyclopedia* found a clear and necessary distinction between the universal and inherent qualities of architectural style and the historical beauties of particular styles. *Style* includes such qualities as symmetry, unity, and proportion. *The styles* include the Greek, the Roman, the Byzantine, and so forth. When Loudon is discussing basic matters of aesthetics, he seems to downplay the historic styles in favor of essential qualities. When he turns to questions of villa building, however, this principled attitude is replaced by a canny and quite open opportunism. Style sells: "thousands of spectators in Europe and America . . . have some crude ideas of what is Grecian and what is Gothic, while comparatively few understand what constitutes a whole in mere combinations of form."[9] In the *Encyclopedia*, therefore, it is possible to find plans for villas in the Grecian style, the Gothic style, the Old English manner, the Italian style, the Anglo-Italian style, the Old Scotch style, the Scotch Baronial, the Castellated, the Monastic Gothic, the Elizabethan, the Swiss, the German-Swiss, the Italian Gothic, the Indian Gothic, and many others.

All of this implies a quite extraordinary pandering to the client, and Ruskin parodies it ruthlessly:

[The villa architect] is requested, perhaps, by a man of great wealth, nay, of established taste in some points, to make a design for a villa in a lovely situation. The future proprietor carries him upstairs to his study, to give him what he calls his "ideas and materials," and in all probability, begins somewhat thus:— "This, sir, is a slight note: I made it on the spot: approach to Villa Reale, near Pozzuoli. Dancing nymphs, you perceive, sir; elegant, graceful. Then, sir, this is a sketch, made by an American friend of mine: Whee-shaw-Kantamaraw's wigwam, King of the—Cannibal Islands, I think he said, sir. Log, you observe; scalps, and boa constrictor skins: curious. Something like this, sir, would look neat, I think, for the front door; don't you? Then, the lower windows, I've not quite decided upon; but what would you say to Egyptian, with hieroglyphics, sir; storks and coffins, and appropriate mouldings above: I brought some from Fountains Abbey the other day. Look here, sir; angels' heads putting their tongues out, rolled up in cabbage leaves, with a dragon on each side riding on a broomstick, and the devil looking on from the mouth of an alligator, sir. Odd, I think; interesting. (1.129)

In some of his most stimulating papers for the *Architectural Magazine,* Ruskin used his understanding of the picturesque to chasten the excesses brought on by Loudon's. Ruskin's ideal, like Wordsworth's, is the Westmorland cottage:

There is no gay colour or neatness about it; no green shutters or other abomination: all is calm and quiet, and severe, as the mind of a philosopher, and, withal, a little sombre. It is evidently old, and has stood many trials in its day; and the snow, and the tempest, and the torrent have all spared it, and left it in its peace, with its grey head unbowed, and its early strength unbroken, even though the spirit of decay seems creeping, like the moss and the lichen, through the darkness of its crannies. The venerable and slightly melancholy character is the very soul of all its beauty. (1.48–49)

This harmony of nature, human feeling, and building form is lost as soon as socially ambitious property owners create "staring, square-windowed, flat-roofed gentlemen's seats, of the lathe and plaster, mock-magnificent Regent's park description rising on the woody promontories of Derwent water" (1.6).

The problem, therefore, was to establish principles that would promote harmony between architecture and landscape. Ruskin's solution was to define the color harmony of the regions of England and then to settle on the manner of architecture appropriate to each. Thus amid the low hills and agricultural lands of southern England, called the simple blue country because the eye sees bluish distances from even the slightest elevation, everything is active, prosperous, and useful. Bright colors, plain brick, and an all-pervading neatness are acceptable in a scene where there is no obscurity, no poetry, no nonsense. In the picturesque blue country, on the other hand, lying at the foot of high hill ranges, we ask for something more, and, because the spirit of this landscape seems to Ruskin to be essentially Greek, he will accept Greek and Roman villas. Greater intricacy is desired in the woody or green country, and Ruskin recommends the complexity of Gothic and Elizabethan villas. He is still far from his late hope for a single, universal style, but he has found in the color harmony of landscape a prin-ciple that chastens Loudon's unlimited eclecticism.

Ruskin also comments on smaller problems of architectural design. He devotes an entire paper, for example, to chimneys. Here again he is op-posed to Loudon, who favored picturesquely irregular outlines with large chimneys for the suburban villas (fig. 6) in his *Encyclopedia*. Ruskin takes the opposite tack. He appreciates the fact that chimneys can give variety to a roofline (his example is Coniston Hall, near Brantwood), but his gen-eral principle, the same one he later invoked to oppose decoration on rail-way sheds, is that utilitarian structures should be left unadorned. "We have no scruple in saying that the man who could desecrate the Gothic trefoil into an ornament for a chimney has not the slightest feeling, and never will have any, of its beauty or its use; he was never born to be an architect, and never will be one" (1.56). He illustrated his own preference with sketches of modest cottage chimneys (fig. 7).

In June 1838 Ruskin announced his intention to offer "a series of essays on the habitations of the most distinguished men of Europe, showing how the alterations which they directed, and the expression which they be-stowed, corresponded with the turn of their emotions, and leading intel-lectual faculties" (1.78). This was very much a Loudonesque enterprise. The immediate occasion was a projected visit to Sir Walter Scott's Ab-botsford. The visit was made, but the series was never begun. This was partly because the *Architectural Magazine* ceased publication with its Janu-ary 1839 issue, but also because, as a letter to Loudon makes clear, Ruskin was deeply disturbed by what he found.

He had gone to Abbotsford expecting the physical embodiment of the imagination expressed in the Waverly novels. Instead, he found something dismaying like Sir Horace Walpole's Strawberry Hill. An Italian fountain was attached to a baronial gateway. The wooden door from the old Tolbooth of Edinburgh appeared in conjunction with a classical architrave. An arch from nearby Melrose Abbey was copied in plaster and made to enclose a fireplace. "This was, to me, the finishing touch," Ruskin wrote Loudon, "for it proved to me at once what without such proof not all the world could have convinced me of, that Scott, notwithstanding all his nonsense about moonlight at Melrose, had *not* the slightest feeling of the real beauty and application of Gothic architecture" (36.17). Scott's home was rich in what might loosely be termed the poetry of architecture, but Ruskin was

Fig. 6. Cottage dwellings in various styles. Encyclopedia of Cottage, Farm, and Villa Architecture (1836).

Fig. 7.   Cottage chimneys. John Ruskin. Architectural Magazine, *1838.*

beginning to want the real thing. He was becoming suspicious of those who loved Gothic merely because it was old, dark, and picturesque.

III

At this point Ruskin was on the verge of a new stage in his understanding of architecture. He was rejecting the atmospherics of Gothic and was ready to investigate the laws that underlay the real thing. That inquiry, however, was postponed for several years. The *Architectural Magazine* ceased publication. Ruskin had his degree to finish, and then the defense of Turner engrossed his attention. He did not neglect architecture. In 1839, encouraged by his mentor William Buckland, he became one of the first members of the Oxford Architectural and Historical Society. He did measured architectural drawings with his Oxford friends. In 1844, as we shall see in chapter 3, he helped decorate one of the first ecclesiologically correct Gothic Revival churches in London. The bulk of his attention, however, was inevitably devoted to the first two volumes of *Modern Painters.* Indeed, the next major step in his architectural education came when he was traveling on the Continent, gathering material for its second volume.

In 1845 Ruskin traveled without his parents, but they required frequent letters home. Since we have Ruskin's journals for his 1840 journey, we are in an excellent position to judge the advance in his thinking.

In 1840 Ruskin had journeyed in search of the picturesque: "Another turn in the hillside brought us in view of Le Puy, the most striking feature of the town being the rock of St. Michael, almost a pillar of basalt crowned by an aerial church. The town a little too white and red in effect but well grouped."[10] Clearly this is the point of view of a watercolor painter. In 1840 Ruskin's eye was constantly charmed by buildings that showed the effect of age and that formed an interesting composition with the land-scape. He liked architecture best when it was part of a hillside. In level Florence, on the other hand, there was "really not a single piece of this whole city thoroughly picturesque."[11] In Pozzuoli he found the temple of Serapis to be a "most picturesque piece of ruin."[12] The pleasures of Rome consisted of such things as an "architrave smashed at one side and built into a piece of Roman frieze, which moulders away the next instant into a porch of broken brickwork."[13]

In 1845 Ruskin's responses are transformed. He is constantly delighted by sights that he had earlier all but ignored. In 1840 he had found Lucca, nestled into its hillside, to be beautifully composed, but on a closer ap-proach he was repelled by the dirty and narrow streets and left after a day. In 1845, by contrast, he barely pulled himself away after a week. His comment on the Church of San Frediano shows the new attitude: "Such a church—so old—680 probably—Lombard—all glorious dark arches & columns—covered with holy frescoes—and gemmed gold pictures on blue grounds. I don't know when I shall get away, and all the church fronts charged with heavenly sculpture and inlaid with whole histories in marble."[14] Ruskin sounds like a man who has discovered a new universe, and there is a quality of greed in his descriptions. He tries to catalog each precious detail. Of San Michele he writes:

> It is white marble, *inlaid* with figures cut an inch deep in green porphyry, and framed with carved, rich, hollow, marble tracery. I have been up all over it and on the roof to examine it in detail. Such marvellous variety & invention in the ornaments, and strange character. Hunting is the principal subject—little Nimrods with short legs and long lances—blowing tremendous trumpets—and with dogs which appear running up and down the round arches like flies, heads uppermost—and game of all descriptions—boars chiefly, but stags, tapirs, griffins & dragons—and indescribably innumerable, all cut out in hard green porphyry, & inlaid in the marble.[15]

After Lucca, Ruskin no longer stands back, integrating landscape and building in a single view. Instead, he crowds in close, delighting in each

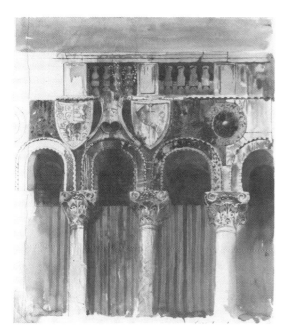

Fig. 8. *Study of the marble inlaying on the front of Casa Loredan, Venice. John Ruskin, 1845. Ashmolean Museum, Oxford.*

Fig. 9. *Below. Detail of Saint Sauveur, Caen. John Ruskin, 1848. Graphite and brown wash on cream paper, 473 mm. × 348 mm. Courtesy of the Harvard University Art Museums (the Fogg Art Museum). Gift: Samuel Sachs.*

new detail. And he no longer finds a special value in the signs of age. As he recalled years later in *Praeterita,* he encountered in Lucca an architecture constructed so expertly and of such incorruptible material that the effects of age were very slight.

The most dramatic sign of Ruskin's new attitude is in his drawing technique. Figure 8, showing the capitals, stilted arches, molding, and marble inlaying of the Casa Loredan in Venice, is an example of his new approach. Figure 9, showing a detail of Saint Sauveur, Caen, shows a slightly freer manner of drawing. In both there is a close representation of inlaid patterns, textural contrasts, and bits of carving. From this time forward Ruskin claimed documentary interest as the chief merit of his sketches. He wrote to his parents that he had learned to draw "very nearly like an architect" and assured them that his drawings were very different from what they were when he "thought merely of a certain kind of picturesqueness." [16]

IV

Most of the elements of Ruskin's architectural education reappear in *The Seven Lamps of Architecture* and *The Stones of Venice.* We can detect the influence of Loudon's associationism, for example, when Ruskin defines the nature of Gothic in terms of the mental characteristics of its creators. The sublime and the picturesque also reappear. The sublime modulates into "The Lamp of Power," losing much of its terror and obscurity along the way. The picturesque comes to be seen as a parasitical quality imposed by time and decay; it is not something that a strong-minded architect would seek for its own sake. But though Ruskin redefines the categories, he preserves his admiration for the visual qualities that they first taught him to admire. He sees echoes of that old standby of danger and awe—the beetle-browed cliff in the propped machicolations of the Palazzo Vecchio—and even as he denounces the picturesque in "The Lamp of Memory," he still expresses admiration for broken lines and vigorous oppositions of light and shadow, especially when they remind him, either by association or actual resemblance, of rocks, mountains, or stormy clouds.

Perhaps the most important legacy from Ruskin's early years was his method of studying buildings with pencil and brush. He always tended to think of architecture in pictorial terms. This is not the only possible approach, and Ruskin has never lacked critics. As an otherwise admiring review of *The Seven Lamps* put it in 1850:

It is quite curious to observe how his examples resolve themselves on examination into good studies for pictures; how he calls our attention only, or chiefly, to the outsides of buildings (except in the case of window tracery, where his profound and striking observations well deserve a separate analysis), how seldom he carries us within the temple, where the true divinity of Christian art has its abode. We could fancy ourselves before a study, by Prout, or a vision, by Turner, as we read.[17]

Architectural critics have been making some variant of this observation ever since.[18] They are right. There are ways of studying buildings that Ruskin scarcely even explores. There is very little of the diagram in his drawings—and the diagram is a form that makes it possible to understand structural systems and proportional relations with unparalleled clarity. There are disadvantages in Ruskin's approach, but there were virtues as well. Architecture was entering a period when it would be asked to provide a wider range of emotional resonance. It would have to express emotions, and it would be expected to have visible kinship with the forms of nature. Ruskin's instinct for the visible forms and emotional associations of architecture was profound. His knowledge of Gothic ornament was unrivaled in range and precision. His drawing enabled him to see new truths about light and shade, about mass and line, about architectural color. His apprenticeship to the picturesque taught him lessons that young architects had been given only sporadic opportunities to learn. No wonder they discovered his books with such enthusiasm.

II

JOHN RUSKIN,
C. R. COCKERELL,
AND
THE PROPORTIONS OF
ARCHITECTURE

"You must not when you leave this room," John Ruskin told an Edinburgh audience near the end of an assault on the classical architecture of the Athens of the North, "refer yourselves to some architect of established reputation, and ask him whether I am right or not. You might as well, had you lived in the sixteenth century, have asked a Roman Catholic archbishop his opinion of the first reformer" (12.71). It is a dramatic picture: the mob jeering in the town square, the embattled reformer tied to the post, the flames licking at his feet as he defiantly tosses his head and shouts truth to posterity. It is necessary to resist the appeal of Ruskin's language and give his opponents their day in court, for they help us define, if only by contrast, the contours of Ruskin's theories.

It is certain that Ruskin expected little sympathy from the architectural profession and deliberately sought converts among the unlearned. His contemptuous references to Vitruvius and Palladio resemble bearbaiting, and the anonymous writer in the *Builder* who signed himself Zeta was merely replying in kind when he expressed a wish to "transform John Ruskin into a Saint Bartholomew, by flaying him alive, without the slightest mercy or compunction."[1] The architects had reason to respond with anger and alarm. They had invested much in the classical tradition, and they had built enduring monuments. If we consider only public buildings under construction shortly before or shortly after the publication of *The Seven Lamps* and *The Stones of Venice,* it is imposible not to be impressed by Sir Robert Smirke's Ionic facade for the British Museum, George Basevi's giant Corinthian columns for the Fitzwilliam Museum, Sir William Tite's imposing portico for the Royal Exchange, the sophisticated archeology of C. R. Cockerell's Ionic order at the Ashmolean Museum, the vast peripteral colonnade of H. L. Elmes's Saint George's Hall in Liverpool, and the Corinthian portico of Cuthbert Broderick's Town Hall in Leeds. Churches were Gothic and gentlemen's mansions often had battlements, but when a building was to be proud, confident, and massive, a classical style was chosen. The new Houses of Parliament were an exception for historical and sentimental reasons. Otherwise, buildings with any pretense of public character—banks, hospitals, insurance office, clubhouses—were built in styles derived from Greece or Rome or from the Italian Renaissance.

For those pleased by this state of affairs, Ruskin's views required careful scrutiny. The best of Ruskin's opponents were considerably more scrupulous in criticizing his views than he had been in his attacks on the classical tradition, and many of their comments are still valuable reading. The most important critic, however, was one who as a matter of policy avoided public comment on his contemporaries.[2] That was Charles Robert Cockerell, one of England's leading architects, professor of architecture at the Royal Academy, and easily the most eloquent defender of the classical tradition. His six dry, scholarly lectures a year were being given (and published, first in the *Athenaeum*, then in the *Builder*) during the same period in which Ruskin was forming and publishing his own views. No other teacher so well represents the accumulated wisdom of early Victorian classicism, and a comparison of his views with Ruskin's shows the choice of doctrines that confronted students of architecture at midcentury.

I

The son of a successful surveyor and architect, Cockerell began his training in the office of Robert Smirke, where he arrived just in time to help prepare the drawings for the Doric portico of the Royal Opera House, Covent Garden. As the years passed, however, Cockerell's understanding of the classical went far beyond the narrow limits of the Greek Revival. It is not too much to say that his sense of the great tradition is much the same as Ruskin's highly flexible use of the word *Renaissance*: it includes the precedents of Greece and Rome, the authority of Vitruvius, the writing of Alberti, the great structures of Palladio, Wren, and Vanbrugh, the doctrines of Sir William Chambers, and the revival buildings of his own day.

Cockerell's prestige was an obstacle to the Gothic Revival, and it is hardly surprising that Pugin should have spoken with contempt of his "vile compounds of Italian detail."[3] Ruskin's attitude was more respectful. There is a letter in the John Rylands Library, written from Ruskin's Park Street address, and therefore to be dated between late 1848 and early 1851, in which Ruskin seeks the older man's support for a proposal to have G. F. Watts paint murals in Cockerell's Taylorian Institute. An 1851 appendix to *The Stones of Venice* refers to Cockerell as "my good friend" (9.430). To some extent, Ruskin accepted Cockerell's archeological writings as a model for his own work. On February 18, 1852, he wrote to his father: "If Fergusson and Cockerell were both at work in Venice, I should not be; but the one works in India, the other in Greece."[4] The two men would probably have met at public lectures during the 1850s, and in 1857 they corresponded in connection with Ruskin's testimony before the National Gallery Site Commission. In January 1858 Cockerell distributed the prizes to art-workmen that Ruskin had donated to the Architectural Museum, and Ruskin, according to the transcript of his remarks that appeared in the *Building News*, began his lecture that evening with both a tribute and an apology:

> they were permitted to meet that evening under the auspices and presidency of their venerable Professor of Architecture at the Royal Academy—one of the most graceful and distinguished designers in the School of Classical architecture—a style distinguished for grace and beauty of design. He felt this the more deeply, because he knew that the Professor of Architecture could not countenance some of those things which he (Mr. Ruskin) might have audaciously or perhaps ignorantly advanced, either in the impulsive haste of a young man, or in a state of mind in which he referred to things which he felt to be false or evil, and where that was not perceived which was associated with the right, the wise, and the good. He knew that Professor Cockerell had much to forgive him, and he felt his forgiveness though he could not adequately give expression to it.[5]

Clearly Ruskin regarded Cockerell with respect, yet in temperament and theory the two men had little in common.

Cockerell's classicism was based on the principle of the module as set forth by Vitruvius and on the theory of harmonic proportions recommended by Alberti and other Renaissance writers. Vitruvius says that an order should be constructed in accordance with a single part that is selected as a standard unit of measurement or module. He takes the diameter of the base of the column (or, in the case of the Doric order, one-half the diameter) as his unit of measurement. By using modules rather than an absolute standard such as meters or feet, an architect shifts his attention from the actual dimensions of a building to the proportional relations between its parts. The thickness of a Doric column will be two modules and its height fourteen. The height of a capital is one module, its breadth two-and-one-sixth modules, and so it goes, with all the figures referring back to one accepted standard. The five orders were valued not simply for their decorative qualities but because they provided the architect with what Rudolph Wittkower has called "the metrical organization of buildings."[6] The orders were the basis of architectural education, and Cockerell was merely repeating traditional advice when, in 1850, he urged his students to "collect examples of the various masters, with reference to the modulus they employed, and to consider their application to actual dimensions— the principle of greatness might be so understood and acquired."[7]

Cockerell spoke as a representative of orthodoxy. The great names of the classical tradition are his guiding presences. He cites Vitruvius, Alberti, Vignola, Palladio, J. F. Blondel, and Philibert Delorme, as if he were drawing up a list of current research for a graduate seminar. Above all he admired Vitruvius, treating his views as nature methodized. Of course he knew that the formulas in Vitruvius's manuscript did not always check out when compared with actual ruins. He was one of those who had done the checking. For this reason Cockerell's tradition is often described in architectural histories as neoclassicism rather than as classicism itself. But this was not a distinction that Cockerell recognized, and he constantly defended the ancient Roman against all modern detractors.

Although his own buildings were dazzling virtuoso variations on classic themes, Cockerell's advice to his students was cautious and conservative. In an age that had seen the revival of the Hindu and Moorish styles, he felt compelled to warn against fads. "A builder with whom he was acquainted," he told students in 1845, "once produced an exceedingly fine portico, so much so that the professor inquired of him how he had designed it. 'Why,' said the man, 'I opened Sir William Chambers' book, and copied it exactly.'"[8] The students were not to follow tradition quite so slavishly, but they were urged never to forget that, as Cockerell put it in 1851, they would always be safe "in the hands of Chambers, whatever be the fashion of the times."[9] One result of this caution was that while Cockerell could approve the growing use of Gothic for religious buildings (though still insisting that the Queen Anne churches had never been bettered), he could only deprecate its wider use. In 1851, the same year in which the first volume of *The Stones of Venice* appeared, he assured his students that to construct hotels and bazaars in Gothic was as ridiculous as it would be to build the Parthenon in a swamp. "Gothic was now in the ascendent," he said, "but the rage for mimicking it would soon pass away. Youth follows blindly, but at mature age we criticize and reflect."[10]

The self-confidence of this remark, set against the growing power of the revival, suggests that Cockerell was a slightly anachronistic figure. When introducing Ruskin at the South Kensington Museum in 1858, Cockerell spoke of himself as "one of the last century, and not of the present century." Though he had admired the wild originality of Beethoven, praised Delacroix, and enthusiastically described the air of Turner's landscapes as "beaming with light, heat, and vegetation,"[11] one would never guess these enthusiasms from either the tone or content of his lectures. It is as though a distinguished literary critic, in an age when Wordsworth, Shelley, and Keats were the triumphant influences, had continued to base himself upon the theories of Samuel Johnson. A revolution in sensibility had occurred, but Cockerell had refused to allow it to alter his views on architecture. He did not speak to, did not seem even to acknowledge, minds nurtured on the medievalism of Scott, the emotionalism of the Evangelicals, the nature imagery of Tennyson's verse. The most passionate young Gothicists ignored Cockerell and embraced Ruskin. That they were right to do so should not blind us to the fact that Cockerell's theories were often very sound, while Ruskin's were, in significant ways, quite simply unarchitectural.

II

The issue in dispute between the two men was whether architecture was the art of proportion or the art of decoration.[12] Ruskin never doubted that it was the latter. His imagination was deeply stirred by the carving of a cable molding or the unexpected contrast of colored stones, but very little moved by geometrical floor plans, double cubes, and juxtapositions of oval with oblong spaces. He was sure that the interest of a building lay not in its utilitarian structure or its plan but in the features "venerable or beautiful, but otherwise unnecessary" (8.28) that were added to it. He ranked styles according to the amount and variety of the ornament they accommodated, criticizing Greek architecture because its ornament was limited and praising the once-despised Venetian Gothic because its decorations were colorful, various, and abundant. He thought the Early English capital unworthy of admiration because it could not be decorated. Cockerell, on the other hand, spoke for the Renaissance tradition when he insisted that the splendor of a building began with the geometrical order of its design and that ornaments were merely added graces—"'nets to catch a customer,' as Philibert Delorme had called them."[13] He cautioned his students against "admiring the *prettiness* of the art—mere matters of detail—long before they were able to appreciate the value of a complete homogeneous whole."[14] He warned against the seductions of pretty drawings that showed only parts of facades or veiled the whole with the use of chiaroscuro or aerial perspective. One need only remember Ruskin's illustrations—always showing portions of buildings, always emphasizing color and shadow—to see how wide was the gap between the two men.

Though Cockerell did not answer Ruskin's views directly, other writers were very quick to assail his equation of architectural beauty with sculpture, color, and ornament. Samuel Huggins, writing "Classical Columnar Architecture and the 'Stones of Venice'" in the *Builder*, maintained that "architecture is the art of the beautiful manifested in structure, of which, by its very nature as a structural art, *form* must be the dominant principle."[15] Ruskin's anonymous critic in the *Illustrated London News* was sure that a

> very essential point of architectural merit is the structural economy achieved in it—determinable by consideration of the relative proportions of the whole areas, and the areas of the points of support; and the relative proportions of the solids and voids in section. These, and other points revealing the creative intelligence of the designer, are the arcana of the art, which the reasoning mind is never tired of contemplating, and in comparison with which mere decorative detail is a matter of but secondary import. But these are the very points in which Mr. Ruskin takes no interest.

By concentrating on ornament rather than on overall design, he added, Ruskin made "the same mistake as it would be to describe the coat instead of the man, and sometimes not even the coat, but the buttons and braid which cover it."[16] Other critics agreed. The anonymous pamphleteer who wrote *Something on Ruskinism* complained that "he looks at everything by itself, labels it a specimen, and puts it by into a pigeon-hole of architectural grammar."[17] Edward Lacy Garbett, the first to discuss Ruskin's theories within the covers of a book, insisted that "the art which engrossed a great part of the attentions of a Phidias, a Michaelangelo, and a Wren is something more than decoration."[18] After Ruskin lectured in Edinburgh, the attacks were redoubled. A writer in the *Scottish Press* complained that Ruskin's views had reference only to the facades of buildings; another insisted in the *Edinburgh Advertiser* that grandeur, repose, and majesty lay only in straight lines and rectangles; and the architects of the city met to solemnly reaffirm the traditional doctrines of proportions. Marriott Field, an English architect who had emigrated to America, told readers of his *Rural Architecture* (1857) that Ruskin neglected the effect of ensemble in favor of minute ornaments.

William Henry Leeds is one of the most interesting of Ruskin's hostile critics because he shared at least some of Ruskin's assumptions. Leeds had been an important contributor to the *Architectural Magazine* under the name Candidus, and he had carried on a controversy with Ruskin on the theory and practice of perspective. Like all of Loudon's contributors, Leeds disliked copyism and thought architects suffered from an unthinking application of rules. Commenting on *The Seven Lamps* in 1849, he agreed that eye and instinct are more to be trusted than the traditional fixed ratios, and he complained that "the doctrine of some, Vitruvius included, would go to convert our art into a sort of barrel-organ, upon which all can grind music alike."[19] He hoped that Victorian architects would develop the style of the Renaissance palaces (what was called "the Italian style") to meet the needs of their own age, and he was a great admirer of the architecture of Sir Charles Barry. Criticizing Ruskin from the point of view of Renaissance principles and Barry's Italian style, Leeds gave the first expression to an opposition that would be very fully expressed in the debates over the Oxford Museum and the Government Offices competition.

Like most of the hostile critics, Leeds complained of Ruskin's heterodoxy. He charged in the *Athenaeum* that Ruskin's "censures are so widely flung about, his denunciations are so dogmatic and curt, his doctrine is so directly counter to all the teachings and practices of our time, and so subversive of nearly all hitherto received authority, that those who are otherwise at variance with each other will make common cause against Mr. Ruskin as their common foe."[20]

Leeds mounts a campaign against Ruskin's heresies in his book *Rudimentary Architecture*. He defends Renaissance design and repeats the now common complaint that Ruskin descants "with tedious prolixity on the forms and carvings of mouldings, and similar *minutiae*." His most important argument is a refutation of Ruskin's attempt to subvert the doctrine of the five orders by reducing them to two: convex and concave.

> Now, were there no objection to this dogmatic assumption—and it is certainly nothing more—it may fairly be alleged against it as a defect, that it makes the entire character of an Order to concentrate in the capital, and moreover, in one single circumstance of it, namely, its general outline or contour. No account is taken of proportions with regard to the column, or of actual bulk in the capital itself (in which last respect the Corinthian differs from the Doric as widely as in every other particular); none of the expression or the degree of it, whether it be that of plainness or simplicity or luxuriance.[21]

For all his complaints against the rigidities of early-nineteenth-century classicism, Leeds found himself defending the proportions of the whole and asserting that Ruskin considered only the part.

Against this barrage of criticism, Ruskin employed all the considerable rhetorical weapons at his disposal. Only once did he even waver. That was when he admitted in the "Reply to Mr. Garbett" appended to volume 1 of *The Stones of Venice* that a distinction could be drawn between the ornament that is intrinsic to a design (presumably capitals, moldings, corbels, and the like) and the additional decoration that may be added later. "That additional decoration is not the architecture," he said; it consists only of "curtains, pictures, statues, things which may be taken away from the building and not hurt it" (9.452). But this was only a short and temporary detour into moderation. Perhaps roused by the resistance he still encountered from many architects, Ruskin pushed his heresy to new extremes. He dropped the moderate paragraphs of the "Reply to Mr. Garbett" from the second edition of the first volume of *The Stones of Venice* in 1858, and he insisted that, as he put it in his 1855 preface to *The Seven Lamps*, what we call architecture is only the association of paintings and sculpture "in noble masses, or the placing them in fit places" (8.11). He reminded his readers that the greatest architects were those who, like Phidias, Giotto, and Michelangelo, regarded architecture as their play and painting and sculpture as their real work. During the 1850s he shifted his stylistic loyalties from Venetian Gothic to the cathedrals of the Ile-de-France solely because they carried so much figure sculpture.

III

Ruskin was not likely to convince the wavering by merely stating his love of ornament in increasingly violent form. The classical view of architecture assumed that beauty derived from harmonious proportions. Against this Ruskin set the expressive power of ornament.

His most impassioned statement came in his 1857 address to the Architectural Association. The AA had been founded in 1847 to help educate the younger members of the profession. It was lapsing into inactivity, and the 1857 meeting was part of a successful effort to revive it. Most of the London architectural world was there, with the younger men probably especially well represented. Ruskin's speech, "The Use of Imagination in Modern Architectural Designs," was thus aimed directly at an audience of architects. The transcript that appeared in the *Building News* will be quoted here, for it indicates audience reaction.

The chairman opened the meeting by listing Cockerell among those who regretted their inability to attend. It was just as well. Ruskin used the evening for a prolonged reductio ad absurdum of the traditional theory of architecture, and it is hard to believe that Cockerell's dignified tolerance could have taken the strain.

Ruskin assumed that architecture should move us with the force and immediacy of a lyric poem. Granting that invention was needed for "the disposition of lines, mouldings, and masses in agreeable proportions," he asked what architects really accomplished with their complicated ratios.

> He thought they would agree with him in saying that the beauty accomplished was not of a pathetic or touching order. They would, however, admit that well-disposed lines in music, properly executed, could rouse the feelings—could give courage to the soldier—language to the silent—consolation to the mourner—more joy to the joyful—more devotion to the devout;—could architects do that by a group of lines?—(cheers.) Could they suppose for a moment that the architectural lines in front of Whitehall could ever dispose the two mute soldiers on black horses under the alcoves to valour?—(a laugh)—or could they suppose that any person feeble in faith was ever made firmer and more steadfast in creed by the proportions of the architraves of the structure in which they were accustomed to worship?—(Laughter.) [22]

Ruskin attempted to replace the manipulation of ratios with that essential element of romantic theory, the sympathetic imagination. He held up a photograph of a carving from the south transept door of Amiens Cathedral showing St. Honoré disputing with his fellow monks:

> How could a man (he continued) produce such a picture as that without sympathy, without entering into, and being able to portray the feelings of others?—(Cheers.) Just think how much sympathy there was in this one picture—sympathy with a man who did not want to be made a bishop—sympathy with the disputing monks—sympathy with all the figures indicated in the photograph. Let them consider how much knowledge was needed in the architect before he could produce such a work. . . . But he might be told that this was sculpture and not architecture at all. Well, could they tell him what was the difference between sculpture and architecture? [23]

There was an answer to that question, but Ruskin did not wait for it. He insisted that in the great ages there had been no difference, except that that which was easy was called architecture and that which was hard was called sculpture. If the two skills were again combined, if architects would again take up the chisel, it would be possible to scatter cathedrals over England like mist upon the waters.

In spite of the enthusiastic audience reaction, much of the comment on

Ruskin's speech was hostile. A writer in the *Building News* found it "scarcely possible to believe that he [i.e., Ruskin] actually gave utterance to such incoherent rhapsody and palpable nonsense."[24] Samuel Huggins insisted that symmetry and eurythmic mass did indeed appeal to the feelings:

> I cannot say whether the charms of proportion and form would go to the extent of consoling me for the unkindness of a mistress, or of awakening in my breast an extraordinary bravery; but I know that a piece of noble architecture, by its general effect, to which the graces of proportion and form were almost the sole contributors, has always had a wonderfully pleasing and harmonizing effect upon my mind. It does not speak to or reason with me as a poem or essay would, but it soothes and elevates me just as music does. And this is the legitimate effect of architecture.[25]

To the younger generation, this no longer seemed obvious. The idea that a building might be regarded as a kind of lyric poem, valued for the intensity of the emotion it conveyed, had already swept the field in church architecture and was already finding expression in competition designs for the new Government Offices. The spirit of the age was on Ruskin's side.

IV

Ruskin denied that architecture was the art of proportion without for a minute denying the importance of proportions in architecture. The kinds of proportions he admired, however, were in sharp contrast to those that had descended from Vitruvius to Alberti and Palladio and finally to Chambers and Cockerell. Their theories stressed order, symmetry, and the subordination of parts to the whole. The proportions Ruskin admired, by contrast, had to be compatible with the spirits of changefulness and redundancy, which he listed among the six defining characteristics of Gothic. Where Alberti and Palladio had compared architectural proportions to the limited ratios of musical harmony, Ruskin compared them to the infinite possibilities of melody. Where Cockerell urged a respect for precedent, Ruskin substituted a romantic emphasis on the individual genius of each architect. "Not by rule, nor by study," he told the members of the Architectural Association, "can the gift of proportionate design be obtained; only by the intuition of genius can so much as a single tier of facade be beautifully arranged."[26]

Ruskin insisted that any single aspect of a structure confronted the architect with an infinite range of beautiful proportions. In the first volume of *The Stones of Venice* he gave as an example the five elements (the height of a shaft, its diameter, the length of the bell stone, its slope, and the thickness of the abacus between shaft and bell stone) that determine the proportions of the capital. Each element could be altered, and "for every change in any one of the quantities we have a new proportion of capital: five infinites, supposing change only in one quantity at a time: infinity of infinites in the sum of possible changes" (9.142). Even within the system he had chosen, an architect would delight in subtle, almost undetectable variations.

At the cathedral on the island of Murano, for example, Ruskin found a simple arithmetical progression between the interval of the nave shafts, the width of the aisle, the width of the transept, and the width of the nave. In the intervals between the arches that ring the back of the semicircular chancel, however, he found a different principle at work. By what Ruskin scornfully termed Grecian principles, each width would have been the same. The actual measurements were as follows:

	Feet	Inches
First interval	6	7
Second interval	7	7
Third interval	7	5
Fourth interval	7	10
Fifth interval	7	5
Sixth interval	7	8
Seventh interval	6	10

The progression is from the widest interval at the center to the narrowest at the extremes. There is a further variation within this pattern, for the architect allowed the second and sixth intervals to be slightly larger rather than slightly smaller than the third and fifth. Above all, no two intervals are precisely the same size.

Ruskin found similar patterns in the arcades stretched across the facades of such Byzantine palaces as the Fondaco de Turchi and the Casa Loredan. His opponents claimed that these patterns were unimportant. Samuel Huggins insisted in 1853 that "the proportion in which Ruskin delights is an invisible one,—that can only be discovered by measurement; and what he most lauds in the early architecture of Venice is a delicacy of proportion that is microscopic, and altogether unappreciable by the eye."[27] Ruskin ignored these arguments and continued to insist that the Byzantine and Gothic architects' exquisite sense of proportion had been crushed by the

mathematical deadness of the Renaissance. In his examination of medieval buildings, he found confirmation for his view that the finest proportions resulted from "a fixed scorn, if not dislike of accuracy of measurements; and in most cases . . . a determined resolution to work out an
effective symmetry by variations as subtle as those of Nature" (8.210).

This insistence on the infinity of possible proportions had important
consequences for the battle of the styles. Cockerell complained that Gothic
had no fixed ratios; columns or supports might be five to fifty diameters in
height and were bounded only by possibility. For Ruskin, this demon-
strated the style's superiority. "It is difficult to express with sufficient force,"
he said in the addenda to his Edinburgh lectures, "the absurdity of the sup-
position that there is more room for refinements of proportion in the relations of seven or eight equal pillars, with the triangular end of a roof above
them, than between the shafts, the buttresses, and porches, and pinnacles,
and vaultings, and towers, and all other double and trebly multiplied mag-
nificence of membership which form the framework of a Gothic temple"
(12.87–88).

Most discussions of proportion after 1853 respond to Ruskin's views.
Sometimes the response is straightforward and negative. T. L. Donaldson,
speaking in 1854, saw a sharp opposition between the old doctrines and
the new. Clearly referring to Ruskin, he said:

> Those who praise the Palazzo del Doge, or the basilica of St. Marco, are silent
> as to the grandeur of the Liberia, or the stupendous nobility of the basilica of
> Vicenza; and Brunelleschi, Bramante, Vignola, Inigo Jones and Wren are ig-
> nored, the principles of sound construction and pure taste are set at defiance,
> and the mind of the student is directed more to the study of the ornamental, as
> the detail of a capital, a leaf, or a flower, than the proportion and expression,
> and character of entire edifices.[28]

But Donaldson belonged to a generation that still knew exactly what it
thought on this subject. Younger architects, whether they considered themselves classicists or Gothicist, were less sure.

A more sympathetic response to Ruskin's views can be found in an 1868
paper by William White entitled "Systematic Proportions in Architecture." White was a prominent Gothicist best remembered today for his
richly polychromatic church at Lyndhurst in the New Forest.[29] He had
conducted his own study of proportions in English Gothic architecture and
had given the results in a lecture before the 1851 annual meeting of the
Ecclesiological Society.

White's 1868 paper pursued two separate but interlocking arguments.

On the one hand, White wants a system of proportions. He stresses the "indispensable necessity of studying and working out, and practicing some definite system of geometrical or arithmetical ratio in architectural proportion." [30] On the other hand, he wants architects to introduce refinements and subtle variations that would spring from individual intuitions. As an example, he cites Ruskin's descriptions of the variations of width between columns in the Byzantine palaces. Though he would not have put it quite this way, White is trying to synthesize Cockerell and Ruskin.

From this point of view, Ruskin's treatment of proportions in his 1857 address to the Architectural Association must have seemed disappointingly incomplete. White relates in his 1858 paper that he spoke to Ruskin after the lecture and subsequently wrote to him. White later published the correspondence. Because this exchange has been overlooked since its first publication in the January 1868 issue of the *Civil Engineer and Architect's Journal,* it will be quoted at length here.

White's first letter enclosed a copy of his 1851 lecture and described his belief that the impressions produced by architectural forms depend in part on geometrical ratios. He stressed that the laws of proportion can be reduced to simple rules:

> Man does not invent them, he only discovers them:—and within certain limits he is justified in inventing rules for the application of them to human purposes,—nay bound to do so if he aims at exercising the re-creative power to which you alluded in your lecture.
>
> It is in this element of your art-teachings—if I may venture to say so—that you appear to me to have just missed the truth: and my belief is, if architecture is ever again to grow into permanence or true grandeur, that alongside of the more purely art element of "expression" there must grow up through the means of convention, a system of development, in the application of the science of such laws. [31]

White's letter was thoughtful and tentative. Ruskin's answer was breezy and dogmatic:

> Thank you for your kind letter, but it is no use my reading anything on this matter, my mind being conclusively made up about it. So far from ignoring proportion I was the first to show the intensely subtle proportions of the Romanesque of Italy, and all the architects at that time derided my arguments, and said they were mere chance differences. But no great designer ever yet thought, or could think, of any mathematical law in designing. If law were of any use you could *teach* design; the nature of a great designer is to do all he does by pure instinct, *scorning law,* except of construction. I know this so positively by experience among living designers, that I would not any more discuss the question. I know in a moment if any painter talks of a law of colour or form, that he

can neither colour nor draw. The laws are there, but he obeys them uncon-sciously—if he *can* design. I have explained this in my various works over and over again: it is one of the things which I know quite as certainly as I do the shapes of crystals and their ways of association. [32]

"This," White very moderately comments, "did not satisfy me, and I could not leave the matter at least without some further protest." He saw that the weak point in Ruskin's argument was the claim that designers scorn laws of proportion and refuse to have conscious knowledge of them. In his second letter he cited Cimabue, who taught his pupils proportions, and a medieval architect who was recorded as having referred in passing to "Arches of the 5th point" as a recognized and well-understood proportion. He also expressed quite firmly his belief that Ruskin was limiting the value of his own books:

I shall not ask you to discuss the question, but you must allow me to record my conviction that your appreciation of the highest elements of art—an apprecia-tion higher than that of anyone whom I know—has blinded you strangely to the perception of other elements, of which I have as strong a certainty as of my own existence. Vol. II., cap. 5, and other similar illustrations of the '*Stones of Venice*,' delighted me, for I had myself observed and appreciated, previously to the publication of that volume, the spirit and intent of similar variation of spac-ings, &c., in English Early Architecture, which you have so well set forth, and of which no one else appears to have attempted so true and so thorough an interpretation. This interpretation, however, in no way militates against, or even touches, the point which I insist upon; it falls quite short of it. [33]

Ruskin's reply was brief:

Thank you for your letter. I agree to all it says. There is no controversy be-tween us on these points. What I mean is, that *cela va sans dire*. Get your poet, and of course he will make laws of metre—get your musician, and he will study his counterpoint; but the thing to be done is to get your nation into a musical and poetical mind, and no teaching of laws will help that. All colouring has been rendered impossible to our youth just now by their infernal laws of colour at Kensington; and you will practically find that if you begin with mathematical laws you will stay there. [34]

This is not, of course, what he had said the first time. In his first letter Ruskin had said that great artists followed laws unconsciously. Now he says that they discuss them—"of course."

But what is disappointing about Ruskin's answers is not their inconsis-tency but the fact that he quite fails to understand that White is giving him an opportunity to raise the entire debate to a new level. He agrees, when pressed, that designers concern themselves with proportions. He will not, however, rise to White's challenge and begin to think about proportions in a way that allows for both system and individual intuition.

Ruskin leaves the Gothic Revivalists and their heirs with an Achilles heel. He leads them to distrust not only classical systems but all systems. This means that his assault on the classicists was incomplete. It was nonetheless effective for quite a long period. Though Cockerell was honored with a place between Barry and Pugin on the pedestal of the Albert Memorial, he lost influence steadily until, as Ruskin's influence began to wane at the beginning of the new century, Cockerell's buildings were rediscovered in A. E. Richardson's dignified volume, *The Monumental Classic Architecture in Great Britain and Ireland during the XVIII and XIX Centuries.* It is one of the ironies of Ruskin's influence, as we shall see, that it was finally defeated early in the twentieth century by much the same doctrines of proportion that it did so much to weaken in the middle of the nineteenth.

III

CHAPEL AND CHURCH: THE RELIGIOUS BACKGROUND TO ARCHITECTURAL THEORY

 WHEN we consider Ruskin's relation to the doctrines of classical architecture, we face a situation that is relatively clear. When we turn to his place in the religious context of his time, that clarity at once disappears. The doctrinal controversies that transfixed the attention of Victorian Englishmen were extremely complicated and are now largely forgotten. Only specialists in the period today recall the effort of the Rev. George Cornelius Gorham to obtain a curate "free from Tractarian error," but in the 1840s it dominated public attention and prompted Ruskin to write an eight-thousand-word essay on the issues it raised. The so-called Papal Aggression of 1851 provoked an even greater furor. Mobs, bonfires, and No Popery placards protested the reestablishment of a Roman Catholic ecclesiastical hierarchy in England. *The Seven Lamps* and *The Stones of Venice* were written when these passions were at their most intense, and we should not be surprised to find them permeated by the spirit of sectarian controversy. The progress of Ruskin's ideas on Gothic during the second half of the nineteenth century cannot be fully understood unless they are first set very firmly in the context of midcentury religious debates.

It is only fair, however, to distinguish between the narrow Ruskin who confronts us in this chapter and the broad, tolerant figure we encounter elsewhere. That can be done by a simple exercise. Read a selection of Ruskin's finest prose. The particular titles will vary from reader to reader, but most lists will include "On the Nature of Gothic," "On the Pathetic Fallacy," "The Two Boyhoods," *Unto This Last*, and selections from *Fors Clavigera* and *Praeterita*. Make a brief summary of the religious positions that seem to be implied. It will be seen that Ruskin belongs to a broad and noble tradition. He scarcely writes a paragraph without showing how thoroughly his mind has been formed by the Protestant discipline of minute study of the Bible, yet he is drawn to such overtly Catholic works as the mosaics at Saint Mark's, the frescoes of Fra Angelico, and the sculptures at Amiens. Surely Ruskin deserves praise as one of those who labored to close the fissure between the Catholic culture of southern Europe and the Protestant culture of the north.

Now make a list of Ruskin's works that deal directly with religious matters. It would include the "Essay on Baptism," some of the footnotes to *The Seven Lamps,* the appendixes "Romanist Modern Art" and "Romanist Bases" in *The Stones of Venice,* the speculations on the nature of the church in *Notes on the Construction of Sheepfolds* (itself originally intended as an appendix to *The Stones of Venice*), and all the passages in the journals and letters that comment on religious matters. Suddenly Ruskin looks unpleasantly narrow. The God implied in the first list has shrunk into a prim moralist who frowns on maypole dancing and watches English tourists abroad to see that they contribute adequate sums to the struggling Protestant churches of France, Switzerland, and the Piedmont.

Part of the difference between the two Ruskins can be explained by chronology. Like most Protestant Evangelicals, Ruskin felt threatened by the forces of Roman Catholicism and Tractarianism. In 1858, however, Ruskin abandoned his Evangelical commitments. His narrowness, therefore, belongs to the 1840s and 1850s, and he repents of it thereafter. He was to pepper the 1880 edition of *The Seven Lamps* with footnotes expressing dismay at the self-confidence of his "rabid and utterly false Protestantism" (8.15). Our sympathies lie with the broadly tolerant Ruskin, but it is the aggressively Evangelical one who confronts us between 1849 and 1853.

I

The religious tendencies that contributed to Ruskin's architectural education during the 1840s were the Evangelical party within the Church of England, the Roman Catholicism of the architect and convert A. W. N. Pugin, and the Ecclesiological Society.

The Evangelicals were Reformation men. They considered that the glorious period of primitive Christianity had given way to priestly usurpation and papal abuse. The sixteenth century had seen a great movement of reawakening, but this in turn had been followed by a weakening of resolve. It was because the Evangelicals saw the Reformation as an unfinished business that they campaigned against Catholic Emancipation in 1829, and they continued to adopt a militantly anti-Catholic tone.

Pugin, by contrast, considered the Reformation an abomination. It was a blow against both the faith he had embraced and the forms of worship that he loved. The subtext of his praise of Gothic was a plea for the conversion of England. The Ecclesiologists, as members of the Church of England, could not attack the Reformation, but they seemed to agree with the Tractarian Hurrell Froude that it was like "a limb badly set—it must be broken again in order to be righted."[1]

The consequences of these religious views can be seen in two Camberwell churches. Camden Church, which no longer stands, was a fair representation of Evangelical preferences. Saint Giles's, the parish church that stood about a mile away, was rebuilt after a fire in the early 1840s and reflected the new doctrines of Pugin and the Ecclesiologists. Ruskin worshiped in the one and helped decorate the other.

Camden Chapel, as it was first called, was built in 1797 by a group of prominent Evangelicals who complained that the gospel was no longer being preached in their parish church. They would have preferred to be part of the establishment so long as they could choose their own Evangelical minister, but when permission for this was refused they opened under the Toleration Act as part of the Countess of Huntingdon's Connexion. They used a modified form of the Church of England service and rejoined the establishment in 1829.

It was in this year that the Rev. Henry Melvill was called to Camden Chapel's pulpit. He was extremely popular. In 1839 the *Metropolitan Pulpit* was able to report that "when a sermon is advertized to be preached by Mr. Melvill, the number of strangers attracted to the particular place is invariably greater than is ever drawn together in the same church or chapel when any of the other popular ministers in London are appointed to preach on a precisely similar occasion."[2] Melvill's sermons helped draw the Ruskins to Camden Chapel in the first place, and Ruskin's letters show that he was still reading their printed versions while writing *The Stones of Venice.*

An old print shows the facade of Camden Chapel (fig. 10), and the plan of George Gwilt's 1814 alterations (fig. 11) shows the layout of the interior. The building was basically a plain brick box, with some architectural pretension provided by a rusticated ground story, four pilasters, a pediment, and a cupola. The interior was a large auditorium designed to bring all members of the congregation within easy reach of the preacher's voice. Seats were provided in pews on the first floor and in galleries held up by

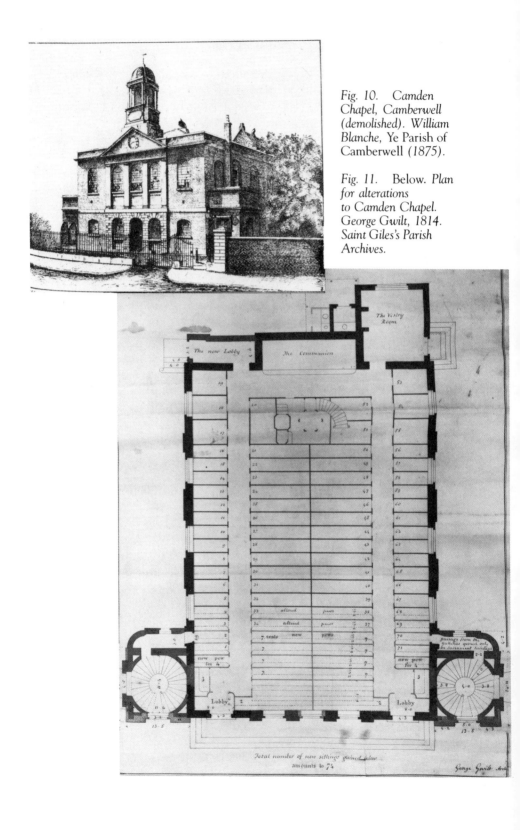

Fig. 10. Camden Chapel, Camberwell (demolished). William Blanche, Ye Parish of Camberwell (1875).

Fig. 11. Below. Plan for alterations to Camden Chapel. George Gwilt, 1814. Saint Giles's Parish Archives.

thin, cast-iron columns. There were two additional small galleries for children on either side of the organ, and transepts were built at the north end
to provide extra seating. The church was laid out north to south rather
than in the liturgically preferred east to west, and its plan had a T shape.
There was no apse or chancel. A small wooden communion table stood
against the wall, but the congregation's attention must have been held by
the tall pulpit.

Camden Chapel was not beautiful, but this was the result of a deliberate
revolt against pride and ostentation. After all, John Wesley himself had
asked after seeing Beverly Minister: "But where will it be when the earth is
burned up and the elements melt with fervent heat?"[3] Such sentiments
tended to militate against Gothic simply because it was widely believed to
be an expensive style.

Pugin and the Ecclesiologists denounced such buildings as Camden
Chapel as mere preaching boxes. They claimed that their obvious cheap-
ness showed a lack of religious fervor, and they insisted that their pilasters
and cupolas were pagan. Pugin held up a dream of lofty arches, majestic
lines of pillars, intricately carved capitals, great rood lofts, and high altars
blazing with gold and jewels. Judged by this standard, Camden Chapel was
the outward sign of inward disgrace.

The explicit Roman Catholicism of Pugin's vision limited its appeal. The
Ecclesiologists, on the other hand, presented many of the same ideas in a
form that members of the Church of England found more palatable. They
argued that the ministering of the sacraments, rather than the preaching
of the gospel, was the most important activity that took place within a
church, and, since this was miraculous, it should occur in an atmosphere
of mystery. The first fact of church architecture should be the separation of
the chancel, intended for the sacraments, from the nave. The boundary
should be marked off by an altar rail, three steps (to symbolize the Trinity),
and often by a rood screen as well. The chancel should be richly decorated
and should contain a stone altar rather than a wooden communion table.

On this basis, the Ecclesiologists rejected nearly every aspect of the
Protestant churches of their day. They were appalled by flat east ends decorated only by the purely ethical teachings of the Ten Commandments.
They vehemently attacked pews (which they insisted on spelling pues) because they wasted space and made churchgoing less attractive to the laboring classes. They opposed galleries in a church, claiming that they destroyed all air of mystery. They did not mention Camden Chapel while
Ruskin was associated with it, but it is easy to guess what they must
have thought. In 1859, while commenting on the 1854 remodeling of the
church, the *Ecclesiologist* expressed blunt views on the older parts of the
building. It called the building "a hideous chapel of ease," said the nave

Fig. 12.   Saint Giles's, Camberwell. George Gilbert Scott, 1844. Illustrated London News, *1844.*

was "frightful," and praised the incumbent for attempting to recast "the old disgustful mass."[4]

What did Ruskin think of Camden Chapel in the 1840s? We do not know, but it seems fair to assume from his growing enthusiasm for Continental Gothic that he was displeased by it. The real question is how much did he know of the new doctrines of church architecture that were in the air. The rebuilding of the nearby parish church of Saint Giles's would have made them common knowledge in the middle-class homes of Camberwell.

On February 7, 1841, Saint Giles's was completely destroyed by fire. The new structure (fig. 12) reflected the influence of Pugin and the Ecclesiologists. As Henry-Russell Hitchcock comments in his *Early Victorian*

Fig. 13. Stained-glass windows, Saint Giles's Church. John Ruskin and Edmund Oldfield, 1844. Law and Mt. Sinai; New Jerusalem; Expulsion of Hagar. Photo: Morgan Wells Associates.

Fig. 14. Stained-glass windows, Saint Giles's Church. High Priest of the Law; Christ as High Priest; Abraham Giving Tithes to Melchesedech. Photo: Morgan Wells Associates.

Architecture, the building was so influential that a spectator today finds it difficult to realize how innovative it was. Ruskin would have seen it with fresh eyes.

The architect was George Gilbert Scott. Like Ruskin, he came from an Evangelical background. His grandfather had written a much-used commentary on the Bible, and his father preached in a church that was even plainer than Camden Chapel. Scott had made his way as an architect by designing a large number of workhouses as well as cheap, archeologically incorrect churches. Saint Giles's was the turning point in his career. Pugin's "On the Present State of Ecclesiastical Architecture in England" had just appeared in the *Dublin Review*. "Pugin's articles excited me almost to fury," Scott later wrote; "I suddenly found myself like a person awakened from a long feverish dream which had rendered him unconscious of what was going on about him."[5] It is a fair guess that Scott did not stress the doctrinal background of his new ideas to the Camberwell parishioners. He always took care to maintain his standing among Protestants. In 1841 he had designed the Martyr's Memorial to Cranmer, Latimer, and Ridley at Oxford. In spite of his efforts, however, his name stirred controversy. The Rev. Thomas Mozley recorded in his *Reminiscences* that "already in 1844 his name was up as one of the Oxford school, and intending church builders were solemnly warned that if they employed him they would find themselves in for the offeratory, the surplice, and much more to follow."[6]

At Saint Giles's Scott had an unusual opportunity. There was a considerable amount of insurance money available after the burning of the old church. There was also a fund drive to which John James Ruskin contributed one hundred guineas. Moreover, the incumbent, the Rev. J. G. Storie, was a man of domineering temperament, fully capable of bullying a timid vestry board. Under these circumstances, Scott felt encouraged to try something ambitious, and he proposed an expensive design. Engravings of the plan were circulated. Modifications were then made, partly to satisfy the wishes of the congregation for something less expensive, partly to meet criticisms published in the *Ecclesiologist*. The resulting church is solid and impressive, with an imposing crossing tower and a tall spire. The interior is disappointing when compared with later Victorian churches, but it must have appeared richly decorated and authentically medieval in 1844. The church has a nave of nine bays and, since Scott heeded the *Ecclesiologist's* advice and abandoned his hexagonal apse, it had one of the earliest deep chancels of the century. Since Scott had adopted Pugin's doctrine of truth to materials, much that was originally designed for plaster was executed in stone. There were galleries, since removed. Class distinctions were observed. The poor kept their place in the "inferior seats," while the "genteel seats" had fancy stall ends carved by "Mr. Pratt's newly invented machine."[7]

The faith of the Camberwell congregation was challenged more than once while the church was being furnished. The piscina, the basin for washing the communion vessels, and the sedilia, the seats for the priests in the chancel, survived the burning of the old church. It would have been natural to include them in the new structure, but both were tainted by the aroma of Romish practices. They were preserved, but only as museum pieces (and have since been returned to the chancel). A similar debate erupted over the new pulpit. Scott proposed one of wood, paneled with porcelain and enameled with sacred figures on a gold ground. Apparently this brought protests not only from members of the congregation but from the bishop as well. For the first time, the record shows Ruskin exasperated by the provincialism of his fellow Protestants. "It is very abominable," he wrote to his friend Edmund Oldfield. "Our Bishops seem to prefer the pro-fane to the Popish, and would admit into their Cathedrals the statue of an actor rather than of an apostle" (12.446).

Ruskin's most direct contribution to Saint Giles's was his collaboration on the design of the great east windows. The original intent had been to have them designed and executed by the London firm of Ward & Nixon. Ruskin and Oldfield felt that Ward's designs were insufficiently medieval and decided to create their own, which would then be executed by the London firm. Ruskin first prepared designs for the window head. These were closer to Michelangelo than to the thirteenth century, so Oldfield prepared a second version, which was the one actually used (figs. 13 and 14). Then the two young men were asked to prepare designs for the five vertical lights. Ruskin's contribution to these windows appears to have been greater. Oldfield was left behind to oversee their execution by Ward & Nixon while Ruskin traveled on the Continent and studied the glass at Rouen and Chartres. But when he applied the lessons of these studies, Ruskin had to be careful not to offend Protestant sensibilities. The win-dows of Chartres, he tells Oldfield on May 22, 1844, are "the perfection of glass painting," but they "represent quaint Romish legends, unsuited either to the comprehension or faith of the Camberwell congregation" (12.437).

The resulting windows are made up of five great lancets, each of which is divided into a series of medallions and bosses. The left-hand light pre-sents the biblical story from the Creation to Moses and the Burning Bush. The second light continues the story from the Exodus down to Ahasuerus' crowning of Esther. The third deals with the Nativity, the Temptation, the Crucifixion, the Resurrection, and the Ascension. The fourth presents such scenes as the stoning of Stephen and the conversion of Saint Paul.

The lancet on the right presents scenes from the Apocalypse. All told there are sixty-nine different subjects and sixty-four patriarchs, apostles, and New Testament figures.[8] These scenes set forth an elaborate typological comparison of Old and New Testament scenes. Unfortunately, the pamphlet that Ruskin and Oldfield issued explaining their work has not survived. It was cited in an article by Mrs. Jameson in the January 18, 1845, issue of the *Athenaeum*[9] and praised in the *Ecclesiologist* for "the testimony it affords to the growing adoption of the symbolical theory."[10]

The contrast between Camden Chapel and Saint Giles's dramatizes a conflict between Ruskin's Protestant faith and his taste for Gothic. In his books Ruskin attempts to resolve this conflict by defending Gothic on grounds that are explicitly Protestant.

II

Both *The Seven Lamps* and *The Stones of Venice* open by setting all that is to follow firmly within the framework of Evangelical thought. This does not mean that the claims advanced are those that Evangelicals are likely to find agreeable but only that Ruskin's way of arguing is one that they will find familiar.

"The Lamp of Sacrifice," for example, is cast in the form of an Evangelical sermon. The orthodoxy of Ruskin's method can be appreciated if his chapter is compared to an actual sermon delivered by Henry Melvill at Camden Chapel in 1839. Melvill was appealing for funds on behalf of a society for building and repairing churches. He was not asking his congregation to support the kind of splendor that Ruskin wanted. He was only asking for more and slightly better Camden Chapels. Nevertheless, he confronted the same ingrained Protestant attitudes that Ruskin would later address. It is possible that Ruskin was present when Melvill's sermon was delivered, and, since it was printed in 1847, he may have relied on it quite deliberately when he wrote his own plea for church building.

Characteristically, Melvill opened with a biblical text: "Then came the word of the Lord by Haggai the Prophet, saying, Is it time for you, O ye, to dwell in your ceiled houses, and his house lie waste?" (Hag. 1:3–4). Melvill first gives a careful reconstruction of the historical circumstances in which Haggai spoke, then goes on to interpret the prophet's words typologically. The principle of interpretation invoked here is that a truth enunciated in physical terms under the Hebrew dispensation will be realized on a more spiritual plane under the Christian one. Haggai demanded a temple in Jerusalem. Christians, freed from the ceremonial law, may build their churches anywhere. They may not, however, do without them. They are required to build houses for the Lord. This brings Melvill to the point that must have especially struck Ruskin:

> We cannot take it as any wholesome symptom which is now to be observed in this country, that, whilst other structures are advancing in magnificances, churches are of a less costly style. If we compare ourselves with our ancestors, it may be said that we build more spacious and luxurious houses; if we want new exchanges, they shall be such as quite to throw the old into the shade; new houses of Parliament, they shall wonderfully outdo what the fire had destroyed; yea, even our hospitals and infirmaries, they shall be almost as palaces compared with those of olden days; but if we want new churches, they shall be as simple and unadorned as possible, contrasting strangely with the vaulted, and arched, and richly-sculptured piles which a former age delighted to consecrate to God.[11]

Ruskin uses much the same method to reach a similar conclusion. He starts by examining the institution of Levitical sacrifice and makes pointed use of a verse from the second book of Samuel: "Neither will I offer unto the Lord my God of that which doth cost me nothing." Ruskin is not as specific in his discussion of historical context as Melvill, but he does establish a central point about sacrifice under the Old Law: costliness was generally a condition of its acceptableness. And this remains true under the New Law; the only difference is that the offering ceases to be strictly sacrificial and becomes thankful in a much wider sense. If men do not offer to the Lord's house, it is because of some deficiency in their faith. And this brings Ruskin to the same point that Melvill had made:

> The question is not between God's house and His poor: it is not between God's house and His Gospel. It is between God's house and ours. Have we no tessellated colours on our floors? no frescoed fancies on our roofs? no niched statuary in our corridors? no gilded furniture in our chambers? no costly stones in our cabinets? Has even the tithe of these been offered? (8.37)

Of course what was the climax of the sermon for Melvill is only the opening stage in the argument for Ruskin. Having comforted Protestant readers with a familiar way of arguing, he at once disquiets them with sharp criticisms of early-nineteenth-century churches. He complains against such standard features as plaster cornices and rose-shaped ventilators in flat ceilings. He inveighs against plaster grained to look like wood, wood gilded to look like bronze, and trompe l'oeil frameworks of pilasters and pediments to enclose real altars. Elsewhere he attacks the "peculiar pompousness" of modern pulpits and wonders how "our congregations can endure the aspect of the wooden sounding-board, attached only by one point of its circumference to an upright pillar behind the preacher; and looking as if the weight of the enormous leverage must infallibly, before the sermon is concluded, tear it from its support, and bring it down upon the preacher's head" (10.445). But it is not primarily the absurdity of the Evangelical church that troubles Ruskin. It is the meanness. Men who have been reborn in the Lord should want to bring Him tessellated colors, niched statuary, frescoes, gilding, and costly stones.

The first chapter of *The Stones of Venice* also opens with an appeal to Evangelical modes of thought:

> Since first the dominion of men was asserted over the ocean, three thrones, of mark beyond all others, have been set upon its sands: the thrones of Tyre, Venice, and England. Of the First of these great powers only the memory remains; of the Second, the ruin; the third, which inherits their greatness, if it forget their example may be led through prouder eminence to less pitied destruction. (9.17)

This prophetic warning is subject to both a broad and a narrow interpretation. The broad one, which modern readers prefer, sees it as asserting in a general way that the greatness of a nation reflects the grandeur of its spirit. The narrower interpretation connects the fates of both Venice and England with the condition of their "*vital* religion" (9.31). The italics are Ruskin's, and the adjective they emphasize was a code word for Evangelical.

The religious argument at the beginning of *The Stones of Venice* would have been especially clear in the charged atmosphere of 1851. Ruskin develops a parallel between Venice and London. The fall of Venice had traditionally been traced to the replacement of the republic by an oligarchy. Ruskin sets this political interpretation aside and substitutes a religious one. The decline of Venice's political prosperity was "exactly coincident with that of domestic and individual religion" (9.23). One of the marks of Venice in her strength was a deliberate exclusion of papal influence from her councils of state. One of the signs of her fall was political submission to Rome. The English legislature, in granting the franchise to Roman Catholics, had exposed itself to the very dangers that the Venetians had so long avoided. Lest the significance of this not be sufficiently clear, Ruskin adds an attack on Catholic Emancipation in Appendix 5: "To have sacrificed religion to mistaken policy, or purchased security with ignominy, would have been no new thing in the world's history; but to be at once impious and impolitic, and seek for danger through dishonour, was reserved for the English Parliament of 1829" (9.423).

It will be observed that this argument has the somewhat startling effect of transforming the Venetians into proto-Protestants. The strategic value of such a maneuver is clear: it shows that an Evangelical faith may be expressed in visual splendor. Indeed, Ruskin argues that Protestantism's suspicion of painting and architecture has been a self-inflicted wound. "It may be a serious question," he warns, "how far the Pausing of the Reformation has been a consequence of this error" (9.45).

The seriousness with which Ruskin interpreted medieval art in terms of a Protestant view of history is illustrated by a passage from the second volume of *The Stones of Venice:*

> Those cornices [i.e., the one on the right in row 3 of fig. 15, and the one in row 4] are the Venetian Ecclesiastical Gothic; the Christian element struggling with the Formalism of the Papacy,—the Papacy being entirely heathen in all its principles. That officialism of the leaves and their ribs means Apostolic Succession, and I don't know how much more, and is already preparing for the transition to old Heathenism, and the Renaissance.
>
> Now look to the last cornice. That is Protestantism,—a slight touch of Dissent, hardly amounting to schism in those falling leaves, but true life in the whole of it. The forms all broken through, and sent heaven knows where, but the root held fast; and strong sap in the branches; and, best of all, good fruit ripening and opening straight towards heaven, and in the face of it, even though some of the leaves lie in the dust. (9.371)

Such an argument seems merely quaint to modern readers. Few of Ruskin's earliest critics found it so, however, and the association of vigorous naturalism with strong religious faith soon underlay a good deal of Victorian stone carving.

In addition to separating Gothic from Catholic theology, Ruskin attempts to disassociate it from any kind of otherworldly mysticism. Thus he goes out of his way to reject the very popular aspiration theory of Gothic. Visitors to the great cathedrals have often associated their height and verticality with intense religious feeling. This poetic insight was elaborated by Pugin, who invoked "the lofty nave and choir, with the still loftier towers, crowned by clusters of pinnacles and spires, all directed towards Heaven, beautiful emblems of the Christian's brightest hope."[12] Pugin was by no means alone in this. The historian E. A. Freeman argued that "in Gothick, the upward tendency in spiritual things, which is its grand lesson, is symbolized by a real physical upward tendency in the lines of the building."[13] In chapter 4 we will find the architectural journalist George Wightwick making a similar argument. Ruskin's friend Coventry Patmore argued the aspiration theory at length in his *British Quarterly Review* article on *The Seven Lamps.*

Ironically, many people think that Ruskin too equated Gothic with an

Fig. 15.   Cornice decoration. John Ruskin. The Stones of Venice, *volume 1 (1851).*

intense pitch of spirituality. His works do reveal one early sympathetic reference to the theory. That was in an 1845 letter to his father, where he defined the difference in feeling between Greek and Gothic architecture by associating the first with endurance and the second with aspiration.[14] He soon adopted another tone, however, and it was presumably the pressure of religious controversy that impelled him to do so. In his published writings Ruskin was stubbornly unwilling to grant that heavenward aspiration played any role whatever in shaping Gothic cathedrals. If they had soaring roofs, it was because their builders, faced originally with the practical need to throw off heavy snow, went on to develop the theme of steepness in a spirit of play: "with the gradual exaggeration with which every pleasant idea is pursued by the human mind, [the Gothic roof] is raised into all manner of peaks, and points, and ridges, and pinnacle after pinnacle is added on its flanks, and the walls increased in height in proportion until we get indeed a very sublime mass, but one which has no more principle of religious aspiration in it than a child's tower of cards" (9.187). In 1854 Ruskin assured an audience in Edinburgh that the competition between citizens of medieval towns over who could build the highest nave resulted from a feeling more nearly "analogous to that in which you play a cricket-match" (12.39) than from any mystical aspiration.

By the time Ruskin reached the middle of *The Stones of Venice,* he had urged his fellow Evangelicals to build splendid churches in a spirit of reverential sacrifice, though not mystical longing, and he had shown that a Protestant spirit could be expressed through Gothic forms. There was one aspect of religious architecture, however, that he had avoided dealing with: its affect on the worshiper. It seemed to him that modern Continental churches were arranged not so much to express emotion as to inspire it—and he mocked those who were "lured into the romanist Church by the glitter of it, like larks into a trap by broken glass" (9.437).

Yet undoubtedly architecture had a legitimate affect, and Ruskin had to decide what it could be. In 1846 he wrote to Dr. John Brown that "I have not been able to come to any steady opinion respecting the real operation of art as directed to religious subjects on the minds of the common people" (36.61). On February 16, 1848, he wrote to his friend the Rev. Edward Clayton: "In your casual reading any passages that bear on the effect of ecclesiastical ornament on *real* religious feeling or national character will be most thankfully received."[15] In 1853, in his chapter on Saint Mark's in *The Stones of Venice,* he set out to solve the problem.

The effort was not a success. As often happens when Ruskin is unsure of himself, he makes too many distinctions, each of which has to be explained and each of which opens the way to a new digression. Eventually the chapter comes to an end with the main issue still unresolved. The stumbling block is easily identified: the men Ruskin had known who possessed a religious spirit that he considered pure and admirable were invariably attracted toward an art that he regarded as deplorable. If they looked at the art of Giotto or Fra Angelico at all, they did so only to be repelled by the Mariolatry and the miracles of the saints that they found there. Their preferred artists were Carlo Dolci, Guercino, Benjamin West, and John Martin—all targets of Ruskin's contempt. Their favorite painting was Salvator Rosa's *The Witch of Endor,* the subject of which was chosen "simply because, under the names of Saul and the Sorceress, he could paint a captain of banditti, and a Neapolitan hag" (9.126). Ruskin could only account for this dismaying situation by saying that the truest faith often leads to the narrowest vision. "I have never yet," he announced, "met with a Christian whose heart was thoroughly set upon the world to come, and, so far as human judgment could pronounce, perfect and right before God, who cared about art at all" (10.124). But if this was true, Ruskin's crusade to awaken his fellow Evangelicals to the value of art was seriously compromised.

On the whole, Ruskin's effort to relate his religion to his architectural views does not show him at his best. One aspect of it, indeed, shows him at his worst. That is his direct, personal attack on Pugin.

By 1951 overwork, ill health, and emotional troubles had brought Pugin close to his final collapse and death. He lamented that he had often been forced to compromise his aesthetic ambitions, cited the Church (soon to be the Cathedral) of Saint George as one in which he had been forced to sacrifice height and proportion to meet conditions laid down by the building committee, and concluded: "I have passed my life in thinking of fine things, studying fine things, desiring fine things, and realizing very poor ones."[16]

Such a remark should have been received with sympathetic silence. Instead, Ruskin chose it as the point of his attack. Lack of funds, he insisted, was no excuse:

> Whatever greatness there was in you, had it been Buonarroti's own, you had room enough for it in a single niche; you might have put the whole power of it into two cube of Caen stone. St. George's was not high enough for want of money? But was it want of money that made you put that blunt, overloaded, laborious ogee door into the side of it? Was it lack of funds that made you sink the tracing of the parapet in its clumsy zigzags? Was it in parsimony that you buried its paltry pinnacles in that eruption of diseased crockets? (9.438–439)

Ruskin softened this by saying that no living architect could design a better finial, but got to the real point when he warned his readers: "do not allow his good designing of finials to be employed as an evidence in matters of divinity, nor thence deduce the incompatibility of Protestantism and art" (9.439).

In spite of this attack, many readers insisted that Ruskin was in Pugin's debt. In 1852, for example, Frank Howard accused Ruskin before the Liverpool Architectural Society of adopting all of Pugin's principles and then, "having dressed himself in Pugin's feathers,"[17] making a personal attack on him. This became so much the accepted view that Ruskin felt compelled to deny it in an appendix to the third volume of *Modern Painters* (1856):

> It is . . . often said that I borrow from Pugin. I glanced at Pugin's *Contrasts* once, in the Oxford architectural reading-room, during an idle forenoon. His "Remarks on Articles in the *Rambler*" were brought under my notice by some of the reviews. I never read a word of any other of his works, not feeling, from the style of his architecture, the smallest interest in his opinions. (5.428–429).

In April 1855 he had said much the same thing in a letter to F. J. Furnivall: "I certainly owe nothing to Pugin,—except two *facts*, one about Buttresses, and one about ironwork. I owe, I know not how much, to Carlyle, and after him to Wordsworth, Hooker, Herbert, Dante, Tennyson, and about another dozen people. But assuredly *Nothing* to Pugin" (5.429). Unfortunately, the two facts Ruskin mentions in the letter are not in the two books he names in the appendix. It is known that he had read and made notes on at least a third book of Pugin's—*The True Principles of Architecture*. The notes survive.[18]

But perhaps the real point to be made is that Ruskin would have been indebted to Pugin even if he had read nothing at all by him. He would surely have seen reviews of Pugin's books—including the very long one in the March 1837 issue of the *Architectural Magazine*. He would have discussed Pugin's ideas with fellow members of the Oxford Architectural Society. Above all, he would have been aware of the influence of Pugin on Scott's design for Saint Giles's. Scott revised his plans in accordance with Pugin's call for reality in construction, and it was precisely this demand that Ruskin later expressed so powerfully in "The Lamp of Truth." There are significant differences between Ruskin's view of Gothic and Pugin's, but Ruskin's denial of any debt can only be explained by the sectarian fervor that gripped much of England at midcentury.

III

How did Ruskin's contemporaries respond to this odd mixture of indecision and excessive passion? The reviews show that religion was a central issue for them, and passages that are today skipped over were then quoted and analyzed at length. Beyond that, it is very difficult to find a common thread. What seemed evidence of the firmest Protestantism to one reviewer was a sign of creeping Puseyism to the next.

Some denied that a direct relation between faith and architectural style was desirable. *Fraser's* begged disputants to "be content to leave to religion and art their several duties—and not to seek to confound the one with the other." [19] *Blackwood's* objected to "the odour of such sanctity" surrounding Ruskin's views, [20] and the *Athenaeum* thought that his claim that cast iron received no endorsement from the Bible would have come better from "a denouncer of the sinfulness of Christmas puddings or the unloveliness of lovelocks, than from so bold and unhesitating a thinker." [21]

On the whole the critics who resisted too close a relation between religion and art represented an older generation. The *Anglo-Saxon* probably spoke for the young when it praised Ruskin for presenting "a solemn view of Art" as "simply *the work* which some amongst us have to do, and which must be done to the glory of God, and for the good of man." [22] Coventry Patmore, writing in the *British Quarterly Review,* welcomed Ruskin's interpretation of Saint Mark's as "a type of the redeemed Church of God" [23] and contrasted his interpretations with the strained symbolic readings of Durandus and the Ecclesiologists. The *Westminster Review* was similarly pleased by Ruskin's interpretation of the cathedral church on Torcello as "a type of the conditions of Christians in all ages" and praised Ruskin as "a Wesley in his way." [24]

Most of Ruskin's reviewers were Protestants and willing to accept his denunciations of Roman Catholicism. Coventry Patmore, still some years away from his conversion, assured readers of the *British Quarterly Review* that Ruskin "takes up the war-cry rising of late from the lips of every honest Englishman against Romanism, and re-utters it in tones that make us think of the blast of Israel's trumpets before the walls of Jericho." [25] The *Gentleman's Magazine* praised Ruskin for teaching that "there exists no necessary association whatsoever, nothing at all of inherent sympathy, between the degraded and degrading Romanism of the twelfth and thirteenth centuries and their glorious architecture." [26]

This last claim is one that a Roman Catholic critic would want to deny, and the *Rambler* did so effectively:

It is indeed a not slightly significant token of the shallowness of the popular religionism of our time, that a man of Mr. Ruskin's acuteness should write a book exalting the religious architecture of the 13th century almost to the level of a work of inspiration, and term it pre-eminently *Christian* architecture, and at the same time believe the Pope to be Antichrist, and gravely propose the repeal of the Catholic Emancipation as necessary to the well-being of England. There is something so transcendently ludicrous in the notion that the Church of Rome is *idolatrous*, and yet that the early mediaeval architecture was the result of the purest Christian faith and feeling that we can only suppose that Mr. Ruskin believes that Cranmer, Luther, and Henry VIII flourished some 700 years ago, and that Salisbury Cathedral was built in the reign of Elizabeth.[27]

This is what we would expect, and it is well put. The surprise comes when we find the *Rambler* denouncing Ruskin for having caught the "peculiar canting style" of the Ecclesiologists. The *Rambler* was no more patient with them or indeed with Pugin himself than with Ruskin. It sought to preserve a respectable distance between dogma and architecture, and its real kinship on this matter was with *Blackwood's* and the *Athenaeum*.

Ruskin's impact on Protestant opinion is difficult to determine. Architectural histories often assert that he made Gothic safe for Protestant congregations. This may well have been his ultimate effect, but it is not evident in the reviews that appeared in leading Protestant publications. They show a striking reluctance to enlist in the Gothic Revival. The *Dublin University Magazine* considered that rational worship required rational architecture and preferred the churches of Palladio and Wren to anything medieval. The *Christian Observer* refused to abandon its opinion that England's only truly Protestant cathedral was Saint Paul's. Its reviewers shrewdly noted that Ruskin's argument for the incompatability of the papacy and great architecture was difficult to apply north of Venice: "Some of the finest churches in England, or anywhere else, must have been building while Boniface VIII was holding the first jubilee at Rome, at the beginning of the fourteenth century. Was Rome ever much worse than at that time? Was architecture ever better?"[28] *Tait's Edinburgh Magazine* looked forward to the day when "all congregations may build as they please, and the architecture will not be considered as any badge of discipline or doctrine."[29]

Many critics went further and insisted that Ruskin was advancing the very trends that he claimed to oppose. The *Dublin University Magazine*, for example, declared,

we cannot help remarking that architectural Puseyism has had no more efficient promoter in England than John Ruskin, and that, until his alarm at the progress of dogmatical Puseyism broke forth in this publication [the first volume of *The Stones of Venice*], no one not honoured with his personal acquaintance could have supposed him to be the decided Protestant he now appears to be.[30]

Matthew Digby Wyatt was disturbed by a "certain mystic quietism about the style of Mr. Ruskin's writing."[31] The *Civil Engineer and Architect's Journal* reviewed the *Lectures on Architecture and Painting* as if it were the dreaded *Tract Ninety* itself:

> The public, who would have shrunk back from openly-avowed Puseyism, listened on a subject of art; they admired his eloquence, his subtlety, his fervour, as they would those of a Jesuit preacher. Profiting by this reception, Mr. Ruskin, having got the ear of the public, has proceeded until he is a recognised missionary of neo-catholicism.[32]

That statement should probably be attributed to William Leeds, who said of Ruskin the same year: "Not only is he avowedly Pre-Raphaelite in his taste but covertly Pre-Lutheran in his sentiments."[33] The *Ecclesiastic* spoke for many when it said that while Ruskin's religious views "appear to be those of a Presbyterian," the actual effect of his books was to bring the doctrines of the Camden Society to those who would never dream of reading the *Ecclesiologist*.[34]

And what of the Ecclesiologists themselves? Clearly their response was crucial to the spread of Ruskin's ideas. Many of them were young clergymen willing and eager to fight for the designs they admired. Their rigid ideas of right and wrong in architectural practice and the sharpness with which they reviewed each new church in their magazine made them a powerful force. Architects either deferred to their opinions or prepared to do a great deal of explaining. Had the Ecclesiologists taken offense at Ruskin's books, as they might well have done, the phenomenon of Ruskinism would have been smaller and more transient than in fact it was.

The *Ecclesiologist's* review of *The Seven Lamps* opens by apologizing for tardiness, and this probably indicates that a good deal of discussion went on behind the scenes. The matter was complicated, as we will see in chapter 6, by the fact that the Ecclesiologists were building a model church in London, and some of Ruskin's doctrines were applicable to its design. By August of 1849, however, the magazine had made its decision: Ruskin's views on architecture were to be welcomed and his views on religion were to be largely ignored. The anonymous reviewers not only praise his views but summarize them in such detail that the articles could almost substitute for the books themselves.

On religious questions, however, their approach was entirely different. The review of *The Seven Lamps* regrets "some unnecessary abuse of the unreformed Church,"[35] but otherwise avoids the topic. The review of the first volume of *The Stones of Venice* begins with a promise to once again abstain "from any lengthened discussion of the continual abuse of the Church of

Rome, and, by implication, of the Church of England, in its Catholic aspect, or of the attack on Mr. Pugin himself, which disfigures this otherwise charming volume."[36] The review of the second volume again promised to avoid disputed questions of theology, and the magazine took this attitude so seriously that a promised article on the highly polemical third volume never appeared. Only once in approximately seventeen thousand words did the reviewers permit themselves an extended analysis of Ruskin's religious position. Their words were carefully measured and are largely accurate:

> It is not as if Mr. Ruskin's *monomania* (for such it is) against Catholicity were at all a necessary consequence of his argument, or at all dependent upon his theory. Fortunately we may adopt, almost without reserve, Mr. Ruskin's principles of criticism without in the least degree sharing his hatred of Catholicity: and Mr. Pugin might learn from Mr. Ruskin,—had not (as is not improbable) Mr. Ruskin learnt it of him,—to loathe all that is false, and mean, and meretricious in art, without being led thereby to idolize so unreal and impossible an "ideal" as Mr. Ruskin's vision of a truthful and art-loving Protestantism. We must confess to a shrewd suspicion, that Mr. Ruskin's vehemence on this point is due to *temper.* His speculations concerning questions of art lead him to one conclusion; his religious prejudices drive him to another, wholly irreconcileable. He cannot harmonize the two, nor part with either; *Hinc illae lacrymae.* Idolizing, as he does, upon conviction, the Campanile of Giotto, or the Frari at Venice, he finds himself loathing the faith of the men who reared them; while, tortured to the very soul by the architecture of the conventicle, and by that high appreciation of art always shown by the Puritan, he struggles against the conclusion that Protestantism is fairly symbolized by the material exhibition it pleases to make of itself.[37]

IV

There is a coda to the story. It might have been a glorious climax had not Ruskin's divorce interfered with one of his few involvements in practical design. In 1853 a project was set in motion for the remodeling of Camden Chapel.

What actually happened has to be pieced together from a variety of sources, and sometimes the record is difficult to interpret. Ruskin finished the last two volumes of *The Stones of Venice* in the spring of 1853. He and his wife Effie traveled to Scotland for the summer and took with them the young painter John Everett Millais. The party was joined there by Henry Acland, who was deep in his maneuvering for the establishment of a natu-

ral science museum at Oxford. He wanted Ruskin to prepare a lecture on
"The Uses of Gothic," which would have been a forthright advocacy of the
Gothic Revival. Ruskin was too busy for this. He was preparing his Edinburgh lectures, however, and these contained a defense of Gothic as an
appropriate style for the nineteenth century. It is not surprising that during
August Ruskin and Millais turned their attention to the problems of modern Gothic design.

In that month Millais wrote to a friend:

> Ruskin and myself are pitching into architecture; you will hear shortly to what
> purpose. I think now I was intended for a Master Mason. All this day I have
> been working at a window, which I hope you will see carried out very shortly in
> stone. In my evening hours I mean to make many designs for church and other
> architecture, as I find myself quite familiar with construction, Ruskin having
> given me lessons regarding foundations and the building of cathedrals, etc. etc.
> This is no loss of time—rather a real relaxation from everyday painting—and it
> is immensely necessary that something new and good should be done in the
> place of the old ornamentations.[38]

On August 17, Millais wrote to Holman Hunt:

> Ruskin and myself are deep in the designing of novel architecture. He is quite
> delighted and astonished at my designs—he thought that we were simply ca-
> pable of copying nature, and that we had no inventions. Now he admits that he
> was awfully mistaken.[39]

Millais's fullest account of his activities came in a long letter, dated August
1853, to Charles Collins:

> Ruskin has discovered that I can design architectural ornamentation more per-
> fectly that any living or dead *party*. So delighted is he that in the evening I
> have promised to design doors, arches, and windows for churches &c, &c. It is
> the most amusing occupation and it comes quite easily & naturally to my hand.
> I think some of the ideas would drive you mad, though I says it, what should
> not. Ruskin is beside himself with pleasure as he has been groaning for years
> about the lost feeling for architecture. When I make a design he slaps his hands
> together in pleasure, & he draws the arches and frames the mouldings for me to
> fill up. The church which will be designed *entirely by me*, (excepting the ground
> plan) will *for certain* be executed shortly as Ruskin is mad that it should be
> begun as soon as the drawings are made. In truth we shall upset all the glisten-
> ing baldheads, Barry, Cockerell, and the like, so completely that we shall have
> to freight a vessel for the New World for them, where they may build Doric
> order Banks for the gold they are finding there—Ruskin believes now I have
> almost mistaken my vocation and that I was born to restore architecture—
> Please say nothing about this, as we don't wish it to become public that we are
> working in consort—

Millais then goes on to other matters but soon comes back to the subject:

> To return to architecture, which I fancy you will like hearing more about than any other subject, I have made several drawings for the church—amongst others a cloister, on which are to be cut in stone all the vices and virtues opposed to each other. The windows I have finished represent eternal happiness, and the struggle for life, to give you a notion of how they are designed (for they are unlike any other windows ever thought of,) the windows form the shape of the window thus [sketch]. I only make this stupid little drawing that you may understand that figures are bended into the form of the porch, or window instead of the rotten old notion of having flowers (which are naturally frail) to support walls. We will have long talks on this interesting subject when I return, Ruskin says these designs I have made smash Margaret St. Church entirely—[40]

None of this enthusiasm centered on Camden Chapel. It is difficult to imagine the Camberwell congregation either needing or paying for cloisters. Nevertheless, Camden Church was about to be remodeled. The Rev. Daniel Moore had succeeded the Rev. Henry Melvill in 1844. He was presumably the same Daniel Moore who in 1844 was named both chaplain and honorary fellow of an architectural college that Alfred Bartholomew was attempting to found in connection with his organization, the Freemasons of the Church.[41] Moore had an informed enthusiasm for Gothic, he was close to the Ruskins, and he knew of Ruskin's association with Millais. The thought of having the artist contribute to his remodeled church must have been attractive. He does not seem to have thought in terms of Millais designing the church. Probably George Gilbert Scott had already been selected for that. Moore's thoughts focused on the stained glass. "Mr. Moore," John James Ruskin reported to his son, "would think the whole pre-Raphaelite school well occupied in setting aside three years pictures and giving their deep thoughts to a window in Camden Chapel."[42]

Apparently Moore did not realize that Millais and Ruskin were already thinking in terms of designing a window. Ruskin did not let on. On November 25, 1853, he wrote to Moore:

> I am much embarrassed by the contents of your letter. I should exceedingly rejoice in Millais giving you a design if we were such masters of glassworking or that his design could be perfectly executed, but I am uncomfortable in the idea of his failing; and of your being disappointed by trusting to him, considering that this kind of design is one which he has never practised—and has hardly thought of.[43]

Ruskin goes on to suggest that there would be nothing wrong with simply copying real examples of medieval glass. However, his friend Oldfield had argued against copying, and Millais seemed to need rest from more demanding endeavors. Accordingly, Ruskin agrees to suggest that Millais try his hand:

> I write therefore to him tonight, begging him not to forget you, only please say to anyone interested in this matter that I cannot and will not answer in any way for the success of the window—It may be one of the finest things done in any age—or it may be a very disgraceful failure, if Millais does not acquaint himself carefully with the capacities of his material.[44]

In fact what Millais sent was either the same design he had written of to Collins or an adaptation of it. It illustrated lines from Tennyson's "The Palace of Art": "And angels rising and descending met / With interchange of gift." Each angel had the face of Ruskin's wife (fig. 16).

Some letters from Ruskin's father, dating from the second week of December 1853, show how the project appeared to a sympathetic but conservative member of the older generation. At first John James was worried that Millais might provide windows with figures of saints. Admittedly every other Anglican church in the area was dedicated to a saint, but this was scarcely appropriate to such an emphatically Evangelical congregation: "We have St. Giles, St. Pauls and St. Matthews, on Denmark Hill but I suppose the Saints don't go down as far as Peckham—I only know it as Camden Chapel now church."[45] Another problem was Millais's controversial reputation as an artist. John James considered him "a beauty of a man" and "high in intellect," but also suspected that "Millais is too grand for working at Peckham and might not please the John Bulls of Camberwell." Ironically, it was the arrival of the design bearing Effie's face that finally wiped away all of John James's hesitations. He was beside himself with ecstasy. On December 12 he wrote: "We were thunderstruck. . . . It is the most angelic painting or fresco I ever set eyes on—all Watts things are dross and lead to this—of the Earth Earthy—this is pure sublimity."[46] In his next letter he adds: "I wonder what Millais will arrive at doing. He is the painter of the age—greater in one way than Turner for I presume at 24 Turner never made such a picture."[47]

Effie's separation from her husband the following year clearly made it impossible to proceed with the window for Camden Chapel. Ruskin did not, however, easily abandon the hope that Millais might yet reform architectural ornament. As late as December 11, 1854, only a few days before their final rupture, Ruskin could still ask Millais: "Have you given up all thought of *architectural* design? I am just getting the workmen to be able to do something—and if you would sometimes do a design for them to carve in wood or stone it would be such a priceless help."[48]

Daniel Moore went ahead with the remodeling. George Gilbert Scott

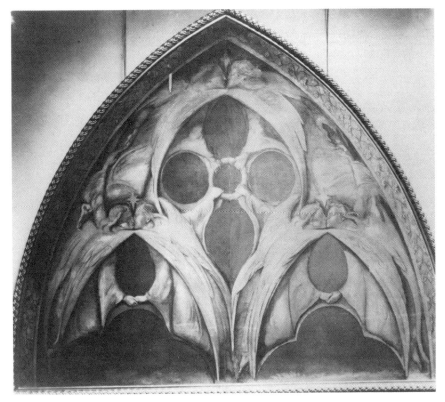

Fig. 16.   Design for a Gothic window. John Everett Millais, 1853. Courtesy of Mary Lutyens.

was the architect, and, as at Saint Giles's, Ruskin helped with the stained-glass windows (fig. 17).

The new chancel for Camden Chapel follows Ruskin's architectural views rather closely. It is, for example, designed in an Italian Romanesque style. Few readers notice, but Ruskin was not especially an advocate of Gothic for churches. In an appendix to the second volume of *The Stones of Venice,* he recommended "the adoption of the Romanesque (or Norman) architecture in our churches, rather than the Gothic" (10.445). This permitted rich decoration without Tractarian associations. It also allowed the use of a basilican plan, which was justified both by the practice of the primitive church and by the Evangelical need for effective acoustics.

Scott had other reasons for turning to the Romanesque style. He was adding to an original structure that derived from the Renaissance. Since the building already had roundheaded windows in the nave, it seemed a logical extension to add a two-bay chancel (used to provide extra seats for

Fig. 17. Chancel for Camden Chapel (demolished). George Gilbert Scott, 1854. Builder, 1854.

the congregation) ending in a round apse with roundheaded arcades surmounted by a half dome. He then had only to replace the original flat roof
with a wagon-headed vault in order to blend the old and the new. Having
found the point where Renaissance and Romanesque harmonized, he was
free to indulge in the new fashion for polychromatic stone and naturalistic
ornament that Camden Chapel's most famous congregant had recently
publicized.

We have only hints as to the discussions that must have taken place between Ruskin, Scott, and Moore over the ornamental part of the addi-
tions. A letter from Ruskin to Moore suggests that there was some alarm
over the abundance of Scott's ornament. Ruskin gives only a little ground:

> I think the design *faultless* and exceedingly beautiful. The appearance of redun-
> dant ornament is caused almost entirely—and very [undecipherable], by the
> two carved columns which are seen so prominently in the interior view. It
> would be easy to leave them uncarved though I think a great pity, but the whole
> effect would then be perfectly simple.[49]

The illustration that appeared in the *Builder* suggests that Ruskin's advice
was taken on this point.

Another controversial matter was the decoration of the new organ. In
this case it is Ruskin who resists excessive ornament. A letter to Daniel
Moore invokes the principle that utility and decoration do not go together:

> All good work involves as its first condition clear declaration of what this
> thing is meant for—and as I have never in my life seen a church organ that I
> admired, I cannot suggest any other merit in the design than that of avoidance
> of any absurd ornament.
>
> In my opinion, all money spent on organ decoration is entirely wasted. An
> organ ought to be as simple as a violin—and I would as soon ask Paganini to
> play on a Gothic fiddle as cumber a church with Gothicism in an organ. My
> own advice in this matter would be to have the thing scrupulously and entirely
> plain of good metal and wood—and of the finest tone possible in this space and
> for the money—and if ever the church is made entirely beautiful like the
> chancel—to keep the organ out of sight.[50]

A second letter went a step beyond scrupulous plainness, but with a significant reservation: "I entirely like its principle—clearly visible *pipes* prettily
coloured; only in this case, the colours are ill arranged, as all modern colouring is, and must for a long time yet be."[51] This is a significant statement
from one of the great Victorian advocates of polychromy, and it should be
remembered when Ruskin's attitude toward his influence is considered.

The final letter concerning Camden Church related to its stained glass.
On April 15, 1854, Ruskin wrote to Pauline Trevelyan:

I have also had to hunt through some books on painted glass to find 13th century squares of design without any popery in them—which might be glazed in
the face of a protestant congregation—at the bottom of the hill. They are
nevertheless very restive; and have nearly protested both their clergyman &
architect into fevers. I advise a little orthodox white-wash and plain lattice,
but the clergyman has a chromatic weakness and I fear, may paint himself out
of the pulpit.[52]

It is ironic that after all of Ruskin's efforts, his Camberwell neighbors were
still so suspicious of the new movement in architecture. Perhaps the remodeled church, partly Renaissance and partly Romanesque, elevated
from its chapel status but still proudly aware of its dissenting origins, will
stand as an appropriate symbol of Ruskin's effort to raise the level of Evangelical taste.

IV

DESCRIBING BUILDINGS: RUSKIN AND NINETEENTH-CENTURY ARCHITECTURAL PROSE

 MUCH of Ruskin's impact was made possible by his literary virtuosity. The classics of the architects' bookshelves—Vitruvius's *De architectura,* Palladio's *I Quattro libri,* Sir William Chambers's *Treatise on Civil Architecture*—offered practical advice and dry prose. George Gilbert Scott, hesitantly publishing his first book in 1850, explains some of the reasons:

> It is . . . one of the disadvantages of the profession of architecture that, though in its own nature highly imaginative, and though it presents a wide field for romantic associations, for antiquarian research, and for philosophical investigation, its actual practice is of necessity so *material* in its character, and so intimately connected with the ordinary business of life, that the architect himself is usually the very last person to give verbal expression to the sentiment or the philosophy of his art; and whatever may be his inward feelings, he seldom rises externally above the ordinary level of the man of business.[1]

This situation would have changed in the Victorian period even if Ruskin had never turned his attention away from landscape painting, for the many battles in the long warfare of the styles encouraged architects to cultivate their literary skills. Pugin's zesty polemics provided a model, but Ruskin went even further, creating a style that not only conveyed information and crushed opponents, but also captured the emotional complexity of great architecture.

It is easy today to forget that many of the buildings Ruskin loved were either denigrated by his contemporaries or given only highly qualified praise. How could he deal with those who found the west front of Rouen overdecorated or Saint Mark's in Venice simply bizarre? Careful argument was not likely to be enough. It would be more effective to take the reader by the hand, place him before the cathedral in Rouen or in Saint Mark's Square, and inspire in him the necessary response. Ruskin's descriptive prose was intended to persuade.

I

We can recapture some of the first impact of Ruskin's style by comparing it with passages by two other writers. One is from Joseph Woods's *Letters of an Architect from France, Italy, and Greece* (1828).[2] The other is from George Wightwick's *The Palace of Architecture: A Romance of Art and History* (1840).[3]

Woods suffered from that clinging to fact that hampered many architectural writers. He opens his account of the cathedral at Amiens by repeating the legends concerning its early history and relics. He tells us that the old cathedral was destroyed by fire in 1218 and that the new structure was begun in 1220. So far this is much the same as the opening to Ruskin's description of Saint Mark's, and it is, in fact, a common guidebook form. Ruskin makes such material an effective prelude to an emotional confrontation with the cathedral. Woods cannot do this. Instead, he goes on to give forty separate measurements of the building, from the length of the front platform (153 feet, 5 inches) to the height of each numeral on the clock (2 feet). Even when he finally turns away from cold facts he cannot lose himself in the object, but continually stands back to compare it to York Minster, Salisbury, Saint Paul's, Westminster Abbey, or to some French cathedrals. This is disappointing in an author who assures us that his "object is rather to communicate the impression produced on the mind of the observer, and to point out the leading sources of that impression, than to enter into *minutiae*."[4]

Nevertheless, Woods's comments on Amiens provide a foil to Ruskin's evocation of Rouen:

> The profusion of ornament in this front is not without its effect, but we endeavour in vain to trace any simple principle of arrangement, and a certain degree of confusion diminishes the pleasure which would otherwise be felt. This objection is applicable more or less to the external of all Gothic buildings, and the more the parts are multiplied the more obvious it becomes: yet it is not a style

of architecture which can succeed without a considerable proportion of ornament, and perhaps even of intricacy. On the inside of a Gothic edifice of the
best periods, although the parts are numerous, yet they all seem to arise from
the mode of construction, and to follow each other so naturally, that the eye
and mind are led from one to the another through the whole system. With the
outside the case is otherwise; the form of no one part seems to depend on that
below it, but each might as well be surmounted by something different as by
that which really succeeds it. The ranges of arches in these fronts have the
effect of dividing the height of the composition into horizontal bands, and
there can be no doubt that in the pointed architecture, the perpendicular lines
should prevail over the horizontal.[5]

This shows Woods at his best, trying to relate the visual characteristics of
the building to underlying principles of design. He is so worried by the
profusion of ornament, however, that he never actually surrenders to the
facade.

If Woods clings to facts and intellectual inquiry, George Wightwick runs
into the opposite danger. He shared the aspiration theory with Pugin and
Patmore, and believed that the essence of Gothic lay in soaring arches and
vertical lines. Woods, with his respect for facts, noticed the power of the
horizontal bands at Amiens, even though he felt that the perpendicular
element "should" prevail. Wightwick, however, ignores such considera-
tions in his description of a typical Gothic cathedral. He leaps at once into
ecstasy:

All that you saw ere you entered the gate of Constantinal Rome only sought to
inform you of the grandeur and the grace belonging to those idolatrous crea-
tions, which, however lofty, still maintain but a horizontal course with Earth:
nor was it till the genius of Pointed Design expanded itself in the glowing atmosphere of Christianized Europe, that Architecture aspired to raise the eye above
the level of mere human perfection, and to give it a 'heaven-directed' aim.
Then sought she, in the long vistas and mounting spires which distinguish the
wondrous temples of Germany, France and Great Britain, to symbolize the ever-
vanishing perspective of Eternity, and the infinite altitude of the Creator above
his creatures. Their lofty pillars seemed rather to spring *from* the earth, than to
rest *upon* it; their aspiring arches, instead of downward pressure, expressed upward continuity; and those windowless walls, which in the Heathen temple,
remain in stubborn solidity to exclude the light, were now pierced on all sides
to admit the beams of divine day. Now sought they to typify, by the sobered
splendour of emblazoned glass, how, through the many coloured medium of
mystery, Heaven poured its dazzling rays, in mercy 'dimmed' for mortal eyes.
Now sought they, in their cruciform plan, to exhibit a symbol of the Everlasting
sacrifice, and in their central crowning tower, an abiding monument of Salvation: whilst, like ever-soaring piety upwards and still upwards rose the 'star-y-
pointing spire,' to seek its *finial* in that heaven where alone the soul's consum-
mation *can* be sought.[6]

This is an emotional response to architecture indeed, though not, as we have seen, one that Ruskin would have admired.

The most effective contrast to both Woods and Wightwick is the final paragraph of "The Lamp of Sacrifice." Ruskin was writing at a time when the sparing use of ornament—the so-called chastity—of the Greek Revival still had force as an aesthetic norm, and at a time when his fellow Evangelicals still looked askance at rich decoration. He presents a painstaking argument against these points of view, but he also recognizes that he must do more. As he said in a letter to his father in 1847, there are some truths that are apprehended only in a certain condition of mind. He could convey them to the reader only "by putting him into that condition, and my endeavour in description would be, not to detail the facts of the scene, but by any means whatsoever to put my hearer's mind into the same ferment as my mind" (22.80).

Here is the crucial portion of Ruskin's paragraph:

> The total number of subordinate niches alone, each worked like that in the plate, and each with a different pattern of traceries in each compartment, is one hundred and seventy-six. Yet in all this ornament there is not one cusp, one finial, that is useless—not a stroke of the chisel is in vain; the grace and luxuriance of it all are visible—sensible rather—even to the uninquiring eye; and all its minuteness does not diminish the majesty, while it increases the mystery, of the noble and unbroken vault. It is not less the boast of some styles that they can bear ornament, than of others that they can do without it; but we do not often enough reflect that those very styles, of so haughty simplicity, owe part of their pleasurableness to contrast, and would be wearisome if universal. They are but the rests and monotones of the art; it is to its far happier, far higher, exaltation that we owe those fair fronts of variegated mosaic, charged with wild fancies and dark hosts of imagery, thicker and quainter than ever filled the depth of midsummer dream; those vaulted gates, trellised with close leaves; those window-labyrinths of twisted tracery and starry light; those misty masses of multitudinous pinnacle and diademed tower; the only witnesses, perhaps, that remain to us of the faith and fear of nations. All else for which the builders sacrificed has passed away—all their living interests, and aims, and achievements. We know not for what they laboured, and we see no evidence of their reward. Victory, wealth, authority, happiness—all have departed, though bought by many a bitter sacrifice. But of them, and their life and their toil upon the earth, one reward, one evidence is left to us in those gray heaps of deepwrought stone. They have taken with them to the grave their powers, their honours, and their errors; but they have left us their adoration.

All of this is intended to clinch an argument by offering an experience. It starts with straightforward discussion of the carving on the west front. Claims are made, examples given. We are directed to an adjoining illustration for further information. The sentences are brief and direct, and convey as much information as such a writer as Woods could possibly desire. Then, with the second sentence in the portion quoted above, the passage modulates into something else. The cadences become more emphatic and the sentence structure more complex; the language reaches toward the condition of poetry. But the emotion presented is quite different from that provoked by the Gothic cathedral in *The Palace of Architecture*. Wightwick's eye followed the vertical lines of the facade upward so rapidly that it seemed to zoom to heaven without ever dwelling on the building. Ruskin, by contrast, seems to look into the facade—through gates, into labyrinths, into depths. The speaker, who a few sentences before was confidently numbering 176 different patterns of tracery, is now lost in dark hosts of imagery, window-labyrinths, and misty masses. This is a vision as intense as Wightwick's and vastly more complex. It is one of Ruskin's strengths to perceive the range of Gothic architecture, the darkness of the shadow as well as the intense points of light, the weight of the stone as well as the airy delicacy of the towers. With the tenth sentence, the passage modulates again. The simpler, shorter sentences act as a kind of recessional, leading us back to something close to the level of ordinary experience.

The multitudinousness of the carving and the richness of Ruskin's response to it are both mirrored in the structure of his sentences. The syntax of Woods's prose makes no special claim on our attention, and Wightwick's soaring verbs are a simple way of gaining a simple effect. Ruskin's literary resources are much greater than theirs, and, accordingly, his language is worth examining more closely.

The second sentence quoted is transitional from the discursive tone of the opening. The central idea—that none of the ornament on the porch is useless—flows naturally from what has gone before, but the dramatic assertion is now stronger: "in all this ornament there is *not one* . . . *all* are visible . . . *all* its minuteness does not diminish." The syntax conveys the sense of a speaker profoundly, passionately moved by what he conveys. Elements are frequently doubled ("not one cusp, one finial . . . grace and luxuriance"), while others stand in antithesis ("does not diminish the majesty, while it increases the mystery"). The sense of the speaker's emotional force is increased by the fact that Ruskin corrects himself in midsentence ("all are visible—sensible rather"), by his use of such emotional terms as "noble" and "majesty," and especially by a sudden burst of alliteration: "its minuteness does not diminish the majesty, while it increases the mystery.

By the third sentence quoted we have broadened our view from a porch at Rouen to styles of architecture—styles sufficiently animate that they can "boast" and be "haughty." By the fourth, we have reached another level of discourse altogether, one that passes beyond argument or assertion to provide a verbal equivalent of Ruskin's most intense experience of architecture. The first ten words of the next sentence can be passed over quickly: "They [i.e., styles that can do without ornament] are but the rests and monotones of the art . . ." An underlying form of the second part of the sentence can be stated as follows:

Subject	Verb	Direct Object	Prepositional Phrase
we	owe	fair fronts, etc.	to its far happier, far higher exaltation

The verb "owe" is used metaphorically, but fits into the grammatical structure of a transitive verb that takes a direct object. The difficulty with the straightforward structure arranged above is that the direct object comes before the prepositional phrase and before the point at which the meaning of the sentence is complete—not an arrangement that would permit it to be elaborated in any great detail. But the meaning of the main clause is, in reality, a very subordinate part of this sentence; it is the elaboration of the direct object that will convey Ruskin's vision of architecture. Accordingly, Ruskin inverts normal English word order by beginning with the expletive "it." This allows him to place the prepositional phrase before the verb: "It is to its far happier, far higher, exaltation that we owe . . ." The direct object now comes at the end, and Ruskin is free to elaborate it into four parallel direct objects, each of which is in turn extensively modified:

> that we owe
> —those fair fronts of variegated mosaic, charged with wild fancies and dark hosts of imagery, thicker and quainter than ever filled the depth of midsummer dream;
> —those vaulted gates, trellised with close leaves;
> —those window-labyrinths of twisted tracery and starry light;
> —those misty masses of multitudinous pinnacle and diademed tower.

It is striking that the longest and most complex of these parallel phrases, the only one in which the modifying participial phrase is itself modified by another phrase, is placed first rather than saved to provide a climax of the series. No doubt Ruskin wants to avoid the formal balance of Johnsonian prose, while still preserving syntactic order in the entire sentence. Yet this is not quite the entire sentence, for Ruskin goes on to conclude with a fifteen-word appositive clause that modifies the entire fifty-one-word direct object: "the only witnesses, perhaps, that remain to us of the faith and fear of nations." Such syntactic richness has a double function. It is appropriate to a sentence that talks about profusion. At the same time, it supports the reader with an underlying coherence, one that is intuited rather than clearly perceived.

Such prose did not delight all of Ruskin's critics. The *Rambler* complained that Ruskin's writing "frequently verges on the unintelligible, through the excessive awkwardness of its construction" and added: "He writes as most fluent people talk, with that slovenly, disjointed, and awkward disposition of his thoughts and expressions, which is scarcely noticed in speaking, but on paper becomes barely intelligible."[7] This, however, was an unusual and rather stingy response. Most readers were so awed by Ruskin's style that his opponents worried that his phrases would distract attention from his assertions. Wightwick, disagreeing with Ruskin at many points, was among those who suddenly drew back in alarm: "the occasionally mysterious tone of his passages, their luxuriant language, deep feeling, and energetic wit, are not unlikely to occasion that sort of vague admiration which may interfere with the practical usefulness of his truths, and leave unnoticed his unquestionable fallacies."[8] Ruskin himself eventually looked back on his early triumphs with a certain rueful amusement, admitting, in a witty self-parody, that *The Seven Lamps* was "overlaid with gilding, and overshot too splashily and cascade fashion, with gushing of words" (8.15).

Nevertheless, an age that stressed the emotional content of architecture required a language that could apprehend and express that content. Ruskin's occasional excesses mattered less than the fact that he had found what was required. It is easy to see how his prose must have overwhelmed young students and clerks accustomed to the informative dryness of handbooks and encyclopedias. To see the full value of Ruskin's method of arguing by impassioned description we must turn to his acknowledged masterpiece, the description of Saint Mark's in *The Stones of Venice*. There Ruskin confronts problems that troubled most young English architects and resolves them through the power and architectonic structure of his prose.

II

Saint Mark's confronts Ruskin with two dilemmas. One is aesthetic: How can an Englishman, raised on the Gothic of northern Europe, adjust himself to the quite different forms of Venetian Gothic? Even if English travelers did not share Woods's surprise at Saint Mark's "lumpy forms" and "enormous, ugly, ill-shaped domes," they would have agreed with his worried comment that "the enrichments are excessively heavy and overcharged, so that the architecture seems made for them, rather than they for the building."[9] Judgments on Saint Mark's were almost uniformly negative before the publication of *The Stones of Venice*, and the earliest reviewers were astonished that Ruskin could praise the building. William Leeds called his opinion "as marvellous as any of the wonders wrought by Aladdin's lamp."[10] Another writer expressed dismay at Ruskin's ultra-admiration for "such truly barbarous architecture, as is that of St. Mark's church and Ducal Palace at Venice."[11] A book was announced for publication entitled *An Attempt to Demonstrate the "Loveliness" of St. Mark's at Venice. By a Candidate for St. Luke's*.[12] Yet these were minority opinions a few months after *The Stones of Venice* was published. Ruskin's description is one of the most successful pieces of persuasion ever undertaken.

Ruskin's second problem is religious: How can a sensibility molded by Protestant austerities not be offended by the lavish Catholicism of Saint Mark's? This was harder to overcome. The paragraphs in which Ruskin attempted to resolve the difficulty in intellectual terms are among the most tedious and inconclusive that he ever wrote. That is why the descriptive passage is so important. The architectonic structure of his prose allows Ruskin to achieve at least a temporary reconciliation of Protestant sensibility and Mediterranean sensuousness.

He begins by sketching the history of the church in a brisk, academic tone. He is, though the reader does not know it, presenting a foil for what is to come, the first in an intricate structure of contrasts. Only once in the first nine paragraphs does emotion intrude. That is when he tells us that the destruction of the body of Saint Mark in the fire of 976 would have deprived the church of most of its revenues had not the casket, in "what appears to have been one of the best arranged and most successful impostures ever attempted by the clergy of the Romish Church" (10.74), miraculously reappeared with the unconsumed body of the saint inside. All of this seems to lead straight toward a discussion of Saint Mark's as it appeared in the nineteenth century.

It is, therefore, surprising to find the tenth paragraph beginning: "And now I wish that the reader, before I bring him into St. Mark's Place, would imagine himself for a little time in a quiet English cathedral town, and walk with me to the west front of its cathedral" (10.78). The abrupt transition alerts the reader to the fact that he is about to read a new kind of prose; it signals him to sharpen his powers of observation. By transporting us from Venice to a place more nearly resembling Salisbury or Wells, it introduces the first in a complex series of contrasts.

The two long sentences that follow are densely packed with detail. There is an underlying structure, however, with key words and phrases serving as signposts on a visual progress. The first sentence begins as an imperative construction and branches out into four adverbial phrases:

Let us go together
—up the more retired street
—through the low grey gateway
—into the inner private-looking road or close
—and so forward till we come to

Each of these adverbial phrases modifies the verb "go," and each ends in a noun that opens the way to further, quite extensive modification. "Into the inner private-looking road or close," for example, is modified by two subordinate clauses:

—where nothing goes in but the carts of the tradesmen who supply the bishop and the chapter, and
—where there are little shaven grass-plots, fenced in by neat rails, before old-fashioned groups of somewhat diminutive and excessively trim houses

The "trim houses" then receive four prepositional phrases of further modification before we finally come to the fourth of the adverbial phrases that bind the sentence together. Yet this description only hints at the outlines of Ruskin's dense structure of freely branching modification. It would be difficult to think of a more appropriate syntactic equivalent for a leisurely stroll.

That, of course, is what it is. Everything is quiet and peaceful and, above all, tidy. We are in the world that Trollope was to explore two years later in *The Warden* (1855). The grass plots are shaven and fenced; the houses are small and trim. The picturesque architecture, with "little, crooked, thick, indescribable wooden gables warped a little on one side," enhances the mood of lovely domesticity. Although the private-looking road hints at the carts of tradesmen, the only inhabitants we see are the canon's children walking with their nursemaids. But above them, on the facade of the vast cathedral, nothing is carefully tended, and as we examine it we become involved in the second of the contrasts. If the dominant actions in the previous sentence were those of leisurely strolling and quiet gazing, the action here is that of looking "up" and "higher and higher up," and "higher still" until our powers of looking are almost overcome. Our quiet scene has been invaded by activity, and Ruskin expresses the frozen action of the architectural facade not with verbs but with adjectives derived from verbs: mouldering, confused, shattered, mocking, swirling, closing, scattering. Where the first part of the paragraph was localized in the nineteenth century, we now move to the greater stretches of historic time and finally, with the images of lichen staining the rocks and rain and wind wearing them, to the still vaster stretches of geological time. By the end of the sentence we have passed entirely into the world of nature, and we hear only "the crowd of restless birds that fill the whole square with that strange clangour of theirs, so harsh and yet so soothing, like the cries of birds on a solitary coast between the cliffs and sea."

The relevance of this scene to Saint Mark's is not yet clear. Some readers have assumed that Ruskin simply wants to show that the Venetian cathedral is quite different from an English one. He has a far more serious purpose, however, and it is hinted at in the eleventh paragraph: for all its apparent solitude, the cathedral has had an undoubted and lasting effect on the hearts of Englishmen. Ruskin does not argue the point; he does not have to. Nor does he explicitly ask what corresponding influence Saint Mark's may have had on the Venetians. That question is planted, however, and carefully held in reserve.

Ruskin's description of the English cathedral was thick with detail, but there was a clear sequence of commands and directions to guide us. In Venice, by contrast, we are battered from all sides and our senses are overwhelmed. We can scarcely make our way. The first sentence locates us in a narrow, crowded alley and assaults our ears with the shrieks of itinerant vendors. The second sentence, instead of describing our progress, tells us what is overhead. The third tells us what is on each side. The difficulty of our progress is mirrored in the syntax. In the second and third sentences, for example, there are no finite verbs. In the opening passage of *Bleak House*, published only two years before this volume of *The Stones of Venice*, Dickens had similarly suppressed finite verbs to portray a world sinking into immobility. Ruskin's purpose is different. Here the world is filled with frenetic activity, though little of it is ours. We are scarcely able to struggle forward. By the last sentence of the paragraph we are still only a few steps further on, and all the while we are assailed by the richest evocation of chaos that could possibly be imagined.

We can make out one thing, however. The signs of Mediterranean Catholicism are everywhere. We can glimpse, in the dark interiors of the shops, the candles that burn before cheap prints of the Virgin. The fruiterer has enthroned his Madonna in a tabernacle of fresh laurel leaves. The less zealous pewterer has let his lamp go out, but at the wine shop the Virgin is enthroned in great glory, surrounded by large red casks and lit by two crimson lamps. In the evening the gondoliers will gather under her image and drink away the money they have gained during the day.

Some Englishmen have been exhilarated by this mixture of the sacred and the profane. Ruskin does not comment on it at all, but simply presses forward. By paragraph thirteen we have gone a yard or two farther, and then suddenly our progress accelerates. We push through the shadow of the pillars at the end of the Bocca di Piazza and suddenly it is as if "the rugged and irregular houses that press together above us in the dark alley had been struck back into sudden obedience and lovely order, and all their rude casements and broken walls had been transformed into arches charged with goodly sculpture, and fluted shafts of delicate stone."

With the English cathedral, Ruskin had begun by describing the quiet world of the close and had risen from sight to vision as his eye moved up the facade. Now he repeats this movement, except that in England the progress was from the peace of the close to the dissonant cry of the birds, while in Venice it is from the jarring noises of the street to the serenity of the cathedral. What we see is simultaneously the facade of Saint Mark's and a vision of heaven. It has, as Ruskin's paradise would have to have, indescribably lovely and subtle color harmonies. There are gold and opal and mother of pearl; there are jasper, porphyry, deep-green serpentine, and rich marbles; there are white domes clustered into a long, low pyramid of colored light. There are figures of angels and carved palm leaves, lilies, grapes, and pomegranates. There are mosaics with gold ground "like morning light when it faded back among the branches of Eden." Decoration is everywhere; above the archivolts it forms "a continuous chain of language and of life." Ruskin describes his vision as "a confusion of delight," and we are not at first tempted to do anything more than immerse ourselves in its verbal rhythms and sensuous harmonies.

Beneath the surface shimmer, however, there is a solid architectural structure and a single rhetorical aim. Ruskin has contrived a complex series of oppositions between the neatness of the English close and the wild solitude of its cathedral, between the jangling streets of Venice and the order of Saint Mark's Square, between the rough-hewn stones of northern Gothic and the gracious color harmonies of Saint Mark's. He has built an arch that still lacks a keystone. Now he introduces yet another contrast—this time between Saint Mark's and the life that goes on before it. He shows an endless procession of soldiers and priests and citizens. He shows idle Venetians reading the papers, an Austrian band blaring, and a sullen crowd that would stiletto every Austrian soldier if it had the chance.

> And in the recesses of the porches, all day long, knots of men of the lowest classes, unemployed and listless, lie basking in the sun like lizards; and unregarded children,—every heavy glance of their young eyes full of desperation and stony depravity, and their throats hoarse with cursing,—gamble, and fight, and snarl, and sleep, hour after hour, clashing their bruised centesimi upon the marble ledges of the church porch. And the images of Christ and His angels look down upon it continually.

At this point we see clearly the single rhetorical aim that lies beneath the variegated surface of Ruskin's prose. He has persuaded us to separate Saint Mark's from the priests who officiate within its walls, from the Austrians who parade before it, and from the idle Venetians who lounge about its base. He has rescued the structure from the nineteenth century and shown that it belongs to the timeless world of imaginative vision. Saint Mark's belongs to those who can respond to it most intensely.

III

There is a Ruskinian influence on architectural prose as well as on architecture itself. In 1850 George Gilbert Scott sounded like a man who was passionate but tongue-tied. By 1857, when Scott published his *Remarks on Secular and Domestic Architecture,* he had gained enormously in flexibility; this was in part because he had, as Coventry Patmore said in the *North British Review,* adopted "not only Mr. Ruskin's ideas, but also, as far as he was able, Mr. Ruskin's style, even to its defects."[13]

G. E. Street was another architect who found in Ruskin's style a vehicle that would convey his own deepest feelings about architecture. In 1855 he published his own description of Saint Mark's in *Brick and Marble in the Middle Ages.* In it he is acutely aware of the contrast between the structural Gothic of northern Europe and the more decorative forms of medieval Venice. Facing the exterior of the cathedral, Street finds himself suspended between Woods's reaction and Ruskin's:

> The west front is certainly most indescribable, and I confess to feeling a doubt, as I looked at it, as to whether it was not more akin to some fairy-like vision, such as in dreams one might see, than to any real and substantial erection of stone and mortar; for, to a mind educated in and accustomed to the traditions of northern architecture, there is something so very *outré* in the whole idea, so startling in its novelty, that it is hard to know whether to admire or not.[14]

Street resolves his doubts when he steps inside, and he does so through a passage of Ruskinian description:

> The deep tones of an organ are heard reverberating through the old building; many people kneel devoutly at their prayers around us; the hot glare of the sun is gone, and in its place a cool, quiet, dim light reveals the whole magnificence of the interior. It is quite in vain to describe this architecturally. The colour is so magnificent that one troubles oneself but little about the architecture, and

thinks only of gazing upon the expanse of gold and deep rich colour all harmonized together into one glorious whole.[15]

Just as Ruskin finds a vision of paradise in the natural decoration of the exterior, so Street finds in "the wild beauty of the pavement," which undulates as if it were "petrified waves of the sea,"[16] a symbol of the sea of life, which the ship of the Church surmounts, and he writes a prose poem to express this insight.

Other Ruskinian echoes can be cited. Here is John Pollard Seddon in an 1851 paper, "The Relation of Architecture to Painting and Sculpture":

> That which [architecture] has to say, is told from one generation to another; is told so clearly, that men may not but hear; and while she shields within her arms the more fragile works of Painting and Sculpture, their voice, whose compass is greater, blends with and becomes one with her own; and history lends its associations and wild legends their awe; and when records have perished, and the voice of tradition is still, so long as one stone will stand upon another, time will but add a charm, and bedeck the mouldering walls with the golden hues of the lichen and the moss, till, beautiful even in death, the last relic is ploughed into dust.[17]

This sort of climax, in which architecture is suddenly seen in the long perspective of centuries as a mute testimony to the heroism of vanished generations, characterizes each chapter ending in *The Seven Lamps* and proved irresistible to many architects. Here is another example from an 1870 paper by the Birmingham architect John Henry Chamberlain:

> They had their reward. . . . The walls may be shattered; the groining of the roof may have fallen; the aisles of their Houses of Prayer may be choked with weeds, or rendered impassable by rubbish; but where there are even two or three stones left standing one upon another, the old life and the old glory are abiding with them. About the broken pillars and the ruined cornices, and all along the lovely lines of the perishing archways, there hangs the spirit of the past; and because that spirit was brave, and because it was pure and unselfish, and full of divine love, it still speaks to the heart and soul of every one of us, who, perhaps, not being all that we might indeed be, have yet enough of strength and nobleness to see, with Lancelot, that we might be better than we are.[18]

All these examples derive from Ruskin's "jeweled" prose. There is, of course, another kind of language in Ruskin's work, best represented by the angry sermon on the modern workman in "The Nature of Gothic." But it is only later in the century, in the publications of William Morris, Halsey Ricardo, and W. R. Lethaby, that we begin to find echoes of Ruskin's prophecies. It was the poetry of description that appealed to the majority of architects. Thomas Graham Jackson provides an instructive example. He will appear in a later chapter as a man whose views were close to Ruskin's during the 1870s, but by the early twentieth century he had moved toward a new, more structural understanding of architecture. Nevertheless, in his old age he could still write: "I always advise my pupils to read, as I did, *The Seven Lamps of Architecture* and *The Stones of Venice*, though I am obliged to warn them that they will not learn architecture from Ruskin, as he considered architecture from a fallacious and unpractical standpoint; but it puts them into a receptive and reverential mental attitude and that, as I found in my own case, is the proper one in which to approach your art." [19]

V

RUSKINISM: ITS VISUAL CONTENT

RUSKIN'S prose conveyed a vision of architecture, but it also offered advice. It did not always give as much as readers expected. "Let him furnish us," demanded the *Christian Observer*, "with designs, plans, and sections, for a few of the buildings most in request; such as churches, courts, schools, hospitals, libraries, museums, club-houses, private residences, railway stations, &C."[1] He never did so, yet there are examples of all these building types that show Ruskin's influence. His advice was sufficiently general that his admirers were not straightjacketed by it, but was specific enough to have visible results. Ruskin's opinions can be itemized under the categories of mass, color, ornament, and the treatment of the workman.

I

The context for Ruskin's specific advice is provided by his sharp distinction between building and architecture. In "The Lamp of Sacrifice" he says that we achieve architecture when we add to mere building "certain characters venerable or beautiful, but otherwise unnecessary" (2.28). The concept of architecture as something added on has troubled many commentators; it raises visions in their minds of sturdy, practical buildings covered with an excrescent growth of decoration. Ruskin's clarifying examples do nothing to calm their fears:

no one would call the laws architectural which determine the height of a breastwork or the position of a bastion. But if to the stone facing of that bastion be added an unnecessary feature, as a cable moulding, *that* is Architecture. It would be similarly unreasonable to call battlements or machicolations architectural features, so long as they consist only of an advanced gallery supported on projecting masses, with open intervals beneath for defense. But if these projecting masses be carved beneath into rounded courses, which are useless, and if the headings of the intervals be arched and trefoiled, which is useless, *that* is Architecture. (8.29)

This places the essence of architecture in features that Cockerell would have considered glorious but secondary and that a modern functionalist would be willing to do without altogether.

Ruskin states the distinction again in his chapter "The Virtues of Architecture" at the beginning of *The Stones of Venice*. This time he asks us to imagine that we are present at the building of a bridge. Ruskin is warm in his admiration for the mental qualities of the builders:

> The man who chose the curve and numbered the stones, had to know the times and tides of the river, and the strength of its floods, and the height and flow of them, and the soil of the banks, and the endurance of it, and the weight of the stones he had to build with, and the kind of traffic that day by day would be carried on over this bridge, all this especially, and all the great general laws of force and weight, and their working; and in the choice of the curve and numbering of stones are expressed not only his knowledge of these, but such ingenuity and firmness as he had, in applying special means to overcome the special difficulties about his bridge. There is no saying how much wit, how much depth of thought, how much fancy, presence of mind, courage, and fixed resolution there may have gone to the placing of a single stone of it. (9.66)

For all this, the man is a builder, not an architect. His concerns are "merely practical" and contain "no reference to architectural principles." It is possible for a man to build this bridge and yet "be merely what Mr. Carlyle rightly calls a human beaver after all." Ruskin assumes a wide gulf between building and architecture, between the calculating intellect and the creative imagination.

To see what is peculiar about this distinction, consider the one piece of architectural theory that everybody knows: Louis Sullivan's dictum that Form follows Function. What this means in detail is subject to endless dispute, but its application to the bridge seems clear. By paying strict attention to practical matters, the bridge builders have created a form that is aesthetically satisfying. But this is what Ruskin will not accept.

Once this is said, however, it must at once be added that there is a complication. In the first half of the first volume of *The Stones of Venice*, Ruskin

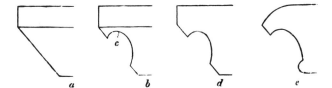

Fig. 18. *Dripstones. John Ruskin.* The Stones of Venice, *volume 1 (1851).*

seems on the verge of overcoming his distinction. His stated purpose is to devote the first half of his volume to construction and the second half to ornament, but instead of dividing them he often seems to establish an intimate connection. In the illustration in figure 18, for example, he sets out to find the most effective shape for a dripstone. The figure at the extreme left is Ruskin's basic shape for a cornice. It consists of a stone with a slanting end, which projects from the wall, and this is in turn protected by a coping stone. The function of this shape is to throw off rain from the wall. The difficulty with the first form is that the rain, instead of falling from the projected portion to the ground, is likely to cling to the slanting surface and run back to the wall. Accordingly the second introduces a hollow. This, however, weakens the projecting part. It is therefore better to use a single piece of stone so that the whole will be stronger at that point. The upper ledge should then be rounded off, as in the form on the right, so that water will not lodge there; a roll should be introduced at the bottom to give further protection to the wall.

Is the resulting dripstone an architectural or a building form? Ruskin, consistent with his initial distinction, thought it was building. Many readers saw no meaningful distinction and blamed or praised him as a proto-functionalist. The *Civil Engineer and Architect's Journal* not only interpreted him as attempting "the determination of forms by the necessities of construction," but accused him of an "over-zealous, over-rigorous application of the doctrine."[2] Coventry Patmore called Ruskin "the first writer who has really attempted to work out the principle which has been often blunderingly expressed by others—namely the direct deduction of most architectural features, short of express ornament, from constructive necessity or 'convenience.'"[3] But a perceptive reviewer in the *Christian Observer* saw that these early chapters in *The Stones of Venice* were really anomalous in the larger body of Ruskin's work:

In the "Seven Lamps of Architecture" he would not allow that the architecture of a building had any concern with its useful purpose—its office was only to add ornament. But now, the greater part of the present volume would be unintelligible, unless the use of the structure, and of every subordinate part of it, was taken as the test of its excellence. In the earlier chapters of the present volume structure is, most legitimately, almost always deduced from function; that is bad which betrays or misconceives it. But when he has finished the discussion of the various essential elements of structure, and proceeds to consider ornamentation—which, in truth, cannot be considered as a separate thing in any of the medieval styles—he seems to forget the principle which has so far safely guided him.[4]

With only occasional inconsistencies, Ruskin maintains his identification of architecture with decoration until the end of his career. It is not surprising that his friend Sir Walter James, evaluating the influence of architectural theorists in 1867, should have concluded that "Pugin has most influenced us in structure, John Ruskin in ornament."[5]

II

Massiveness was one of the qualities that Ruskin demanded most emphatically: "Mass of everything, of bulk, of light, or darkness of colour, not mere use of any of these, but breadth of them: not broken light nor scattered darkness nor divided weight, but solid stone, broad sunshine, starless shade" (8.134). But Ruskin's idea of mass is quite distinct from what his architectural contemporaries meant when they referred to the disposition of the masses. He does not dwell, as other writers do, on the interrelated masses of nave, crossing tower, transepts, choir, and radiating chapels. What he means rather, is that a building should convey a sense of the quantity and weight of its materials. Its walls should be thick and its doors and windows recessed so that this thickness will be dramatized.

Some of Ruskin's discussion of massiveness recapitulates eighteenth- and early-nineteenth-century admiration for the sublime, but there are two important differences. One is that he replaces the earlier stress on terror with a new emphasis on secure strength. Buildings may occasionally intimidate with an overhanging cornice, but they reassure with a firm base and heavy piers. Ruskin's sublime is triumphantly calm rather than darkly menacing. The other revision in the traditional theory is Ruskin's de-emphasis on great size. Magnitude is a matter of psychological perception rather than actual measurements. Sublimity begins when any form reaches the degree of magnitude that will make a living figure look less than life size beside it. Even architecture of relatively modest size could have a visible kinship with mountain forms.

Ruskin's admiration for effects of mass carried with it a preference for what he called surface as against linear Gothic. The distinction is made clear in figure 19, which reproduces plate 12 from volume 2 of *The Stones of*

Fig. 19.   Linear and surface Gothic. John Ruskin. The Stones of
Venice, *volume 2 (1853).*

Venice. The head of a niche from Abbeville (on the left) represents foliation decorated by more foliation; it is linear, nervous, and, in Ruskin's
words, hardly stronger than a piece of lace. The head of the niche on the
right, from Verona, presents a solid mass of stone which contrasts with a
bold mass of shadow below the trefoil. The broad surface of the stone is
unpierced, and the mass of it is thick and strong.

Ruskin's call for combined mass of stone and breadth of surface leads him
to urge a basic simplicity in the shapes of architecture. His preference is for
forms that can be inscribed within a circle or that in their main outline
approach a square. These forms present large areas of surface at the same
time that they make possible the psychological impression of great size. To
show its magnitude, a building must have one continuous, visible bounding line. Once this line is broken, the building's size can no longer be esti-
mated. Moreover, the eye is always drawn to the terminal lines of a facade,
and in buildings that tend toward the square, such as the cathedral at Pisa,
these lines are removed as far as possible from the spectator.

It is especially to be noted with respect to the Palazzo Vecchio and other mighty
buildings of its order, how mistakenly it has been stated that dimension, in
order to become impressive, should be expanded either in height or length, but
not equally: whereas, rather it will be found that those buildings seem on the
whole the vastest which have been gathered up onto a mighty square, and
which look as if they had been measured by the angel's rod, "the length, and the
breadth, and the height of it are equal;" and herein something is to be taken
notice of, which I believe not to be sufficiently, if at all, considered among our
architects. (8.108)

This does not mean, however, that architects are forbidden to stretch their
facades into rectangles. If grace and proportion require an elongation in
one direction, an architect may still achieve the sense of power by confronting the spectator with "a continuous series of any marked features
such as the eye may be unable to number; while yet we feel, from their
boldness, decision, and simplicity, that it is indeed their multitude which
has embarrassed us, not any confusion or indistinctness of form" (8.110).
Thus an architect may use arcades, aisles, and ranges of columns, extending them just to the point where the mind starts to become bewildered.

It is not only mass of stone that Ruskin demands, but broad masses of
light and shade as well. This is justified by a psychological appeal. Ruskin
believes that shadow in architecture affects us by a kind of human sympathy. It is an equivalent expression for "the trouble and wrath of life, for
its sorrow and its mystery" (8.116–117). No building is truly great unless
it has "mighty masses, vigorous and deep, of shadow mingled with its surface" (8.117).

Ruskin made the attention given to masses of light and shade the basis
for his distinction between the healthy phases of Gothic and its decline. It
is a line that he finds possible to draw very precisely, and it is perhaps clearest in the evolution of window tracery. In the earliest traceries, attention is
fixed on the forms of the penetrations rather than on the stone itself. The
forms become more elaborate and the tracery steadily thinner as we proceed from the earliest examples, but it is still the form of light against
darkness that commands our attention rather than the tracery itself. At a
certain point in the history of Gothic, however, a watershed is passed. The
architect stops dividing his window into masses and begins to emphasize
linear forms instead. Stone traceries are made to seem as light and flexible
as thread; they pass in and out of one another. To Ruskin, this is the deca-
dence of Gothic. His preference is always for geometrical plate tracery, in
which forms are punched out of stone. He never extends his praise to curvilinear tracery, and he shocked his contemporaries by speaking with contempt of the "detestable perpendicular" (8.108).

Ruskin's call for mass and breadth was aimed directly at contemporary practice. It is a useful exercise to examine Gower Street near the British Museum from Ruskin's point of view. We need not share his indifference to the art of proportion to see that it lacks what he most demanded: a sense of weight, a conviction of strength, a contrast of broad light and deep shadow. It is easy to see why Ruskin should have exclaimed in dismay that English architecture was "small and mean, if not worse—thin, and wasted, and unsubstantial" (8.135–136).

In place of the flat surfaces of Gower Street, the new Victorian street-scape was to have "sloping roof, jutting porch, projecting balcony, hollow niche, massy gargoyle, frowning parapet" (8.135). This was to be the beginning of the reform of English architecture. "Until that street architecture of ours is bettered, until we give it some size and boldness, until we give our windows recess, and our walls thickness, I know not how we can blame our architects for their feebleness in more important work; their eyes are inured to narrowness and slightness: can we expect them at a word to conceive and deal with breadth and solidity" (8.136).

No part of *The Seven Lamps* was more immediately influential than "The Lamp of Power." The reviews show clearly how much Ruskin was giving forceful expression to a feeling that was already half formed in the hearts of his readers. To be sure, there were a few hostile voices. Matthew Digby Wyatt quoted the long passage beginning "the relative majesty of buildings depends more on the weight and vigour of their masses than on any other attribute of their design" (8.134) and denounced it as "a piece of nonsense."[6] *Blackwood's*, defending the Greek Revival rows of Edinburgh, protested that it is "regularity, giving, for instance, to the whole side of a square the appearance of a single building, which makes our streets so beautiful."[7] But these voices were a decided minority. The *Ecclesiologist* urged that "The Lamp of Power" be "studied carefully" and declared that "there are golden counsels in it for the architect."[8] William Whewell, reviewing *The Seven Lamps* for *Fraser's*, summarized Ruskin's call for massiveness with particular sympathy. A reviewer in the *Church of England Quarterly Review* hoped that Ruskin would have even more to say about the subject in a future volume and assured his readers that "The want of shadow in English building, arising from the absence of deep recesses and bold projections, and the appearance of *papery thinness* which modern Gothic exhibits, display an insensibility to the value of light and shade in a *facade* that is painfully evident in the new Houses of Parliament."[9] E. L. Garbett employs a long quote from Ruskin in opposing the "false principle, called lightness, which has, unfortunately, during the last century or two, crept into the architecture of this country."[10] Coventry Patmore, writing in the *North British Review*, was happy to endorse Ruskin's advice for remedying "the errors of modern house architecture."[11]

III

Ruskin's enthusiasm for color was just as timely as his demand for mass. Polychromy was not unheard of in the 1840s. Ruskin was acquainted with examples in James Wild's Christ Church, Streatham, and Thomas Henry Wyatt's Church of Saints Mary and Nicholas, Wilton. The use of color in most early-nineteenth-century architecture, however, was both rare and hesitant.

A report in the *Builder* on a discussion at the Royal Institute of British Architects (RIBA) shows something of the range of contemporary attitudes at midcentury. It is especially interesting in that the leading members of the institute were classicists rather than Gothicists. For them both the Palladian tradition and the Greek Revival discouraged the use of color. On the other hand, archeology had now shown conclusively that the Grecian temples were originally polychrome. Accordingly, the institute's members gathered to discuss Francis Cranmer Penrose's *Investigations of Athenian Architecture* (1852) and its implications for architectural practice.

C. R. Cockerell represented the old guard. He had himself explored the use of polychromy in Greece, but he invoked the climatic argument against its use in England: "it should be introduced with very great reserve in this grey climate, although it may have been happily and properly applied under a more brilliant sky."[12] Edward I'Anson agreed that the prevailing feeling was against color. T. L. Donaldson, on the other hand, was willing to experiment. He pointed out that "the marble arch in Oxford-street was a cold, dead, tasteless monument; but if marble of different colours had been employed for the columns, the frieze and the panels, it would be more expressive and more beautiful."[13] And Sydney Smirke was unexpectedly lyrical: "Let the student inquire why the blossom of the rose never looks so charming as when contrasted with its own green leaves; and why the purple and yellow streaks on the corolla of the pansy make the humble little plant one of the most lovely.[14] Ten years earlier such a meeting would have been unanimous against the use of color. Now opinion was divided.

Amid such disagreement, a firm voice could have great effect. "I believe it to be," said Ruskin in *The Stones of Venice*, "one of the essential signs of life in a school of art that it loves colour; and I know it to be one of the first signs of death in the Renaissance schools that they despised colour" (10.109).

Ruskin discussed many different ways of achieving polychromatic effects. The use of natural colors of stone was his deepest love. He also supported the device of strengthening brick walls with horizontal bands of stone as well as zigzag and diaper patterns. But his most original contribution to Victorian discussions of polychromy was his defense of encrustation.

Many of the buildings Ruskin admired in Italy had plain brick facades to which were attached thin slabs or crusts of marble. This gave an appearance of great richness but also seemed to violate one of the most fundamental beliefs of the Gothic Revival. Pugin and the Ecclesiologists had established truth and reality as among the chief virtues of architecture. A building was not to convey a false idea about the material of which it was made. Ruskin had endorsed this standard in "The Lamp of Truth" when he condemned the graining of wood to resemble marble and the use of cast-iron ornament to imitate stone. The same standard would seem to condemn the facades of a great many Italian Gothic churches.

But Ruskin argues that this is not so. Provocatively, he defends not only the use of marble slabs but also the application of stucco. If there was any point on which Pugin and the Ecclesiologists had carried the day, it was in their condemnation of the "unreality" of the stucco facades on so many Regency buildings. It must therefore have been startling to find Ruskin defending Italian facades on which applied stucco had been used as a ground for diaper patterns:

> What? the reader asks in some surprise,—Stucco! and in the great Gothic period? Even so, but *not stucco to imitate stone.* Herein lies all the difference: it is stucco confessed and understood, and laid on the bricks precisely as gesso is laid on canvas, in order to form them into a ground for receiving colour. (11.26)

The saving principle was that of confession. If stucco was used, it should be obvious. If marble was attached to a brick surface, the rivets should be shown. Then there would be no falsehood and no unreality.

In his chapter "St. Mark's," Ruskin gives detailed rules for the encrusted style. Since its buildings depend on jewel-like splendor, we must not expect them to exhibit great size; instead they should spread low walls before us like the pages of a book and provide us with shafts whose capitals we may touch with our hands. The materials employed must indeed be precious, for only their great beauty can release them from the obligation to do constructive work. Since the slabs of marble do not bear weight, the plinths and cornices that surmount them must be light and delicate. Decoration will necessarily be shallow in its cutting, and therefore the sculptor must abandon three-dimensional naturalism. Shafts of different sizes and of varied marbles will contribute to the richness of the whole. Ruskin's principle of confession and his analysis of the encrusted style met with widespread applause. "We have seldom read anything better done," said the *Guardian.* "It is indeed obvious, if we reflect upon the matter, that an architecture of precious marbles and an architecture of freestone must be governed by different rules, but Mr. Ruskin is certainly among the first to seize the true spirit of these two great schools, and to lay down certain definite principles for the guidance of our judgment respecting them."[15]

Ruskin was one of the men most responsible for the Victorian interest in polychromy. He was not, however, the only one. The group of writers, designers, and teachers around the great English administrator Henry Cole were also concerned with the topic. The Cole group, which included such men as Owen Jones, Richard Redgrave, and Matthew Digby Wyatt, had organized the Great Exhibition and controlled the Government Schools of Design. Their views were extremely influential and were usually opposed to Ruskin's. He, for his part, disliked everything they ever did. He called their Crystal Palace a cucumber frame, denounced Cole's illustrated children's books, and wanted his system of art education rather than theirs taught in the Government Schools of Design. Not surprisingly, the Cole group will frequently help define the nature of Ruskin's views by contrast.

Their most important spokesman on the question of polychromy was Owen Jones. He was well known for his careful studies of the Alhambra, and his *The Polychromatic Ornament of Italy* (which dealt with the sixteenth century) preceded *The Seven Lamps* by three years. His *The Grammar of Ornament* (1856), with its chromolithographed plates, must have been in the library of every Victorian architect and designer. His views on architectural color were well known, and their opposition to Ruskin's was often noted.

Jones had been a rather hesitant participant in the 1852 discussion at the RIBA:

> The question of introducing colour in this country was altogether a distinct one. He did not think the time had arrived for us to do so; indeed, we were not able yet to devise an architecture of our own. When we had made our own buildings, we might colour them according to our own modes of thought; but at present we transplanted a Greek temple into England; and, in his opinion, the colouring on it would be no more out of place than the building itself.[16]

In other words, the question of color was secondary to that of creating a new architectural style. At midcentury all discussions of a possible new style centered around the Crystal Palace, and, not surprisingly, Jones's decorative scheme for Paxton's building was a daring and influential effort in architectural polychromy. He began with the knowledge that the south side and the whole of the roof of Paxton's building would be covered with canvas in order to prevent a buildup of midday heat. If the building were painted a simple tint of white and then illuminated in such a monotonous way, the myriad parts of its cast-iron construction would lose all distinctness.

The solution was parti-coloring. "It would everywhere," Jones explained, "bring out the construction of the building." [17]

Jones then turned to art history for further guidance. He discovered that in the best periods the prevailing colors in decorating were the primaries: blue, red, and yellow. Blue, which retires, was placed on the concave surfaces, and yellow, which advances, on the convex ones. Red, the color of the middle distance, was used for horizontal planes, and neutral white for vertical ones. Thus, Jones employed color to define and express structure.

Ruskin's attitude toward the relation between color and structure was dramatically different. He argued, in a passage that Matthew Digby Wyatt dismissed as a "piece of dogmatic heterodoxy," [18] that color would never follow form but should always be arranged on a different system. He modified this slightly in the first volume of *The Stones of Venice,* permitting the use of colored bands to express the internal division of floors, but in general the separation of color from function remains characteristic of his thought.

As Jones turned to art history to develop his views, so Ruskin turned to nature. He pointed out that the stripes of a zebra and the spots of a leopard do not precisely coincide with the divisions of its anatomy. If the separation of color and form characterizes nature, why not architecture as well? Today, after Darwin, we would explain animal coloring in functional terms—as camouflage or as a means of display. To Ruskin, trained in natural theology and accustomed to regard nature as the art of God, it seemed obvious that the spots of a leopard could provide guidance to an architect. He therefore set down rules for the separation of color and form:

> Never paint a column with vertical lines, but always cross it. Never give separate mouldings separate colours . . . and in sculpture ornaments do not paint the leaves or figures (I cannot help the Elgin frieze) of one colour and their ground of another, but vary both the ground and the figures with the same harmony. Notice how Nature does it in a variegated flower; not one leaf red and another white, but a point of red and a zone of white, or whatever it may be, to each. In certain places you may run your two systems closer, and here and there let them be parallel for a note or two, but see that the colours and the forms coincide only as two orders of mouldings do; the same for an instant, but each holding its own course . . . in all cases it is a safe rule to simplify colour when form is rich, and *vice versa;* and I think it would be well in general to carve all capitals and graceful ornament in white marble, and so leave them. (8.177–178)

It is clear that Ruskin's separation of form and color was diametrically opposed to Jones's system.

Ruskin was also at pains to deny that any system was possible. Color, like proportion, was a matter of intuition. Ruskin told an audience of architects and art-workmen at the Architectural Museum that while he did not want to deprecate the value of Owen Jones's work, he wanted to free them from the notion that they could do nothing without rule. The *Builder* quoted him as saying:

> We were told as a rule that there were three primary colours,—red, blue, and yellow,—and that these primaries would occur in every composition; that these three colours always existed in a ray of light in the proportions of 8, 5, and 3, and that in these proportions they neutralized each other and produced white light: then, said the scientific gentlemen, "because these colours occur in a ray of light, you should always put them into your colour compositions in just such a manner as that each colour may be neutralized by its neighbor." How absurd was all this. . . . There, said the lecturer—producing at the same time an orange—is as fine a yellow as you can have. If the scientific man were asked what colours should be introduced with it in a composition, he would reply, "Well, eight of red, and five of blue." But what said Nature? She gave neither red nor blue, but, placing the orange in the midst of bright green leaves, enabled you to look on one of the most beautiful objects in existence—an orange grove. (12.501)

Ruskin thought that the finest colors were indescribable, and he demanded an emotional resonance from color that cannot be reduced to any system. "No colour was really valuable," he told his audience at the Architectural Museum, "until it was gradated. The great beauty of colour consisted in a sort of twilight melancholy,—a dying away; no colour was in fact of use till it appeared to be dying" (12.503).

Finally, Ruskin felt that the system of disposing color in separate areas destroyed its brilliancy. Color always needs to be tempered, and Ruskin finds it a principle of the best Gothic that if a mass of red is to be set beside a mass of blue, a piece of the red should be carried into the blue and a piece of the blue into the red. This is why diaper, zigzag, and checkered patterns always enrich color effects.

IV

Ruskin's demands for color and mass come together in his discussions of the wall. He was not one of those admirers of Gothic who felt that the style reached its glory when it dissolved into a skeletal frame. He loved the earlier phases of the style when visible strength was all important, and he was willing to see an architect forgo decoration altogether so long as the wall conveyed impressions of security and power to the imagination.

Ruskin found Renaissance walls deficient in these qualities, even when they seemed designed specifically to secure them. Rustication, for example, met with his entire contempt:

> It is . . . sometimes supposed that rustication gives an appearance of solidity to foundation stones. Not so, at least to anyone who knows the look of a hard stone. You may, by rustication, make your good marble or granite look like wet slime, honeycombed by sand-eels, or like half-baked tufo coated with concretions of its own mud; but not like the stones of which the hard world is built. Do not think that Nature rusticates her foundations. Smooth sheets of rock, glistening like sea waves, and that ring under the hammer like a brazen bell— that is her preparation for first stories. (9.350–351)

Similarly the Palladian motive, such as that on the facade of the Army and Navy Club in figure 20, looked to Ruskin like "two half-capitals glued, as it were, against the slippery round sides of the central shaft" (11.46). Still worse was the kind of exhibited masonry employed on the main floor. Here the architect, as if worried that his wall might appear weak, has overcompensated and attracted more attention to each separate stone than abso-

Fig. 20.   Army and Navy Club, Pall Mall. Parnell and Smith. Building News, 1860.

lute conditions of strength require. "The device was thought ingenious at one period of architectural history," Ruskin observes; "St. Paul's and Whitehall are covered with it, and it is in this I imagine that some of our modern architects suppose the great merit of those buildings to consist" (9.90). It was also used on Soane's Bank of England, leading Ruskin to wonder sarcastically if the lines were not intended to be symbolic of account books.

Another characteristic of early-nineteenth-century wall design that met with his disapproval was the growing use of cast-iron columns on the ground floor to support brick or masonry loads above. This had great appeal in commercial architecture because it concentrated support and allowed generous room for plate glass windows and display space. It also destroyed the idea of stability by making it appear that the weight of the building was carried only on narrow columns and thin sheets of plate glass.

What was it, then, that Ruskin asked for in wall design? His first requirement was that a wall should appear organized. Nothing could redeem a flat, monotonous surface, and the sameness of smooth ashlar walls should be avoided. A wall should be organized vertically into base, body, and cornice and further divided horizontally into areas of concentrated strength, such as piers and buttresses, and the areas that come between, which Ruskin calls the wall-veil. If forced to build in small stones, which tend toward sameness and diminish ideas of power, an architect should introduce larger blocks for contrast or employ massive stones for shafts, columns, lintels, and architraves. Diversity of size and color should give each stone an imaginative presence. Ruskin illustrated his views in the first volume of *The Stones of Venice* by juxtaposing the revealed masonry of Arthur's Chocolate House with a spandrel from San Pietro, Pistoia.

The sense that each part of the wall is doing its proper work will endow it with qualities that we associate with living things. Ruskin asks that walls be not only organized but animate. This view underlies the frequent metaphors that enliven the otherwise rather technical discussions in the first volume of *The Stones of Venice*. Thus the base of the wall is like the paw of an animal, string courses are epochs in a wall's existence analogous to periods of rest and reflection in human life, and the cornice is like a crown.

Ruskin's word *wall-veil* was his most dramatic contribution to architectural terminology. Its sudden popularity among pupils and clerks was an early sign of the approaching Ruskinian wave. It was annoying to old-guard architects who thought it part of his mysticism and poetry. It may be confusing to modern readers, since it has a similarity to the modern term *curtain wall*. But while the suggestion of a certain diaphanous lightness seems to cling to the wall-veil, this is not part of Ruskin's meaning. Here, in the most "functionalist" part of Ruskin's work, we see how independent his aesthetics are from his concern with structure. A wall-veil may not need massiveness in order to support, but it should have mass anyway, and Ruskin devotes considerable attention to finding ways to secure it.

Characteristically, Ruskin's views on the wall-veil grow out of his study of nature. Many of the noblest mountains—the example cited is the Matterhorn or Mont Cervin—are built up of stones so imperfect and friable that they would seem unable to bear any weight at all. The mystery is solved—and we are struck with "intelligent reverence for the great Builder" (9.87)—when we discover that a large quantity of loose and slaty shale is held together by a thousand bands of quartz. This is not, to be sure, the only way for nature or man to build a wall. Some materials are at once so strong and so abundant that they do not require strengthening. The kind of wall most associated with Ruskin's influence, however, is one in which horizontal bands of a stronger material alternate in rich polychromy with the bands of a weaker one. Thus we may have bricks alternating with rolled pebbles or hewn stone alternating with brick. Ruskin justifies such banded wall construction on every possible ground: it suggests to the imagination the horizontal space of interior rooms; it symbolizes the alternation of light and darkness in human life; and, by echoing the natural courses of rocks, it gives to a building some of the qualities of a geological structure.

V

Ruskin placed great, even excessive demands on ornament. Of course he recognized that decoration was not appropriate to all buildings. If a structure had a bluntly utilitarian purpose, it would achieve its own rough dignity without decoration. If resources were limited, an architect should stress power and mass rather than beauty. Moreover, Ruskin had little enthusiasm for such buildings as the Houses of Parliament where ornament was spread evenly over the facade, and he urged architects to concentrate their decoration. But with all these qualifications, Ruskin still defines a perfect building as "one composed of the highest sculpture (organic form dominant and sub-dominant) associated with pattern colours on the flat or broad surfaces" (8.186). His example is the Cathedral of Pisa, and this is a very richly decorated ideal indeed.

He insisted that ornament should be readable and ridiculed the Army and Navy Club (fig. 20) because the sculpture under its cornice was too small to be clearly seen from the street below. He also urged architects to remember that a building would be seen from various distances and that they should therefore design ranks of ornament. From a distance, we see great masses, black windows, and broad cornices. Coming closer, our attention shifts to traceries, shafts, and pinnacles. Closer still, we pick out niches, statues, knobs, and flowers.

Once he had established the importance of ornament, Ruskin faced three controversial questions: (1) How much freedom should be given to the carver of it? (2) How naturalistic should it be? and (3) What should be its proper relation to structure?

Ruskin's call for the workman's freedom was one of the most continuously fruitful aspects of his influence throughout the nineteenth century. It was also one of the most misunderstood. Here it is only necessary to clear up two frequent misunderstandings.

First, Ruskin did not advocate handing over the architect's function to his workmen. It is important that this be clear because something of this kind was in fact urged during the 1870s. Ruskin's respect for hierarchy was too ingrained ever to allow him to propose such a thing. He discusses architects in relation to their workmen in just the same terms as he defines the responsibilities of kings toward their subjects. They are to guide and serve at once. They are to allow their workmen freedom in executing, but the responsibility for determining the extent of this freedom is theirs alone.

Second, Ruskin's defense of the workman does not entail any concessions to incompetence. Ruskin praises imperfection, but this is a paradoxical concept. It can best be understood in relation to what was fast becoming the craftsman's chief rival—the machine. By the 1850s it was clear that most forms of ornament could be produced mechanically in large volume and at small unit cost. In Lambeth, for example, the Messrs. Cox were using a wood-carving machine driven by steam.[19] The architect or designer had only to bring a model of the foliage, figure, scrollwork, or diaper pattern that he wanted. It would be set on one side of the machine and a point on a metal rod would move over its contours. This would, in effect, pass directions to the rapidly whirring cutters on the other side of the machine, which would then, making six to seven thousand revolutions per minute, carve equivalent contours onto a block of wood. The fine points would then be finished off by hand. The resulting piece was not only inexpensive but had a higher degree of technical finish than comparable handwork.

What charge could be brought against such ornament? Ruskin's strategy was to turn its seeming advantage into a glaring weakness. Perfection was

monotonous. Ornament produced by machine, or by workmen who function as machines, had a look of monotonous sameness to it, a look of equal
effort everywhere. The imperfect products of a free workman, by contrast,
have qualities of life and subtle variation that can only be given by the
human hand.

Ruskin's next question was the degree of naturalism that architectural
decoration ought to show. His fundamental doctrine was that the forms
that are loveliest in architecture are also those that are commonest in nature. This at once put him in conflict with two influential trends in Victorian opinion.

One held that there is an inevitable conflict between nature's curves and
architecture's right angles. W. H. Leeds insisted that the forms of architecture are altogether conventional and admit the imitation of natural forms
only in details:

> Even in those details . . . which are borrowed from plants and foliage, an ab-
> stract and formalized imitation, instead of a direct and mimic one, ought to be
> adopted. Nature may very properly be looked to for fresh hints and *motifs*, but
> it is a great error to attempt, as some seem inclined to do, to engraft botany
> upon architecture.[20]

The *Edinburgh Advertiser*, responding to Ruskin's lectures, praised the
Greeks because "they rarely introduced the forms of the vegetable world
into their architecture, and, when they did, always symmetrised them,—
or, in other words, took away from them an appearance of life, the reality
of which they could not possibly retain in stones."[21]

The members of the Cole group took a rather different position. They
actively promoted the use of natural forms as ornament but also insisted
that they should be rigorously conventionalized. We can see what they
meant in a shop front by Owen Jones (fig. 21) and in an illustration from
Christopher Dresser's *Art of Decorative Design* (fig. 22). The latter represents plant forms that have been carefully ironed out and made strictly
geometrical. Lest a reader confuse this kind of ornament with that recommended in *The Seven Lamps*, Dresser explicitly contrasts Ruskin with
Jones, "a man who, by his works, has manifested his knowledge of ornament, and who has given forth more real practical information respecting
the decorative art in his propositions . . . than Mr. Ruskin has in his much
more voluminous writings."[22]

Any reader of the Victorian architectural press would have been aware
of this contrast between Ruskin's views and Jones's. An 1857 article in
Building News, entitled "Iron Architecture," for example, tells the reader

Fig. 21. Details of shop front in New Bond Street. Owen Jones. Journal of Design and Manufactures, *1850.*

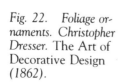

Fig. 22. Foliage ornaments. Christopher Dresser. The Art of Decorative Design *(1862).*

that instead of listening to Ruskin's lectures he should "carefully digest the one that was recently delivered at the Institute by Owen Jones" in order to learn that "true art consists in idealizing upon, and not in copying from, nature."[23] As late as 1889 we find J. L. Roget telling readers of the *Architect* that "Mr. Ruskin would obey the presumed injunction of nature by copying the most frequent of her forms," while "Mr. Owen Jones would follow her dictates by imitating the most common qualities of her forms."[24]

So we have Ruskin firmly situated in nineteenth-century opinion as a defender of naturalism. This is accurate so far as it goes. Was he also a defender of slavish imitation?

He sometimes seems so. In *The Stones of Venice* we find him responding to Raphael's famous dictum—as restated by E. L. Garbett—that "the artist's object was to make things not as Nature makes them, but as she WOULD make them."[25] Ruskin rejects the principle that we should alter what we find in nature and asks sarcastically if an artist could possibly improve a daisy—"or a pease-blossom, or a moth, or a mustard-seed, or any other of God's slightest works" (9.407). This sounds like a very pretty piece of Victorian naturalism indeed. Ruskin spoke in the same vein when, at a meeting of the Society of Arts in 1857, he replied to remarks by George Wallis, headmaster of the Birmingham School of Art. Wallis had reiterated the Cole group's frequent objection to the naturalistic carpets that resembled meadows more than they did floor coverings. Ruskin answered:

> They had heard . . . an ungallant attack upon the ladies for promoting a base manufacture of carpets, admitting the complete imitation of flowers. He could not blame the ladies in this, chiefly because he knew a most respectable and long-established firm, engaged in carpet manufacture on an extensive scale, which conducted its business on the principle Mr. Wallis opposed. He referred to the firm whose head partners, the months of April and May, supplied a large part of the world with green carpets, in which floral design was largely introduced, and he believed generally to the satisfaction of the public. (16.427)

This sounds like Dickens's satire against the Cole group in the first chapter of *Hard Times*, a book Ruskin admired. However, it leaves Ruskin in the unfortunate position of defending not only naturalism but also the sentimental excesses of popular taste.

Ruskin seems to have been content to appear a spokesman for a naïve form of naturalism if that was the price of sharpening public perception of the disagreement between himself and his opponents. But he qualifies his naturalism significantly when he is not engaged in controversy and has time for qualifications.

Acknowledging in "The Lamp of Beauty" that architecture cannot accommodate a totally imitative treatment of natural forms, he urges the carver to "abstract" certain features from the whole for detailed attention, while presenting others in a more symbolic manner. This is illustrated in figure 23, where the flow and outline of leaves in moldings at Rouen are precisely reproduced while their serrations and veinings are only indicated. The contrast of these leaves with Dresser's plant forms is very striking. Ruskin warns, however, that even such abstraction as he permits must not be overdone: "a purely abstract manner, like that of our earlier English work, does not afford room for the perfection of beautiful form, and . . . its severity is wearisome after the eye has been long accustomed to it" (8.171). Ruskin's position in "The Lamp of Beauty" is that ornament must be based on natural form, that as it rises on the scale of being it will become more imitative, that even at the highest pitch of naturalism some element of

Fig. 23. Leaf moldings. John Ruskin. The Seven Lamps of Architecture (1849).

abstraction is always needed, but that this should not be carried so far as to eliminate vitality and grace.

To some critics this was not enough. Coventry Patmore complained in the *British Quarterly Review* that "this fine critic falls into the universal error of regarding Gothic leafage as nothing more than an imitation of nature."[26] He thought Ruskin's comments on abstraction insufficient to account for the very great difference between Gothic carving and natural foliage. He was sure that the mere reproduction of hop or hawthorne leaves would give a totally un-Gothic impression, and as proof he cited the failure of attempts in the *Builder* to base spandrel decorations on a direct imitation of natural fact (fig. 24). Patmore argued that foliage became architectural only when enclosed within the bounds of a geometrical outline.

Ruskin agreed. It was not often that he capitulated to a critic, but in his chapter "The Treatment of Ornament" in the first volume of *The Stones of Venice* he gives detailed consideration to all the factors that might combine to limit the naturalism of Gothic foliage and he draws attention to the "valuable remarks" (9.304) in Patmore's article. Ruskin's principle of ab-

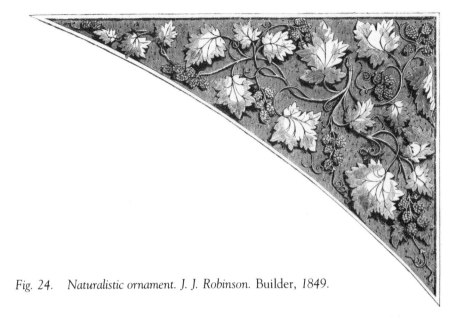

Fig. 24.   Naturalistic ornament. J. J. Robinson. Builder, 1849.

straction had allowed a carver to select certain features of a leaf for imitation and to leave others out. He now tells the carver to subtly alter the form of the leaf itself:

> You must not cut out a branch of hawthorn as it grows, and rule a triangle around it, and suppose that it is then submitted to law. Not a bit of it. It is only put in a cage, and will look as if it must get out, for its life, or wither in the confinement. But the spirit of the triangle must be put into the hawthorn. It must suck in isoscelism with its sap. (9.305–306)

Patmore was able to report in a later edition of the *British Quarterly* that "Mr. Ruskin adopts [our] views as far as relate to the essential character of Gothic foliage, and reclothes them in splendour of words, which we, and all living critics besides himself, might well envy."[27]

On the questions of the proper relation between decoration and structure, Ruskin is less ambiguous. Here too his view can be differentiated from the dominant trend in architectural thought.

The most common position among Gothic Revivalists was that laid down in the first paragraph of Pugin's *True Principles*:

> The two great rules for design are these: 1st, that there should be no features about a building which are not necessary for convenience, construction, or propriety; 2nd, that all ornament should consist of enrichment of the essential construction of the building. The neglect of these two rules is the cause of all the bad architecture of the present time.[28]

Pugin then declared his distaste for ornaments that were "actually constructed" as against those that formed "the decoration of construction." This is more than just a play on words. Pugin is attempting to establish a relation in which ornament completes and glorifies structure while remaining subordinate to it. His example is the flying buttress, in which a piece of essential construction is converted into a light and airy decoration. This formulation was accepted by the Cole group and rephrased in Owen Jones's *Grammar of Ornament:* "Construction should be decorated. Decoration should never be purposely constructed."[29]

This returns us to Ruskin's distinction between building and architecture. The formula advanced by Pugin and Jones, which was extremely well known throughout the nineteenth century, would seem to offer Ruskin a convenient escape from his excessively sharp opposition between the two. Characteristically, he refuses to take it. He did not comment on the subject during the 1850s, but his attitude was no doubt consistent with that expressed in an 1873 Oxford lecture. There he presented a photograph of Saint Zeno at Verona and observed that "a disciple of Mr. Pugin" would no doubt claim that it "was nothing more than the decoration of this construction" (23.87). But it seemed to Ruskin that there was no sense in which the carving could be said to be subordinate to the structure. In the porch the architect—Ruskin calls him the sculptor—had created a variety of surfaces. Some were chosen for carving, others not. There was no pattern in which the structurally more important members were given special emphasis. Whatever relation existed between structure and decoration was an extremely loose one.

It is possible to define Ruskin's view of architecture by citing his opinions and by contrasting them to the views of other influential writers. Once we have located his place in contemporary debates, however, we have still not defined Ruskinism. For that we need an additional element, one that Ruskin himself was not able to supply. The missing ingredient is a viable concept of a nineteenth-century style.

VI

RUSKINISM AND THE SPIRIT
OF THE AGE

 No dictionary of architecture defines the adjective *Ruskinian*, but it is in frequent use nonetheless. Ruskin scholars say that it ought not to be, that it is vague and often misapplied, but architects, architectural historians, and tour guides remain confident that it is possible to stand before a warehouse in Birmingham's jewelry quarter or a row of homes in Clapham and pronounce them to be in some way Ruskinian. Their use of the term implies a confidence that it means something, and often a molding or piece of mosaic work can be traced back to a particular passage or illustration. But there is something more involved, something that cannot be found in *The Seven Lamps* or *The Stones of Venice*.

The central fact about Ruskinism as a historical phenomenon is that it achieved a large measure of independence from Ruskin himself. It developed in ways that he did not recommend and often in ways that he did not admire. Victorian architects were strong-minded men, and the demands of Victorian society were imperious. Not surprisingly, the men and the society took Ruskin's words and applied them in unexpected ways. Even at the Oxford Museum, where Ruskin was on the spot and where his advice was actively solicited, there is a certain disharmony between his vision of architecture and the use to which it was put. In many other cases there is a bristling tension. Since this is the case, we cannot define Ruskinism solely by examining Ruskin's words. We need to know what problems and imperatives were in the minds of the young architects who read them.

The evidence of the *Builder* and the *Civil Engineer and Architect's Journal* is clear: architects were preoccupied by the question of style. They had reached the point where they could reproduce the forms of the past with great precision. If designing in the Gothic style meant simply choosing features from the two hundred illustrations to Bloxham's *Principles of Gothic Ecclesiastical Architecture,* then the revival could proceed without delay. But architects wanted an idea of style that went beyond the mere appeal to precedent. They did not find such a concept in Ruskin. They therefore reached their own solution and absorbed his visual recommendations into it. The fundamental paradox of Ruskinism, and the chief source of tension in its development during the second half of the nineteenth century, is that Ruskin's visual enthusiasms are integrated into a quite un-Ruskinian concept of style.

I

The great question at midcentury was whether the revival of a past style was consistent with a progressive age. Many complained that architects had become mired in precedent. It was not only the medievalists who were vulnerable to this criticism. When the 1847 designs for the Army and Navy Club in Pall Mall showed a striking resemblance to Sansovino's Palazzo Cornaro, a correspondent who signed himself Anti-Copyism complained to the *Builder* that "poor architecture appears to have got into a terrible fix; its career is terminated, and it presents the curious anomaly of an art, which continues to be practised, having come to an impassable full stop."[1] The charge of copyism was made even more vehemently against the Gothicists, for the style they admired seemed to reflect a way of life that had vanished. Stylistic preferences really expressed attitudes toward the nineteenth century. The Gothicists could say with Pugin: "I hate the modern boastful spirit which would exalt the mechanical superiority of our age at the expense of all that is admirable in the past."[2] Others, like Robert Kerr, found it inconceivable that a people who had passed the Reform Bill and built the railroads would be content with the architecture of "bloodthirsty, beef-eating barons" and "disgusting, filthy-minded monks."[3]

The charge that the Gothicists were reactionary copyists was made with great zest in the hostile reviews of Ruskin's books. *Blackwood's* found it simply incredible that a writer should scorn the glories of industrial progress:

> Was it better that a few lazy monks should be employed in illuminating missals, than that hundreds of thousands should be employed in wood-cutting, metal-engraving, and lithography, to disseminate a knowledge of art far and wide among the people. We do not hesitate to express our belief that there is more

thoughtful and intellectual work performed in one month within the compass of Great Britain, than was given to the artificers of all Europe in twenty years during the Gothic period.[4]

The *Athenaeum* too wondered why Ruskin persisted in looking backward: "What has commercial life of the nineteenth century to do with the Gothic? what has the Army, the Bench or the Bar?—what has the emigrant or the optimist?"[5] Even a sympathetic reviewer like the one who wrote in *Sharpe's London Journal* could not help regretting

> the evident bias of our author in favour of past times, and his depreciation of our existing civilizations. This vein runs through the entire book. . . . Our steamboats, our railroads, our suspension bridges—with the manifold application of scientific discovery to the promotion of human progress and enjoyment—are the great works of *our* age, although in architecture we may be clumsy imitators of those who have preceded us.[6]

The charge that Ruskin was blind to the great achievements of his own age was made with special vigor by the group around Sir Henry Cole. Matthew Digby Wyatt complained in the *Athenaeum* that Ruskin's prejudices were "so strong, his affinities so wire-drawn, his antipathies so unsupported by even common sense, that we have stared equally at the conclusions at which he has in many cases arrived and at the extraordinary mental process by which he appears to have reached them."[7] In the *Journal of Design and Manufactures* he drew a clear distinction between the Cole group's approach to art and architecture and Ruskin's:

> He seems to us to have altogether a very lopsided view of railways and railway architecture and not to have any consistent theory of mechanical repetition as applied to art. Moreover, instead of boldly recognizing the tendencies of the age, which are inevitable, perceiving the wide distribution of certain kinds of art, and the positive good that is in this;—instead of considering the means of improving these tendencies and results, he either puts up barriers against their further developement, or would attempt to bring back the world of art to what its course of action was four centuries ago!—as easy a thing as to put the world itself back. Our course in this nineteenth century may be hateful if you please; denounce it, but as it *is* our course, wise men should recognize the fact, and try, by all the light that God gives them to direct it rightly.[8]

Ruskin was curiously acquiescent before this charge. He wrote to Cole that "there is much truth in what you say respecting the inevitable tendencies of the age; but a man can only write effectively when he writes from conviction—and may surrender the hope of being a guide to his age, without thinking himself useless as a drag" (36.105).

II

The hostility between Ruskin and those more sympathetic to the spirit of the age crystallized over whether a new style ought to be invented that would express the concerns of a new epoch in the world's history. The members of the Cole group had helped dramatize this possibility with their work on the Crystal Palace of 1851. Here the so-called railway materials of cast iron and plate glass were employed in a building that was a symbol of progress. Its admirers must have shared Matthew Digby Wyatt's hope that "new materials would hasten the day when the great problem would be realized of an original style, consistent with the wants, the spirit, and importance of this our nineteenth century."[9] Until this happy day arrived, however, the Cole group was willing to settle for an eclectic use of motifs from all periods and cultures. They thus dissented from Ruskin's position without offering any clear alternative to it.

Coventry Patmore was another critic disturbed by Ruskin's hostility toward the age. He wrote many articles on architecture before achieving fame with *The Angel in the House*, and many of them were reviews of Ruskin's books. Since they were all published anonymously, Patmore was free to develop rather different lines of thought in different periodicals. In certain magazines it is possible to see him accepting most of Ruskin's view of architecture.[10] In others, he experiments with the idea of a nineteenth-century style based on iron and glass.

The spirit with which Patmore approaches the question is expressed in his 1846 review of the second volume of *Modern Painters*:

> "Progress" is the word written on our banner,—Progress is the article of our faith, which we cannot resign—the advocacy of Progress is the object of this periodical, from which it may not depart—we assume Progress not as an historical accident, but as an essential attribute of man, without which he does not fulfill the conditions of his being. To all exaltation of the middle ages, with their courage and their piety,—with their atrocity and their superstition, with their virtues and their vices,—we are determined opponents.[11]

This sounds like the *Athenaeum* or *Blackwood's* or the *Journal of Design and Manufactures*. It is hardly surprising that Patmore was impressed when he came upon a pamphlet by a little-known architect named Vose Pickett that argued that new principles of construction and a new system of decoration would emerge from the use of iron. A few years earlier Pickett had tried to persuade the directors of the Army and Navy Club to employ iron for their new clubhouse. He was much derided by his contemporaries, but the success of the Crystal Palace must have given new force to his arguments.

Patmore's most remarkable comments on iron architecture as the basis for a new style occur at the beginning of his review of the last two volumes of *The Stones of Venice* in the *North British Review*. Here he begins by contemplating a paradox: "All railway travellers who trouble themselves with 'trifles' of this kind will agree with us when we declare, that, as a general rule, whenever artistic effect has been attempted in the places in question, the result has been a display of almost hopeless imbecility; but, on the other hand, where no such effect has been sought, it has often been obtained." [12] Ruskin said something similar to this. Warning against the decoration of railway stations in *The Seven Lamps,* he declared that "railroad architecture has, or would have, a dignity of its own if it were only left to its work" (8.160). Patmore, however, goes far beyond granting the stations dignity. Unlike Ruskin, he is fascinated by the functionalist vision of a new style arising out of strict attention to utility:

> leave 'style' to take care of itself, as it always will, if you trust it; make your furniture strong and unpretending, as befits rough and hasty usage; do with your 'artistic effects' of all kinds, what the song recommends little 'Bo-peep' to do with her sheep; 'leave them alone, and they'll come home,' and bring their decorative appendages behind them. Wherever mechanical operations are carried on upon a large scale, as in the Railway, there is sure to be enough to amuse and delight the eye. What can be more pleasing, in its place, than the light iron roof, with its simple, yet intricate supports of spandrels, rods, and circles, at Euston Square, or the vast transparent vault and appropriate masses of brickwork at King's Cross? What 'fine art' that we could have time to understand on a Railway journey could equal the beauty of the throbbing engines, or the admirably calculated reticulation and intersection of the iron lines at some great junction? [13]

This is one of the many statements made in the early 1850s that sound enough like twentieth-century theory to engage modern sympathies.

At this point we have a curious phenomenon: the Victorians seemed about to invent the International Style. At one time architectural historians blamed them vehemently for not doing so. Yet their failure does not seem to have resulted from any lack of enthusiasm for the task. Perhaps the new technology was not developed enough to allow for a new style. Perhaps the Victorians were too deeply imbued with historicist modes of thought to accept an architecture that broke dramatically with the past. There must be many reasons why the promised new style was stillborn. Ruskin's opposition was only one of them, but it was an important factor.

Ruskin did concede in "The Lamp of Truth" that the time was probably

near when new architectural laws would be developed for metallic construction. This, however, was more a strategic concession than a hope.
Ruskin at once went on to assert that "all present sympathy and association" (8.66) limited architecture to traditional materials. He carefully restricted the use of iron in ways that precluded its use as the basis of a new
style. It was to be used as a binding material, as Wren had used it around
the spire at Salisbury, but not as a support. This practice made sense in the
seventeenth century because the veins of Wren's iron were of very unequal
strength. A column of such iron would have been unreliable in compression. Nineteenth-century improvements in manufacture, however, had
eliminated this difficulty. By Ruskin's day cast iron was valuable primarily
for its strength in compression. It was the combined thinness and strength
of the cast-iron columns that was encouraging changes in design. To abandon it as a support, as Ruskin urged, would have been to forgo its most
innovative uses. Certainly it would have forestalled any possibility of developing a new style based on iron construction.

Ruskin was quite sure that the much-talked-of new style was a will-
o'-the-wisp. This was his claim in his January 1857 address to the Architectural Association entitled "The Use of Imagination in Modern Architectural Design." The attack on the classical doctrine of proportions
contained in this address has already been described in chapter 2. The
speech also contained an onslaught against stylistic originality. As before,
the text given in the *Building News* is quoted because it indicates audience
reaction:

> Perhaps the first idea of a young architect might be that it was incumbent upon
> him to invent a new style, worthy of modern civilization in general, and of
> England in particular, worthy of the days of improved machinery and tele-
> graphs—quick as steam, and sparkling as electricity—(A laugh). But he would
> ask whether, if an inventive architect in England was to invent a new style, and
> to have a county or province given to him for his invention, was every archi-
> tect, therefore, to invent a new style? Could they have more than one guiding
> head—one Columbus? If they sailed in company, what was to become of all the
> Columbuses?—(A laugh.) And when a new style was invented, could they do
> more than build in a style that was previously invented, or in styles that were
> already known? He would grant them that a new style might be invented—
> a style different from all styles hitherto known—such an one as that in which
> the capitals, instead of being at the top, might be placed at the bottom of the
> columns—(a laugh)—one in which buttresses would exchange their present
> position altogether, and one in which the proportions of lines should be so
> composed as to be neither crooked nor straight—(Continued laughter). The
> speaker carried out this idea at some length, enumerating other absurdities
> which might be introduced in a new style. But still (he continued), he would
> ask, when that had been accomplished—what after that?—what next? A

scheme might be originated which was merely fantastic and a bubble. And if they would not be content with Palladio they would not be content with Paxton—(A laugh, and cheers).[14]

That seems to have closed the matter; very little more was heard about a new style for the rest of the century.

III

But the original problem still remained: the Gothicists had to show not only that their style was lovely but that it was also expressive of a progressive age. Unless they could do this, they might be asked to design some lovely churches but they would not be awarded railway stations, hotels, museums, clubhouses, libraries, and mercantile exchanges.

How did Ruskin help them in this endeavor? The answer is that he did not—at least not directly. He seems to emerge in "The Lamp of Obedience" as a forthright defender of "absolute copyism" (8.257). A young architect, he says, should learn his art as a student learns Latin, following the rules and imitating the masters. Only very slowly would he progress toward the point where, as a master of the language, he could take a license:

> We must first determine what buildings are to be considered Augustan in their authority; their modes of construction and laws of proportion are to be studied with the most penetrating care; then the different forms and uses of their decorations are to be classed and catalogued, as a German grammarian classes the powers of prepositions; and under this absolute, irrefragable authority, we are to begin to work, admitting not so much as an alteration in the depth of a cavetto, or the breadth of a fillet. (8.257)

As an architect reaches maturity, he will be allowed "to change or to add to the received forms, always within certain limits" (8.257). Decoration might be open to innovation. Architecture would change, though as slowly as language itself, and Ruskin can imagine a new style arising as a result of long evolution rather than individual invention. Ruskin's advice is as conservative as it could be without banishing change altogether. Indeed, it sounds like the advice of a confirmed classicist.

This posed a problem for his admirers. But a still greater one arose when Ruskin tried to name the style to which architects should be obedient. "We want *some* style," Ruskin insists. Yes, but which one? Suddenly Ruskin wobbles. He offers not a rule but a set of possibilities: "The choice would lie I think between four styles:—1. The Pisan Romanesque; 2. The early Gothic of the Western Italian Republics, advanced as far and as fast as our art would enable us to the Gothic of Giotto; 3. The Venetian Gothic in its purest development; 4. The English Earliest Decorated" (8.258). It is as if a humanist of the early Renaissance had hesitated between the choice of Chinese, Persian, and Latin learning. To be sure, Ruskin chooses his Latin: the earliest phase of English Decorated, perhaps enriched with decorative elements from French Gothic and protected from another decline into Perpendicular. This is essentially what the Ecclesiological Society had been urging for some years. The difficulty was that a young architect who followed this advice, without altering a cavetto or a fillet, would have had to ignore the fascinating information about Italian architecture that Ruskin had just given him. Yet if there is any single element that has stamped certain architects as Ruskinian in the eyes of Victorians and in those of posterity, it is the use of Italian and French elements in free combinations that were emphatically original and somehow felt to be appropriate to the progressive nineteenth century. The fact that this mixture was not advocated by Ruskin matters less than the fact that it was the all but inevitable result of the publication of *The Seven Lamps* and *The Stones of Venice.*

Clearly the initiative lay with Ruskin's readers. We can see how they seized it by examining a book and a church. The book is *Progress in Art and Architecture* by John Pollard Seddon. The church is All Saints', Margaret Street, designed by William Butterfield. The church was begun in 1849, just after *The Seven Lamps* appeared. The book was published in 1852, after the first volume of *The Stones of Venice* had been published.

About John Pollard Seddon's admiration for Ruskin there can be no doubt. He has followed Ruskin's enthusiasms through France and Italy, he has adopted many of Ruskin's views, and even his illustrations imitate those of *The Seven Lamps* (see figs. 25 and 26). We have already seen that he could adopt Ruskin's prose style. Here, if anywhere, is a Ruskinian architect. Yet Seddon parts company with Ruskin at a crucial point. He entirely shares the Crystal Palace spirit. "Progress," he proclaims, "the crown of the past, the hope of the future, is at once both the noblest privilege and the bounded duty of man."[15] For Seddon, the "brilliancy" of *The Seven Lamps* is sadly clouded over in its closing pages:

so much so that truly "The Lamp of Obedience," the last of the series, is fearfully quenched in gloom; for in it we are forbidden all hope of advancing our art until we can again merge the profession into a band of freemasons as of old, and "teach our architecture at our schools from Cornwall to Northumberland, as we would teach English spelling and English grammar;" and it is proclaimed

Fig. 25.   *Capital from the Ducal Palace,*
Venice. John Ruskin. The Seven Lamps of
Architecture *(1849).*

Fig. 26.   Below. *Capital from the Ducal*
Palace, Venice. John Pollard Seddon. Progress in Art and Architecture *(1852). By*
permission of the British Library.

that "until a universal system of form and workmanship be everywhere adopted and enforced, our architecture will languish in the dust:"—that "the only chance for architecture rests upon the bare possibility of obtaining the consent of architects and the public to choose a style and use it universally."[16]

Seddon is sure that this thralldom is opposed to the spirit of the age; it belongs to the epoch of feudalism and monastic compulsion. Ruskin can enjoy whatever comforts pessimism affords, but Seddon will not abandon his faith in progress:

> Mr. Ruskin himself fears the impossibility of uniting architects into a body of freemasons, but asserts that with that he has nothing to do; yet indeed we have something to do with its possibility, for the present is one phase in the general development of society,—one page in the history of its progress, to which the world has not arrived by mere chance. To deny the possibility of further progress in any branch of human skill or knowledge is to assert that Providence is at fault, which is absurd: we may be sure that we shall never be placed in a position where our duty should be impossible.[17]

Seddon shares the architectural enthusiasms of *The Seven Lamps,* and he favors Gothic in the battle of the styles. But it must be a modern Gothic.

He attempts to achieve this apparent hybrid by adopting most of Ruskin's views but rejecting his recommendations on style. He explodes with impatience at the whole question: "The day has passed when the works of a nation should be reckoned in the aggregate, and their growth described as regularly as that of a vegetable. We want neither a new nor a universal style; it were better that we know nothing about styles; the very name of them is a bane and a hindrance to the architect, however useful to the antiquary."[18] This sounds for a moment like Patmore's recommendation to let style take care of itself as railway engineers do. It also, as Henry-Russell Hitchcock observes, sounds like Walter Gropius.[19] But the resemblance is accidental. Seddon's passage is really a verbal gesture of annoyance at those who think of style in glossary or textbook fashion. He does not want to have to choose between Early Middle Pointed and Late Middle Pointed. For that matter, he does not want to follow Ruskin in choosing between the Pisan Romanesque and the early Gothic of the western Italian republics. What Seddon wanted was simply a Gothic of the nineteenth century, one that would draw on the forms and associations of all medieval styles in order to employ the new materials and meet the new demands of a progressive age.

A similar reconciliation of Ruskin's influence with the idea of progress occurs in the church of All Saints', Margaret Street (figs. 27 and 28). It is unlikely that either William Butterfield, the church's architect, or Alexan-

Fig. 27.   All Saints', Margaret Street. William Butterfield. Builder, 1853.

der Beresford Hope, its chief patron, were devoted to Ruskin to anything like the extent that Seddon was. They wanted to mark a new stage in the ecclesiological movement and to show that Gothic was a style capable of meeting needs and assuming forms unknown in the fourteenth century.

In its early days, the Ecclesiological Society had encouraged the strict observation of English precedent in church architecture. This was what Beresford Hope called the "Anglo-parochial age" of ecclesiology.[20] In the late 1840s, however, the Ecclesiologists turned to new concerns that copyism could not solve. They sought to build new churches for the mis-

Fig. 28.   All Saints', Margaret Street (interior). Builder, *1859.*

sionary lands of England's slums. The rambling association of church, rectory, and parish school suited to a rural parish was obviously impractical
on the crowded streets of London or Manchester. They inevitably found
themselves abandoning copyism in favor of what they called development.
   The complex of church and related buildings on Margaret Street was

intended as a model for the urban minster. The buildings were made more compact and taller than a similar complex in the country would have been in order to make efficient use of the small lot available in a crowded city and to drink in light from above the surrounding buildings. Another important innovation was the use of exposed brick rather than stone. Butterfield used some features, such as sash windows and exposed cast iron, which had no medieval precedent at all.

There is a real question as to how far Ruskin influenced All Saints' and, through it, the architecture of the 1850s. At one time it was common to see Ruskin as the prime progenitor of Victorian Gothic. Kenneth Clark's *The Gothic Revival* (1928) gave its concluding chapter to Ruskin and did not mention All Saints' at all. That imbalance was corrected in 1954 when Henry-Russell Hitchcock titled the final chapter of his *Early Victorian Architecture* "Ruskin or Butterfield?" He traced many parallels between Ruskin's views and All Saints', but also stressed Butterfield's originality and argued that "only after 1855 did a more peculiarly Ruskinian and Italianizing current, readily differentiated from the earlier stream flowing from the Butterfieldian spring in Margaret Street, become significant."[21] Since then there has been a tendency to see Butterfield's church and Ruskin's books as representing divergent tendencies. George L. Hersey argued in *High Victorian Gothic* (1972) that "Ruskin's influence was antithetical to the ecclesiologists' achievement" at All Saints'.[22] He interprets Ruskin as encouraging a more nearly symmetrical, classicizing architecture than we see in Butterfield's complex grouping and irregular outline.

My own view is that it is right to draw a distinction between Ruskin and All Saints' but wrong to draw anything so clear-cut as an antithesis. I have found no evidence that Victorians saw an opposition between Ruskin's ideas and the innovations of the church on Margaret Street. On the contrary, the Ecclesiologists were at pains to mute such disagreements with Ruskin as they had, and admiring reviewers of Ruskin's books often cited All Saints' as an example of the kind of architecture that Ruskin's doctrines would encourage. The phenomenon we face in the early 1850s is Ruskin *and* Butterfield.

Paul Thompson shows how this situation developed.[23] He points out that *The Seven Lamps* was published in May of 1849. If the plans for all Saints' were completed by June of that year, there was very little room for any influence from Ruskin. Thompson, however, presents evidence that the plans were altered between June 1849 and March 9, 1850, when they were finally submitted to the Metropolitan Building Office. They were changed because, as Beresford Hope wrote to a friend, "the aesthetic possibilities of different materials have become more and more clear, and the present scheme is that of a church whose character shall arise from *construction* and not from *superaddition,* namely that the pillars shall be *made of granite* and not pointed middle like those at St. Barnabas (Pimlico), the diaper shall be an encrustation of tiles, and not the track of a paintbrush, and so on."[24] The effect of the changes, according to an April 1850 issue of the *Ecclesiologist,* was to make the church

> a practical example of what we are very anxious to see tested, viz. constructional polychrome. The material of the building, and of the appended clergy and chorister-houses is to be red and black brick, arranged in patterns, with stone windows and bonding in the church. Internally, there is to be a use of coloured marble, which was of course impossible in the middle ages. Geometrical mosaic work in tiles is also to be introduced and, above all, the building is to be arranged with a view to frescoes of a high order of art.[25]

Not all of these changes relate to *The Seven Lamps,* but some clearly do. Ruskin's book contained a major argument for constructional polychromy, and it recommended checkered and zigzag patterns. It also urged that color be independent of architectural form, and this is the case with Butterfield's walls. But it is characteristic of All Saints' that even where Ruskin's influence seems most clear, it is still mixed with other, quite different sources of inspiration. For example, Ruskin urged architects to give their attention to "geometrical colour mosaic" (8.219), and Butterfield clearly did so in his spandrels for the nave. But searching for actual specimens to study, he turned to Matthew Digby Wyatt's *Geometrical Colour Mosaics of the Middle Ages* (1849).

George L. Hersey turns around the question of how far Ruskin influenced All Saints' and asks how far it influenced Ruskin. This is a valuable step, and we may extend it to ask how far it created the context in which Ruskin's books were interpreted. It would have been quite natural to think of Ruskin's doctrines in terms of the *Ecclesiologist's* call for development.

Basically, All Saints' captures Ruskin for the cause of Gothic modernism. Like Seddon, the *Ecclesiologist* noted Ruskin's pessimism in "The Lamp of Obedience": "Mr. Ruskin ends his fascinating volume in gloom and evil augury."[26] By the last chapter of *The Stones of Venice,* however, that gloom has vanished. The church proved that modern Englishmen had the capacity for Gothic design:

> It is the first piece of architecture I have seen, built in modern days, which is free from all signs of timidity or incapacity. In general proportion of parts, in refinement and piquancy of mouldings, above all, in force, vitality, and grace of floral ornament, worked in a broad and masculine manner, it challenges fearless comparison with the noblest work of any time. Having done this, we may do anything. (11.229)

Moreover, Ruskin now endorses an eclectic version of Gothic:

It is hardly possible at present to imagine what may be the splendour of buildings designed in the forms of English and French *surface* Gothic, and wrought
out with the refinement of Italian art in the details, and with a deliberate resolution, since we cannot have figure sculpture, to display in them the beauty of
every flower and herb of the English fields. (11.230)

Ruskin does not quite say that he is an optimist and a supporter of progress,
but this omission must have been unnoticed by many of his readers.

The Ruskinism of the 1850s and 1860s is a synthesis of Ruskin's own
views and those of his admirers. It contains a major area of tension: Ruskin's ideas are used to help create a style expressive of the age. By the mid-
sixties, however, Ruskin would startle his admirers by asking whether the
commercial and industrial ideals of the nineteenth century could possibly
be expressed in beautiful architecture.

VII

BENJAMIN WOODWARD AND
THE FORMATION OF
RUSKINIAN GOTHIC

 It is difficult to discuss Ruskin's impact on English architecture with any seemly order. If we proceed by topic—
say from the Government Offices competition to the
study of Italian Gothic to the popularity of naturalistic
carving—we divide individual architects and lose the
sense of their careers. If we proceed by architects, we find that such broad
topics as the design of civic buildings and the new interest in brick have to
be repeated in each case. The only solution is a compromise, with its at-
tendant inconsistencies, repetitions, and sudden leaps sideways.

Fortunately, certain rough divisions suggest themselves. A natural break
occurs in the early 1870s. Before that time we have the first impact of Ruskin's ideas in the fifties, a sort of Ruskinian craze in the early sixties, and a
growing conviction on the part of both Ruskin and his best admirers that
what they had created was not wholly good. This is the period of visual
Ruskinism, when the most obvious signs of his influence are such features
as stone bands in red brick walls and arches with rounded intrados and
pointed extrados. During the seventies both Ruskin's theories and the
Gothic Revival undergo reevaluation, while Ruskin himself continues to
develop his ideas in ways that were original, maddening, and fruitful. This
ushers in a period of moral Ruskinism in which architects show less interest in polychromy and more in the nature of work. All of this breaks down
into a series of chapters proceeding from the 1850s to the remarkably slow
fading of Ruskin's influence in the twentieth century. But this chronologi-
cal division cannot be followed consistently for there were two archi-

tects—Benjamin Woodward and John Henry Chamberlain—whose Ruskinism was so pervasive and complex that they require separate chapters. Chamberlain died in 1883, and his career thus spans our two historical periods. Woodward, because he died from tuberculosis in 1861, belongs almost entirely to the fifties.

I

No one did more than Benjamin Woodward to give practical application to Ruskin's ideas. Most other leading Gothicists had been decisively affected by the Ecclesiological Society before they read *The Seven Lamps,* but Woodward, in spite of his early interest in Pugin, was free to mold his Ruskinism in a comparatively pure form. The result was highly influential. When Lord Palmerston was thwarting George Gilbert Scott's plans for the Government Offices, Woodward's Oxford Museum was rising on a spot that commanded national attention. The Irish stone carvers he brought to England set the fashion in naturalistic foliage for decades to come. The merger of the Pre-Raphaelite movement with the Gothic Revival, one of Ruskin's dearest ambitions, was accomplished at the Oxford Union. Several talented young men, including R. St. John Tyrwhitt, John Hungerford Pollen, Edward Burne-Jones, and William Morris, were first attracted to architecture by the ferment surrounding Woodward's buildings. In effect, Woodward created the visual forms in terms of which Ruskin's ideas would be understood. More than one Ruskinian building turns out to be one that is clearly based on the Oxford Museum.

In spite of his key position in the development of Victorian architecture, Woodward is an elusive figure for the historian.[1] Shy and silent by temperament, he did not leave that trail of lectures, articles, books, and letters to the editor by which Scott, Street, Seddon, and others can be tracked. The biography planned after his death was never written, and his formative years are obscure. He appears to have been born in Ireland in 1815 and was originally articled to a civil engineer. His true love, however, was architecture, and by 1846 he was associated with Sir Thomas Deane. (Three generations of Deanes were involved with the firm, and, since all were named Thomas, they are slightly confusing. The eldest, Sir Thomas Deane, was mayor of Cork as well as an architect. His son, with whom Woodward was most closely associated, continued the firm after 1861 and eventually took his own son into partnership.) The eldest Deane's work had usually been classical. The firm's major Gothic designs of the 1840s, Queen's College, Cork, and the Killarney Lunatic Asylum, were produced after Woodward joined the firm; it is probable that he was largely responsible for them.

A comparison of Queen's College (fig. 29) with the Trinity College Museum (fig. 30) shows the nature of Ruskin's impact. It would be difficult to imagine more sharply contrasting designs. The most obvious influence on the first is Pugin, who advocated that each separate function of a complex should be expressed in the elevation. The result would be picturesque variety, based not on a frivolous desire for scenic effect but on a sound respect for planning and function. At Queen's Woodward was following Pugin's lead in seeking an architecture of picturesquely broken outlines and juxtapositions of parts. At Trinity College, by contrast, he was following Ruskin's dictum that a building, to show its magnitude, should have a single bounding line from top to bottom and from end to end.

There is something else surprising about Woodward's design: it does not at first glance look like a Gothic Revival building. This is because at Trinity College Woodward faced the delicate problem of designing a medieval building for a classical environment. He needed a style that would mediate between two traditions. He found it in the appendix "Renaissance Ornaments" in the first volume of *The Stones of Venice,* where Ruskin explains that the transition toward the Renaissance began with a Byzantine revival in which architects replaced their Gothic pointed arches with seemingly more archaic round ones. Ruskin cites the Palazzo D'Ario as typical of this phase and reproduces a detail from it—a polychromatic "eye," which Woodward promptly borrowed for his own facade. Woodward used other sources besides Ruskin, notably the round-arched garden facade of Charles Barry's Travellers' Club and some illustrations of Venetian palaces that appeared in the *Builder* during 1851, but it seems clear that the stylistic keynote of his building came from Ruskin. His partner Thomas Deane later echoed Ruskin's appendix when he said that the museum was "in the style of the fifteenth century Byzantine period."[2]

Beyond this stylistic debt, the Trinity College Museum reflects the overall conceptions of architecture set forth in the chapters "The Lamp of Power" and "The Lamp of Beauty." Like Ruskin, Woodward tends to separate the two. From a distance, we see the building's power—its compact shape, its broad surfaces of stone, its cornice set against the sky like a horizon. Only when we come closer do we see the carved beauty of the moldings and capitals.

It was here that Woodward employed the carvers who achieved fame as

Fig. 29.   Queen's College, Cork. Deane and Woodward. Builder, 1848.

Fig. 30.   Trinity College Museum, Dublin. Deane and Woodward. Building News, 1858.

the archetypal Ruskinian workmen. The man in charge was a Mr. Roe of Lambeth, but he was assisted by three Irishmen: James and John O'Shea and their nephew Edward Whellan.

Unfortunately, the backgrounds of these men are even more obscure than Woodward's own. Eve Marion Blau conjectures that they would have studied at the Government School of Design in Cork, which paid more attention to such crafts as wood and stone carving than its English counterparts. She also thinks that they worked with Woodward at Queen's College and that in their work there they drew on illustrations by James K. Colling of the carvings at the Southwell chapterhouse then appearing in the *Builder*. This is an interesting possibility, for the Southwell carvings represent the naturalistic extreme in Gothic ornament. Since the Queen's work was finished by 1848, it appears that the bias of Ruskinian craftsmanship was set before *The Seven Lamps* was even published.

The O'Sheas also exemplify the more uniquely Ruskinian doctrine that carvers should be given a large measure of freedom in carrying out their work. A writer in the *Builder* notes that "the architects are seeking to carry out views lately advocated, by leaving the *design* of the ornament to the workmen themselves, in order to obtain variety; the only assistance being verbal instructions from the architects by geometrical forms &c."[3] The success of the Trinity College Museum in publicizing Ruskin's view of craftsmanship is indicated on page 171 of the March 29, 1856, issue of the *Builder*. At the bottom of the page is the latest installment in a series of attacks on Ruskin and Pre-Raphaelitism. At the top is a careful engraving of two "Workmen's Capitals" from Trinity, along with a note stressing that it is to the workmen alone that "the whole of these sculptures are owing."[4]

This juxtaposition is significant for the progress of Ruskin's influence. At a time when his doctrines were still under widespread attack, Woodward's version of them was widely admired and available for imitation. A writer in the *Builder* noted that the style of the museum was being copied in Dublin. William Allingham wrote in May 1855 to his friend Dante Gabriel Rossetti: "Yesterday in Dublin I saw but hastily the part-finished building in Trinity College, which is after R's own heart. Style early Venetian, I suppose, with numberless capitals, delicately carved over with holly leaves, shamrocks, various flowers, birds, and so on. There are also circular frames here and there in the wall, at present empty, to be filled no doubt with eyes of coloured stone. Ruskin has written to the architect, a young man, expressing his high approval of the plans; so by and by you cognoscenti will be rushing over to examine the Stones of Dublin."[5]

II

It is remarkable, in retrospect, that a competition should have been required to select Woodward as architect of the Oxford Museum. Not only was he experienced with the museum type, but his admiration for Ruskin enabled him to sympathize with the broad outlook of those who had campaigned for a natural history museum in the first place. Many of the losing competitors felt ill used, and some complained in bitter letters to the *Builder* and the *Athenaeum*. They had been asked to enter a competition in which planning and program requirements were carefully set, but they must have quickly realized that they were being judged by unstated intellectual and aesthetic standards as well. The most striking feature of the building that now faces Parks Road is the consistency of the intellectual purpose that governs it from plan and elevation down to the smallest decorative detail. It achieved this coherence because Woodward was able to express a vision that already existed in the minds of the museum's backers. It is a vision in which science, art, and religion are reconciled, one best expressed in a sentence from Sir Thomas Browne's *Religio Medici*, which was at one point intended to be carved on one of the museum's walls: "Nature is the Art of God."

We are accustomed today to think of science as conflicting with religion and separated from art. In the 1830s, however, when John Ruskin and the museum's chief advocate, Henry Acland, were students together at Christ Church, such divisions were by no means inevitable. Both young men came from pious Evangelical backgrounds. Both studied geology and collected fossils. Both sketched architecture and belonged to the newly formed Oxford Architectural Society. The first president of the society was the Rev. William Buckland, canon of Christ Church and reader in minerology and geology. Buckland was author of one of the famed Bridgewater treatises in which the intricacies of the natural world were painstakingly explored as manifestations of the divine plan. (The important architectural historian William Whewell was author of another.) Thus all the concerns later expressed in the Oxford Museum were integral parts of Ruskin's and Acland's intellectual outlook. There were, to be sure, hints of coming discord. The study of fossils had persuaded Buckland that the biblical time scheme needed reinterpretation, and in the 1850s, while the museum was being built, Ruskin would complain that the geologists' hammers were torturing his dreams. Such doubts could be repressed, however, in the days before the 1859 publication of Darwin's *On the Origin of Species by Natural Selection*. Ironically, that book appeared just as work on the museum was winding down. The pre-Darwinian faith of Ruskin and Acland is symbolized in the carving that appears over the apex of the arch at the museum's entrance: it shows an angel holding an open Bible in one hand and a nucleated cell in the other.

Ruskin and Acland held that nature should be studied as a mode of revelation. This was not a view that had traditionally been held at Oxford. The few lecturers in science were ill housed and poorly equipped. There was no single building—or even any adequate room—for their collections and laboratories. Art and architecture, though sometimes objects of enthusiastic amateur study, were not taught at all. Ruskin and Acland wanted to remedy both deficiencies. Acland, who had become Lee's reader in anatomy in 1844, quoted *Modern Painters* in defense of his study of nature and crusaded for a chair in art as well as a science museum. Ruskin, in the third volume of *The Stones of Venice,* argued that the natural sciences were allied with Gothic humility rather than Renaissance pride, and he complained that "until the last year or so, the instruction in the physical sciences given at Oxford consisted of a course of twelve or fourteen lectures on the elements of Mechanics or Pneumatics, and permission to ride out to Shotover with the Professor of Geology" (11.259). From the beginning, then, the scientific, artistic, and religious aspects of the Oxford Museum were connected. What was needed was an architect who could affirm these connections in actual stone.

Although the competition seems unnecessary in view of the extraordinarily close match between Acland, Ruskin, and Woodward, it was unavoidable in the context of the 1850s. Acland's struggle for a science facility was difficult enough.[6] It would have been doomed had he complicated the question with any pronounced views on architecture. The resulting competition served to highlight the confusion of style characteristic of the early 1850s.

The competition designs went on public display on October 30, 1954. The *Builder* gives a breakdown of the choices presented:

Gothic, of all kinds	12
Greek more or less German in treatment	3
Roman, more or less after Wren with pedimented porticoes, columns & c.	4
Italian, more or less Barryan or Palatial	6
Elizabethan	1
The Order of Confusion	2
Original, Crystal Palace work tacked on to various regular book details	3
Abominations, about	2
Total	33

The *Builder's* critic tried to be fair to all designs, but clearly thought that the museum should be in the medieval, collegiate style of Oxford. He was prepared to admire Greek, Roman, or Renaissance entries, but not to recommend them. The Gothic entries as well failed when brought to the test of local associations: "The styles selected are rather ecclesiastical than collegiate, and have a tendency to Nuremberg and Ratisbon sympathies rather than to those of Oxford or Cambridge."[7]

The entry of Edward Middleton Barry, Sir Charles Barry's son, reflected this diversity in a dramatic way. Having, as the *Civil Engineer and Architect's Journal* put it, "entered on the matter with a determination to go in and win,"[8] he submitted four different designs under the motto *Fiat justitia ruat coelum* (Let justice be done, let the heavens fall). All had different elevations, but three had the same plan. One, labeled B, was Roman. Another, labeled C, appears to have been late Gothic with four centered arches and octagonal bays between angle buttresses. A and D were both Italian Renaissance entries, with columns carrying a classical entablature and balustrade. They seem to have been distinguished by different plans. Both were in the Renaissance style that Sir Charles Barry had used on the main facade at the Travellers' Club and elsewhere. *Fiat justitia* A had some features, including projecting wings and a recessed central portion, in common with Cockerell's Ashmolean. The *Builder's* critic liked the plan of D even more, so much so that he regretted that "the style adopted is not the one we should have thought most to be preferred for Oxford."[9]

The *Athenaeum* confirms the *Builder's* view of the competition and adds additional detail:

> Of the whole thirty-three designs scarcely half-a-dozen indicate a predilection for classical traditions. The dreary asceticism of the first and middle-pointed school of ecclesiology,—emulating in an entire absence of grace the naive transcripts of nature, so painfully elaborated by the votaries of pre-Raffaelism,—dominate over and trammel the independence of too many of the competitors. In exceptional cases, Ruskinism lifts up its head; in some others, the coldly monumental style of Schinkel, and the Bavarian modification of the antique, find adherents.

He praises Barry's entries because "the stubborn stone-work of the walls and the brittle elements of the glassy roof are alike subdued to consistency with one another, through subordination to one common modulus of order and proportion."[10]

The *Builder* also published a comment on the competition by the architectural historian James Fergusson. He had been one of the sharpest critics of copyism a few years earlier and one of the warmest advocates of a new style expressive of the age. The Oxford entries showed too clearly that no progress had been made toward an answer to the style question. He was

especially annoyed that E. M. Barry should have submitted multiple elevations for a single plan: "It proves . . . only too clearly how little meaning
there is in modern architecture, that, like a masquerade suit, it will fit anybody, or conceal anything."[11] Nevertheless, he too endorsed one of Barry's
proposals. He chose the Renaissance design on the grounds that the Italian
style, because it lacked the perfection of the Grecian and the Gothic, was
one in which progressive development was still possible.

None of the journals showed much interest in the design that Woodward
submitted (fig. 31) under the motto *Nisi Dominus aedificaverit domum* (Unless the Lord build the house, the builders labor in vain). The *Builder* did
not mention it at all, and the *Athenaeum* only cited it in passing. Yet *Nisi
Dominus*, along with *Fiat justitia A*, was one of the six designs sent on for
more detailed examination by two outside assessors. *Nisi Dominus's* chances
should have worsened when the assessors reported that although none of
the designs could be constructed for the stipulated thirty thousand pounds,
Fiat justitia would come closest. Nevertheless, *Nisi Dominus*, along with
Fiat justitia, was one of the two designs presented to Convocation.

Woodward's version of Gothic must have been a surprise to his fellow
revivalists. The Oxford Architectural Society, led by the antiquary John
Henry Parker, had become a stronghold of those who urged a revival
of native English Gothic. Like many Ruskinian designs that were to follow, *Nisi Dominus* was hard to pin down to a specific source, but it was
certainly foreign. Commentators described it variously as Lombardo-
Gothic,[12] Rhenish Gothic,[13] Romanesque Gothic,[14] and Early English
Decorated with a very strong tinge of southern Gothic.[15] One disappointed
competitor claimed that it was copied from a monastery on the Rhine, but
neglected to say which one.[16] A professor called it "Veronese Gothic of the
best and manliest type in a new and striking combination."[17] The debt that
all recognized was described by the *Building News* in 1859: "we have been
told that the architects stared so long and so steadily upon Mr. Ruskin's
'Seven Lamps,' that they have quite destroyed their eyesight for everything
that is not reflected in Mr. Ruskin's mirror, and that he has availed himself
of their pitiable condition to overwhelm and bury them in his 'Stones of
Venice.'"[18]

Like the Trinity College Museum, *Nisi Dominus* is indebted to "The
Lamp of Beauty" for its ornament and to "The Lamp of Power" for its outline and mass. As at the Trinity College Museum, the picturesque asym-
metry of the early Gothic Revival is rejected in favor of a central tower
with nearly symmetrical wings. Considering the additive nature of Woodward's planning, with a chemistry laboratory here and a dissecting yard
there and a curator's house somewhere else, the compactness of the main
facade is remarkable. This can be related to Ruskin's call for a single

bounding line. Ruskin also says that if a building is to be stretched into a rectangle rather than gathered together into a square, "a sense of power may be communicated to this form of magnitude by a continuous series of any marked features, such as the eye may be unable to number; while yet we feel, from their boldness, decision, and simplicity, that it is indeed their multitude which has embarrassed us, not any confusion or indistinctness of form" (8.110). This seems a fair description of the arcadelike sequence of Woodward's windows. The fact that the bilateral symmetry is disrupted by different windows on the left and right extremes of the ground floor has practical justification in terms of lighting different kinds of interior spaces, but may also reflect Ruskin's view that a master of Gothic proportions will deliberately vary from strict symmetry as a sign of life. The only features of *Nisi Dominus* that cannot be readily justified by a Ruskinian text are the decorative buttresses. Not that Ruskin was opposed to buttresses, but he thought an excessive reliance on them to be a vice of early-nineteenth-century Gothic. They were in fact omitted when the building was constructed.

Although hard evidence is difficult to come by, it seems clear that Woodward's victory was the result of backstage maneuvering by Henry Acland. He was the chief crusader for the museum, an intimate friend of Ruskin's, and one of the great academic politicians of the century. Since he had enough to do merely defending the idea of a separate building devoted to the natural sciences, Acland tended to avoid public involvement in the aesthetic side of the controversy. He did, however, urge Ruskin to speak at Oxford on the modern uses of Gothic, and he conferred with Ruskin at Glenfilas in 1853. He was presumably the author of an anonymous pamphlet on the competition, which appeared in December 1854. The pamphlet avoids the battle of the styles and defends *Nisi Dominus* against *Fiat justitia* on practical grounds. First, *Fiat justitia* put the odor-producing chemistry laboratory and dissecting yards within the mass of the building while *Nisi Dominus* put them outside. Second, *Fiat justitia* violated the instructions by including a basement, thus producing a building of three stories rather than the stipulated two. Finally, *Fiat justitia* was not easily extendable as future needs might require. Barry had designed a tightly organized building and asked the university to erect only two-thirds of it at present. The result would look unfinished. Such incompleteness, however, was appropriate to Gothic, and Woodward's plan for a quadrangle with one side removed met the requirement of extendability. Acland thus stressed practical matters, but differing evaluations of classic and Gothic were implied. Ruskin did not say a great deal about architectural planning, but he was clear on the question of Gothic's adaptability. Its builders never "suffered ideas of outside symmetries and consistencies to interfere with the

Fig. 31.   Oxford Museum. Deane and Woodward. Builder, 1855.

real use of what they did" (10.212). It was a virtue of Gothic building that it was never finished. One of Acland's rival pamphleteers alluded to the Ruskinian nature of his arguments when he asked if *Nisi Dominus* were an example of the "Gothic 'imperfection'" which had recently become popular.[19] Apparently the argument for Gothic adaptability proved convincing. On December 12, 1854, *Nisi Dominus* was declared the victor.

III

It was only now that Ruskin himself entered the picture. He was at first reluctant to commit his energies to the controversy. Shortly before the competing designs were put on display, he wrote to Mrs. Acland that there was no use his troubling about them "because they certainly won't build a Gothic Museum and if they would—I haven't the workmen yet to do it, and I mean to give my whole strength, which is not more than I want, to teaching the workmen, and when I have got people who can build, I will ask for employment for them."[20] By December 11 he had studied the plans, concluding that *Fiat justitia* was a commonplace and contemptible imitation of Sansovino and Palladio but that *Nisi Dominus*, "though by no means a first-rate design, was yet quite as good as is to be gotten in these days, and on the whole good" (16.xliii). His eagerness rose as the final vote approached. He wrote to Lady Trevelyan:

> Of the Oxford museum—no news yet. The "Quantities are being taken out" as they say. It is not *certain* yet that Woodward has it—depends still on confirmation till it is sure—I do not trouble my head much about the matter—as soon as it is secure to Woodward I will set to work upon various monstrosities for his advantage.[21]

When the final decision was made, he wrote to Acland:

> I have just received your telegraphic message from Woodward, and am going to thank God for it, and lie down to sleep. . . . To me this is a kind of first fruits for sowing of which "I knew not whether I should prosper." I am glad after all, it is at Oxford.[22]

Ruskin was not simply pleased that a design he had influenced was going to be built. He expected to be an active participant. He wrote to Acland:

Now then—indeed. The great good of this matter is that Mr. Woodward is evidently a person who will allow of suggestion and is glad of help—though better able himself to do without either than most. But there seems to be something quite providential . . . in the way my work is being laid out for me at present . . . here in this college with you and Woodward both ready to do anything possible with money.[23]

To Lady Trevelyan he was even more succinct: "Acland has got his museum—Gothic—the architect is a friend of mine—I can do whatever I like with it."[24]

Against this last statement we should no doubt put William Tuckwell's recollection that Ruskin often suggested improvements "which silent Woodward sometimes smilingly put by."[25] We should also recall that Ruskin was extremely busy during the period that the museum was under construction, finishing the last three volumes of *Modern Painters,* issuing his *Academy Notes,* cataloging the Turner watercolors, teaching at Working Men's College, and producing such works as *The Elements of Drawing, The Elements of Perspective, The Harbours of England, The Political Economy of Art,* and *Unto This Last.* We may reasonably wonder how much time he had left over for the museum. Yet Ruskin's capacity for work was prodigious, and it appears that his involvement was nearly as important as legend says it was.

It is certain that he played a large role in seeking the participation of artists and advising on disputes. Having failed to merge the Pre-Raphaelite movement with the Gothic Revival at Camden Chapel, he set out to accomplish the same goal at the museum. He vowed to "get all the pre-Raphaelites to design me each an archivolt and some capitals & we will have all the plants in England and all the monsters in the museum."[26] To Acland he wrote enthusiastically of getting

Millais and Rossetti to design flower and beast borders—crocodiles and various vermin—such as you are particularly fond of—Mrs. Buckland's "dabby things"—and we will carve them and inlay them with Cornish serpentine all about your windows. I will pay for a good deal myself, and I doubt not to find finds. *Such* capitals as we will have! (16.xlv)

Millais's relation with Ruskin was soon ended, and Rossetti, though he talked of painting a mural of Newton gathering pebbles on the shores of the Ocean of Truth, never worked at the museum. Nevertheless, the merger Ruskin dreamed of took place during the 1850s at the Oxford Union, and this was to have important consequences for the rest of the century.

Ruskin was also active in an ongoing debate over just how and where

the museum was to be decorated. He wrote in an undated letter to Jane
Carlyle that he had "designed and drawn a window for the Museum at Oxford and have every now and then had to look over a parcel of five or six
new designs for fronts and backs to the said Museum" (5.xl). In fact, Ruskin was extremely concerned with decorating the exterior of the museum,
in contrast to Woodward who was emphasizing the interior. Ruskin had
been dissatisfied with the facade from the beginning. Moreover, emphasis
on the exterior decoration was consistent with his view that architectural
ornament ought to teach and inspire. In 1858 Ruskin wrote to Acland: "I
press on people the duty of decorating outside rather than in—my main
principle being simple life, and richly bestowed public joy—nor do I think
the inside of a museum in much *need* of decoration and hence my obstinate
answer to Woodward."[27] He made his own designs for the main front and
said that one of them was carved. It was presumably the one shown in
figure 32, which was referred to in the 1870s as the Ruskin Window. He
also proposed modifying the lower range of windows on the main front and
urged traceried balconies for some of the upper windows. He contributed
thirty pounds for this purpose and published his own design for such a balcony in the book that he and Acland issued, *The Oxford Museum*. Much of

Fig. 32.   The Ruskin
Window of the Oxford
Museum. Architect,
1872.

Ruskin's contribution to its pages was actually an appeal for his conception of the building as a dramatic piece of public rhetoric.

As resistance to the expense of the museum grew, and as Woodward's illness forced his frequent absence, Ruskin's fund-raising and supervisory activities grew in importance. This produced some strain. On December 20, 1858, he exclaimed in exasperation to Lady Trevelyan: "I've done with architecture and won't be answerable for any more of it. I can't get the architects to understand its first principles & I'm sick of them. I'll go into the clouds again [i.e., into the chapter on clouds in *Modern Painters*, vol. 5]. That's the country to live in."[28] The next month he wrote to his father from Oxford to say that he was inspecting the color and stone decoration at the museum. By March 1859 he was complaining again: "What a nuisance these Oxford people are—making one refuse so often and often—I've told Woodward fifty times that I'm busy at present and yet they keep at me."[29] In January of 1860 we find him thanking Ellen Heaton for a donation and adding that "it will enable another window to be carved in the front of the building, under my immediate direction, as the architect, Mr. Woodward, is ill and had to go to Madeira for the winter, and I was obliged to take the conduct of the decoration while he was away."[30] All told, Woodward spent the last three winters of his life in Madeira, Algiers, and the south of France.

It is certainly appropriate to say that the immense emphasis placed on decoration at the Oxford Museum reflects Ruskin's ideas, and it is no doubt also true that his involvement with Woodward affected in turn the way he stated his principles. His stress on decoration was given new intensity after he became associated with an architect who shared his view of the prime importance of ornament. It is, as Ruskin said it ought to be, the expression of the building's meaning. Ruskin had shown how Saint Mark's could be regarded as an illuminated prayer book. His museum is a Bridgewater treatise. Its columns illustrate the geology of England, and their capitals display its flora and fauna. Its forms and colors exemplify what Ruskin saw as the principles of Nature herself. Its lecture rooms were illustrated with appropriate murals, such as R. St. John Tyrwhitt's mountain forms in the geology room. The statues of the inner court represent the history of science from Archimedes to Jenner. Ruskin, Woodward, and Acland had created the first example of an important Victorian architectural genre—the Illustrated Building.

None of this, however, closes the question of how closely the museum expresses Ruskin's views. He himself was inclined in later years to make large and discouraged claims for his role. In an 1877 letter to R. St. John Tyrwhitt he said: "For the Museum, of course it is I—not Acland—who am answerable for it. Woodward was my pupil. I knew from the moment he allowed iron work, it was all over with the building; nor did I ever approve the design—but it was a first effort in [the] right direction."[31] The interesting aspect of this passage is that the statement about the ironwork tends to contradict the implication of Woodward's docility. The Oxford Museum confronts us with the same problem that we face with all Ruskinian architecture: that of determining how far Ruskin's doctrines were altered when they were applied by his admirers. The Oxford Museum may well be the most obviously Ruskinian building ever constructed, but even it reveals fissures between Ruskin and Ruskinism. They can be seen most clearly in the stone carving and in the ironwork of the inner court.

The O'Sheas were the stuff of legend, and no one who has ever read the anecdotes about dignitaries of the university finding themselves carved as parrots and owls is likely to think of the Oxford Museum without visualizing a rollicking band of lighthearted Irishmen setting about their work with untutored skill. Their playfulness, at least, was real enough, and it is not surprising to read in one of James O'Shea's very few surviving letters that he "would not desire better Sport than putting monkeys cats dogs rabbits and hares, and so on, in different attitudes on those jambs."[32] But the O'Sheas and their cousin were also serious men, devoted to their craft and eager to create a new kind of architectural ornament. O'Shea speaks of adding "Beauty to the Building that i canot Explain only with my Hammer and Chizel,"[33] and neither spelling nor syntax obscures his sincerity. The O'Sheas' carving was widely illustrated and it was soon imitated. As early as March 29, 1856, the *Builder* was reproducing work in the style of the O'Sheas from a Baptist chapel in Preston, with the significant comment that "freedom was permitted to the carvers."[34] As much as anyone, it was the O'Sheas and Whellan who set the pattern for naturalistic carving in Victorian architecture.

It is possible that the skill of the O'Sheas and Whellan led to an extension of Ruskinian doctrine. In *The Oxford Museum* Ruskin lays it down as a principle that *all* architectural ornamentation should be executed by the men who design it. Clearly this was not originally the practice at the museum. Sophisticated artists were invited to provide designs that the O'Sheas would carve, and even Lady Trevelyan and a Mrs. Brodie "lent their aid" in "arranging" two or three of the capitals.[35] But most of the work looks as if it came from only a few hands working on common principles. It seems likely that the O'Sheas and Whellan not only took advantage of the freedom allowed them but extended it to the point where they did their own designing. Ruskin had originally thought that workmen capable of building in Gothic did not yet exist. The discovery of the O'Sheas must have been profoundly encouraging.

The Oxford carvers were encouraging in a more practical way as well:

they were extraordinarily quick at their work. As a result, the carving was relatively inexpensive. This mattered, for Convocation was protesting the museum's expense, and some members were attempting to have Woodward replaced over the issue. The general public, moreover, worried that decoration was expensive, and Ruskin's talk of a lamp of sacrifice cannot have calmed their fears. In his lecture "The Political Economy of Art," Ruskin was able to report that Thomas Deane had assured him that workers freed from repetitive labor worked more quickly and therefore at less expense.

The most obviously Ruskinian aspect of the carving is its naturalism, and it is here, paradoxically, that Ruskin's own attitude becomes problematic. Some form of naturalism was clearly part of the museum's program. Ruskin stated the principle quite clearly: "all art employed in decoration should be informative, conveying truthful statements about natural facts, if it conveys *any* statement" (16.214). The carvers took this to heart and decorated the museum with loving studies of palms, ferns, mallows, irises, aloes, wheat, barley, oats, Indian corn, sugar cane, and many other plants.

We saw earlier that Ruskin had two rather different positions on the degree to which ornament should be naturalistic. He accepted Coventry Patmore's criticisms of *The Seven Lamps* and restated his views in *The Stones of Venice*. The Oxford carvers seem to be paying attention only to *The Seven Lamps*. They often seek the spontaneity of nature at the expense of architectural function.[36]

In the first volume of *The Stones of Venice*, Ruskin argues that the duty of a capital is to express a transition between support and load. The carver can do this by taking advantage of the central fact of plant life and rooting his carving where it rises from the column. He can give it an elastic and upward spring at the abacus—the topmost element in the capital which carries the load. Both these things are done effectively in the two top capitals on figure 33. The ferns rise from the annulet. They have delicate touches of spontaneity, but the regularity with which they are disposed gives them some of the stiffness of stone. They embody the idea of support as they meet the octagonal abacus. Some of this is still true of the capital at the lower right, but it is difficult to associate ideas of load bearing with those gracefully bending plant forms or with the frog and snipe hopping among the stems. The corbel at the lower left, by contrast, is simply a graceful bouquet arbitrarily placed in front of an architectural form.

How much did Ruskin encourage this extreme naturalism? My guess—it is only that—is that he may have supported it enthusiastically at first. He often urged artists to follow nature trustingly as a first step in their education, though he expected that later they would rise to a more imaginative interpretation of natural facts. All the participants at the museum seem to have been carried away by the first step in this two-stage process. Ruskin

Fig. 33. Capitals and corbel from the Oxford Museum. Builder, 1859.

found his own design for a wrought-iron spandrel to be excessively naturalistic. Writing in 1858, he realized that a more conventional treatment
of the iron bars, and a more constructive arrangement of them, would have
"given vigourous expression, not of the shape of leaves and nuts only, but
of their peculiar radiant of fanned expression" (16.234). He made similar
criticisms of the carving. Of the fern capital in figure 33 he says that "while
beautiful, [it] is not yet perfect Gothic sculpture; and it might give rise to
dangerous error, if the admiration given to these carvings were unquali-
fied" (16.231). In other words, it was necessary to pass beyond imitative
naturalism. In later years Ruskin described O'Shea as a man who "too
easily thought, in the pleasure of his first essays, that he had nothing to

learn" (22.525). Thus Ruskin clearly distanced himself from the naturalism of the Oxford Museum carving. But it was the work of the O'Sheas
and Whellan that came to represent what the public understood to be Ruskinian stone carving.

The ironwork of the inner court is next in fame to the carving, and its
relation to Ruskin's principles is even more complicated. Ruskin said in his
1877 letter to Tyrwhitt that he knew it was all over with the building as
soon as Woodward allowed iron. And many commentators have seen an
anomaly in Ruskin's association with a building that was, in Acland's confident words, an experiment to "try how Gothic art could deal with those
railway materials—iron and glass."[37] After all, Ruskin's antipathy toward
railroads and iron was notorious. Should we not assume that there is an
absolute dichotomy between the body of the Oxford Museum and its iron
and glass inner court? Many writers assume this. Nikolaus Pevsner writes
in his guide to Oxfordshire that "Ruskin had denied with his usual hys-
terical emphasis that these materials could be vehicles of art. Yet—self-
contradictory as always—he seems to have had no objection to the iron
tracery of the museum."[38] Robert Furneaux Jordan takes a different tack in
his popular history of Victorian architecture when he assures his readers
that the roof was anathema to Ruskin and caused his resignation as advisor
to the museum. But Pevsner and Furneaux Jordan contradict one another,
and Ruskin, when he criticized the museum in the 1870s, was projecting
backward his later dislike of iron. During the 1850s his attitude was more
ambivalent and more interesting.

It is helpful to remember that the crucial figure in the design of the inner
court was not Woodward but Francis Skidmore of Coventry. He was a modern Gothicist, a man who believed in using Gothic principles to build in
nineteenth-century materials for nineteenth-century needs. In 1855 he
told the Architectural Museum that cathedrals could be constructed as
iron frames, with the interstices filled with ceramics, marble, and noble
frescoes, and with ample use of crisp iron foliage. Skidmore's views were
entirely compatible with those of such men as Acland, who saw the museum as a vindication of Gothic as a modern style.

The progressiveness of Gothic, to be sure, is not one of Ruskin's favorite
themes. It belongs rather to his admirers. But there are other senses in
which the inner court follows Ruskinian principles.

It is important to remember—and this is why Pevsner's charge of self-
contradiction will not stick—that Ruskin distinguishes between cast iron
and other types. The choice at the Oxford Museum was between cast iron
and wrought iron.

The two materials are distinct both chemically and in terms of the ways
they can be used. Wrought iron is a ductile material, easy to shape when

heated. Cast iron has a higher carbon content; it is easy to melt and to cast, but rather brittle once it has hardened. Wrought-iron ornament is made by a craftsman who wields a hammer. Cast-iron ornament is produced when melted iron is poured into a mold. Many nineteenth-century businessmen admired it because long rows of identical Corinthian columns could be mass-produced. Ruskin despised it for the same reason. He tended to use it as a symbol of all the age's faults—much as people today use plastic.

Skidmore and Woodward shared Ruskin's attitude toward cast iron, at least to the extent of first trying to build the entire inner court in wrought iron. This was a daring experiment because it was well known that cast iron is strongest bearing vertical loads while wrought iron is most effective resisting horizontal pressures. The heavy load of the glass roof would seem to have called for cast-iron columns. Wrought iron, however, was easier to reconcile with Ruskinian principles.

A writer in the *Building News* declared that the resulting shafts were graceful and that the spandrels "were filled with exquisite foliage." Unfortunately, it was soon found that the wrought-iron shafts were bending under the weight they had to support. The court was reconstructed with "the small bases [giving place] to larger ones, the groups of pipes to large shafts, the arched piping to strong solid arches." [39]

The present court is still faithful to Ruskin's principles so far as this is practicable. The arborescent form of tall columns with branching capitals maintains the link between architecture and nature (fig. 34). The distinction between the undecorated cast-iron columns and the decorative wrought-iron foliage follows Ruskin's dichotomy between utility and beauty. Finally, Skidmore was careful not to let his iron look deceptively like stone. The revealed bolt heads show the material of which they were made.

The next problem was painting the iron. In this connection the 1858 lecture "The Work of Iron in Nature, Art, and Policy" should be considered. It is one of Ruskin's less successful efforts, and no Ruskin scholar has ever been detained by it for long. Parts of it, however, seem to be an indirect expression of the discussions over the inner court at the Oxford Museum. Ruskin defends the decorative potential of iron and worries over the problem of coloring it.

One thing was sure: iron needs protection against dampness and rust. Paint of some sort is a necessity. We have seen that Owen Jones painted the Crystal Palace in a way that emphasized form. Should Woodward do the same? Or should he follow Ruskin and make color independent of form? The answer in the Tunbridge Wells lecture is an anticlimactic but still interesting piece of indecision: "The difficulty of colouring ironwork rightly, and the necessity of doing it some way or other, have been the principle

Fig. 34. Ironwork, Oxford Museum. Builder, 1860.

reasons for my never having entered heartily into this subject; for all the ironwork I have ever seen look beautiful was rusty, and rusty iron will not answer modern purposes" (16.423). Ruskin is quite correct. Rust is indeed lovely, and it would have provided the right monochrome for complicated capitals. It is used now in COR-TEN steel, but it was not available for the uses of the Oxford Museum.

But Woodward and his collaborators had to do something. They seem to have discussed the subject at length, but we have only the most tantalizing hints as to the progress of their debate. The *Building News* reported that the first attempt featured rich greens and chocolates, with a fair admixture of bright hues. This was good enough in the opinion of the anonymous writer, but he thought a second version better still. Alas, he does not describe it. He only mentions that "a few ancient people" thought that it was "overdone." There was a third version, and the ancient people triumphed:

> one day we found in corner of the court one column among the groups presenting a very remarkable appearance, and looking very much as if it has been drawn through a river of bread-sauce, or as if some foul animal with an unwholesome tongue had licked it. In our innocence we thought that some fresh experiment was about to be tried, and that this was a "first coat," destined to receive something better. Nothing of the kind! It was itself an experiment, and what was more, was considered a vast improvement on the earlier colouring; and behold, the leprosy has spread and infected every column in the place. The ironwork is accordingly for the time destroyed; the shafts look like huge slate pencils, alternating with vast Bath-sticks, and the entire place has been quakerized to the utmost. . . . But what a pity it is that so noble a work as this should be so marred by being, as it were, cut short in its growth! It is all the invention and creation of this century, except the finishing touches, which have been derived undiluted from the wishy-washy age of neat gentilities which has passed. [40]

The conflict seems to have been between a vibrant, unorthodox combination of colors and a safe brown, and Ruskin appears to have been in the conservative camp. In 1858 he urged postponing any controversial plans for the interior decoration of the building: "Leave it for future thought; above all, try no experiments" (16.225). On January 6, 1859, when the wishy-washy gentilities were accomplished, he wrote to his father: "I've been over the Museum carefully. All the practical part, excellent. All the decorative in colour, vile. It is the best error to make of the two" (16.lii). This recalls Ruskin's wish that the Rev. Daniel Moore would consider good, plain whitewash for the walls of Camden Church. Once again we find Ruskin not quite a Ruskinian.

IV

Two other designs by Woodward should be mentioned. Both helped shape the contemporary reception of Ruskin's thought, and both date from the time when the Oxford Museum was under construction. *

The Crown Life Assurance building in Blackfriars (fig. 35) was destroyed ten years after it was constructed to make way for a railroad, but detailed descriptions survive in both the *Builder* and the *Building News*.[41] It

---

* There is another Ruskinian commercial building of the 1850s with which Woodward's name has been associated. On January 15, 1855, Ruskin wrote to Lady Trevelyan: "I have got an order to build a bank! The banker says it must look like a bank. I return answer I am very sorry—but it will look like a church—if he provokes me—I will make it look like a bank, of flowers" (*Reflections of a Lifetime: John Ruskin's Letters to Pauline Trevelyan,* ed. Virginia Surtees, London: George Allen and Unwin, 1979, p. 98). Virginia Surtees speculates that this is a reference to Woodward's Crown Life Assurance building. This commission, however, was not awarded to Woodward until August 1856. Contemporary references make it more likely that Ruskin was working with an architect named George Truefitt.

A member of the Ecclesiological Society, Truefitt had submitted one of the two lonely Gothic entries in the Army and Navy Club competition. Reproduced in the 1847 volume of the *Builder,* it is interesting for its use of the central tower and symmetrical wings later employed at Oxford and also for the fussy decoration that covers it. In 1850 Truefitt published his *Designs for Country Churches.* These, compared with this Army and Navy Club entry, allow us to guess that he has been favorably impressed by Ruskin's call for mass and power. The idea of a closer association with Ruskin would have appealed to him.

On March 28 Ruskin wrote to Lady Trevelyan: "Of the bank—no news yet. The working drawings are being made and Rossetti is considering what mythological and philosophical information will be best for the minds of the clerks." By October 13 the *Builder* quoted Alfred Baily as telling a meeting of the Architectural Association: "He believed he was justified in saying that they would shortly see a building in the north of England erected from Mr. Ruskin's designs, with the constructive assistance of an architect. He [the Chairman], for one, was delighted to hear it. They were rather tired of his singular recipes, and were anxious to see the pudding itself. Let them wish it every success, and may it be as rich and juicy as the mind that made it. But if it should turn out a failure, if it should prove flat, crude, and indigestible, then by every architectural stomach in the kingdom they would not spare him." We do not know what happened next. All that is certain is that the *Builder* wrote in its January 19, 1856, review of the Architectural Exhibition: "Mr. Truefitt has erected a new room in the Yard at the 'Old Bank,' Blackburn. (195), where there is a 'lean-to' roof, in the trussing of which a perforated leaf-work pattern is introduced. This room is, we believe, the work for which Mr. Ruskin was said to have been applied to for designs; but the completion without his assistance seems to show that the original arrangement was not carried out."

Fig. 35.   *Crown Life Assurance building (demolished). Deane and Woodward. Building News, 1858.*

was striking for both its carving and its polychromy. The O'Sheas and Whellan created a great variety of flora and fauna, with a chase of animals up and down the gable over the main entrance. Interior friezes designed by John Hungerford Pollen featured foliage, birds, and animals. The colors, except for the red spirals on a bronze background painted on the rain pipe, were those of natural stone. Materials included red and gray granite, red brick, and Portland stone, as well as various types of marbles in the eyes on the third floor. The *Building News* specifically commented that no sham or "compo" embellishments were used. The result impressed the writer for the *Builder.* Though he worried that polychromy would distract attention from structure and give London's buildings "what Sir Charles Barry has well called a Tunbridge-ware-like appearance,"[42] he praised the Crown Life building as the city's "best exemplification of artist-like application of colour."[43]

An even more important design in terms of public perceptions of Ruskin was Woodward's proposed Foreign Office in the Government Offices competition of 1857 (fig. 36). One writer noted that it was "an inspiration from the 'Stones of Venice,'"[44] a second complained that "the whole smacks of the Stones of Venice and the Seven Lamps more than is suitable to an edifice which is not to be a department of the Doge,"[45] and a third claimed

Fig. 36. Design for Foreign Office, Government Offices competition. Deane and Woodward. Illustrated London News, *1857.*

that Woodward's entry, "both from the evidence which is on the face of it, and from report, owes much to Mr. Ruskin."[46] This last claim refers to a rumor that Ruskin had not only advised on the design but had actually prepared some of the drawings for it, a claim widely enough circulated that Ruskin rose to deny it at a public meeting in May of 1857. "He was quite unable," he was reported to have said, "to design buildings of the kind, and he never dreamed of interfering in any way."[47]

The first half of this statement is undoubtedly true, but the second is more doubtful. Ruskin and Woodward were in close association, and it is difficult to believe that they did not discuss the project very seriously. Certain parts of Ruskin's January 1867 lecture, "The Use of Imagination in Modern Architectural Design," especially his suggestion that good architecture ought to inspire the guards at Whitehall with military ardor, might have been uttered with Woodward's submission in mind.

The Crimean War had only recently ended when the competition for the Government Offices was announced. It had been a popular war, in spite of the administrative scandals connected with it. The painters of the Royal Academy were celebrating English heroism, and both Ruskin and Woodward were eager to do the same in architecture. As at Oxford, the building's intellectual and emotional content was to be expressed through ornament. The major difference was that here, instead of a treatise on natural theology, there would be a Victorian *Iliad.*

Figure 37 shows some of the carving that John Hungerford Pollen designed for Woodward's entry. It was to be placed low where it could be read, as Ruskin always urged, and its subjects were to be both dramatic and inspiring. There are panels in low relief on the base of the building, standing figures on the piers of the first floor, mounted figures on the second, and actual battle scenes rising up and over the pointed arches. The *Builder's* critic complained of a "deficiency of the special architectonic character,— the framework of lines, and the order in masses,—which most conduces to the effect of sculpture itself."[48] But Ruskin had anticipated this objection four months earlier in his talk at the Architectural Association. Granting that there was an architectural manner of sculpture, he nevertheless rejected the idea that sculpture had to be the subordinate art. He went on to say that the forthcoming competition offered "a fine opportunity for bringing forward, and for popularizing, as it were, the art of sculpture—an art so intimately and beautifully allied to that of architecture."[49] In his unpublished notes on the competition, apparently prepared with a view toward publication, he called for buildings that would "tell us what it is good for us to know, and make us feel what it is good for us to feel." As an example, he instances a building that might "show us even in feeble and rude bas-relief, how the soldiers stood in the last struggle at Inkerman" (16.xxxii).

Fig. 37.   Portion of design for Foreign Office. Deane and Woodward. Sculpture by John Hungerford Pollen. Builder, 1857.

At the very least, then, Woodward's and Ruskin's thoughts were proceeding along the same lines, and the rumors that Ruskin participated in forming Woodward's entry are understandable. They must have also been encouraged by the nature of a competition that Ruskin had set at the Architectural Museum the previous year. The prize was to be given for a bas-relief within a quatrefoil, similar to those at the Cathedral of Amiens, which would illustrate some incident connected with the Crimean War. The bas-relief was to contain between two and twelve human figures, some principal and others merely representing the presence of an army or multitude. It was also to contain foliage or architecture, which was to be either Gothic or modern English but not Grecian in character. The names of the principal figures were to be legibly sculptured, and if horses were introduced, their indicated pace was not to be faster than a trot. No attention would be paid, in judging the prize, "to delicacy of execution, or quantity of labour; but solely to ingenious disposition of masses, grace of line, and truth of expression." [50] This was very nearly a dry run for the Government Offices. O'Shea was one of the two carvers who competed. He offered *The Queen Presenting the Victory Medals to her Soldiers.* The other competitor, Mr. Chapman, portrayed *General Windham Leading His Men to the Attack of the Great Redan.* [51] Ruskin was not satisfied by either entry, and, rather than award a prize, made a cash payment to each carver.

V

The association of Ruskin and Woodward was an extremely important one for both men. It conditioned Woodward's career, and it helped persuade Ruskin that English architecture could be reformed. The pessimist, who in 1849 had hoped for no more than a few experiments in geometrical color mosaic, had by 1857 become such an optimist that he could urge the young members of the Architectural Association to become sculptors as well as architects. Yet by 1861, when Ruskin was asked to contribute to a memorial volume for Woodward, he had reverted to his original pessimism. He wrote to Henry Acland:

> I'm very sorry for Woodward. Rossetti's brother could do the work you want better than anybody else, if it was in any bricklayers rate of wages likely to be paid for. If it is not—truly—it had better not be done. There is nothing whatever to criticise in the Oxford Museum or this other thing [the Oxford Union]. Nothing bad and nothing good. [52]

Perhaps this discouraged tone results from the fact that Woodward's death, combined with the university's unwillingness to spend further funds, meant that the Oxford Museum was doomed to be forever unfinished. That would be cause for temporary despair, but in fact Ruskin's words in 1861 are entirely consistent with all that he had to say about the museum in later years. We must therefore ask what he thought went wrong.

Before we can answer that question, however, it will be useful to look at two other evaluations of the museum. The first is James Fergusson's. The second is that of an anonymous critic who wrote a detailed series of articles on the Oxford Museum for the *Building News* in 1858 and 1859.

Fergusson's discussion comes at the end of his *History of Modern Architecture*. There he accuses both the classic and Gothic revivals of copyism, but it is clearly the Gothicists who exasperate him most. The Oxford Museum, designed to be "Gothic in conception, Gothic in detail, and Gothic in finish," strikes him as their ultimate absurdity. He thinks its inner court clumsy and awkward, its lecture rooms cold and drafty, and its library long and ill proportioned. "You take a book from its press, and are astonished to find that men who could spend thousands on thousands in this great forgery have not reprinted Lyell's 'Geology' or Darwin's 'Origin of Species,' in black letter, and illuminated them, like the building, in the style of the thirteenth century." The one point Fergusson praises in the museum is the pillars with their capitals, which surround the inner court: "they are good precisely because they are not Gothic. The shafts are simply cylinders of British marbles; the capitals adorned with representations of plants and animals, as like nature as the material and the skill of the artist would admit of, and as unlike the Gothic cats of the facade as two representations of the same class of objects can well be made."[53] This brief praise for the work of the O'Sheas and Whellan, however, soon gives way to the observation that the chemistry laboratory, modeled after the abbot's kitchen at Glastonbury, looks as though it ought to house an alchemist rather than a scientist. Fergusson measures the museum by the test of progress and it fails.

It is all the more surprising, therefore, to find the critic in the *Building News* measuring the building by the same standard and giving it very high marks indeed. The writer's identity is unknown, but it is clear from his observations that he was close to the museum over a period of years. It is also clear from other articles he wrote under the title "The Liberty of Labour" that he was a warm admirer of Ruskin. He expects Woodward's building to deal a death blow to "the rotten system of antiquarian conservatism" and lay the foundation stone for "an English style of the Twentieth Century, which shall grow up as the Anglo-Saxon free constitution and free Church are growing up, to be the wonder and admiration of the world."[54]

Moderns are not more likely than Victorians to reach a settled verdict on the Oxford Museum. It is one of the most continuously fascinating buildings of the nineteenth century, and it certainly falls short of complete success. Both its strengths and weaknesses reflect contradictions in the mid-Victorian mind. Three of them can be identified.

The first is the ambivalent attitude toward the lamp of sacrifice. Clearly the Victorians were willing to spend on their important buildings. They wanted them to be ornate, to be built of precious materials, and to last for centuries. But they also believed in double entry bookkeeping and control of expenses. Ruskin and Woodward were asking for a virtually open-ended commitment. Convocation called a halt, and the result is a building that is rich and fascinating in some parts, bare in others.

The second contradiction is that Victorians wanted buildings that testified to their enduring beliefs at a time when those beliefs were in rapid transition. In the case of the Oxford Museum we have a temple of Natural Theology built just on the eve of the publication of Darwin's *Origin of Species*. The first major public dispute over Darwin's theories, the confrontation between T. H. Huxley and the bishop of Oxford, took place at the museum in 1860. It is very awkward to put a sermon on God and nature into stones if it will need instant revision.

Ruskin never yielded in his call for sacrifice, and he never gave in to Darwinism. The third contradiction, however, was one that he came to see very clearly. Henry Acland said that he hoped the museum would "go down to posterity as the production of the middle of the nineteenth century."[55] The writer in the *Building News* thought it achieved this; James Fergusson thought that it did not, but both agreed that this was the text by which it should be judged. His experience with the Oxford Museum helped persuade Ruskin that the architecture he loved could not be reconciled with the age in which he lived. He did not see this in the midfifties, at least not clearly. When he spoke about his relation with Woodward to a Dublin audience in 1868, however, he had made up his mind: "the architecture we endeavoured to introduce is inconsistent alike with the reckless luxury, the deforming mechanism, and the squalid mystery of modern cities" (18.150). But by the time Ruskin achieved this conclusion, his ideas had acquired an autonomous momentum among architects. They had become indissolubly linked with the cause of Gothic modernism.

VIII

THE 1850s: THE STRUGGLE
FOR A VICTORIAN GOTHIC

A survey of the 1850s reveals an ironic contrast between the fortunes of Gothic Revival architects and Ruskin's attitude toward their achievement: they move from struggle to success while he proceeds from hope to discontent. The extent of his disillusion was not made clear, however, until the following decade. So far as the general public was concerned, Ruskin appeared during the 1850s as an active supporter of the Gothic Revival. His views were sought, and, when they were not always forthcoming, they were eagerly guessed at. Four of the leading architects of the decade—George Gilbert Scott, George Edmund Street, John Pollard Seddon, and Alfred Waterhouse—were quite consciously concerned with absorbing and applying his ideas. Inevitably, they transformed them in the process.

I

We have seen that George Gilbert Scott and Ruskin first came into contact at Saint Giles's, Camberwell. They met again in 1846 when, according to the *Ecclesiologist*, E. A. Freeman's paper on geometrical window tracery given at the Oxford Architectural Society "gave rise to some valuable remarks from Mr. Rusken [sic], of Christ Church, Mr. Jones, of Queens, and Mr. George Gilbert Scott."[1] Their contacts became more frequently in the 1850s, and Scott was lavish in his praise of Ruskin's work:

I cannot trust myself with the task of commenting upon the works of this most
eloquent and remarkable writer. This, however, is quite certain, that no man,
Pugin alone expected, has so strongly influenced the undertaking we have in
hand, and no single individual, not himself a professed artist, has in our times
exercised so wonderful an influence over the art of his day. Our opponents de-
test him as they did Pugin and the ecclesiologists before him, and find in his
writings abundant grounds for reiterating, according to their custom, the charges
of enthusiasm, inconsistency, and the like. It is probably that all unflinching
reformers are more or less open to such charges; but in spite of all this, the
effect of his writings has been enormous, and in the main, beneficial.[2]

This is deeply felt, but it is also subtly qualified: "Pugin alone accepted, in
the main beneficial." Scott was not an uncritical admirer. He integrated
what he considered the best of Ruskin's ideas into larger, more acceptable
contexts.

As was also the case with Street, Seddon, and Waterhouse, Scott's reading of Ruskin was closely connected with his study of European Gothic.
He had traveled abroad during the 1840s, but without any dramatic effect
on his architecture. He had visited Belgium in 1844, not realizing, as he
said in his *Recollections,* that France would have taught him more. He
reached France in 1847, but his 1850 book on restoration still treated
Gothic as an essentially English phenomenon. It was not until 1851, after
both *The Seven Lamps* and the first volume of *The Stones of Venice* had appeared, that he made his way to Venice.

His first reactions and those of his traveling companion Benjamin Ferrey
are precisely what we would expect from two disciples of Pugin: "The Venetian Gothic, excepting the Ducal Palace, disappointed me at first, but
by degrees it grew upon me greatly. Ferrey was enraged at it, and I could
continually hear him muttering the words, 'Batty Langley,' when he heard
it spoken favorably of."[3] Batty Langley, of course, was the eighteenth-
century architect who had produced an inadvertently amusing reconciliation of "Gothick" with the five orders. Ferrey was later to conclude his
memoir of Pugin with an attack on the Venetian element that had entered
English architecture. Scott, on the other hand, talked with Ruskin in Venice, considered his views carefully, and was eventually as responsible as
anyone for what became known as Anglo-Venetian Gothic.

He did not, however, simply convert. He always warned that Venetian
elements were to be used with caution. Most of the features that attracted
him in Italian Gothic related either to its urbanity or its richness of color
and material. Simple outlines, arcaded windows set in walls without but-
tressing, and bold cornices might generate an urban sublime. Rich materials showed how a commercial society might celebrate its own prosperity.
Like Ruskin, Scott relished the beauty of stone, and he would set a polished granite shaft as if it were a rich jewel.

When Venetian elements seemed to lead away from the northern emphasis on structural integrity, however, it was always the latter that emerged victorious. That happened when Ruskin explained the virtues of the encrusted style. Scott accepted the claim that there was no sham involved. He restated the principle of confession, noting that at Saint Mark's the slabs are placed with their longest dimension *vertical*, as if to prevent any thought of their pretending to be constructional. But though he accepted the theoretical validity of the encrusted style, Scott was very cagey about actually using it. Thin slabs of colored marbles, he urged, should be restricted to panels and other subordinate, clearly nonstructural areas. Always a synthesizer, Scott absorbed Ruskin's Venetian Gothic into a framework that had been provided by Pugin and the *Ecclesiologist*.

Scott's most important act of synthesis occured in an 1857 book entitled *Remarks on Secular and Domestic Architecture, Present and Future*. We saw in chapter 6 that Ruskin's influence would have been very limited if architects had not evolved an essentially un-Ruskinian conception of Gothic as a progressive style capable of expressing the aspirations of a proud industrial nation. Scott was not the only man who helped solve this problem, but his book was long, detailed, and highly influential with both the public and the profession.

His reconciliation of the conflicting demands of reverence for the past and enthusiasm for the present centered on his concept of the *point de départ*. The Victorian architect should go back to the point of perfection that Gothic had reached just before its stiffening into perpendicular and make that his point of departure. On that basis he was to "press forward, to develope, to make the revived style our own, to adapt it in every way to our own wants."[4] His Gothic would express the characteristics of his own age: its unequaled knowledge of past styles, its devotion to natural history, its use of new materials, and its creation of new forms of commercial and civic organization. The Victorian Gothic architect would be able to say, as Scott himself did, "I am no medievalist."[5]

Scott's preferred method of arguing was to set up two extremes and then choose the middle path between them. His favorite choice is between Gothic purism and nineteenth-century practicality. Purism, for example, would always cover windows with pointed arches. Practicality prefers square windows in domestic architecture. Scott the compromiser concludes that the pointed arch is scarcely practical for rooms of ordinary height and that the square window should be freely used in domestic architecture. Where the height of a staircase or a great hall makes it possible, however, the architect should at once revert to the pointed form.

Another question was whether Gothic domestic windows should be mullioned. While mullions had medieval precedent on their side, sash windows had been, in Scott's rueful words, "registered with Magna Carta,

Habeas Corpus, and Trial by Jury as the Englishman's birthright."[6] Purism is sacrificed once again. The mullioned window is the most beautiful in the abstract, but Scott knew that Butterfield had used sashes in the choir school and clergy house at All Saints' and that Ruskin, in his Edinburgh lectures, had recommended placing sashes behind stone tracery. Scott accepts the comprehensive view, even suggesting that sashes be hung in grooves within mullions so as to slide in the usual manner.

In this spirit, Scott goes on to discuss doorways, roofs, chimney shafts, woodwork, ceilings, grates, staircases, floors, metal work, color decorations, painted glass, brick, and terra-cotta. He insists that the Gothic architect embrace all modern innovations. He can use plate glass and cast iron. He can employ flat or high-pitched roofs. He can Gothicize such non-Gothic elements as the dome (as Scott did in his baths at Brighton) and the grand staircase (as he did as Saint Pancras's).

Careful observers recognized that Scott's concept of style was both different from Ruskin's and an advance. A little dialog that appeared in the November 28, 1857, issue of the *Builder* maps out one version of the possible viewpoints:

> *Ruskinius.*—Italian Gothic is the style that should be chosen for a groundwork; none other is so fitted for sculpturesque treatment.
> *Donaldo.*—Nay; Greek art is the most perfect; the mind should first be imbued with a love of the most perfect styles.
> *Scotonius.*—I disagree with both of you. Fourteenth-century Gothic should be chosen as the *point de départ.* Revive classic art,—what will be the effect? A resurrection of the dry bones of antiquity, without one spark of vitality. Gothic art is the only one that reflects, even at this day, the living sentiments of the homely English mind.[7]

It will be noticed that Ruskin is thought to be a forthright advocate of Italian Gothic. It will also be noted that though Scott is made to disagree with both Ruskin and the classicist T. L. Donaldson, it is only Donaldson's views that are actually rejected.

It would be too much to say that Scott laid the charge of copyism to rest, but he seized the initiative for the Gothic camp. The *Builder's* review was characteristic: "These are certainly the principles on which the revival should be carried on, and would, doubtless, result in a style adapted to, and representing the age, but which, we are disposed to think, would not have very much in common with fourteenth century Gothic."[8] Leslie Sutton, writing in the *Building News,* was even more emphatic: "Gothic architecture, as taught by Mr. Scott, is no longer medieval."[9] A long review in the *Times* explained that Pugin and Ruskin had failed to convince the English public that Gothic was suited to anyone except monks and crusaders. It was Scott's achievement to crown "the labours of both Pugin and Ruskin by an assertion of the freedom of Gothic architecture from antiquarian restraint, [and] by a detailed exposition of the perfect ease with which mediaeval art can adapt itself to every modern appliance."[10] The Rev. Charles Boutell made clear the ultimate implications of Scott's style in an 1858 address to the Architectural Association: "You look back upon the 'Early English,' the 'Decorated,' the 'Perpendicular,' and the Elizabethan Gothic,—the VICTORIAN Gothic is your own."[11]

Like Ruskin, Scott felt that the renewal of architecture required a re-birth of craftsmanship. To this end, he played a leading role in organizing the Architectural Museum (fig. 38). Intended for the education of "our humbler class of artists, such as our carvers and decorators,"[12] the museum sponsored lectures by the leading architects and theorists of the revival. It also made available a large collection of plaster casts of Gothic carvings as well as brass rubbings, seals, prints, photographs, and original specimens of work in stone, wood, metal, and stained glass.

Ruskin was an active and enthusiastic supporter of the museum. In 1853 a report on its collection declared that "The fine head of St. Simeon, from the church of Venice of that name, presented by Mr. Ruskin, is specially worthy of a visit, it being singularly noble for that early time, the date being 1417."[13] Ruskin also gave casts of sculptured panels from Rouen and Notre Dame, capitals from the Ducal Palace, and a series of English royal seals. He also lent his drawings of Continental architecture. In 1854 he

Fig. 38. Architectural Museum, Westminster. Builder, 1854.

gave three lectures that were advertised for "Students and Art Workmen in Decorative Art only."[14] In 1855 he joined Scott, the Rev. Charles Boutell, and others in addressing an audience of between three and four hundred. Competitions were an important part of the museum's activities, and Ruskin set problems and offered prizes. In 1856 the *Builder* described the response to one of his challenges in these terms:

> a large capital of Venetian Gothic character came from Ireland without any name or address. The other competitors were George Galpin, whose capital exhibited between conventional foliage on four sides that number of groups illustrating the parable of the Prodigal Son; W. Sandilands, a smaller work, wherein palm trees form the foliage, and a scriptural allegory is set forth by groups between the stems (ruder and less learned than the last, but more original); and W. Farmer, who sent two specimens, formed, one of the vine, the other of the rose, ivy, maple, and vine conjoined.[15]

The next year, as we have seen, Ruskin set a very ambitious task on a subject derived from the Crimean War. His speech at the prize giving in 1858, according to the *Times,* had four hundred present.[16] He maintained his interest in the museum after it was absorbed into the South Kensington complex and in 1865 offered a ten-pound prize for work in opaque enamels on copper.

Ruskin's and Scott's names were closely linked in the controversy that followed the Government Offices competition of 1857. There is some irony in this, for Ruskin gave Scott only lukewarm support. His name was frequently invoked in the debate nonetheless, and in ways that reveal much about his impact on the Victorian public.

Victorian competitions were often murky, but that for the Government Offices was more tangled than most. The buildings were to be among the most prominent in Westminster and were expected to have a decisive impact on architectural trends. Accordingly, there was a great deal of maneuvering between the classicists and the Gothicists. The former seemed at first to be victorious. The winning designs could be traced back to either the French or Italian Renaissances. The main result of the 1857 judging for the Gothic party was that several of its leading members—Scott, Woodward, G. E. Street, and the partnership of James Prichard and John Pollard Seddon—gained premiums and a good deal of publicity. The government, however, was under no obligation to accept the winning designs. Scott had warm supporters in Parliament, including Lord John Manners, an associate of Disraeli in the Young England group, and Lord Elcho, who had attended Ruskin's Edinburgh lectures. By 1858 they had succeeded in having Scott appointed architect for the entire complex, and there the matter might have rested.

Unfortunately for Scott and his supporters, a change of government brought in Lord Palmerston as prime minister. Palmerston was in his seventies, and his views on architecture had long been formed. He held all the opinions about Gothic that Pugin, the Ecclesiologists, and Ruskin had labored to refute: it was Jesuitical, it was uncomfortable, and, above all, it was gloomy. Scott's designs were rejected. He then tried to compromise with Palmerston by turning to the Byzantine and Saracenic styles in the hope that they would provide a via media between Gothic and classic. It was to no avail. The prime minister was witty, jaunty, and firm. At last Scott, to the dismay of his supporters, gave in. With the assistance of Matthew Digby Wyatt, he produced the classic building that now stands opposite the Banqueting Hall.

The significance of this protracted affair in terms of Ruskin's influence thus lies in the controversy rather than in the structure that was actually built. Public interest was even greater than it had been three years previously for the Oxford Museum. Ten thousand people came to Westminster Hall (fig. 39) on the opening day to see the 217 designs, 7,000 on the second day, and 10,000 again on the third. The *Builder* observed that

Fig. 39. *Public display of Government Offices competition.* Illustrated London News, 1857.

"the body of London architects seemed each day transported *en masse* to Westminster."[17]

In spite of the diversity of entries, the competition was interpreted as a straightforward contest between the classic and the Gothic. Ruskin, as we have seen, was most closely associated with Woodward's entry, but he was also regarded as an overall leader of the Gothic cause. The *Building News* reported that "if the votaries of the Italian style are large in number and powerful in their champions, the small band of Gothic supporters, under the inspiration of Mr. Scott and Mr. Ruskin, exhibit a degree of vigour and ability which has gained attention for them."[18] Both architects and the public watched with fascination as the struggle between Scott and Palmerston went on in heated parliamentary debates and in the columns of the *Times*. The classicists seemed to lose the argument even as they won the battle. The *Building News* observed in 1860 that "many who entertained no decided opinion, either one way or another, have been converted by the love of fair play natural to most Englishmen, into ardent supporters of Gothic architects."[19] And all this discussion inevitably brought Ruskin's ideas before a larger public. "Above and beyond all," said the *Daily Telegraph* after an 1861 debate in Parliament, "it is a Godsend, a windfall, an apocalypse to Mr. Ruskin."[20]

The most striking feature of Scott's design was the degree to which it drew on Continental styles of Gothic. Scott's Foreign Office is shown in figure 40. He said in his *Recollections:*

> I did not aim at making my style "Italian Gothic;" my ideas ran much more upon the French, to which for some years I had devoted my chief study. I did, however, aim at gathering a few hints from Italy, such as the pillar-mullion, the use of differently coloured materials, and of inlaying. I also aimed at another thing which people consider Italian—I mean a certain squareness and horizontality of outline. This I consider pre-eminently suited to the street front of a public building. I combined this, however, with gables, high-pitched roofs, and dormers.[21]

The "foreignism" of Scott's designs caused some resentment among those members of the Gothic camp who defended the purity of English models. The Oxford historian E. A. Freeman spoke for this group when he regretted that the leading Gothic designs in the competition, including Scott's, "exhibited those mistaken theories of architecture which had recently obtained so much influence in the country, and which he expressed by the word 'Ruskinism,' as he considered that Mr. Ruskin in his unintelligible volumes had been principally their promoter."[22]

Observers noted similarities between Scott's Foreign Office and the Oxford Museum. The effort to placate Palmerston led Scott to draw even

Fig. 40.   Design for Foreign Office, Government Offices competition. George Gilbert Scott. Building News, 1857.

more heavily on that aspect of Woodward's style that represented a synthesis of medievalism and the early Renaissance. In August of 1860 he presented a design (fig. 41) that, as he said later, employed the Byzantine style "toned into a more modern and usable form by reference to those examples of the renaissance school which had been influenced by the presence of Byzantine works."[23] He was presumably thinking of the Trinity College Museum. He must also have been aware of another Woodward design in the same vein that was even closer to hand—the Crown Life Assurance offices in Blackfriars. Lord Elcho, one of Scott's chief supporters, led a delegation of M.P.'s to Woodward's building and during a debate presented the prime minister with a photograph showing the Assurance offices and the two Renaissance buildings on either side of it. The building on the right was labeled "Palmerston Ornate," the nearly identical but slightly less ornamented one on the left was marked "Palmerston Pure," and Woodward's in the center was identified as "What London would be if Palmerston would allow it."[24] Palmerston would not allow it. He dismissed Scott's design as a mongrel sort of affair, complaining that the architect had simply designed pointed windows and then given them rounded tops. He wanted, and soon got, his Italian Renaissance offices.

Classical architects played an active role in the debate, and they made it

Fig. 41.   Proposed Foreign Office, 1860. George Gilbert Scott. Drawings Collection of the Royal Institute of British Architects.

clear that they considered Ruskin as much their opponent as Scott. The most active and influential among them was Sir William Tite. Though he had visited Ruskin in Venice in 1852, he felt no temptation whatever to abandon his classical loyalties. He told the RIBA in 1855 that

> one gentleman (Mr. Ruskin) admired to the very echo the Ducal Palace at Venice—a feeling which he regretted should exist among the architects of England. . . . He thought that architects and architecture were much indebted to Mr. Ruskin, but he regretted that his lot had been cast in Venice; for of all the ugly types of Gothic architecture to be found on the continent, that of Venice was, in his opinion, the most ugly.[25]

During the years before the Government Offices competition, Tite watched the growing strength of the Gothic party with dismay. In 1856 he complained that there had been no competitors for the architectural medals of the Royal Academy because these were offered for classic styles, while "the young architects of the day are studying medieval church architecture to the abandonment of other studies."[26]

A member of Parliament himself, Tite was in a perfect position to lobby both before and behind the scenes. On two occasions—at a November 1859 meeting of the RIBA and in a July 1861 debate in Parliament—he combined his campaign against Scott's designs with swinging attacks on

Ruskin. Granting the moral value of the lamp of truth, Tite insisted that it could not be lit in Venice. Conceding Ruskin imagination and fancy, he denounced Ruskin's "imperfect knowledge and consequent dogmatism." He said of Ruskin's Edinburgh lectures: "They appear to me to be very unimportant, and often nonsense, as may be seen in the remarks on the pointed form of the leaves of the ash-tree, which seems to be adduced as a reason why the pointed arch should be preferred—(a laugh)."[27] He quotes Ruskin's six rules in the addenda to his printed lectures, which exalt decoration at the expense of proportion, and dismisses them as self-evidently absurd. His most effective tactic is one that he used in both 1859 and 1861. In the third volume of *The Stones of Venice* Ruskin devotes over four hundred words to the Casa Grimani as the principal example of Renaissance architecture at its finest. While sincere, Ruskin's praise is essentially a strategic maneuver designed to prepare the way for the passionate denunciation of the Renaissance that follows. Tite did not bother to explain this on either occasion. He simply quoted Ruskin's entire passage, culminating in the claim that it was the Roman Renaissance in its purity—represented by such buildings as the Casa Grimani, the Town Hall at Vicenza, Saint Peter's, Saint Paul's, and Whitehall—that was the true antagonist of the Gothic school. "To that opinion," Tite told his fellow members of Parliament, "he entirely subscribed."[28] The House responded with cheers.

Ruskin's name also figured prominently in journalistic debates over the Government Offices:

> What is there either to motive or to justify such lawlessness, such gross violation of all architectural syntax and prosody? No authority can be found for it in any noble edifice that has not been maimed, or else left imperfect. John Ruskin, after his "Sir Oracle" fashion, assured us that the front of York Minster is no better than "Confectioner's Gothic." We only wish, then, that we could get some of the same confectionary at Whitehall. If so be that Gothic we must have, by all means let us call in the confectioner, and see what he can do for us, since we positively sicken at Scott's *secular*.[29]

Some assumed that Ruskin was a power behind the scenes and that his purposes were intricately Machiavellian: "That Mr. John Ruskin defends Mr. Scott as a means of advocating the archeological merits of Mr. Street, and claims impartial judgment for Free Gothic, in the hopes of supplanting it with ascetic medievalism, is too patent to call for further proof or comment."[30]

It is a sign of Ruskin's importance in mid-Victorian architectural discussions that he held a central position in the debate over the Government Offices without ever issuing any emphatic pronouncements on the subject once the competition had been decided. All we have to reveal his attitude is one inconspicuous public statement and some private letters.

The public statement was made in February 1859 before a meeting of the Architectural Photographic Society. The main lecturer was G. E. Street, who was talking on Venice. Ruskin was there to introduce him. In the course of his remarks Ruskin touched on the conflict over the Government Offices:

> the saddest thing in all that debate was the total absence of perception by the assembly, of the connection existing between the Gothic architecture and our own constitution. It was said to be a remnant of the dark ages, but it never seemed to occur to the speakers that the English Constitution was a remnant of the dark ages, and it seemed rather more desirable that the building for the purposes of our Government should be in the style of those noble vaults under which our sovereign worshipped, than in that of the edifice which was near them, and with the central window of which such associations were connected—associations not altogether such as we should like to revive. [31]

In other words, build in the style of Westminster Abbey rather than in that of the Banqueting Hall, before a window of which King Charles was beheaded. Scott and his design are not specifically mentioned.

Another expression of Ruskin's opinion came in October of 1859 when a letter, signed only with the initials E.A.F., appeared in the *Times*. The author was the historian E. A. Freeman, who had overcome his objection to the foreign elements in Scott's design at least to the extent of defending it against those who claimed that Gothic was too expensive:

> Gothic may be as rich as you please or as plain as you please. ₁ᴧlian cannot. Mr. Scott designs a highly ornamented building. Of course, such a highly ornamented building is best, but you may cut out every bit of ornament and still leave it perfectly good. In Gothic you want nothing but a good outline, pointed arches, and chamfered jambs. Rich mouldings, capitals, foliage, crockets, pinnacles, &c., are all so much the better if you can get them, but you can do perfectly well without them. Keep Mr. Scott's outline, and strike out every inch of ornament, and you still have a handsome Gothic building. You cannot do this with a Classic design. [32]

Ruskin was so struck by the good sense of this argument that he wrote to the *Times* asking for the name behind the initials so that he could send on his congratulations. Freeman, presumably still angry over Ruskin's praise of Italian Gothic and his denunciation of the perpendicular style, angrily accused the newspaper of breaching a confidence. [33] The next year, writing in the *National Review,* he carefully disassociated himself from the Ruskinian elements in Scott's design:

Since Mr. Ruskin began to abuse English and French Gothic, and set up Italian in their stead, we have had a sort of counter revolution against the true Gothic movement. Northern Gothic has been discovered to be "savage," English perpendicular to be "detestable," and etc. . . . Nearly all inferior architects have been bitten with this madness; even Mr. Scott himself has not been quite unhurt.[34]

Freeman's dislike of Ruskin became one of the passions of his life. In 1887 he insisted that "the influence of Ruskin had swept away all that was rational" in English architecture,[35] and his biographer recorded that "among the authors whom he most disliked were Plato, Carlyle, and Ruskin, in no one of whom could he see any merit."[36]

Ruskin's best-known reference to the Government Offices occurs in a letter dated August 1859 to Eneas Sweetland Dallas:

Nice sensible discussion you're having in England there about Gothic and Italian, aren't you? And the best of the jest is that, besides nobody knowing which is which, there is not a man living who can build either. What a goose poor Scott (who will get his liver fit for a *pâté de Strasbourg* with vexation) must be not to say at once he'll build anything! If I were he, I'd build Lord P. an office with all the capitals upside down, and tell him it was in the Greek style, inverted to express typically Government by Party. Up today, down tomorrow. (36.315)

This appeared in Kenneth Clark's influential book *The Gothic Revival* and has been used ever since to show that Ruskin's opinion of Scott was a very low one. But Ruskin realized that he had said more than he intended and wrote again to clarify his views. The second letter, dated September 10, 1859, is in the Pierpont Morgan Library; the relevant passage is as follows:

It is more important to correct a mistake I have inadvertently caused you to make respecting my opinion of Scott—I think him an able and admirable architect—as far as architects reach in these days—I like his book exceedingly—much better than some of my own—For Barry and his son I have on the contrary unmitigated contempt—But I do not care to stir in the question—because neither Scott nor anybody else can build either Gothic or Italian at present—all real work in those styles depends principally on the mastery of figure sculpture—all modern architecture is spurious—and must remain so until architects become sculptors—their doing so does not in the least depend on the adoption of any style for their public buildings—and therefore I said that Scott—who in the modern way can design with great facility—ought to be able to build Lord Palmerston anything he likes.[37]

Taken together, these letters suggest that Ruskin's attitude toward Scott and the Government Offices was a complicated one. First, he was disgusted with the English public for engaging in the controversy at all. The Italian was detestable, the claims of Gothic were obvious, and there was no need for argument. Second, he felt that Scott deserved support and was concerned lest an influential writer for the *Times* have any doubts on that score. Third, he liked Scott's *Remarks on Secular and Domestic Architecture* "exceedingly." Fourth, Scott is only an admirable architect "as far as architects reach in these days." He is still only an architect when he ought to be a sculptor. Fifth, it is far more important that architects become sculptors than that they adopt any particular style for their public buildings. It may have been the complexity of his views, and the need to qualify his admiration for Scott, that kept Ruskin from entering the debate in which his name was so often invoked. It appears that he tactfully refrained from mentioning his reservations to the architect. Scott justified his final submission to Lord Palmerston with the claim that "even Mr. Ruskin told me that I had done quite right."[38]

II

Ruskin's approval of Scott was tentative and came with reservations attached. His attitude toward G. E. Street was much more positive. In 1888 an anonymous writer in the *Architect* recalled:

> I was once talking with Mr. Ruskin about architecture, and as he was in a desponding mood he descanted upon the shortcomings of English architects. Our censor was able to make out a long indictment. It began, as I remember, with the treason which had been committed against the buildings in Oxford under the guise of restoration, and it ended with the defects which were to be found in certain buildings of the time that were supposed to be examples of Italian Classic. Mr. Ruskin's belief for the moment was that English architects were unable to appreciate the work of their forefathers, and were incompetent to copy conventional forms which were supposed to be subject to the most precise rules. It is not necessary that I should endeavour to bring back what I urged in reply. What is now clear to me is that, when the names of so many who would not be enlightened by the "Seven Lamps" were mentioned, I introduced Mr. Street's name as if inquiring how he could be affected by the indictment. "Street," said Mr. Ruskin, "is a fine fellow," and he uttered the words with an enthusiasm that surprised me.[39]

Although Ruskin would occasionally adopt a sharp tone in disputing some of Street's analyses of Italian buildings (especially his dating of the parts of the Ducal Palace), he maintained his enthusiasm for Street's architecture.

George Edmund Street was born in Essex in 1824 and articled to an architect in Winchester. He came to London in 1844, where he entered the office of George Gilbert Scott. He lived in Camberwell and frequently attended matins at Saint Giles's. He set up his own practice in 1848. A friendship with Benjamin Webb gained him a commission to design buildings at Wantage for an order of Anglican nuns, and this led to his appointment as diocesan architect to the bishop of Oxford. He traveled to France in 1850 and to Germany and Belgium in 1851.

Street's interest in Ruskin was connected with his knowledge that the new task facing the Gothic Revival would be the design of secular buildings in urban settings. This would require a Gothic style suffused by certain qualities normally considered classical: breadth, repose, symmetry, and horizontality. Italian Gothic seemed to present just such a synthesis.

That was the lesson Street drew when he praised James Wild's Saint Martin's Northern Schools (fig. 42) as a pattern for urban architecture. This building is often cited as an early example of Ruskinism. It may be, since its cornerstone was laid four months after the publication of *The Seven Lamps*,[40] or it may be an independent phenomenon. What matters is that Wild used Italian Gothic sources to create a building clearly suited to a narrow urban street. In the fall of 1853, Street made his third trip abroad and published the results in *Brick and Marble in the Middle Ages; Notes on a Tour in the North of Italy* (1855).

Ruskin is a dominating presence in this book, so much so that one writer sourly referred to Street as Ruskin's "umbra."[41] Street himself says in the preface: "No man need or can profess his acquiescence in every one of the opinions which [Ruskin] has propounded, but as an architect I feel

Fig. 42.   Saint Martin's Northern Schools (demolished). James Wild. Builder, 1849.

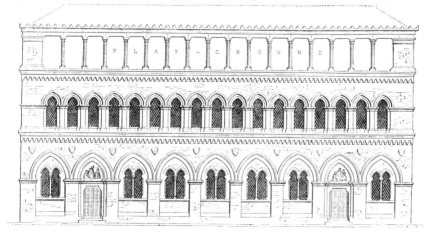

strongly that a great debt of gratitude is owing to him for his brilliant advocacy of many truths in which every honest architect ought gladly to acquiesce."[42] As with Scott, however, praise is accompanied by careful reservation. *Brick and Marble* reflects an inner debate over Ruskin's theories and the values of southern as compared to northern Gothic.

Street's first and deepest commitments were to Pugin and the Ecclesiologists. Judged by the standard of Pugin's true principles, the structural clumsiness of southern Gothic, with its excessively thick walls and constant recourse to tie-rods, was a scandal. Against this background, Ruskin's preference for southern over northern Gothic must have come as a shock. The northern variant of the style, in Ruskin's view, neglects "perfect grace and quiet truthfulness" in favor of a multiplication of small forms and an exaggerated piquancy:

> those who study the Northern Gothic remain in a narrowed field—one of small pinnacles, and dots, and crockets, and twitched faces—and cannot comprehend the meaning of a broad surface or a grand line. Nevertheless the Northern school is an admirable and delightful thing, but a lower thing than the Southern. The Gothic of the Ducal Palace of Venice is in harmony with all that is grand in all the world: that of the North is in harmony with the grotesque Northern spirit only. (9.188)

Ruskin's distinction is summed up in figure 19, which shows linear Gothic from Abbeville on the left and surface Gothic from Verona on the right. The first, he says, is weak in masonry and broken in mass while the second is strong, simple, and yet perpetual in its variety. Throughout much of his journey, Street was debating the relative merits of the two forms of Gothic.

He reveals his northern loyalties with his constant condemnation of the structural naïveté of Italian buildings. He condemns the constant trefoiled ornament of the south as "always unsatisfactory, because unmeaning and unconstructional."[43] He regrets that in Venice architecture was never "essentially constructional in the sense in which it was in our own land."[44] Yet he also appreciates the classic repose of southern Gothic and worries that the very skill of northern builders led them into aesthetic errors as they lost the calm of quadripartite vaulting and plate tracery in the linear nervousness of lierne vaulting and curvilinear tracery. Street questions the verticality and aspiration of northern Gothic and begins to share the southern view that "perfect rest was the only allowable state for a perfect building."[45] By the time he heads north he has almost been won over. Standing before the west front of Strasbourg Cathedral, he almost shares Ruskin's preference for the universal spirit of Southern Gothic over the more limited appeal of the northern:

after the simple, unbroken facades of Italian churches, with their grand porches and simple breadth of effect, there is really something which so entirely destroys all repose in a front covered as this is with lines of tracery, and niches, and canopies in every direction, as to leave, I confess, a painful feeling upon the mind of the restless nature of the designer's thoughts.[46]

When he stands awestruck in the nave, however, his faith in the north is restored. Later, especially after his careful preparations for the Lille competition of 1855, Street would be very emphatic in asserting the superiority of French over Italian Gothic.

Street states the lessons he draws from Italy in significantly different ways at two different times. In his 1855 book he tends to restrict himself to what may be termed architectural features—mouldings, tracery, balconies, and so forth. Three years later, however, when Street lectured "On the Future of Art in England" to the Ecclesiological Society, he had gone even farther down the path of Ruskinism. He is now sure that architecture is incomplete unless it merges with the other arts. He looks to Italy not for its columns and moldings but for its murals and carvings. He complains that the training of too many architectural workers has been narrowly architectural rather than generally artistic; he hopes to see someone venturing to do something in more than one department of art. He praises Alexander Dyce's paintings at All Saints', Rossetti's reredos at Llandaff Cathedral, and, above all, the murals at the Oxford Union. He makes his closest approach to a complete acceptance of the Ruskinian faith: "Three-fourths of the poetry of a building lies in its minor details."[47]

Street's career in the 1850s thus shows him gradually accepting Ruskin's most important ideas. It also shows him arguing with George Gilbert Scott over the proper interpretation of one of them.

We saw in chapter 6 that while Ruskin never wavered in his faith that all beautiful forms of ornament were derived from a close and loving study of nature, he was uncertain as to the degree to which nature should be conventionalized for architectural purposes. Different architects, citing different passages from Ruskin's work, and sometimes the same passage, could defend rather different compromises between naturalism and conventionalism.

Street's first statement on the matter seems to lean toward the more naturalistic extreme. This occurs in his 1853 pamphlet urging Gothic as the style of the proposed Oxford Museum. There he says of the fourteenth-century architects:

They took nature as their guide: with her they went into the meadows and the woods and culled all that was most beautiful in colour and in form, and applied it to the use of art. If they carved a figure it was a true reproduction of a living form: not conventionalized so far as to be unlike nature, but just so far as to stereotype, as it were, nature's most perfect mood.[48]

In 1853 naturalism required emphasis and defense. Five years later taste had changed so much that Street felt obliged to adopt a different stance. When he did, he found himself embroiled in an unexpectedly bitter controversy with his former employer.

The forum for their disagreement was a series of lectures at the Architectural Museum. This had become, under Scott's leadership, something of a center of the naturalistic approach. Street, therefore, felt obliged to warn his audience that excessive naturalism was a fault in architectural ornament, that nature needed to be conventionalized when placed in an architectural framework, and that earlier (more conventional) rather than later (more naturalistic) examples of Gothic foliage should be chosen as models. As Street told an audience a few years later, "he had educated himself very much upon the system which Mr. Ruskin had himself argued for of old," and he had learned that "what is required of architectural sculptors is that their work should be a noble abstraction of nature, not a mere imitation of natural forms in the crude sense of the term; not the mere reproducing of the outline of a leaf or of a flower."[49]

Scott was angered by Street's advice. The next lecture was his and, to be sure of his audience, he inserted a notice in the *Builder* saying that since it was "intended especially for carvers and art-workmen, he is anxious that they should be made aware of it, and that they should come early and take the seats from which they can best see any illustration he may make use of."[50]

The audience that listened to these lectures must have been puzzled by some of the distinctions presented. Street had distinguished between "the conventionalized idealization of nature," which he favored, and the "conventionalizing of nature herself,"[51] which he did not. Scott's arguments were equally subtle. The examples, at least, were clear. Street recommended the twelfth-century carving at Notre Dame as giving "the very essence of natural forms, without any of the vulgarity (as I think I must call it) of the direct imitation of nature."[52] Scott urged the study of carving from the second half of the thirteenth century and especially praised the very naturalistic foliage of Sainte Chapelle. Scott insisted that the carver "who wishes to take nature as his guide" should study "every form and every curve, every tendency and habit" of the living plant and be able to hit off its real character.[53] He was willing to see, in a phrase that he borrowed from plate 6 of the second volume of *The Stones of Venice*, the natural form brought "into service." Street was willing to leave the forms of nature farther behind: "the best capital ever sculptured in direct imitation of nature could never require a tithe of the thought, power, or sense of beauty and fitness, which are evidenced by a really fine piece of conventional sculpture."[54]

Two things must be stressed about this debate. One is that both men are self-consciously adopting Ruskinian positions. The other is that Scott's Ruskinian position is winning the greater applause. Street was bitterly aware of this. He stressed the fatal similarity between Gothic naturalism and the worst tendencies of Victorian popular taste:

> consider how easy the descent is, if we once consent simply to copy natural forms. Nothing, it seems to me, can be easier: any one may take ivy leaves and twist them about into pretty patterns; and I protest that I know few things which seem to me to be more likely to ruin much of our work than the way in which this is coming to be the fashion. Undoubtedly there is something fascinating in an artificial age like this in the idea of taking unaltered nature for our guide; but the whole virtue of Nature as a guide is when she is held under proper restraint. Otherwise, I confess I do not see where we are to stop. If direct imitation of Nature be a good thing, then Grinling Gibbons is a good master for our carvers, and those men are not so far wrong who light gin-palaces with gas branches made in the shape of an arum, or a lily with white porcelain flowers, green leaves, and brass stalks; nor those who made cornice poles with terminations carefully copied from fuchsias gathered by giants.[55]

In a subsequent letter to the *Builder*, Street reiterated his view that Scott's defense of naturalism encouraged some of the laziest tendencies of the age: "I submit that, considering the character of most modern work, it is, to say the least, a safer course to protest, as I did, against the flagrant '*vulgarity*' of the '*direct*' imitation of nature, than to address a crowd of working men, whose present tastes are so avowedly naturalistic, as Mr. Scott did, in a general condemnation of my protest. The very applause his remarks elicited from them must, I think, have made him suspect how very far he was from doing good."[56]

How did Ruskin's influence appear in Street's buildings? It is well to remember that Street remained—by the vagaries of an architectural practice rather than by intent—primarily a church architect until the last great work of his career. We must therefore turn to two churches. The first is so minor that Henry-Russell Hitchcock does not even mention it in his very thorough essay on Street's work in the 1850s. The second is one of the masterpieces of Victorian architecture.

The church of Saint Paul stood on Herne Hill not far from the Ruskin home. It had been built in the 1840s by a Mr. Alexander and was apparently not to Ruskin's taste. When it burned he immediately, according to

Fig. 43.   Facing page, top. *Saint James-the-Less*. G. E. Street. Builder, *1861.*

Fig. 44.   Facing page, bottom. *Capital from Saint James-the-Less. Photo: author.*

Fig. 45.   Above. *St. James-the-Less (interior).* Building News, *1862.*

his own account "called on the different members of the congregation, and congratulated them on the occurrence" (16.462). He praised Street's rebuilt church as "pure beyond anything he had seen in modern architecture." It was especially remarkable for "a piece of colouring admirably introduced," and he doubts that "it could be excelled by any of the colours in ancient art" (16.463). John Unrau suggests that this statement refers to the bands of Devonshire marble in the piers of the nave.[57] Ruskin's statement provides one of the few instances in which he praised the color sense of a Victorian architect.

There is a fine discussion of Saint James-the-Less (fig. 43) in John Summerson's *Victorian Architecture*, but the definitive comment is Henry-Russell Hitchcock's: "Thus might Heaven itself have been decorated by the Victorians!"[58] Street covers every surface with some color, some pattern, or some intricate piece of craftsmanship. Walls are enlivened by contrasts of red brick, black brick, stone, and red and yellow glazed tiles. Some nave columns are made of polished red Aberdeen granite encircled by shaft rings, while others are inlaid with spiral patterns. The capitals in the nave (fig. 44) feature great stiff leaves pierced by drill holes to increase the contrast between light and shade; between the leaves figures act out the Parables and Miracles of Christ. The arches are given notched intrados. The wooden roof of the nave is covered with blue, red, green, and white arabesques enclosing portraits of patriarchs, kings, and priests. The chancel arch (fig. 45) is decorated by G. F. Watts, whom Ruskin had praised in *The Stones of Venice* as the only English artist capable of design in color on a large scale. The pulpit is lavishly carved. There are elaborate inlaid mastic designs on the chancel arch, and there is also, as at Saint Paul's, Herne Hill, a central cross of Irish marbles decorated by balls of Derbyshire spar. One is often moved to sympathize with those aesthetes of the 1870s and 1880s who denounced their elders for not appreciating the value of a plain, undecorated surface. At Saint James-the-Less it does not matter. Because the details are so fine, we readily accept the premise that all have equal claims on our attention.

The direction of Street's career changed in the course of the 1860s. The Italian Gothic element in his work diminished, and his last great work, the Law Courts in the Strand, draws on English precedents and associations. Yet these buildings are still associated with Ruskin's name for good though slightly complicated reasons.

In 1872 Coventry Patmore, reviewing Charles Eastlake's *History of the Gothic Revival*, remarked that while he thought Ruskin's indirect influence had been largely for the good, his direct influence had been for the bad. Ruskin himself often decried his influence, but in this case he disagreed: "the fact to my own notion is otherwise. I am proud enough to hope, for instance, that I have had some direct influence on Mr. Street; and I do not doubt but that the public will have more satisfaction from his Law Courts than they have had from anything built within fifty years" (10.459). One need only look at the Law Courts to see that they are far less obviously Ruskinian than Saint James-the-Less. White Portland stone has replaced constructional polychromy, and there is no attempt to employ carving and sculpture to transform the building into a textbook on the English constitution. The Law Courts may be Ruskinian in spirit but they are not so in detail.

Why, then, was Ruskin proud to claim a direct influence. It is possible that he had not seen the particular designs for the Law Courts and was basing his comment on the totality of Street's career. But there is another, more topical explanation. Like the Oxford Museum and the Government Offices, the Law Courts were the subject of a well-publicized competition. This time, however, the classicists were on the defensive and the only question was which of the Gothic designs would be accepted. The classicists, however, regrouped their forces and made Street's winning entry the focus of a furious assault. James Fergusson was once again one of the doughtiest warriors, still advocating the cause of E. M. Barry and the modern Italian style. In this context, Ruskin's statement may be regarded as a public declaration of support for Street. It was interpreted in just this way. A leading article in the *Architect*, probably written by E. W. Godwin, Street's most active defender, noted that most of the outcry came from nonarchitects and concluded: "Outside the profession there is but one man (Mr. Ruskin) whose opinion on the nature and value of a Gothic design would have any weight for us, and he supports Mr. Street."[59]

III

We have seen in chapter 6 that John Pollard Seddon absorbed Ruskin's influence in 1851 and 1852.[60] We will see in chapter 9 that during the 1860s he became an important critic of the excesses of some of Ruskin's admirers. His work during the 1850s is important not only for its intrinsic interest but because it allows us to refer to the activities of his older brother, Thomas Seddon, and his partner, John Prichard.

Thomas and John Pollard Seddon came from a line of London cabinetmakers. Ironically, their family firm pioneered in methods of furniture production that were opposed to the spirit of Ruskinian craftsmanship. In an essay entitled "Design and Industry through the Ages," Nikolaus Pevsner used the Seddon factory to illustrate the growing separation of design from execution and the increasing replacement of craft processes by division of labor.[61] These were the very trends that Thomas Seddon set out to reverse.

Thomas Seddon had worked as a designer for the family firm and, like many others at midcentury, had become alarmed by the inferiority of English to French art manufactures. Henry Cole and his circle responded to this situation by reorganizing the Government Schools of Design. Influenced by *The Seven Lamps*, Thomas Seddon set out to organize a system that would be quite unlike the government schools. Neville Warren, Seddon's collaborator, complained that the Cole group treated workmen "more as machines which it is desired to improve than as men of thought and understanding." He insisted that the new institution in Camden Town was "not in any degree a school of design."[62] As John Pollard explains in a memoir of his brother, the Government Schools enforced a distinction between designers and workmen. The favored students attended day sessions; workmen came only at night, and their distinctive dress marked them off. At the Government Schools, students were taught to draw either from a book of outlines or from prints of classical and Renaissance ornament. At the North London School, as in Ruskin's classes at Working Men's College, they were taught to draw from natural objects. The Government Schools trained designers whose work would be realized by machines. At the North London School, by contrast, men employed in the workshops of Clerkenwell, Kentish Town, Camden Town, and Gray's Inn Road were shown how they might both design and execute.

Thomas Seddon also attempted to influence the workers at his family's factory. He encouraged them to study natural forms and to work freely in realizing the basic design submitted to them. "This, however," as John Pollard explains, "was up-hill work. When they were apprentices, they had learned to carve oak and ivy leaves, and they saw no use in continually reverting to the fields and the garden."[63]

There were other difficulties as well, and the labor of organizing the North London School undermined Thomas Seddon's health. Ironically, the school itself soon fell under the control of the Cole group. Thomas Seddon pursued his career as a painter, accompanied Holman Hunt on a journey to the Middle East, and died on a second journey there in 1856. He might have been mourned as a martyr to art, but Ruskin's eulogy at a memorial meeting in 1857 proposed him as a type of all the young men blighted by England's commercial and industrial system.

John Pollard Seddon went into partnership with John Prichard. Their firm produced many churches and restorations as well as a design for the Government Offices. It also produced two buildings that show Ruskin's influence in quite different ways. One was Ettington Park; the other was the Cardiff Post Office.

It was Prichard who was responsible for the design of Ettington Park (fig. 46), though Seddon sometimes supervised construction.[64] With Prichard, we have another architect who owed loyalties to both Pugin and Ruskin. The former was the more enduring influence on his career. He had trained under Pugin's principle assistant, and in 1859 he described himself as "a true disciple of Pugin."[65] The most striking features of Ettington Park, however, are its polychromatic wall-veil and its sculptural decoration, and both of these reflect Ruskin's doctrines.

The client E. P. Shirley must have played an active role in shaping the design. This gentleman was introduced into Disraeli's novel *Lothair* under a fictional name and was described in these terms:

> The other country member, Mr. Ardenne, was a refined gentleman who loved the arts. He had an ancient pedigree, and knew everybody else's, which was not always pleasant. What he most prided himself on was being the hereditary owner of a real deer park; the only one, he asserted, in the country. Other persons had parks which had deer in them, but that was quite a different thing. His wife was a pretty woman, and the inspiring genius of archaeological societies, who loved their annual luncheon in her Tudor Halls, and illustrated by their researches the deeds and dwellings of her husband's ancient race.[66]

Shirley wanted an architectural style consonant with his own vivid historical imagination. Ettington Park was originally Tudor, but had taken on a Palladian form with later improvements. The new alterations were to transform the exterior, giving more dramatic presence to the building and letting in more light. Shirley first sought a design from G. E. Street and, failing to get one that pleased him, then turned to Prichard.

Both men were clearly thinking along the lines being explored at the Oxford Museum. Prichard visited it while preparing his plans, and E. P. Shirley, who had attended Magdalen College, was presumably the Mr. Shirley who defended Woodward's cause at an 1858 meeting of Convocation.[67] The Oxford Museum showed Prichard how he might satisfy his client's romantic antiquarianism while still producing a building that, as the *Building News* put it, "would have been impossible in the age to which its style is referable."[68]

Ettington Park reflects three aspects of the Ruskinism of the 1850s. First, it unites elements of French and Italian with English Gothic. Second, it is a striking example of constructional polychromy, making use of five different stones in a horizontally banded wall. Third, and most dramatically, the building exemplifies Ruskin's argument that "it is in becoming memorial or monumental that a true perfection is attained by civil and domestic buildings; and this partly as they are, with such a view, built in a more stable manner, and partly as their decorations are consequently animated by a metaphorical or historical purpose" (8.225).

Fig. 46.   Ettington Park, Warwickshire. Prichard and Seddon. Building News, 1869.

Fig. 47.   Sculptured panel, Ettington Park. Photo: author. Courtesy Ettington Park Hotel. Stratford on Avon, England.

Built to last and built of local stone, Ettington Park (fig. 46) seems to grow naturally out of the surrounding countryside. The large sculptured panels on the facade (fig. 47) grow out of the family's history as well. Their subjects were chosen by Shirley himself, designed by H. H. Armstead, and carved by Edward Clark. They begin with the Saxon thane Sewallis founding the church at Ettington and come down to the committal of Sir Robert Shirley to the Tower by Oliver Cromwell. One panel shows Sir Thomas Shirley crusading in the Holy Land, where his page is bringing him the head of a vanquished Saracen; another shows Sir Ralph Shirley bidding farewell to his wife and child as he leaves with Henry V for France. In addition to the fourteen panels, there are shields and crests, heads of monarchs on corbels, and full-length statues in carved niches. If the Oxford Museum was a Bridgewater treatise in stone, Ettington Park is an architectural *Stemmata Shirleiana.*

The Cardiff Post Office sheds light on the way in which Ruskin's influence was absorbed into street architecture. It is especially interesting for its dramatic use of polychromatic brickwork (fig. 48).

Nineteenth-century interest in the aesthetic possibilities of brick precedes the publication of *The Seven Lamps* by only a very short time. There had, of course, been a golden age of brick architecture lasting from the second half of the seventeenth to the second half of the eighteenth century. Even during the best period for brick, however, it was considered inferior to stone, and by the early nineteenth century, it was regularly covered with a layer of stucco, which was lined in imitation of stone jointing. Pugin and the Ecclesiologists led the way in using brick without disguise. In 1847 the Rev. Thomas James published a pamphlet entitled "On the Use of Brick in Ecclesiastical Architecture." There is no way of knowing whether or not Ruskin read it, but both writers call attention to James Wild's Christ Church, Streatham. It is clear that aesthetic trends were shifting when *The Seven Lamps* appeared, and the process must have been speeded by the repeal of the tax on bricks in 1850.

Ruskin mentions the material only once in *The Seven Lamps*. His emphasis was on the natural colors of stone. Many of his comments, however, seem applicable to brick, and Coventry Patmore concluded an article in the *North British Review* by specifically inviting Ruskin to "confer a vast benefit upon our cities by shewing us what are the essential and peculiar artistical capabilities of brick architecture."[69] The most important passage on brick in *The Stones of Venice* is clearly a digression, one that looks as though it had been added to satisfy the demands of readers. It warns architects that "our fields of good clay were never given us to be made into oblong morsels of one size" (10.303) and points out that bricks can be used for arches and plinths as well as for the mass of a structure. The brickfield,

Fig. 48.   Design for post office, Cardiff. Prichard and Seddon. Building News, *1857.*

Ruskin now proclaims, would be the best academy for England's architects for some half century to come.

It was not long before a reference to Ruskin was all but obligatory when brick was discussed. In 1853 the *Builder* assured its readers that "much of the architecture of Italy (as we are reminded in turning over Mr. Ruskin's pages) serves to force upon consideration our ignorant neglect of the real use of brick.[70] In 1854 the Rev. Thomas James (who might himself have claimed priority) quoted Ruskin in support of polychromatic brickwork.[71] Both Street's *Brick and Marble in the North of Italy* (1855) and Scott's *Remarks on Secular and Domestic Architecture* (1858) discussed the material at length. The Architectural Exhibition soon began to feature drawings with such titles as *Designs for Brickwork on Aesthetic Principles* and *Decorative Brickwork Applied to the Exterior of a Building without Disturbing the Lines of Architectural Design*. In 1861 the *Building News* observed that "whether owing to Ruskin or Street's *Brick and Marble,* one now comes on a parti-coloured brick building on the corner of every street."[72] In 1864 the same magazine ran a well-illustrated series on brick architecture that quoted Ruskin and analyzed examples of the recent use of colored and molded brick. In the same year a writer surveyed the transformation of Leicester by the new brickwork and concluded that "all the poetic invitations of Ruskin had not been in vain."[73]

There is a major irony in all of this. It lies in the fact that Ruskin's influence on English brickwork was coincident with the transformation of brick making by mechanical processes. Hand molding is a craft process, and Ruskin could reasonably say that the bricks made by it "became precious, or otherwise, just in proportion to the hand-work upon them, or to the clearness of their reception of the hand-work of their mould" (8.85). Hand-molded bricks, moreover, showed attractive variation in surface and tint. Technical advances were changing this even as Ruskin wrote. Mass production created smooth brick with uniform surface and color. New clays were exploited, more controllable kilns were introduced, and bricks were offered in a much wider range of colors than before. The Poole Manufacturing Company announced in 1856 that it could offer brick in buff, French white, blue, green, maroon, or any other color. Their bricks could be glazed to resist soot and molded into a variety of convenient shapes. Proud of their product and eager to gain publicity for it, they announced that they were willing to give free bricks for an important building by an important architect.[74]

There is no evidence that Seddon took them up on this offer, but his post office was clearly intended as a display piece to show the proper use of brick. Assuming that picturesque verticality would be out of place on city streets, Seddon draws on his experiences in Italy. The building (fig. 48) recalls such Venetian palaces as the Palazzo da Mosto and the Palazzo Loredan, and the continuous imposts at the springing of the arches stress the horizontal. Seddon uses rounded Byzantine arches on the first two stories and segmental ones above. On the far right of the ground floor, however, he spans a narrower opening with a rounded intrados and a pointed extrados.

Most of the facade was of red Bridgewater bricks. The architects, said the *Building News*, later regretted that they had not used the even brighter orange-red local bricks.[75] For the voussoirs of the ground floor arcade they used alternating glazed maroon bricks and unglazed white bricks. Around these they placed a ring of purplish black glazed bricks, and then another ring of polychromatic voussoirs, alternately of colored glazed brick and green Bridgend stone. In the string course above the arcade, two courses of maroon bricks enclose a rich brown cement band bearing the name of the building in gold block letters. The treatment of the first floor arcade is a more restrained version of that on the ground floor: each tympanum is filled in with alternate Caen stone and green Bridgend stone, with a central panel of polished Irish green marble. The brick and stone combination of the ground floor string course is repeated in the cornice with the addition of Minton's chocolate tiles and Caen stone. Above that is a row of alternate white and red bricks set diagonally, and then a molded stone coping. The exterior woodwork was painted in shades of rich brown, picked out with blue and red, and Minton's tiles, "of varied and brilliant colour" said the *Building News*,[76] were used beneath the ground floor windows. This is an astonishing composition, as rich, though not as influential, as Woodward's Crown Life Assurance Office. The citizens of Cardiff must have been startled.

IV

Alfred Waterhouse was born in 1830 into the family of a Quaker cotton merchant.[77] His apprenticeship was under Richard Lane, a Manchester architect whose civic buildings featured Doric or Ionic porticoes. His own enthusiasms were medieval, however. He later recalled that he was carried away by "the teaching of Pugin, Scott, and, above all, of Ruskin," and as soon as his pupilage was over he "was off to North Italy, to dwell for a time among those marvels in marble, stone, and brick which had been so irresistibly commended in the 'Seven Lamps of Architecture' and the 'Stones of Venice.'"[78] When, on his return, he found himself designing a sugar warehouse that required much light on the ground floor and none above, his thoughts naturally turned to the Doge's Palace (fig. 49). His Royal Insurance buildings (fig. 50) made a freer use of Venetian Byzantine and Gothic elements.

It was Waterhouse's victory in the Manchester Assize Courts competition of 1859 that established him as a leading architect. There was no doubt a paradox in the presence of a dominating Ruskinian building in the center of what Asa Briggs has called the shock city of the industrial revolution.[79] It is not really so startling, however, in the context of the 1850s. Ruskin's response to urbanism and industrialism during that decade was to demand reform; his angry claim that Manchester could produce no good

Fig. 49.   Friar and Binyon Warehouse, Manchester (demolished). Alfred Waterhouse. Victoria and Albert Museum.

art came later in his career. His defenses of beauty, moreover, were exactly what a sizable body of Manchester opinion wanted to hear. Ruskin's lectures had been among the high points of the Manchester Art Treasure's Exhibition of 1857, and he lectured again to large, appreciative audiences in 1859 and 1864. Many elements in his theory of architecture appealed to Manchester's parvenu appetite for mingled self-glorification and self-improvement. He showed how the rich materials and lavish decoration of a building could return the beauty of nature to a crowded city, acknowledge

Fig. 50.   *Royal Insurance buildings, Manchester. Alfred Waterhouse.*
Building News, *1862.*

the medieval roots of English law, and at the same time claim kinship with
the great merchant cities of the middle ages. Such arguments for Gothic
proved compelling, and the Assize Courts marked an epoch in Manchester's architecture.

In addition to their general debt to Ruskin, the Assize Courts (fig. 51)
owe particular debts to Woodward and Scott. The Oxford Museum influenced Waterhouse's use of decoration. Thomas Woolner, who did the free-
standing statues for the museum court, provided enough models to keep
two carvers employed in Manchester full time. There were statues of great

legal figures from Alfred the Great to Sir Matthew Hale as well as carving of such subjects as the Judgment of Solomon. The O'Shea brothers and Edward Whellan came north to supply foliage and bosses. James O'Shea carved an elaborate screen for the judges' residence. Skidmore provided the decorative ironwork.

Waterhouse's larger ideas on architectural design echoed Scott's work with the Government Offices. The statement to the jury acccompanying Waterhouse's submission stressed the economy and adaptability of Gothic, both points at issue between Scott and Palmerston, and stressed that there was nothing in the style to forbid the use of ordinary sash windows of almost any width up to six feet, glazed with single sheets of plate glass. In August of 1859 one of Scott's supporters in Parliament was able to twit Palmerston with the news that "at Manchester the Gothic style had recently been selected for a building at a meeting attended by many men of business, with a Quaker for the chairman (Laughter)."[80] The laughter reflected the belief that Gothic was the preserve of Puseyites and Tories. By proving this wrong, Waterhouse gave new force to Ruskin's claim that Gothic was a universal style.

Ruskin was delighted by the Assize Courts. He visited them in 1863 and wrote to his father that they were "much beyond everything yet done in England on my principles" (18.lxxv). He thought the great hall (fig. 52)

Fig. 51.   Manchester Assize Courts. Alfred Waterhouse. Builder, 1859.

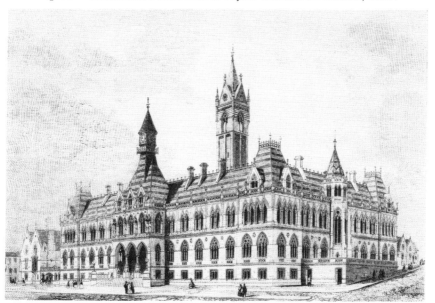

Fig. 52. *Manchester Assize Courts—great hall. Builder, 1865.*

one of the finest things he had seen and praised the stained glass and the sculpture. He must have been especially impressed to learn that the clerk of the works, Henry Littler, had as a young man copied out the whole three volumes of *The Stones of Venice*, tracing every illustration.

In later years Waterhouse had two interesting reservations about the first wave of Ruskinian enthusiasm in English architecture. One relates to stone carving. He came to believe that the work of the O'Sheas and Whellan looked better when only half-worked and concluded that they needed to put more thought and less work into their foliage. Whether foliage should be naturalistic or conventional seemed to him of secondary importance. What really mattered was that each leaf should appear to grow from the bell of the capital, that its curves should maintain the general form intended by the architect, and that the foliage should be vigorous and severe.[81] In effect, Waterhouse shares in the reaction against the first wave of Ruskinian carving that was expressed by Ruskin himself in the 1859 letters on the Oxford Museum.

Waterhouse's other reservation concerned the use of polychromy. If too blatant, it tended to outshine architecture rather than to serve it. Near the end of his career Waterhouse recalled that Ruskin had "fired imaginations with descriptions of colour harmonies more bewitching than many produced by the brush" but that "the result was not always what could be desired."[82] He traced several reasons for this, including the sooty atmosphere and the vulgarity of popular taste. Ruskin's pessimism over the future of Victorian architecture may be more understandable if we realize that Waterhouse himself became discouraged about the prospects for polychromy. "He had long hoped to see the dusky towns of England brightened by colour," he said in 1891, "but he feared it would not come about in his time."[83]

The Assize Courts provide an appropriate climax to the progress of Ruskinism during the 1850s. One the one hand, Ruskin's influence is spreading, expressing itself in an ever greater variety of buildings. It takes diverse forms in the work of such original architects as Woodward, Scott, Street, Prichard, Seddon, and Waterhouse, but there are always common elements: a borrowing from foreign, and especially from Italian, Romanesque and Gothic buildings; a preference for simple building shapes that convey a sense of mass; an attention to color in natural stone, brick, or tiles; a preference for ornament that tends toward the naturalistic; and a use of sculpture and stone carving to tell a story, point a moral, or preach a sermon. By 1859 it must have seemed genuinely possible that a reborn Gothic could become the universal style of the world's richest industrial nation. Yet at just this point, the strains begin to show. During the 1860s one set of Ruskin's admirers became sharply critical of the rest, and Ruskin himself began to see the contradiction between the architects' hope that Gothic might express the age and his own growing suspicion that industrialism and fine architecture were incompatible.

IX

THE 1860S: TRIUMPH AND DISPERSAL

 THE number of Ruskin's admirers among architects increased dramatically after the Manchester Assize Courts, and his influence became correspondingly diverse. In very general terms, two separate trends appear. On the one hand, many architects used inspirations from *The Stones of Venice* in startling and opportunistic ways. On the other, such men as John Pollard Seddon, William Burges, and E. W. Godwin mounted an attack on the Ruskinian craze and presented their own purer version of the master's teaching.

I

The basic fact about English architecture during the 1860s is the failure of the effort to evolve a common style of the age. The 1862 index to the *Builder* tells the story:

> Style, a new: another cry for, 447; can we form, 484, 504; crying for, 518; the way to, 518; how can it be formed, 537; on the possibility of, 556; thoughts of a mechanic about, 590; hints as to, 631; combinations the only method of creating, 663; question, 700; why not a, 720; why not a new language? 772, 826.

Styles: can two flourish together? 250; of architecture, history of the modern, 865; see also "Classic" and "Gothic."

The difficulty was not merely that the classic and Gothic parties remained divided but that each tended to split into diverse trends. R. P. Pullan, William Burges's brother-in-law, was able to discern four separate trends among the Gothicists: the antiquarian, which followed precedent closely; the new light, which sought to develop a uniquely Victorian style out of the Gothic; the eclectic, which mixed different styles to the point of impropriety; and the school of development, which treasured associations with the past but proceeded forward from a *point de départ*.[1] It is a measure of the diversity of Ruskin's influence that his name can be associated with all these trends.

This, of course, raises the question of how firmly Ruskin's influence can be associated with any of them. If it were not typographically inconvenient, it would be useful to employ not just quotation marks but multiple sets of them. Thus the Oxford Museum, for all Woodward's originality and Ruskin's discontent, is Ruskinian. George Corson's Leeds warehouse (fig. 53), on the other hand, is "Ruskinian." But what about Vickers and Company's distillery on Victoria Street (fig. 54)? That is ""Ruskinian."" John Taylor's railway station at the bottom of Herne Hill (fig. 55), with its Italian Gothic moldings and polychromatic brickwork, is """Ruskinian.""" The Crossness Pumping Station, with its Italian Gothic arches and its interior court decorated with cast-iron foliage (fig. 56), is very handsome but undeniably """"Ruskianian."""" It is difficult to imagine how many quotation marks are needed for the many factories that belched their smoke out of attenuated campaniles (fig. 57).

Two developments of the 1860s deserve special attention. One is the popularity of Byzantine and Italian Gothic designs. The other is the growing interest in an eclectic or a latitudinarian approach to style.

When Scott and Street advocated the study of Italian Gothic in the 1850s, they warned against exoticism. But this quality of foreignness was soon deliberately cultivated. Certain commercial buildings in Bristol are said to exemplify a style nicknamed "Bristol Byzantine."[2] Foster and Ponton's Philosophical Institution and Library (fig. 58), also in Bristol, derives its shape and proportions from the Ducal Palace, though it is French Gothic in many of its details. Venetian Gothic proved extremely popular in Manchester, as we see in Thomas Worthington's Memorial Hall (fig. 59) and Edward Salomons's Reform Club (fig. 60).

George Somers Clarke brought an obviously Mediterranean note to London. Though he had traveled and must have had well-crammed note-

Fig. 53.   Leeds warehouse. George Corson. Builder, 1861.

Fig. 54.   Vickers and Company Distillery. Mayhew and Calder. Builder, 1865.

Fig. 55.   Herne Hill Railway Station. John Taylor. Building News, 1863.

Fig. 56.   Cast-iron capital from Crossness Pumping Station. Photo: author. By permission of Thames Water Authority (England).

Fig. 57   Suggestions for factory chimneys. R. Rawlinson. Builder, 1857.
Fig. 58.   Facing page, top. Philosophical Institution and Library, Bristol. Foster and Ponton. Builder, 1870.
Fig. 59.   Facing page, middle. Memorial Hall, Manchester. Thomas Worthington. Builder, 1865.
Fig. 60.   Facing page, bottom. Reform Club, Manchester. Edward Salomons. Builder, 1870.

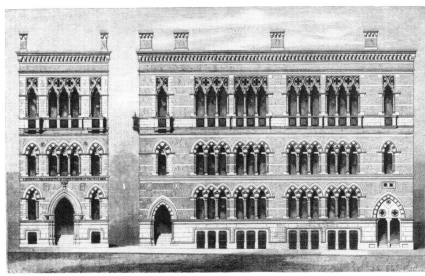

Fig. 61. *General Credit and Discount Company, 7 Lothbury Street, London. George Somers Clarke. Building News, 1868.*

Fig. 62. *General Credit and Discount Company (detail). Photo: author.*

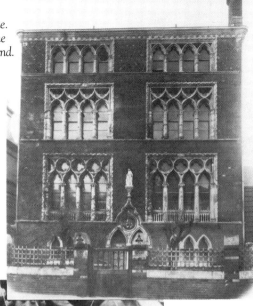

Fig. 63. School for the blind, Brighton. George Somers Clarke. Photo: Royal Commission on the Historical Monuments of England.

Fig. 64. School for the blind, Brighton (detail). Photo: Royal Commission on the Historical Monuments of England.

Fig. 65. Dock House of the East and West India Dock Company. A. Manning. Building News, *1877.*

Fig. 66. Warehouse for Messrs. Barran and Sons, Leeds. Thomas Ambler. Building News, *1879.*

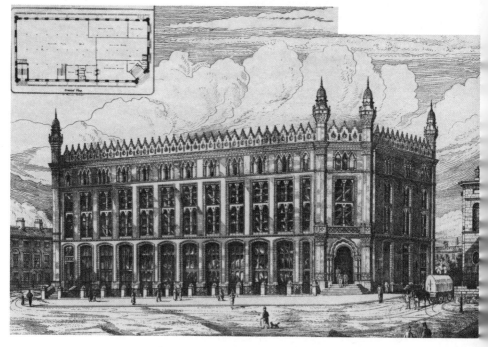

Fig. 67. Manchester ware-house. J. E. Gregnan. Builder, 1850.

Fig. 68. Below. Mark Lane offices. George Aitchison. Building News, 1864.

Fig. 69. New warehouses, Southwark Bridge Road. Henry Jarvis. Builder, 1864.

Fig. 70. Registered Land Company, Cannon Street. Fred Jameson. Building News, 1866.

Fig. 71.   Throgmorton Street offices. T. Chatfield Clarke. Builder, 1870.

Fig. 72.   Proposed Chelsea Vestry Hall. Henry and Sidney Godwin. Builder, 1858.

Fig. 73. Tavistock
Chambers. Charles
Gray. Builder, 1857.

Fig. 74. Grosvenor Hotel.
James Knowles, Jr. Builder, 1861.

N° I

N° II

A

B

Fig. 75. Above. *Ornament for the Grosvenor Hotel.* Building News, 1863.

books in which to draw, his debts to Ruskin are often quite obvious. The handsome marble eye that decorates his ornate General Credit and Discount Company offices at 7 Lothbury near the Bank of England (figs. 61 and 62) is drawn from the first volume of *The Stones of Venice*; it is the same device that Woodward had used at the Trinity College Museum. The windows on Clarke's Seamen's Orphan Asylum in Wanstead seem inspired by the illustrations to Ruskin's chapter "Gothic Palaces." The carving on his school for the blind in Brighton (figs. 63 and 64) attempts to inspire and instruct according to Ruskin's principles.

The tendency to use flashy but ill-digested elements from medieval Italy grew as the years went by. Examples include the Dock House of the East and West India Dock Company (fig. 65) and the clothing factory and warehouse for the Messrs. Barran and Sons in Leeds (fig. 66). There were both emotional and practical reasons for this.

The emotional rationale is that Bristol, Manchester, and London were mercantile cities and that Venetian styles were therefore appropriate on associationist grounds. Ruskin himself made this argument. Moreover, southern styles encouraged an ostentatious display of building materials, which testified to the wealth of a commercial firm. The Dock House, for example, used Box Ground stone relieved with red Mansfield stone in the voussoirs, red Aberdeen and blue Peterhead granite for the polished columns, gray Cornish granite for the plinth, and various colored marbles for the decorations at the angles.

Practical reasons for turning to medieval Italy included convenient floor plans and the ease of relating facades to internal structure. Northern Gothic, as the architects of the Dock House explained, would have sacrificed space by "recessing portions of the structure, from which much of the effect of a Gothic building is obtained."[3] Italian Gothic, however, allowed plans with continuous floor space.

With his discussion of the wall-veils of Italian Gothic, Ruskin contributed to the solution of another problem that Victorian architects faced in commercial structures. By the middle of the nineteenth century, a building's floors were normally supported by rows of cast-iron columns. These freed the external wall from much of its load-bearing function and allowed a generous provision of windows. Renaissance architects, however, found it difficult to take advantage of this opportunity. Their canons of proportion restricted the amount of void in relation to solid. An effort to solve this problem can be seen in figure 67, where the architect provided dressings for only every other window in his Manchester palazzo; he presumably hoped that those left bare would not count in the general effect. Ruskin showed how Italian Gothic could unite generous window-openings with the much-desired sense of massiveness. By encouraging his readers to think not in terms of walls but in terms of arcadelike sequences in which the support function was gathered into heavy columns or piers, he created the opportunity for almost continuous fenestration. George Aitchison's Mark Lane office building (fig. 68) provided an example of such a commercial wall-veil.[4]

For these reasons, a Ruskinian commercial style, borrowing heavily from Woodward's Crown Life Assurance building and Waterhouse's Royal Insurance buildings as well as from Italy, developed during the 1860s. Its characteristics include window arcades, a mixture of richly colored materials, arches with round intrados and pointed extrados, sash windows, naturalistic carving, and rather spiky ironwork (often provided by Skidmore). Figures 69, 70, and 71 show examples.

Exotic as they often were, the architects who merely borrowed from medieval Italy did not produce the most eye-popping Victorian buildings. That honor was reserved for those who called themselves eclectic, latitudinarian, or even (they appear to have been the first architects to claim the term) Victorian. Though they borrowed freely from the work of Woodward, Scott, Street, and Waterhouse, they were regarded with considerable antagonism by the leaders of the Gothic school. Opportunism was the least of the charges against them. Nevertheless, their work was an effort to solve a basic dilemma in Gothic Revival thinking about style.

The rationale for the new eclecticism of the sixties appeared in some articles by Leslie Sutton in the 1858 volume of the *Building News.* He urged that George Gilbert Scott's inclusive approach to Gothic be extended even further. He envisioned an architecture in which elements from the most heterogeneous styles could be combined in wholly original ways. He hoped that the much-longed-for new style would develop out of this, but in the meantime he was willing to settle for mixtures. Discussions of style among the Gothicists had moved from Ruskin's emphasis on obedience to Scott's call for development and now culminated in a frank demand for the very liberty that Ruskin had opposed in the first place. Eclectic Gothic, said Sutton,

> refuses to slavishly follow precedent; it treats antiquarianism and archeology as curious studies of dead art, which should not be allowed to impose control upon living art—dry bones that it is impossible to clothe with fresh and living beauty, and it demands that liberty which is the essence of thought. This absolute freedom is necessary for the successful adaptation of Gothic art to modern requirements, and also for its concordance with the progress of civilizations.[5]

No designs by Sutton appear in the architectural press, but some idea of what he had in mind is provided by the proposed Chelsea Vestry Hall by Henry and Sidney Godwin (fig. 72). The accompanying description in the

Builder described it as "eclectic Gothic, founded on the Italian Gothic style, adapted to the present age."[6]

This freewheeling approach began to appear quite regularly on the walls of the annual Architectural Exhibition and in the architectural press. The quality now sought was described with the slang term *go*. One of the most prominant architects with "go" was Charles Gray, whose work (fig. 73) was regularly praised for its inventive use of polychromatic brickwork. He also employed oppressively heavy arches and, as the *Building News* put it, stumpy columns "having capitals carved in leafage such a short distance from the ground that, to use the words of Mr. Ruskin, you may touch them with your hand."[7]

The hope that polychromatic brickwork, naturalistic carving, and Italian Gothic features might blend into an original style found an important expression in Thomas Harris's *Examples of London and Provincial Architecture* (1861). Harris used expensive color plates and described the work he admired as Victorian rather than Gothic. One of his young men, John Henry Chamberlain, was among Ruskin's most interesting and committed admirers. It was widely felt, however, that Harris had gone too far, and the *Building News* spoke for many when it protested the "jubilant chirrupings and crowings about 'Victorian Architecture.'"[8]

Another sign of the stylistic freedom that developed during the 1860s was the extent to which Ruskin's views on decoration were adopted by avowed classicists. There was suddenly a widespread interest in finding a compromise in the battle of the styles. One dramatic sign of this trend was James Knowles's Grosvenor Hotel. Knowles was quoted in chapter 2 as one of Ruskin's many classicist critics. During the 1850s, however, he began to give some ground. A young man who had shortly before called Ruskin "crazy" was by 1855 willing to concede the truth of Ruskin's often-stated view that the English people would never truly love triglyphs. They loved flowers and would always prefer crockets to dentils. Knowles's answer was to keep his basic classical allegiance but to explore a new kind of ornament:

> In an arch. of our own day we may take dignity—repose—& calmness, sufficient power, catholicity, etc. from the Classic—but over this a sweet & wooing growth of life must run—the flowers must love & clasp it—& sympathies & affections must cling round it for inticements—at the least symbols & not abstract forms—"Pure classic" is not companionable nor *alive* enough for the English people.[9]

The Grosvenor combined classic repose with the new, more companionable decoration (figs. 74 and 75). Its ornament consisted of roses, peonies, lilies, ivy, and broad bands of foliage. The *Building News* described this work in entirely Ruskinian terms:

Though the closest imitation of nature has here been attempted—even to the representation of veinings and serrated edges—the compact groups of the leaves and the severe outlines with which they are confined have entirely prevented the weak and spiritless effect which is often too apparent in naturalistic designs. The stems and other details on what may be called the *bell* of the cornice have a very slight projection.[10]

Knowles was less attracted, however, by Ruskin's doctrine of truth to material. The running ivy leaves were cast in cement, which was then painted to look like stone.

II

Faced with this deluge of Ruskinisms, John Pollard Seddon, William Burges, and E. W. Godwin warned that many architects were seizing all that was easy in Ruskin's books and ignoring all that was essential. We have already encountered Seddon. Burges and Godwin were among Ruskin's best and most-talented admirers during the 1860s (though, ironically, Ruskin's only published reference to Burges was a slighting one). Their early careers can be briefly summarized.

Born in 1827, William Burges received a copy of *Contrasts* from his father as a fourteenth-birthday present and by seventeen was already a member of the Ecclesiological Society.[11] He was articled in the office of Edward Blore and in 1849 entered the employ of Matthew Digby Wyatt. He did research, illustrations, and some of the articles for Wyatt's *Metal Work and Its Artistic Design* (1852) and *The Industrial Arts of the Nineteenth Century* (1853–1854). He traveled abroad extensively during the early 1850s. He spent the entire winter of 1853 in Rome, where he was in close contact with Frederick Leighton and George Aitchison, both of whom were enthusiastic about Ruskin's books.[12] Not surprisingly, the two designs that established his reputation showed his mastery of foreign styles of Gothic. One was his entry in the Lille Cathedral competition of 1856; the other was his submission for the Constantinople Memorial Chapel competition of 1857. The first was a study in early French Gothic, with short columns, bold forms, and plate tracery; the second was Burges's first and last effort in Italian Gothic.

One of Burges's early projects with Ruskinian connections was the little book that he and the French antiquary A. N. Didron put together on the capitals of the Ducal Palace. When Burges and Didron met one another in 1856, they discovered that they had both been inspired by *The Stones of*

Venice to study the capitals in detail and they decided to pool their investigations. They needed some illustrations, however, and neither had sufficiently detailed drawings. Burges told his collaborator that Ruskin had donated plaster casts of some of the capitals to the Architectural Museum. It
might be possible to make engravings from photographs of them. It was
apparently Didron who asked permission, and Ruskin, "*avec la bonne grâce
d'un gentleman anglais,*"[13] agreed. The capitals were photographed in London; then tracings were made from the photographs in Paris and sent to
Burges so that he could correct them against the actual casts. They were
then engraved (fig. 76) and published in the *Annales archéologiques* and in
Venise; iconographie des chapiteaux du palais ducal.

Burges's notes on the capitals show him following Ruskin's lead, correcting some of Ruskin's details, and, most significantly, narrowing Ruskin's
focus. Ruskin is interested not only in deciphering the subject of each
capital, a difficult job in itself, but also in relating the carvings to a tradition of typology and symbolism that pervaded medieval and Renaissance
art. Thus he is constantly stopping to compare the capitals to similar por-
trayals of virtue and vice in Dante, Giotto, Spenser, and Bunyan. The
capitals are interpreted as expressions of moral insight. To Burges and
Didron, by contrast, the iconographical scheme is merely an excuse for
sculpture. The same contrast between Ruskin's broad moral interests and
Burges's narrowly artistic concerns will reappear during the 1860s.

E. W. Godwin was born in Bristol in 1833.[14] His early diaries show that
he sketched local churches and other medieval buildings, read the publications of the Ecclesiological Society, and studied several buildings by Butter-

*Fig. 76.   Engravings of Venetian capitals that Ruskin presented to the Architectural
Museum.* Annales archéologiques, *1857.*

field. A letter published in the *Builder* in 1857 shows that Godwin had wholeheartedly accepted the view that Gothic was the style of progress:

> I believe, and sincerely hope, in spite of the opposition of the champions of the "Classic," that a style will *grow upon* the hitherto but little understood *principles* of the Mediaeval style, as different as that of the fourteenth from that of the twelfth century, and as conformable to the progress of invention. I ask,—would such a style be *Medieval?* would not such a style be *Gothic?* For who amongst us will presume, for instance, to tether down to a time or people or creed, such forms as the trefoil and the quatrefoil.[15]

Like Scott and Street, but more cloyingly, Godwin expressed the religious basis of the revival. The task of architecture, he said, only reflects the greater purpose of man, which is

> to restore that likeness within us which has become so obscure by the accumulation of sin; and, with more faith, more hope, more love, exercise a deeper sympathy with all the glorious creations of the Great Good, and we shall find our architectural skill will reflect, as in a glass, the image of this likeness, and, endowed with the *life* of the inner man, approach more nearly the excellence of those works which God himself pronounced to be so "very good."[16]

Clearly Godwin was as yet far being that man whom Max Beerbohm would call "the greatest aesthete of them all."[17]

The message of Seddon, Burges, and Godwin during the 1860s began with a simple warning. As Burges put it:

> No man's works contain more valuable information than Mr. Ruskin's, but they are strong meat, and require to be taken by one who has made up his mind, or, as Carlyle would say, "anchored to a formula." To such a man, "The Stones of Venice" is an architectural romance full of information and instruction, but to one in search of a style and just beginning his architectural life it is almost destruction.[18]

Under Ruskin's spell, architects were inflicting on the English streetscape an architecture that was designed for a sunnier climate than England's and for an architecture of marble rather than of stone.

They were also, in Burges's view, indulging a vulgar fascination with architectural "bits"—colored tiles, stumpy columns, notched moldings, chamfered edges, foliage that covers a building until it "looks like a petrified arbour," and string courses that jump "up and down in a most spasmodic manner."[19] All these features could be traced to one line or another in Ruskin's books.

Many of the architectural debates of the 1860s came down to a matter of which sentence in Ruskin the writer wanted to quote. Those who emphasized moldings and chamfers pointed to the careful discussion of these features in the first volume of *The Stones of Venice*. Those who took the opposite view cited "The Lamp of Power." Thus the writer of "Brick Architecture" in 1864 could assure his readers, "'A great artist,' says Mr. Ruskin, 'habitually sees masses, not edges.'"[20] Seddon, Burges, and Godwin insisted that Ruskin's great lessons were the value of massiveness and the intimate connection between architecture, sculpture, and painting. They warned against self-consciously foreign designs and against excessive emphasis on minor details.

Godwin, for example, complained that many architects were so emphasizing applied decoration that the true designers of their buildings were the firms that manufactured colored tiles, stained glass, carved pulpits, and florid capitals. He was distressed by the incongruities that resulted from the mixture of northern and Italian Gothic. Thus he complains that Waterhouse "adopts large, traceried windows for the ground floor of his Manchester Assize Courts, and then solemnly pauses until he has read the 'Stones of Venice' before completing his English ecclesiastical-looking basement with a story of marked Italian domestic character."[21] Like Burges, he pointed to the popularity of Venetian Gothic as one of the menacing phenomena of the day:

> The architects who practice in this style flatter themselves that they at least are *en rapport* with the great art critic of the age. It would be manifestly unjust to call Mr. Ruskin their leader, and yet it is doubtless to Mr. Ruskin that we are indebted for their very existence. . . . whoever will take the trouble to glance at the illustrations in the volumes of the Building News and other architectural journals will soon discover that all Anglo-Venetian Gothic is pretty much alike, that one example is as tame as another, that they are utterly opposed to Mr. Ruskin's real teaching, and that they are as far removed from the Gothic of Venice as a bleached mutilated skeleton is from the glowing living body. We do not for a moment wish to say that this infliction is Mr. Ruskin's fault. It is his misfortune, but not his fault, that his works should be skimmed instead of *read.*[22]

It was Seddon who led the most aggressive assault on the eclectic and overdecorated versions of Ruskinism. The occasion was the opening of Bassett Keeling's Strand Music Hall in 1863. Contemporary attention to this building was immense—some fifty notices appeared in various newspapers and journals.[23] The Strand facade (fig. 77) was a narrow one. Behind it were dining rooms, refreshment bars, kitchens, and a passageway that led to the music hall itself. This was a dramatic sight, for Keeling had suspended his ceiling from an iron roof so that he might place his lighting between the two and so diffuse the illumination through a ceiling of col-

Fig. 77.   Strand Music Hall. E. Bassett Keeling. Building News, 1863.

ored glass, opal, and prisms. The richly decorated hall must have been spectacular. The explorer Richard Burton said that "although he had seen many things, he had never experienced, under one roof, anything quite like that remarkable building."[24]

The outcry was immediate. Keeling, who was young, brash, and keen for Gothic as a progressive style, proclaimed that his building displayed a manner of "design, arrangement, and decoration, so far novel and unusual as to remove it from the jurisdiction of the pedantry of art."[25] He called his design Continental Gothic; he called it eclectic; he called it an example of latitudinarianism; and he seemed not to care whether it was said to exemplify a style or a no-style. The *Building News* simply described it as an effort "to adopt the Continental or modern eclectic Gothic feeling, or whatever better name can be found for it."[26] In spite of this wilderness of labels, the building's connections with the Ruskinian phase of the Gothic Revival are obvious. The Strand facade is similar to both Woodward's Crown Life Assurance building and Waterhouse's Royal Insurance Company offices. O'Shea worked on the Strand Music Hall, and Keeling's use of copper foliage to provide capitals for iron columns recalls Skidmore's work at the Oxford Museum. Keeling's building represented an extreme of Gothic modernism, conspicuously divorced from the high ethical idealism that normally underlay the revival.

Seddon, one of the creators of the style being caricatured, now became extremely vigorous in his denunciation of "Acrobatic Gothic." He mocked the carvers who were filling their capitals and corbels with daisies and buttercups as well as exotics from the squire's hothouse. He warned architects to avoid the "hair-stand-on-end style" in which "knobs, bosses, and balls, notches and chamferings with villainous spiky iron-work, still usurp the place of quiet, well-studied detail."[27] The Strand Music Hall attracted so much wrath because it seemed an epitome of all the faults of the new licentious Gothic. Every curved line was serrated, every edge was chamfered, and the omnipresent polychromy—with balls of granite and serpentine and polished pillars and patterned brickwork and Minton's tiles and Carrara marble—destroyed any possibility of respose: "the highest jinks and most comic capers that may hereafter be performed upon its stage or within its walls, cannot be otherwise than in harmony with those which have been already played by [the architect] in actual stone, brick and iron."[28]

Burges, Seddon, and Godwin proposed a two-part solution to the ills of the Gothic Revival. One part was a new stress on the masculine qualities of simple massing, balanced composition, continuity of horizontals, and bold, unchamfered corners. In effect, they were returning to "The Lamp of Power" and interpreting it in terms of thirteenth-century French Gothic. The other part of their program was a serious application of Ruskin's claim that "architecture is only the association of sculpture and painting in noble masses, or the placing them in fit places" (8.11).

Burges was so impressed by Ruskin's novel view that he could proclaim that all the reforms of Pugin and the Ecclesiologists had produced "mere architecture, or, rather, the bones of the building without the flesh."[29] Henceforward, the task of architecture was to tell wondrous stories. In

1858 he told the Ecclesiological Society that "the architects of the present day should begin to be what the architects of the twelfth and thirteenth centuries were—not only architects but painters and sculptors as well." [30] They should know how to dispose frescoes in buildings, how to separate them by bands, how to allow for height of situation. They should be able to design sculpture, even though it would have to be executed by other hands. Surveying the International Exhibition of 1862, he concluded that "when we see one architect designing stained glass windows, another secular and domestic plate, a third furniture combined with colour, and fourth sculpture, we feel that this is surely a right good beginning and that there is no occasion to despair of the result." [31] It was even possible to look ahead to the time when the full Ruskinian program would be fulfilled: "Most certainly the present generation will not see men like Donatello, and so many others of his age, who were equally good in all the fine arts; but if the present movement goes on, it will surely be no unreasonable expectation that such men may appear some two generations hence." [32]

The architectural expression of these hopes can be seen in the first version of Burges's proposed speech room for Harrow (figs. 78 and 79), in Seddon's design for alms houses in Fulham (fig. 80), and in Godwin's Northampton Town Hall (fig. 81). This last building was, as Godwin later recalled, "entirely founded upon *The Stones of Venice*." [33]

In 1862 Godwin explained the philosophy underlying his building to the ratepayers of Northampton. His lecture begins, like so many of Ruskin's own essays of this period, by warning against the view that art is a luxury:

> That feeling is by no means new. It arose with the spirit of the Renaissance; and, until that debased spirit of wild voluptuousness and unrestrained freedom be subdued and cast out from among us as an unclean thing, the position of art, in all its nobility and in all the power of its moral and religious teaching, will never be fully and fairly realized. If, on the other hand, the arts were but united again, how great would be their influence upon one another. [34]

Painting, for example, would lead architects to moderate those violent contrasts in polychromy that had been mocked as streaky bacon. It would also teach them to keep their patterns "flat, conventional, and unobtrusive," and it would demonstrate that "flowers are not meant to be trampled on." That lesson owes more to Owen Jones than to Ruskin, but the lessons of carving might have come straight from *The Seven Lamps*:

> Then, too, sculpture, if we treated her properly, might come out of her hiding place, and show how she could cut the histories of our cities and of our civil and religious freedom at the corner of the street, at a less cost than enriching cornices and balastrading parapets which people never strain their necks to look

Fig. 78.   *Proposed speech room, Harrow on the Hill. William Burges. Architect, 1872.*

Fig. 79.   *Proposed speech room, Harrow on the Hill (interior). Architect, 1872.*

Fig. 80. *Alms houses, Fulham. John Pollard Seddon.* Building News, *1877.*

at; and, if they did, would probably be none the wiser. She would tell us that the money we throw away upon egg and dart borders, to enrich the mouldings of our public buildings, would almost pay for large angle sculptures, which, while they soften the harsh angles of our walls, would convey some valuable lesson to the passerby. But then, of course, they must be placed as though to be seen, not stuck up in pediments for the especial amusement of the servant girls across the way.[35]

Not since Woodward's Government Offices design had anyone taken so seriously Ruskin's claim that "there should not be a single ornament put upon great civic buildings without some intellectual intention" (8.230).

Fig. 81.   Northampton Town Hall. E. W. Godwin. Building News, 1861.

Fig. 82. Carving from the Northampton Town Hall. R. Boulton. Building News, 1865.

Godwin faced a practical problem in carrying out an ambitious sculptural program—he had to find a carver prepared to go beyond stock designs and naturalistic foliage. The town fathers, not surprisingly, had their own candidates for such profitable employment, but Godwin fought for his own man, who had read and been inspired by *The Stones of Venice*. This was presumably R. Boulton of Worcester, though some of the sculpture was done by a Mr. Nichols and the capitals and smaller pieces were executed by Mr. Edwin White (fig. 82). There was a great deal of work to be done: there are full-length statues and deeply carved capitals; there are tympana and heraldic shields carved in low relief; there are moldings and traceries; there is a cornice and a pierced parapet; there is even a mason's mark on the base to remind the passerby that the building is rooted in medieval traditions of craftsmanship.

The next problem was to ensure that the carvings would not conflict with one another and produce a confused jumble. The solution lay in Ruskin's insistence that ornament should always be designed with regard to the distance from which it would be seen. We do not see a building all at once. Rather, we see it progressively:

> first, for example, the great masses,—the buttresses and stories and black windows, and broad cornices of the tower, which give it make and organism, as it rises above the horizon, half a score of miles away: then the traceries and shafts and pinnacles, which give it richness as we approach: then the niches and statues and knobs and flowers, which we can only see when we stand beneath it. At this third order of ornament, we may pause, in the upper portions; but on the roofs of the niches, and the robes of the statues, and the rolls of the mouldings, comes a fourth order of ornament, as delicate as the eye can follow, when any of these features may be approached. (9.301)

Approaching from a distance, though it would have to be a good deal less than six miles, the spectator cannot fail to be struck by the bold, simple masses of the Northampton Town Hall. Godwin uses the same combination of broad, arcaded facade, central tower, and steep gable that Woodward had employed at the Oxford Museum, but the darkness of the recessed windows and the very sturdy appearance of the tower, with its deep louvers, provide a greater play of light and shadow and a more powerful sense of mass than Woodward's building. As we approach, our attention shifts to the large statues. They show figures ranging from Saint Michael (patron saint of the corporation) and Saint Patrick (said to have been born nearby) to Richard the First (who granted the town's first charter) and John Dryden (who wrote *The Hind and the Panther* at Rushton Hall). Moving closer still, our attention shifts to the tympana of the ground floor windows. These show episodes in Northampton's history, including the erec-

Fig. 83. Archivolt on the Duomo of Murano. John Ruskin. The Stones of Venice, volume 2 (1853).

tion of an Eleanor cross, the trial of Thomas à Becket, the execution of Mary Queen of Scots, the Battle of Naseby, and the Great Fire of 1675. Between the windows of the first story are eleven different fables from Aesop, and on the ground floor capitals we see such subjects as men branding cattle and the town fire brigade at work. Finally, below the ground floor windows and at eye level are a series of heraldic shields representing both the prominent families and the important crafts of the town.

There are other ways in which the Northampton Town Hall shows Ruskin's influence. The triangular ornaments on the ground floor facade, for example, are quite obviously derived from the illustrations to the second volume of *The Stones of Venice* (figs. 83 and 84). Similar but more natu-

Fig. 84. Carving from the Northampton Town Hall. Photo: author.

Fig. 85. Carving from the Northampton Town Hall. Photo: author.

ralistic carvings in the porch (fig. 85) might have been specially created to illustrate Ruskin's view that carvers should abstract certain features of nature, such as the outlines of leaves, while leaving others, such as the internal veining, only lightly indicated. The most surprising piece of Ruskinism, however, is one that the spectator might not ordinarily notice at all but that, if Ruskin is correct, he ought to feel unconsciously: the division of the ground floor into seven bays of slightly varying widths. "No doubt at first sight the seven arches appear to be all of about the same span," Godwin said in an article in the *British Architect* in 1878, "but I read what Ruskin said about the charming building produced by having a series of arches of different widths. He went into ecstasies over the west front of St. Mark's Venice, because they were of different widths, producing a beautiful wave like harmony."[36]

III

In spite of their own impressive achievements, Burges and Godwin began to show signs of unease at the prospects of the Gothic Revival during the mid-1860s. They did not lose confidence in their own principles, but they despaired of their fellow architects ever achieving the much-longed-for unity of purpose. "Until the question of style gets settled," Burges said in 1865, "it is utterly hopeless to think about any great improvement in modern art."[37] So long as this was the precondition for progress, things would look bleak indeed. Godwin complained of the 1867 Architectural Exhibition that

> A restless wandering to and fro from the ends of the earth, trying Italian Gothic one year and French Gothic the next, experimenting with the Renaissance today, and may be the Egyptian tomorrow, is the sort of thing which is no doubt very enticing to a young antiquary who had studied well the history of art, but which the young architect should, nay must, eschew, if he desires to see architecture once again a growing living art.[38]

The next year Burges appeared to have given up all hope:

> If we copy, the thing never looks right, however servilely the mouldings . . . may have been imitated. The same occurs with regard to those buildings which do not profess to be copies: both they and the copies want spirit. They are dead bodies; they don't live. We are at our wit's end and do not know what to do.[39]

Seddon alone remained an optimist. As late as 1872 he was still proclaiming the inevitable victory of the Gothic cause. But Burges and Godwin knew in the mid-1860s that this confidence was unfounded. They did not doubt the validity of their own version of Ruskinism. They still advocated an architecture of mass and sculptural ornament. They also knew, however, that though superb individual buildings might be created, the common style of the age would never materialize.

Things had reached this pass when the Queen Anne style suddenly became fashionable in the early 1870s. The magnificent architecture of the
thirteenth century had suddenly been replaced by the debased mannerisms
of the seventeenth. And what made matters worse was that this new development was being led by men whom Godwin had once counted among
the "good knights of the Gothic army."[40] The situation was actually more
complicated than Seddon, Burges, and Godwin realized, as we will see in
chapter 12, but it seemed clear to them at the time that both Ruskin and
Gothic had been repudiated. The problem was whether or not to adjust to
the new climate. Seddon persisted in the faith he had lived by and became
one of the Queen Anne style's harshest critics. Burges created brilliant individual works, while complaining of the architectural masquerade around
him. Godwin denounced the new movement and then leapfrogged it. He
ceased to be a Gothicist and became an aesthete.

The transition must have been all the easier in that Godwin had never
truly shared the passionate religious commitment that underlay the revival. The lugubrious words on art and faith quoted earlier simply reveal a
young aspirant aping his elders. He dropped such piety forever when he
decided to live with Ellen Terry, whose husband, the painter G. F. Watts,
refused to grant a divorce. His commitment to art, on the other hand, was
the passion of his life. It is no wonder that he hit it off with the painter
James McNeil Whistler. The earliest results of this friendship were seen in
his furniture design, but his architecture was soon transformed as well.

Shortly before the Whistler-Ruskin trial began, Godwin lectured to a
group of architectural pupils and assistants in Manchester on "Some Buildings I Have Designed." It was an appropriate moment to reconsider the
shifting loyalties of his career, and he reminisced at length about the
Northampton Town Hall and his debt to *The Stones of Venice.* He was, considering the emotions surrounding the trial, very gentle toward Ruskin.
But he was also very firm in saying that the Ruskinian connections between sculpture and architecture had never been realized:

> there was no building in the country that they could refer to and say, Look at
> this painting, or this sculpture; it is all one—one glorious work of art. Their
> sculpture was a disgrace, wherever they turned—whether they went to the
> Northampton or the Manchester Town Hall, or wherever they went, it was uni-
> formly dull. Hardly a man in England yet knew how to sculpt architecturally.[41]

The Northampton Town Hall was not even very logical, for it should have
been vaulted throughout the ground floor, and it was certainly not appropriate to its time. Godwin no longer saw any hope in revivalism or in the
concept of the *point de départ:*

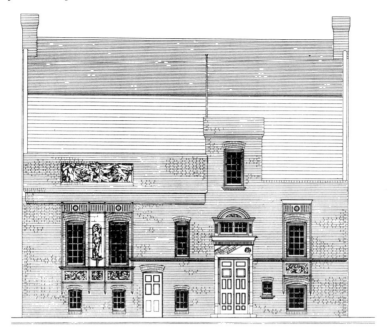

Fig. 86. White House, Chelsea. E. W. Godwin. British Architect, *1878.*

don't take up any one [style] and say, "That is my line of departure; I will work on this line," because, after they had worked for a time the fashion would change. Depend upon it, Gothic architecture had had its knell sounded. So long as Mr. Street lived we should have a little of it now and then. So of Queen Anne architecture; we should see much of that. . . . then, having played all the scales and variations, Queen Anne architecture would die before they had time to turn around.[42]

His advice was to forswear allegiance to a style—or at least to treat style as a matter of personal willfulness. If asked what style their building was, the young men were to say, "It is my own."

What Godwin now admired is exemplified by the combined studio and home that he had designed the year before for Whistler. At first glance, White House (fig. 86) resembles the simple Georgian townhouses that Ruskin had so despised. A closer look reveals a Japanese subtlety in the reticent surface ornament and in the disposition of dark apertures on the plain white surface. The polychromy is of the subtlest kind: hard white brick, green Eureka slate for the roof, white Portland stone for the doorway, with the doors themselves, the window frames and other woodwork painted a plain gray blue. There is no sculpture. Ironically, the Metropolitan Board of Works demanded changes in Godwin's design, including the provision of relief sculpture, which would have made the building more Ruskinian. Godwin made changes in his design, but ignored most of them in construction.

With his White House, Godwin turned away from the problem, so important in the 1850s and 1860s, of expressing Victorian aspirations in great civic buildings, and he accepted a task characteristic of the 1870s and 1880s—that of designing homes in which the exterior, the interior decorating scheme, the dress of the inhabitants, and even their ideas and moods might all display a pervading aesthetic unity. But the unity of art and life is an ideal that Ruskin advocated with increasing fervor in the later part of his career, and Godwin was as much concerned with the basic ideal of the unity of the arts in White House as he was in the Northampton Town Hall. There is thus an element of continuity between the early and late phases of Godwin's work. It is also useful to recall that in 1884 Godwin designed the interior of a home across the street from White House for Oscar Wilde. In 1882 Wilde had lectured in North America, preaching a mélange of aesthetic doctrines derived from Whistler, Godwin, Pater—and Ruskin. Clearly Ruskin's influence on the new world of late Victorian England is more complicated than might at first appear.

X

RUSKIN VERSUS THE
PROFESSION

Ruskin's disillusion with the Gothic Revival occurred while his influence on it was at its height. This suggests that his thinking during the 1860s evolved quite independently of that of his admirers. But there was one era where their concerns coincided—that of education. It was clear that if Ruskinian ideals were to be realized, both workmen and architects would require a very different training than any that they had received. There were many discussions of the subject, and Ruskin's name was often invoked. On the whole, it is easier to find evidence of his impact on the training of architects than on the education of workmen. The picture that emerges in each case, however, is much the same: his ideas appeal strongly to the more idealistic in each group, but are finally defeated by the age's dominant tendencies toward machine production among workmen and professionalization among architects.

I

Ruskin's impact on the education of workmen was conditioned by his distinction between building and architecture. He was not primarily concerned with the education of bricklayers, carpenters, and stonemasons. His remarks are nearly always directed toward the man who made the decoration—the Art-Workman, as he was then called.

That left a large body of workmen to be considered, especially in an age that loved ornament. Ruskin kept his ideal of imaginative handwork before the public by giving his patronage to the Architectural Museum, by teaching at the Working Men's College, and by speaking before such bodies as the Saint Martin's School of Art, the Saint Matthew's Working Men's Institute, and the Mechanic's Institute in Bradford. The frequency with which he was invited to speak at such organizations suggests that his views were popular, but it is difficult to find particulars. The comments of a Mr. Ash following Ruskin's address to the Annual Conversazione of the Saint Martin's School of Art in April 1858 are therefore of considerable interest.

Mr. Ash (workmen, no matter how skilled, rarely found their first names used in print) was a foreman with the firm of Hart and Son, ecclesiastical and domestic ironworkers. They worked in brass and wrought iron for such architects as Butterfield and Seddon. They were an important part of the movement toward naturalism and toward the original use of medieval motifs. Mr. Ash was sufficiently strong for freedom from precedent that in April of 1856 he rose at the Architectural Museum to protest against one of the tasks set for a competition:

> He reprobated strongly its being described as in the style of the latter part of the thirteenth century, as tending to fetter the invention of the competitors. He said that Mr. Ruskin had made *his* a subject of the nineteenth century by prescribing subjects illustrative of the Crimean war, and had also stated that possibly the works of the competitors might be used in conjunction as the monument of some of those who had fallen in that war, and he (Mr. Ash) suggested that the iron screen might form a grille round such a monument, but if so, it should be a work, not of the thirteenth, but of the nineteenth century.[1]

We have noticed that Ruskin himself never explicitly embraces the slogans of Gothic modernism. His admirer seems unaware of the omission.

Mr. Ash was also a strong supporter of the principle that "architecture embraced not only artists, but artisans."[2] He wanted a class for practice and working drawings, where the artisan might join with the junior architect. He wanted a school where stonemasons and bricklayers would be called upon to give elementary lectures and where students would hear "the practical thoughts of practical men."[3] Founded in 1854, Saint Martin's was one of the nearest approaches to this ideal. Though affiliated with South Kensington, it was open to ideas from the Gothic movement. It offered night classes that attracted builders, engravers, lithographers, engineers, carvers, gilders, jewelers, cabinetmakers, house carpenters, upholsters, watch engravers, and even a pastrycook. It would be foolhardy to assume that all these men were animated by a Ruskinian vision of craftsmanship, but Ash made it clear that this was the vision that inspired the school.

Rising to thank Ruskin for his 1858 address, Ash praised "the liberal manner in which he had contributed to the development of art amongst the artisans of this metropolis."[4] He went on to urge manufacturers to play a more active role in the education of their workmen. He wanted them to join with the district schools of art in arranging excursions to Lincoln, Beverly, and York, and also to permit shorter hours so that they could attend evening classes. Hart & Son paid the entrance fee for each apprentice who attended Saint Martin's School. It also paid one shilling a month toward the student's expenses and a further two shillings and sixpence so long as his work was satisfactory. Thus the apprentice himself had to pay only two shillings for a year's classes.

Ash also encouraged his apprentices to undertake a more Ruskinian approach to their labor than the Government Schools encouraged. He had noticed in previous years that none of his workers' names appeared on the prize list:

> To what did they attribute the cause? The apprentices said, "We have no Gothic copies; our heads and hands are in the practice, but we have no theory; here everything is Classic. Shall we do anything for the annual meeting?" His (Mr. Ash's) answer was, "Yes, try what you can show your fellow-students, what you can not only design, but also make, for that occasion." Now the result was that on one of the tables in the room one of the apprentices had his candlestick, another his lock-plate, another his hinge front, another his door-knob. There the meeting had not only their thoughts brought forth, but the results in the work of their hands.[5]

The significance of this is twofold. First, the apprentices united design and execution instead of merely designing for machines. Second, they turned their backs on copying classic patterns in favor of a free application of medieval principles. Ash told students to look forward to the day when "they should not be tied down to the earth all the days of their lives by copying of egg and tongue, volute and ovolos, like so many carving machines, but that they should all be able to revel in their own fancies which nature had given them as intellectual beings, who possess a heavenly soul as well as an earthly body."[6] He was greeted with cheers.

Taken simply by themselves, Mr. Ash's comments suggest that Ruskin's attitudes toward craftsmanship were warmly welcomed by skilled artisans and young apprentices alike. But the firm of Hart & Son was a special case, and the preponderance of evidence indicates that Ruskin's opinions made little headway among those whom they were intended to benefit.

One example appears in a series of articles published in the 1862 volume of the *Building News*. Signed by C.B.A., they bore the title "The Home and Out-Door Education of Artist-Workmen, Their Proper Work and Their Way to It." C.B.A. is critical of the educational methods Ruskin was using at the Working Men's College (he objects to the neglect of outline and the excessive emphasis on drawing), but he is a thorough Ruskinian on basic principles. He denies that there can be any dividing line between artist and art-workman, wants necessary labor made mentally interesting, and objects to the treatment of workers as mere human machines.

Against this background, C.B.A.'s encounter with an actual workman is of considerable interest. He describes watching a potter work with astonishing manual dexterity at the production of clay candlesticks:

> Not the slightest hint could be got at from most attentively observing him that his mind was at work, or that he was thinking over the business, or that he looked for any given effect as a result of his hand-work. No; it was all pure manual quickness, and skill, and finger practice; that is, in the proper potter's art, solely considered manually. . . . When all was over—for we stood it out to the end, and thus lost nothing—our worthy friend, before gathering together his clay into one indiscriminate ball, threw an admiring glance along his rows of candlesticks, and pots, and railing-spikes, and objects looking like large acorns, and of truly pre-adamite interest, and which would probably have puzzled Professor Huxley himself had he found them in a dry state anywhere— we took the liberty of asking him whether he had ever seen the pottery in the British Museum? and reminded him of what the Etruscans had accomplished with the self-same potter's wheel. His reply was, that he had often seen them, but was unable to understand them, or to see how *he* could make use of them.[7]

This was discouraging, since one of the major efforts in workmen's education was to make available models from the past for study. If workmen could see no point in this, their products were unlikely to improve. C.B.A. was still more discouraged in that his potter was by no means mentally obtuse. A member of a cooperative society, a warm admirer of Richard Cobden, and an enthusiastic free trader, he had lively opinions on every subject but his craft.

William White reached similarly discouraging conclusions after talking to ironworkers in the north of England. He found them completely uninterested in whether a given piece of decoration was produced by craft processes or industrial ones. "It is a mere mercantile calculation as to whether machinery or hand-labour shall be employed in the execution of a given work, and as to how far it will pay to produce fresh machinery, dies, or gauges." Worse, insofar as the workers had a preference, it was on the side of machinery: "It is considered unworthy of the age to put to hand-labour that which machinery is capable of executing,—and this as a matter not merely of economy but of art."[8]

Similar testimony can be found late in the century in a speech by the Birmingham merchant William Kenrick to the National Association for the Advancement of Art. Although Kenrick identified himself as one who largely accepted "the doctrines of Mr. Ruskin and Mr. Morris," he had to concede that he lived in a world that was very little governed by their teachings. Like Mr. Ash and C.B.A., he thought the problem was one of education. The difficulty was that it proved much easier to establish schools than to draw workmen into them: "Such schools they look upon with jealousy and suspicion, believing them to be intended for the middle classes. They will tell you what they want are cut and dried rules for doing their work better and more expeditiously."[9] Kenrick thought this attitude would pass in time, but the date of his address was 1891.

Most observers had become disillusioned with the art-workman long before. In the rare instances where he could be persuaded to accept a creative role, complained the *Building News*, he was likely to produce "something small in parts, weak in line, and 'naturalistic' in character, instead of the broad simple forms [the architect] would probably prefer."[10] Even the normally optimistic Seddon despaired:

> The truth was that such a creature [as the artist-workman] at present did not exist, and how to get one seemed to be an insuperable difficulty, unless it were, perhaps, in the class of carvers. Carvers were a class of men who had been so trained as to be able to think a little for themselves; yet the difficulty of getting anything respectable in that branch was immense, and in metal work there was very little indeed that was decent. In the works of Mr. Skidmore . . . there was great excellence, but that was mainly owing to the fact that Mr. Skidmore was himself an artist, and had devoted much study and superintendence to the work, but that gentleman had recently stated that he had completely failed in obtaining or educating a single artist workman.[11]

In this situation there seemed no choice but a return to what Ruskin had called servile ornament. A writer in the *Building News* lamented that architects had no choice but to prepare full-sized drawings of subjects so that they could be reproduced without even the variation that would come from altered dimensions: "Of course such a method of directing the art-workman degrades him to the level of a mechanic, but there is no alternative."[12]

II

Victorian architects, unlike art-workmen, were able to shape their own educational institutions, and it was natural that the men who designed Ruskinian buildings should wonder if it were also possible to train Ruskinian architects. The standard mode of architectural training in Victorian

England was the apprenticeship system, supplemented by whatever classes and lectures might be offered by such organizations as the Royal Academy or the Architectural Association. It was widely agreed that this was inadequate. Each attempt at reform, however, faced not just how students ought to be trained but what an architect ought to be.

There were three competing possibilities. One was to unite the profession of architect with that of the engineer. Another was to base education on the classical orders and systems of proportion. The third was to produce architects who could paint and carve and who had mastered the crafts. This was the Ruskinian ideal. The battle between the contending parties lasted into the twentieth century. The Ruskinians lost it as architecture developed into a closed profession taught in schools dominated by sophisticated classicists. Before their defeat, however, they mounted two major campaigns. The second of these was led by Norman Shaw and W. R. Lethaby in the 1890s. The first belongs to the early and mid-1860s. Among its first leaders was a man named Randall Druce.

Druce was a leading member of the Architectural Association, and he was especially concerned with the educational needs of the younger aspirants to the profession. He consistently adopted a Ruskinian point of view, insisting on architecture's connections with the other arts and crafts. In June of 1859 he told an audience that he had read *The Seven Lamps* "with eagerness," praised Ruskin's lecture "The Influence of Imagination in Architecture," and insisted, perhaps a little defensively, that he had "never seen anything strange in [Ruskin's] writings."[13] In November of the same year he told an audience that architecture should tell stories, inspire, and instruct. Thus an asylum might show Jesus healing the blind and a workhouse might be distinguished by "a subject contrasting manly independence with idle dependence, and distinctly showing the assistance to be given the aged and unfortunate."[14]

This clearly required an architect who had mastered more than draftsmanship and the five orders. Druce found his model for architectural education in medieval and Renaissance Italy. There every architect had received his earliest training in some other art or craft. Thus Nicola, Giovanni, and Andrea Pisano had all started with sculpture, Giotto and Arnolfo had been painters, and Orcagna and Brunelleschi had trained as goldsmiths. Bramante had begun as a painter, and Sansovino had studied sculpture and worked in metal before turning to architecture. Because they were skilled in the sister arts, each of their buildings could be "a perfect work of combined architecture, sculpture, and painting."[15]

The ideal was that no architect should be trained in architecture alone. Realizing it was less simple. In 1860 Druce took a first step by helping to organize a class in wood carving for architects, but the campaign soon moved beyond this training in the minor crafts. William Burges took up the cause and insisted that architects, as an essential part of their educa-tion, should learn to draw the human figure.

The necessity of figure drawing is not one of Ruskin's themes. His own training did not include it, and, whether from prudery or other reasons, he rarely discusses the nude. Nevertheless, skill in drawing the figure was ab-solutely essential if architects were ever to realize his conception of their art as one in which "the sculpture and painting were, in fact, the all in all of the thing to be done" (8.10). There were two reasons for this. One—the best one—was that no other kind of drawing trains the hand and eye so well. The second, more practical reason was that to achieve a union of architecture, painting, and sculpture, an architect would have to design his own sculptures and frescoes even if others were to execute them. Lack of skill in figure drawing condemned architects to notches, chamfers, and manufactured ornament.

The campaign for a broadly artistic architectural education opened with a speech by George Gilbert Scott before the Architectural Association in March of 1864. Carefully avoiding Ruskin's extreme position that "the same person should be a sculptor and a painter as well as an architect," Scott took the intermediate view that the architect should be the chief artist, "director of all the artists employed in carrying out that one great art which comprises and unites all the others."[16] His studies should include animal drawing, designs from natural foliage, and, above all, the human figure. Following Scott's talk, the association pledged itself to support a plan for architectural education.

The next step was made by E. J. Tarver in an April 1864 paper, "Figure Drawing Applied to Architecture." He echoed Scott's views and pointed to G. F. Watt's widely admired new fresco in Lincoln's Inn Hall and to the stat-ues at the Oxford Museum as showing the direction in which architecture ought to move. He finished by calling for the establishment of a life class—a call endorsed in the following discussion by both Seddon and Burges. The class was established with E. J. Poynter as the instructor, but the results were not encouraging. Only thirty-six pupils attended, only twenty-five were architects, and only fifteen of these came regularly. This was enough to prompt one of the first expressions of the discouragement that pervades Burges's later writings: "If architecture means only surveying and valuing, the sooner Mr. Tarver shuts up his class the better."[17]

Nevertheless, the movement entered a new, broader phase—one that involved Ruskin himself. A Committee on Architectural Education was organized with representatives from the Royal Institute of British Archi-tects, the Architectural Association, and the Architectural Museum. Rep-resenting the latter organization were Alexander Beresford Hope, Joseph Clarke, Benjamin Ferrey, and John Ruskin. It is not easy to know what transpired in committee meetings, but a discussion recorded in the *RIBA*

Transactions indicates that Scott pressed for figure drawing and that Ruskin supported Scott. Beyond that, the situation is unclear, and the committee seems to have been unable to decide exactly what it wanted. Ruskin's ideal of an architect who was also a painter and a sculptor was clearly impractical, but it was difficult to fix on any clear goal short of this. Some sort of school was apparently needed. The problem of setting goals was reflected in the difficulty of finding its name. Scott was sure that the new institution

> should not be called a "School of Architectural Decoration." He did not view it even as a school of architectural drawing. He was puzzled, he confessed, to coin a name for it. It was really a school in which architects might learn those branches of art which were not exactly architectural but bore strongly upon architecture. It was, as he had said, a point of union between architecture, and sculpture, and painting. A "School of Art for Architects" was a name he had thought of, and that was, he thought, about as good a name as they could get, though it was not a school for architectural drawing merely.[18]

Scott's reference to "those branches of art which were not exactly architectural" shows how much he was hanging back from Ruskin's ideal. Burges was willing to go much further, but he too had to be practical. The meeting finally agreed, with Scott proposing and Burges seconding, that the school should be called the School of Art Accessorial to Architecture.

It perhaps goes without saying that the school was never founded. The major result of this discussion so far as Ruskin was concerned was an invitation to address the RIBA on "An Enquiry into Some of the Conditions at Present Affecting the Study of Architecture in Our Schools." This paper does not, however, provide a climax to the campaign for a better kind of architectural education. Ruskin, characteristically, had his own crusade to pursue. Accordingly, his paper on the study of architecture should be considered together with another major utterance of the 1860s—"Traffic." The circumstances surrounding both lectures show how complex and ironic the relations between Ruskin and Victorian architects had become.

III

The ostensible purpose of "Traffic" was to advise the citizens of Bradford on a style for their new wool exchange. The town was typical of the newly prosperous northern cities that were so often the recipients of Ruskin's advice. Its prosperity was based on the manufacture of machinery for the woolen trades as well as on the making of the cloth itself. It had grown from 13,000 people in 1801 to 104,000 in 1851, and by 1881 it would reach 183,000. The social evils that accompany rapid growth were all present, but the town fathers must have been pleased by their social progress. They had strengthened their municipal government, incorporating the town in 1847, and they had concerned themselves with improving the drainage, paving the streets, and educating the poorer classes. They felt entitled to a dramatic piece of municipal self-advertisement, and the new exchange was intended to provide it.

Eleven architects were asked to submit designs.[19] Some, like Scott, Street, Waterhouse, and Burges, were nationally known representatives of the Gothic Revival. Philip Webb and Norman Shaw, both of whom had worked in Street's office, were rising young men, and they brought the number of Gothicists to six. Cuthbert Broderick, on the other hand, was the designer of the Leeds Town Hall (fig. 87), a building so little to Ruskin's liking that in the preface to his Edinburgh lectures he asked the citizens of Leeds not to build it. Lockwood and Mawson, in whose office Broderick had trained, was a well-established local firm, and the remaining entrants had local ties as well. By the time of the competition deadline, Scott, Street, Webb, and Waterhouse had all withdrawn. This left William Burges and Norman Shaw to represent the Gothicists. Burges's design does not survive, but Shaw's is illustrated in figure 88. As the crucial decision ap-

Fig. 87. Leeds Town Hall. Cuthbert Broderick. Builder, 1853.

Fig. 88.   Design for the Bradford Exchange competition. R. Norman Shaw. Building News, *1871.*

proached, the contest was essentially narrowed down to Burges and Shaw on the one side and Henry Francis Lockwood on the other.

Lockwood's strongest supporter was a civic leader named Henry William Ripley. His interest appears to have been less in the style of the Exchange than in the ceremony that would surround the laying of the cornerstone. He was struggling for control of the local Liberal party and expected that the ceremonial visit of Prime Minister Palmerston would aid his plans. The

Gothicists were led by Aldam Heaton, whose sister-in-law, Ellen Heaton, had been patronizing the Pre-Raphaelites under Ruskin's direction and had contributed to the Oxford Museum.

Ruskin stayed at Heaton's home during his visit to Bradford and was filled in on the local situation. Lockwood, after he won the competition, complained to the *Bradford Observer* that his enemies had brought in Ruskin just prior to the final judging with the object of denying him the prize. He was right. It would have been most undiplomatic of Ruskin to use his public platform to endorse a design by a member of the Gothic party, but he did the next best thing by urging the audience to consider the great beauties of Waterhouse's Assize Courts in Manchester. Ruskin's address was not, however, a straightforward plea for Gothic. As often when he was asked to do a simple thing, he did something complicated instead. He set out to make his audience rethink the nature of architectural style.

Ruskin begins by transforming his topic into a challenge: "I do not care about this Exchange," he tells his audience, "because *you* don't" (18.433). The thirty thousand pounds they are about to spend is the equivalent to them of a new coat to a single man, and they have turned to Ruskin as a respectable architectural man–milliner who can tell them the newest and sweetest thing in pinnacles. Ruskin's audience has assumed that taste is a matter of fashion. He tells them instead that it is an expression of morality, and it is clear that the true morality of Bradford grows out of the worship of the Goddess of Getting On. The appropriate architectural expression of this faith would involve a frieze decorated with pendant purses and an inner chamber housing a large statue of Britannia of the Market. Ruskin does not consider commerce irredeemably vulgar. One purpose of *The Stones of Venice* was to show the architectural effects of greatness of spirit in a commercial city. But Venice maintained the vitality of its private faith while Bradford, though building lovely Gothic churches for its Sunday worship, expresses its true spirit in its warehouses and factory chimneys. It is the moral problem that matters; solve that and style will take care of itself. In the meantime, it will do little good to construct Gothic buildings without the Gothic spirit.

Ironically, it was just such a building that the citizens of Bradford built (fig. 89). Although H. F. Lockwood regarded Ruskin as a man of "brilliant genius" but "incomprehensible theories,"[20] he actually built a very passable piece of secular Gothic. He was unprejudiced about style and could build in Italian Gothic, French Renaissance, or Roman classic with equal skill. He studied Scott's proposed Halifax Town Hall, and he searched Bradford's past for heroes worthy to decorate his facade. The spaces between the spandrels are punctuated by the heads of such worthies as Sir Walter Raleigh, Sir Francis Drake, Titus Salt, Robert Stephenson, Richard

Fig. 89.   Bradford Exchange. Lockwood and Mawson. Builder, 1964.

Arkwright, James Watt, W. E. Gladstone, Richard Cobden, and Lord Palmerston. They are disgracefully skimpy, but are undoubtedly Ruskinian—or """"Ruskinian."""" In 1877 a donor made the pantheon complete by providing the large central hall with a dramatic statue, not of Britannia of the Market, but of John Bright.

At Bradford we have both an ironic triumph of Ruskin's influence and some of the elements that would bring about its transformation. There is a major Gothic architect, William Burges, who tried with great integrity to fulfill the side of Ruskin's thinking that identified architecture with painting and sculpture. There is a good professional man, Lockwood, who was willing to adopt Gothic if that was the fashion. There is Norman Shaw, only a few years away from abandoning the strict tenets of the Gothic Revival. Finally, there is Ruskin himself, now thinking of style in terms quite different from those of his admirers. Style remained the primary question for them, but was now only a secondary one for him.

But few architects perceived the new direction of his thought. The reports on "Traffic" that appeared in the architectural press were brief. G.H.G., writing in a May 1864 issue of the *Building News*, could quote with unruffled approval Ruskin's statement that taste was an index of morality.[21] E. W. Godwin, arguing in a June issue of the *Builder* against Lockwood's design on the ground that he had underestimated his costs, simply assumed that Ruskin was on his side: "I refrain from entering on the fine art question. If Mr. Ruskin fails to set the people of Bradford right, it is surely vain for me to hope, within the compass of a note, to attempt anything of the sort."[22] A gulf was opening between the Gothic Revivalists and their prophet, and they did not seem to know it.

When Ruskin addressed the RIBA in May of 1865, however, the evidence of his disenchantment could not be ignored. Some of the special interest of this occasion lies in the fact that the lengthy discussion following Ruskin's lecture was recorded in the institute's *Transactions*. This was one of the few occasions on which architects were able to confront Ruskin directly.

Both the lecture and the responses should be considered in two contexts. The immediate one is the controversy over the proper training of architects. Ruskin does not mention either Burges or Seddon among the architects he chooses for special praise (he does cite Godwin), but he endorses their position on architectural education: he wishes to see the profession of architect united "not with that of the engineer, but of the sculptor" (19.35), and he asserts that the architect should learn to draw "quick and firm sketches of flowers, animals, drapery, and figures, from nature, in the simplest terms of line, and light and shade" (19.37).

A more general context is provided by the mood of self-congratulations that many Gothic Revivalists felt during the early sixties. The fifties had been a time of struggle; in the late sixties men such as Burges began to feel that something was wrong, but in the first half of the decade, everything seemed headed in the right direction. A. W. Blomfield expressed the new mood in an 1861 address to the Architectural Association:

Fourteen or fifteen years ago, when Mr. Ruskin wrote that beautiful simile of the Mountain Ridge, the culminating point of Gothic art, up to which all had been progress and after which all was decline, he expressed a doubt whether the stir he saw going on was a real awakening or only a movement among dry bones. Since that day something more tangible has been done: his call has been answered by some at least. A band earnest, if small, and though small, ever increasing, have girded themselves for the work and are again pressing steadily onwards. After the long night in the trampled plain, they are again climbing the mountain side; the mists are rising, they see clearly before them the point where travellers of another day began to descend, and to their upward gaze a new morning is already gilding the summits of more distant and more glorious heights.[23]

Against this optimism, Ruskin offered something that sounded very much like despair. "All lovely architecture," he told his audience, "was designed for cities in cloudless air":

But our cities, built in black air which, by its accumulated foulness, first renders all ornament invisible in distance, and then chokes its interstices with soot; cities which are mere crowded masses of store, and warehouse, and counter, and are therefore to the rest of the world what the larder and cellar are to a private house; cities in which the object of men is not life, but labour; and in which all the chief magnitude of an edifice is to enclose machinery; cities in which the streets are not the avenues for the passing and procession of a happy people, but the drains for the discharge of a tormented mob, in which the only object in reaching any spot is to be transferred to another; in which existence becomes mere transition, and every creature is only one atom in a drift of human dust, and current of interchanging particles, circulating here by tunnels underground, and there by tubes in the air; for a city, or cities, such as this *no architecture is possible* [emphasis added]—nay, no desire of it is possible to their inhabitants. (19.24)

Nothing like this had been heard before among Victorian architects. They had, to be sure, worried obsessively about smoke-laden skies. An 1859 article in the *Builder,* for example, calculated that 3 million tons of coal a year were consumed in Manchester and Salford alone and that thirty-six tons of sulphuric acid were formed in the atmosphere during the same period.[24] In 1860 an article observed that sulphuric acid acted on the clay in certain common stones, forming an impure sulphate of aluminum, which was then washed out of the stone by rain, leaving the grains of silica to crumble away.[25] In 1861 the *Building News* quoted R. W. Billings's warning that pollution was rendering architectural color useless.[26] An 1864 article in the *Builder* expanded on the point:

where coloured materials are used, and not glazed or polished, no architect can satisfy himself exactly on what principle he should design. He may follow the present, and we fear most pernicious, fashion of strong colours, saying that the smoke of two or three years will tone them down; or he may make colour subordinate and a pleasing variation, instead of dominant over form; in which case, that part of his design which was expressed through the element of colour will after a similar interval of time disappear altogether.

The writer noted that at the Alliance Fire Office in Bartholomew Lane, "lines of black and white, caused by soot, and rain divided into streams by the water leaf ornament, are marked on the fascia below, so as to give the appearance of bad, or pointed imitation of, fluting."[27] At Cockerell's Sun Fire Office, the detail had been so obscured by pollution that it contributed nothing to the building's general effect.

Victorian architects thought incessantly about smoke. What they did not do was treat it as a symbol. They thought of it as the source of a practical problem in design, one that they could not solve. To Ruskin, by contrast, it was an emblem of modern life, the sign of social and industrial conditions that made good architecture impossible. Architects who had gathered at the RIBA to consider the next step forward for their profession were startled to hear one of their leaders proclaim: "I have seceded from the study not only of architecture, but nearly of all art; and have given myself, as I would in a besieged city, to seek the best modes of getting bread and water for its multitudes, there remaining no question, it seems to me, of other than such grave business for the time" (19.38).

In the discussion that followed, architects were able to talk back to their most celebrated critic. Some praised his eloquence while avoiding or dismissing his ideas. T. L. Donaldson said that Ruskin's words "touched so high a chord, they appealed to feelings of so lofty a nature, that it was impossible to give at once expression to those emotions, which were called forth by such a theme so powerfully treated."[28] Matthew Digby Wyatt turned over a string of adjectives and finally concluded that only *ébloui* "could adequately define the mixed state of surprise, delight, and general acute excitement in which the fiery essay the meeting had heard left him."[29] He did not, however, see such a close and direct relation as Ruskin did between art and morality, and he was sure that Ruskin's vision of an El Dorado of art was much too impractical for architects who had their living to earn. J. W. Papworth agreed with Digby Wyatt and stressed that his acquiescence in the proposed vote of thanks did not at all imply approval of what had been said.

The most interesting of Ruskin's hostile critics was Robert Kerr. He was a man whose opinion would be heard. A founding member of the Architectural Association and an active participant in the RIBA, Kerr was both a successful architect and an important architectural journalist. His contributions frequently appeared in the *Builder* and the *Building News*, and after

1870 he wrote leaders for the *Architect*. He served as professor of architecture at King's College, and in 1891 he enlarged and updated James Fergusson's *History of Modern Architecture*. He was an influential figure, and Ruskin was one of his constant themes.

His first major statement on the subject was quasi-sympathetic. It came in an 1860 speech, "The Battle of the Styles." There Kerr divided the Victorian architectural world into four camps. The first advocated Barry's Italian style, the second supported eclecticism, the third (which included the Pre-Raphaelites) pursued the science of ecclesiology. Kerr associated this last group with the strict development of medieval precedent and felt that Ruskin did not quite fit into it. He therefore placed him in the fourth camp of the latitudinarians:

> But the high priest of all latitudinarians was Mr. Ruskin. Not to speak of his elegance of diction and graceful form of thought, which were but the superficial covering of solid matter beneath, the honest pluck and audacity at the root of all was delightful. He might compare with John Bright! Talk of looking before you leap! he neither looked nor leaped: with one stroke of his pinions he was amongst the clouds and winds: a moment more and he had reached the goal of his endeavour: how he had reached it the clouds and winds only knew; but let them shake him in his seat who could. [30]

Unfortunately, Kerr does not offer any extended definition of his term. In part he seems to mean any iconoclastic willingness to break with precedent. Thus he associated Ruskin with E. B. Lamb (whom Ruskin had met in the 1830s) and with W. H. Leeds (who had assailed Ruskin vigorously in the 1850s). These two names, however, do not connect Ruskin with any participants in the battle of the styles that was going on in 1860. John Summerson suggests that Kerr is thinking of those architects who were treating Gothic in a spirit of originality—George Truefitt, Charles Gray, and C. F. Hayward. [31] This seems very plausible. It is striking that a few years later Bassett Keeling, under attack from Seddon and others, would defend himself as a latitudinarian. Whatever the case, Kerr stopped discussing Ruskin in a friendly tone after the address to the RIBA.

Kerr's remarks were longer than those of any other speaker at the 1865 meeting. He too praised Ruskin's "eloquence and imagination," but then assailed him for identifying architecture not only with sculpture and painting but also, most perniciously of all, with poetry. The architect, Kerr insisted, was "a professional man—a servant of the public for the efficient design of buildings—precisely like the engineer." [32]

For the rest of his life Kerr continued to reiterate his view of Ruskin as a dreamer, a poet, and an amateur. In November 1865 he announced that architects could not follow Ruskin's advice if they were angels of heaven—

"and, even if they could, John Bull would not appreciate it, because he loved that which was practical." [33] In 1869 he contrasted Pugin "the practical architect" with Ruskin "the speculative enthusiast." [34] A year later Ruskin was still a high priest, but now "the High Priest of a faith which directly identified Architecture with Poetry." Kerr tells readers of the *Architect:* "Mr. Ruskin is a writer of poetical criticism in poetical style. Whether, indeed, he deals with art, the love of his youth, or with Political economy—in middle age the object of his demented dalliance, his wooing is the same—poetry wrapt up in poetry." [35] In 1884, addressing the RIBA on "English Architecture Thirty Years Hence," Kerr recalled the days when "the specious, reckless, often meaningless rhetoric of his charming writings stirred up a vague and spurious sentimentalism, which, without benefiting architecture, was doing infinite damage to the architect." [36] He had his final word in an article written shortly after Ruskin's death in 1900: "Sentimental emotion was the root and branch of his being; in dreamy quietude and gentleness when it might be so, in volcanic impulsiveness when otherwise; the restless soul never quite sober, often intoxicated with inspiration not to be expressed." [37]

Ruskin's supporters at the 1865 meeting were less forceful than his opponents, in part because they were puzzled by the direction his thought was now taking. William White agreed that the instruction of architects should differ from that of engineers. It should be founded on beauty, and "in all nature the most beautiful objects, as he thought he had learnt from Mr. Ruskin's writings, were those which apparently were the least to be regarded as utilitarian." [38] G. E. Street wondered if he might not have misunderstood Ruskin at several points. He was especially disturbed that Ruskin had so casually accepted the label of naturalist. He endorsed, however, Ruskin's insistence on "the necessity of a religious feeling about art"; [39] in other words, he was quick to agree with the part of the speech that coincided with his own deeply held views. Alexander Beresford Hope complained that Ruskin suffered from "a sort of 'end-of-the-world-is-coming idea.'" It was, he warned, "the duty of those who had their part to play in the world's progress to throw off such feelings." If gaudy architecture was being created, it was at least an improvement on the no-architecture of Baker Street. He called on Ruskin to "cheer-up" and to "recognize great prospects for his own principles in the future, which he was now too modest and too sensitive to recognize for himself." [40]

Seddon spoke in Ruskin's defense, and he continued to serve as the counterweight to Robert Kerr in professional forums during the next decades. Seddon had protested against Ruskin's pessimism in 1852, and he still saw no reason to despair. He seemed not to believe Ruskin's claim that he had seceded from the study of architecture. Certainly Seddon never seceded from his admiration for Ruskin's work. His firmest statement on the matter came in 1870 when Elijah Hoole presented "A Summary of Mr. Ruskin's Earlier Architectural Criticism" to the RIBA. Kerr rose from his seat to deliver his now customary assault on Ruskin. Seddon responded:

> I cannot agree with Professor Kerr that [Ruskin's views] are of an unpractical nature, nor has he, in my opinion, pointed out in what respects he considers them to be so. Since Mr. Ruskin's first words were published many years have passed, and many minds—practical minds—have been devoted to the subject, and have developed further and carried out independently similar principles to those suggested by that writer, but I must say—I speak for myself, and think I may do so for others,—that many minds have been influenced by him, even in their practice, while certainly the enthusiasm of numbers has been kindled by his eloquence. It seems to me there are many things which are now regarded as truisms, but which were not considered truisms at the time, and simply taking the chapter on Truth, I should support the whole gist of the arguments it con-tains. I think its forcible pleading was greatly needed, considering the faults which pervaded architecture at that time, from the neglect of veracity both in construction and ornamentation. In calling the attention of the public and the profession to the simple maxim that architecture, like all other things, should be founded upon honesty and truth, Mr. Ruskin did great service, and you may take every one of his chapters in the same way, and find that they contain valu-able instruction and advice. Thus the chapter on Life in Architecture, if you consider the general bearing of it, lays down many important principles which were not previously recognized, and which are scarcely recognized thoroughly yet, and therefore I contend that Mr. Ruskin is to be looked upon as a great teacher of the principles of architecture as well as other arts, and that the pro-fession, as well as the public at large, owe him great thanks for the able services which he has rendered them.[41]

Seddon reaffirmed his faith at Abermad, a house he designed in Wales. He included in it a stained-glass window containing all seven lamps of architecture.

IV

Although Ruskin's criticisms of the Gothic Revival had been thoroughly formulated by February of 1864, he was still comparatively restrained in presenting them to an audience at the Working Men's College:

> In architecture, though great things were being done in England—less, perhaps in London than in other parts, owing to peculiar restrictions and conditions

which might be unavoidable; and most notably in Manchester, where, besides the magnificent museum, were many noteworthy specimens of the Gothic style—the present generation of Englishmen would pass away before any true appreciation of the glories of Gothic architecture was arrived at.[42]

A year later, in his address to the RIBA, Ruskin singled out six architects for praise: Butterfield, Woodward, Scott, Street, Waterhouse, and Godwin.

This, however, was very nearly the last public occasion on which Ruskin had anything good to say about a Gothic Revival architect. From the mid-1860s on he constantly decried his own influence. He declared in his preface to the 1874 edition of *The Stones of Venice:*

> I would rather, for my own part, that no architect had ever condescended to adopt one of the views suggested in this book, than that any should have made the partial use of it which has mottled our manufactory chimneys with black and red brick, dignified our banks and draper's shops with Venetian tracery, and pinched our parish churches into dark and slippery arrangements for the advertisement of cheap coloured glass and pantiles. (9.11)

He saw his influence (wrongly, since it was completed in 1848) in Butterfield's Saint Augustine's College, Canterbury, and attacked its cloisters as "the multiplication of the stupidest traceries that can be cut cheapest" (8.128). He ridiculed John Loughborough Pearson's bank on Oxford's High Street and insisted that the only result of the Gothic Revival was that "sometimes behind an engine furnace, or a railroad bank, you may detect the pathetic discord of its momentary grace, and, with toil, decipher its floral carvings choked with soot" (18.151).

Ruskin's comments on Alfred Waterhouse's Natural History Museum provide a striking instance of his new attitude. In 1863 he had praised Waterhouse's Assize Courts as the finest work yet done in England on his principles. Now, confronted by Waterhouse's delicate polychromy and profuse ornament, Ruskin is appalled. He wrote to the curator of Waterhouse's proposed museum at Sheffield: "I . . . felt really myself yesterday in the new London Museum as if I could do, anyhow, something better than that. Its absurd outside and dismal inside are the worst bit of jobbery we've done yet, in London!"[43] In a second letter he added: "They have made such an accursed mess of the Nt. Hist. Brit. Mus. at Kensington that I am rather picqued to show what can be done with proper light and illustrations at Sheffield."

Yet in spite of his ferocious comments on Gothic Revival buildings, it is very hard to find evidence that Ruskin actually changed his mind about his architectural doctrines. His attitude is epitomized by a statement he made in 1876: "I have been correcting my Stones for the printer, and find it mostly all right, but the advance of my mind since I wrote it!—it is like editing a volume of baby talk, without any fun in it" (24.xxv). The advance of Ruskin's mind affects his social views. He puts his architectural opinions in a new context, but the opinions themselves are not found wanting. Ruskin peppered his 1880 edition of *The Seven Lamps* with lamentations for the fate of his book in a land where the only living was billsticking, but he was still sure that "the actual teaching of it is all right" (8.xlvii).

Ruskin's despair might have brought the Ruskinian phase of English architecture to an end. Instead, his new social views raised important questions about how his architectural teachings were to be applied. Instead of gently declining in the 1870s, Ruskinism entered a new and highly creative phase.

XI

JOHN RUSKIN, JOHN HENRY CHAMBERLAIN, AND THE CIVIC GOSPEL

 IF architecture expresses its society, then there is considerable irony in the fact that Victorian cities, made prosperous by coal, steam, railroads, and division of labor, should have so often celebrated their importance with Ruskinian buildings. There was an inevitable contradiction between Victorian capitalism and Ruskinian ideals. In the hands of an unusual architect, however, this contradiction could give way to a synthesis, and it is in this light that the career of John Henry Chamberlain should be viewed. Many architects who came of age in the 1850s and 1860s were eager to achieve a visual Ruskinism. Many were anxious to serve the needs of England's commercial and industrial centers. Others—a smaller number—responded to the moral imperatives of the Guild of Saint George. Chamberlain was the only architect who did all three: he absorbed the enthusiasms for Italian Gothic, polychromy, and naturalistic ornament; he was very nearly the official architect of the Birmingham Liberals; and he served as cotrustee of the Guild of Saint George. Of all those who created Ruskinian buildings for Manchester or Birmingham or Leeds or Leicester, none found the underlying kinship between Ruskin and his age more skillfully than John Henry Chamberlain.

Some, of course, denied the possibility of such a kinship and stressed the incompatability between Ruskin's doctrines and the proud spirit of their cities. Joseph Cowan, leader of the Northern Reform League and M.P. for Newcastle, expressed his sense of this opposition in an 1881 speech, "The Rise and Strength of Great Towns," at the Middlesborough Jubilee in 1881:

Middlesborough is an epitome of modern times—of that irresistable and victorious civilization which has for its foundation industry and freedom—freedom of thought, of labour, of sale and exchange, which is the building principle of commercial success. . . . I have a sneaking sympathy with the plaintive wail that Mr. Ruskin and others so often . . . raise over a vanished and irrecoverable past. But the Fates are against them. The minister of civilization preaches from the railway car and the telegraph.[1]

Joseph Chamberlain, a friend and client but not a relation of John Henry Chamberlain's, expressed a milder form of the same annoyance when, as mayor of Birmingham, he set out to defend his town's machine-made goods against arts and crafts critics. Their complaints were, he said, nothing but "Brummagem Ruskinism, without the genius and eloquence and originality which made self-assertion tolerable and eccentricity enjoyable."[2]

Ruskin, for his part, showered the new cities of the industrial revolution with unrelenting abuse. He usually chose Manchester for emphasis, but Birmingham did as well. It was just as smoky and, with all its small workshops in the metal trades, probably noiser. The very idea of fine art and architecture in such a place seemed impossible.

This opposition had a political side as well. Birmingham, as John Bright once said, was Liberal as the sea was salt. Ruskin was usually perceived as a Tory. When the Liberal Club at Glasgow University put forward John Bright as their candidate for the lord rectorship, the Conservative Club promptly asked Ruskin if they might advance his name. He replied that he held opinions concerning lands and rents that the Conservative Club would be far from sanctioning and said in a subsequent letter to the Glasgow Liberal Club that he cared no more for Disraeli and Gladstone than for two old bagpipes operated by steam. Nevertheless, Ruskin's respect for hierarchy and his dislike of equality and electoral reform made him define himself in *Praeterita* as "a violent Tory of the old school" (35.13), and he was constant in his antipathy toward Liberalism. He defined it as "the squinting leading the squinting (27.180) and said he hated it as he did Beelzebub. A Tory only in a paradoxical sense, Ruskin most emphatically declared himself an "illiberal" (27.14).

This contrast between Ruskin and Liberalism can be related to the alignment that emerged in the 1850s between Toryism and Gothic on the one hand and Liberalism and the Italian style on the other. The clergymen who studied ecclesiology also tended to be passionate Tories, and Lord John Manners, Scott's chief defender in Parliament, had been a leader of the Young England movement. Thus the Gothicists tended to be allied with a political cause, regardless of the wishes of individual architects among them. It is doubtful that E. W. Godwin greatly cared which party governed Northampton, but, as the *Building News* observed, his victory in the Town Hall competition was a result of the connection that many people made between Gothic architecture and conservatism. It complained of a tendency to make art parties coincide with political parties:

> The battle of the styles has spread into fields which its stoutest knights never dreamt of. So long as the "octogenarian jocular" is at the head of the Government, the country is pledged to a Palmerston edition of Palladio as the style for all public works and this mongrel Anglo-Italian style can count its supporters on the Whig side of the House of Commons as accurately as if it were a question of the extension of the suffrage or a vote of censure on the Lord Chancellor. . . . It is well known in Northampton that the Conservative majority of the Town Council obtained for the town a "Gothic" Hotel de Ville. It is equally well known that had the Liberals been in a majority a "Classic" hall would have been built.[3]

The evil was dissolving even before the *Building News* protested. Just as Unitarians had adopted the style of the Ecclesiologists, so Liberals accepted Gothic. The Bradford Exchange is an example. But Chamberlain did more than simply design Gothic buildings for Liberal clients. He employed Ruskinian Gothic as an essential instrument of the Liberal social program and made this synthesis the foundation of his career.

I

Chamberlain was born on June 26, 1831, in Leicester, where his father was minister to a congregation of Calvinistic Baptists. He was articled to a local architect named Goddard and then spent an interval of study in London. In 1856, after a journey to Italy and an abortive attempt to set up practice in his native Leicester, he decided to try Birmingham where he had some wealthy relatives. Years later, writing in the *Building News*, he quoted a letter of Pugin's: "I went to Oxford through Birmingham, the most hateful of all hateful places. A town of Greek buildings, smoky chimneys, low radicalism and dissent."[4] Chamberlain was a radical and a dissenter, but must have otherwise agreed with this assessment. Among the town's impressive buildings were the Birmingham Banking Company, with its free-standing Corinthian columns, the Curzon Street Goods Station, with its giant Ionic portico, and the Birmingham Town Hall, a copy of the Temple of Castor and Pollux in the Roman Forum. These classic buildings maintained their pomp amid crumbling rookeries and tangled, unpaved streets. When Prince Albert visited the city in 1855, the *Builder* noted that "every place on that occasion was positively flooded with liquid slimy mud: the air itself was foul, and the thousands who thronged the streets must have been literally steeped in mud."[5] The pleasantest feature of nineteenth-century Birmingham was surely the nearby suburb of Edgbaston, where topiary and stucco gave relief from the rigors of the town.

Chamberlain was already a fervent admirer of Ruskin when he arrived in Birmingham. The first expression of his enthusiasm came in 1852 when he received a medal from the RIBA for an essay entitled "On the Introduction of Colour, including Painting in Fresco, to promote or heighten the effect of architectural composition generally." Here he argued for polychromy, defending Ruskin's view that colour should be treated as something distinct from form.[6] Most of Chamberlain's other writings of the 1850s show him adopting and expanding Ruskin's arguments. He inveighs against the Greek Revival and Renaissance styles. He denounces the deceptive use of materials. He delights in ornament, insisting that it can never be supplied by machine but only by the constantly varying touch of the craftsman. He insists that the minor arts languish when divorced from architecture, and, though he never pursued the unity of the arts as Burges and Godwin did, he paid lip service to the ideal that an architect should also be a painter and sculptor.

Chamberlain inaugurated his career in Birmingham with two notable buildings: a shop in Union Street for his uncle's firm of Eld & Chamberlain and a house in Edgbaston for Mr. Eld. The house (fig. 90), is the more picturesquely irregular of the two buildings, with a large, gabled porch of the kind that Ruskin had recommended in his Edinburgh lectures as symbolic of domestic good feeling. Chamberlain had argued in his 1852 essay that broad surfaces should be treated simply and that vivid, sparkling, or contrasted colors should be reserved for smaller parts. Thus the brightest color effects in Mr. Eld's house are in the geometrical tile mosaics that fill the arch heads (fig. 91). The store (fig. 92) is more compact, as befits its urban setting. Its principal facade is almost square. Chamberlain seems to have associated himself at this early point in his career with those architects who combined aggressive modernity with polychromatic brickwork. His designs were praised in the *Builder* alongside those of Charles Gray, and his Union Street store was illustrated in Thomas Harris's *Specimens of Victorian Architecture*. From the point of view of such men as Burges and Godwin, Chamberlain had gotten himself entangled on the wrong side of the Gothic Revival.

It was the popular side, however, and we may wonder why these two buildings did not at once launch a successful career. The answer seems to be that Chamberlain was a pioneer in a cause that very soon became a craze. If Ruskinism was only a matter of polychromy and Italian Gothic

Fig. 90.   House for
Mr. Eld, Birmingham. John
Henry Chamberlain. Photo:
author.

Fig. 91.   House for Mr.
Eld, mosaic decoration.
Photo: author.

Fig. 92.   Store for Eld & Chamberlain. John Henry Chamberlain. Thomas Harris,
Examples of the Architecture of the Victorian Age (1862).

details, then anybody could do it. By February 1863 the *Builder* noted that
Birmingham architects were running wild after the colored-brick style. It
mentioned in particular a Lombardo-Gothic house by Hubert Bland in
Great Hampton Street and a grocer's shop modeled after Orcagna's loggia
on the Piazza Vecchia. Chamberlain found some work to do. He designed a
Giottesque chimney for the local waterworks and performed some tasks for
Lord Lyttleton, but commissions were few. In 1864, when Lord Lyttleton
offered a chance to design a cathedral in Christ Church, New Zealand,
Chamberlain almost emigrated. If he finally succeeded in his adopted
town, it was because of the position he came to occupy among a remarkably adventuresome group of civic leaders.

Examine any aspect of public life in Birmingham during the 1860s,
1870s, and early 1880s and you will find the same names appearing again

and again on every committee and in support of every major cause. Chamberlain became one of those names, an integral part of Birmingham's interlocking directorate. He took a house in Edgbaston, where he met other rising young men—including the future leader of the Birmingham Liberals, Joseph Chamberlain. Both were active in the Birmingham and Edgbaston Debating Society. On January 30, 1861, John Henry Chamberlain, along with Samuel Timmins and William Kenrick, argued the negative and Joseph Chamberlain the positive on the proposition that "the works of the English novelists since the days of Scott are superior to those of their predecessors." John Henry was president of the society in 1861–1862 and was succeeded the next year by Joseph.[7] The young architect also entered into a partnership with an engineer named William Harris. It lasted only a short time, but bore fruit later when Harris became one of Joseph Chamberlain's chief political lieutenants and organizer of the Liberal caucus.

Throughout the 1860s we find Chamberlain extending the sphere of his civic life. He joined George Dawson and Samuel Timmins in campaigning for free public libraries, and he served on the committee to establish a Shakespeare Library. He was honorary secretary of the Birmingham Archeological Association and vice-president of the Royal Society of Arts. As an architect, he designed the Paradise Street extension of E. M. Barry's Birmingham and Midland Institute in a Gothic style. As an up-and-coming civic leader, he revitalized the institute's operations, making it the town's center for artisans' education. In 1859 he lectured there himself on Pre-Raphaelitism in painting, sculpture, and architecture, and in 1865 he invited a Dr. Hodgson to speak on "Mr. Ruskin's Political Economy." He also encouraged his friends to share his aesthetic interests. Thus the 1867 annual meeting of the Birmingham Architectural Society featured not only Chamberlain as president but also his former partner William Harris as vice-president and such associates as Samuel Timmins and John Thackeray Bunce (editor of the *Birmingham Daily Post*) as honorary members. Chamberlain became, as one of his obituaries put it, "a Liberal of the Liberals"[8] and was never happier than when officiating at some political meeting. Yet he constantly proclaimed himself a Ruskinian, citing Ruskin constantly in public lectures, exhibiting his collection of Ruskin's books (fig. 93), and serving as trustee of the Guild of St. George. Near the end of his life he was elected a councilman. The *Times* report on his funeral in October 1883 indicates the remarkable place he had come to hold in his adopted city:

> The funeral procession comprised two sections, one starting from the residence of the deceased, consisting of immediate friends and mourners, and the other and larger section, which was marshalled at the Council-House under the direction of the Mayor, composed of members of the Town Council, the local

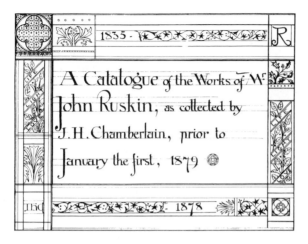

Fig. 93. *Title page.*
A Catalogue of the
Works of Mr. John
Ruskin (1878). *Man-
chester City Council:
Cultural Services
Department.*

magistrates, the School Board, the Committee of the Midland Institute, the
Royal Society of Arts, the School of Art, and Architectural Association, and
other public bodies with which the late Mr. J. H. Chamberlain had been connected. The streets along which the procession passed were crowded, and
closed shops, drawn blinds, and flags half-mast testified in many places to the
high esteem in which the late Mr. Chamberlain was held.[9]

This gives a remarkable picture of the corporate life of Birmingham's elite
and clearly shows that Chamberlain was near the heart of it.

But Chamberlain gained more from the Birmingham Liberals than
simply a network of organizations and a set of influential friends. He acquired a social philosophy known as the Municipal Gospel or the Civic
Gospel. Its most eloquent spokesmen were ministers: George Dawson
(originally Baptist but later nondenominational), H. W. Crosskey (Unitarian), Charles Vince (Baptist), and R. W. Dale (Congregationalist).
Chamberlain joined Dawson's Church of the Savior and was on friendly
terms with the others. From them he heard an emphasis on the promise of
urban life that provided a counterweight to Ruskin's passionate despair. "A
town," Dawson said, "is a solemn organism through which shall flow, in
which shall be shaped, all the highest, loftiest, and truest ends of man's
moral nature."[10] R. W. Dale expressed the century's most un-Ruskinian
sentiment when he admitted, after a visit to Lake Lucerne, that it did not
make him "feel half the thrill I have sometimes felt when I have looked
down on the smokey streets of Birmingham from the railways as I have
returned to work from a holiday."[11]

Dawson, Crosskey, Vince, and Dale preached the redemption of urban
life, and their congregations carried it into practice. Dale, recollecting

those exciting days after death had taken some friends and the Unionist split had divided others, invoked their special mixture of camaraderie and idealism. "The time was," he recalled, "when I used to have a smoke with [Joseph Chamberlain] and John Henry Chamberlain and Timmins and the rest as often as twice or three times a week. . . . In those days the Liberal party in Birmingham was in many respects like a secular church." [12] Certainly this group of friends expressed their faith with the true fervor. They brought the water and gas works under municipal control. They campaigned for free public libraries and mounted a major crusade for free, nondenominational schools. They passed a new building code and improved the town's sanitation. They founded an art gallery and an art school. They embarked on a major slum clearance scheme and drove a new street through the heart of town. Above all, they built. Not surprisingly, there was a great deal of work available for a well-connected architect. Chamberlain extended Barry's Central Reference Library in a Lombardic style, redecorated the interior of the Town Hall in a classical manner to harmonize with the Greek Revival exterior, and designed many of the new branch libraries. He designed private homes for many leading citizens, including Highbury for Joseph Chamberlain and The Grove for William Kenrick. He designed for the town corporation, producing waterworks, pumping stations, hospitals, baths, a dispensary, a lunatic asylum, a school of art, and thirty board schools. He did this by uniting his Ruskinism with the Civic Gospel.

II

Chamberlain's architectural philosophy can be found in his *Introductory Lecture on the Offices and Duties of Architecture* (1858) and in the series of eight papers on "Gothic Architecture and Art" that he contributed to the *American Architect and Builder's Monthly* in 1870 and 1871.

His first principle was what he called the Law of Compensation: an architect must replace in his own way all the natural beauty that the city dweller has lost. [13] He does this, Chamberlain said in 1858, by studying nature, getting her lessons by heart, and by at last weaving them into his building until "it speaks out truths drawn from the light and darkness, from the river and the cloud, from the rock and field and tree." [14] A hostile critic at once complained that this "outstrips by far the Oxford Graduate," [15] but it was the faith that Chamberlain lived by. "If in respect to ornament," he told an audience in 1879, "they could not go to nature and say 'the idea of this ornament is derived from nature,' or if on the contrary they could say 'it is in direct opposition to the teaching of nature,' then they might be sure it was not ornament, it was not to be considered as ornament, and was most probably a monstrosity."[16]

Chamberlain's second principle is that the architect has a direct and rather prosaic social responsibility. Most of the mid-Victorian architects who felt Ruskin's influence pursued the architectural plums. It is difficult to imagine any of the men described in earlier chapters designing Peabody estates or concerning themselves with sanitation in areas of decaying tenements. Chamberlain, by contrast, gave such matters careful thought. His *Introductory Lecture,* for example, contains a very clear-eyed passage on incest—the very common result of raising large families in a single room. "Perhaps some may think or say that dealing with these things is foreign to the office of Architecture," Chamberlain writes, "but indeed with these things lies the very chief concern of Architecture."[17]

Chamberlain's third principle is that architecture testifies to the moral worth of the culture that produced it. In its lowest form, this produces only ostentatious self-display. At a higher level, it supports Joseph Chamberlain's strategy of using impressive architecture to enhance the prestige of the municipal corporation. At its highest level, it produces John Henry Chamberlain's Ruskinian view that "the art of any nation is the measure of that nation's capacity for admiration and power of expression."[18] Once this claim was accepted, the task of remaking the nineteenth-century urban environment became a compelling necessity. H. W. Crosskey, minister of the Unitarian church that Joseph Chamberlain attended (and that John Henry Chamberlain attended after George Dawson's death), described members of the town council "dwelling on the glories of Florence, and of the other cities of Italy in the Middle Ages" and "dreaming that Birmingham too might become the home of a noble literature and art."[19] Chamberlain's close friend John Thackeray Bunce pursued this imperative in a remarkable article, "Art in the Community," for the September 1877 issue of the *Fortnightly Review.* He adopted very nearly the entire Ruskinian program, not only quoting at length from *The Stones of Venice* and urging the claims of Gothic but also encouraging stone carvers to portray such subjects as the anti–Corn Law agitation and the struggle for the Reform Bill.

Amid these signs of loyal discipleship, there is one Ruskinian doctrine that Chamberlain pauses over and eventually rejects. That is the distinction between building and architecture. As we have seen at the beginning of chapter 5, Ruskin begins both *The Seven Lamps* and *The Stones of Venice* by defining architectural beauty as something that is added to constructional necessity. To many mid-Victorians these passages sounded just right. Chamberlain was one of the first among Ruskin's admirers to find them puzzling.

His discontent did not at first break out into open disagreement. In his 1858 "Inaugural Lecture" he seems to accept Ruskin's distinction, but not until he has explained it at length and, in effect, explained it away. He begins by quoting Ruskin's words in *The Seven Lamps:*

> Let us therefore confine the name [of architecture] to that art which taking up and admitting as conditions of its working the necessities and common uses of the building, impresses on its form certain characters venerable or beautiful, but otherwise unnecessary. Thus I suppose no one would call the laws architectural which determine the height of a breastwork or the position of a bastion. But if to the stone facing of that bastion be added an unnecessary feature, as a cable moulding, *that* is Architecture. (8.29)

But from this, Chamberlain worries, "the ordinary reader is in danger of obtaining the impression . . . that to change building into Architecture nothing more is necessary than to add ornamental features to its own natural ugliness."[20] He sets out to clarify the subject by taking the example of a low wall such as might be used to enclose a garden. To protect it from the wet, it is necessary to top it off with a row of wide coping stones, their edge projecting a few inches over the face of the wall to throw off the rain. The resulting form has an ugliness that cannot be redeemed by the addition of a cable molding. The challenge is to introduce beauty into the coping itself by shaping it into beautiful forms of varying light and shade. The architect must begin his work by drawing grace out of utilitarian forms. Only when this basic work is completed may he "knit the framework of his roofs together with the flowers of the forest, and people the deep shadows of his doorways with the likenesses of the great and noble, or adorn them with the carved records of deeds of worth and heroism."[21] Chamberlain has replaced Ruskin's sharp distinction between building and architecture with a graded continuity. And this, he says, is what Ruskin really means.

It may be, but Chamberlain seems dissatisfied with this account of his master's teaching, and whenever he returns to the subject, as he quite regularly does, he sounds more like Pugin or Viollet-de-Duc than like Ruskin. In 1860 he told the Birmingham Archeological Association that "all Gothic sculpture commenced in the decoration of the constructional features of the building."[22] In 1863 he repeated that "the ornamentation must spring out of the original construction."[23] In 1870 he insisted that architectural beauty "springs from necessity, and is at least based on usefulness."[24] In 1879, thirty years after its publication, Chamberlain reevaluated *The Seven Lamps.* He discussed the book very thoroughly, restating its formulations and praising its influence. The distinction between building and architecture, however, received short shrift. It was an idea, he said, which he "ventured to contest."[25]

What caused this shift? Perhaps it was merely an architect's love for the practical side of his work, but there is another possibility as well. Throughout his career Chamberlain followed Ruskin's principle that architecture should reflect the laws and forms of nature. During the 1860s he encountered views of nature that were significantly different from Ruskin's.

The crucial element was the appearance of Darwin's *Origin of Species* in 1859. Where Ruskin saw in nature a clear separation between beauty and utility, evolutionary biology implied that what man perceives as beauty had originally an entirely practical function.

Ruskin's view is clearest in the second volume of *Modern Painters* (1846), where he cites the examples of the movement of an ostrich and the action of a shark's dorsal fin. Both appear beautiful so long as we delight in their appearance of energy. Both are drained of beauty as soon as we conceive of the skeletal frame within and "substitute in our thoughts the neatness of mechanical contrivance for the pleasure of the animal" (4.154). "It is by a beautiful ordinance of the Creator," Ruskin tells us, "that all these mechanisms are concealed from sight, though open to investigation; and that in all which is outwardly manifested, we seem to see His presence rather than his workmanship, and the mysterious breath of life rather than the adaptation of matter" (4.155).

In the 1860s Chamberlain encountered a different view of nature in the work of "such great and good men as Charles Darwin, and Alfred Wallace, and William Bates."[26] Their influence can be seen in his lectures entitled "Gothic Architecture and Art" when he pauses to illustrate a point by describing some baby flatfish that he had observed at the seashore. They lay at the bottom of the water, just even with the sand.

> I suppose most persons, if asked what the color of sea-sand is, would say, in an indefinite and vague manner, that it was a sort of yellowish-brown; and yet it is full of strange and subtle and various shades of colour—brown, and gold, and purple, flecked with white, and with every colour and shade seen to perfection, with the clear, shallow water running smoothly over it. Now, these little fish, lying in their natural position, flat upon the sand, were not in any way to be distinguished from the sand around them. . . . They were mottled with brown, and gold, and purple, with little flecks of white here and there, and looked like living sand.[27]

The explanation of the color of the flatfish—that this loveliness results directly from a strictly utilitarian need for camouflage—is wholly at variance with Ruskin's habits of thought. Chamberlain concludes that nature shows us "the law of necessity in perfect combination with that of beauty."[28] Not surprisingly, many of his lectures in the "Gothic Art and Architecture" series are devoted to showing how the loveliest forms of architecture arise out of the neatness of mechanical contrivance. Thus Chamberlain, though in most respects a self-consciously faithful disciple of Ruskin, was also one of the first to reevaluate his teachings in light of the new evolutionary biology. He would not be the last.

III

A good deal of Chamberlain's work still stands. Highbury, the impressive home he designed for Joseph Chamberlain, is carefully preserved. His Shakespeare Memorial Room has been restored. A room from The Grove, his home for William Kenrick, has been installed in the Victoria and Albert Museum. The Birmingham School of Art, with its magnificent terra-cotta rose designed by Chamberlain and executed by Samuel Barfield, is still standing. The town square still contains the memorial fountain that John Henry Chamberlain designed for Joseph Chamberlain. (A monument for George Dawson, with a Gothic canopy by Chamberlain, has been removed.) Two aspects of Chamberlain's work should be discussed here as showing both the strengths and limitations of his Liberal idealism. They are his board schools and his plan for the Civic Improvement Scheme.

The board schools are rightly listed among the Birmingham Liberals' proudest achievements. The struggle for them occupied much of their energies during the 1860s and 1870s, and it was Joseph Chamberlain's leadership of the National Education League that first made him a national figure. The struggle was between the Anglicans and the Catholics, who favored voluntary schools associated with religious bodies, and the Liberals and Dissenters, who advocated compulsory education without religious instruction. Forster's Education Act of 1870 was by no means a complete victory for the Liberals since it gave the new board schools the role of filling in the gaps in the voluntary system, but it did allow each municipality to elect a school board, levy taxes to support the new schools, and require attendance of children between five and thirteen. Birmingham at once set to work, and the first school board was elected on November 28, 1870. Ironically, the Tories turned the complicated system of staggered voting to their advantage and won eight of the fifteen seats. The Liberals managed to elect their leaders—Joseph Chamberlain, George Dawson, and R. W. Dale—and in the next election of 1873 they swept the field. John Henry Chamberlain was appointed architect to the board from the beginning, and his work for it constitutes a major part of his output. Five schools date from 1873, two from 1874, three from 1875, six from 1876, six from 1877, and nine more were built during the following six years.

The probable appearance of the schools had been a subject of controversy during the campaigns of the 1860s. Church schools were built in a style hallowed by religious and historical associations, and they had benefited from the ecclesiological movement. The board schools, accommodating unprecedented large numbers at a cost acceptable to the ratepayers, might well have been cheap and plain. Sebastian Evans, a Birmingham Tory, had forseen this possibility in a nightmare vision:

> A dismal house which I knew was a school . . .
> The one word "League" grim lettered in black.
> 'Twas the dismallest house the world ever saw
> Where to pray to God was to break the law.[29]

In London E. R. Robson turned to the newly popular Queen Anne style to meet this challenge. Chamberlain, by contrast, went ahead with the style he had forged in the previous decades.

The law of Compensation guided both siting and design of the board schools; each was designed to bring light, fresh air, and beauty to a gritty urban environment. Chamberlain's typical school (fig. 94) was a gabled structure built of red brick with terra-cotta ornament used to add texture and color. Borrowings from Italian Gothic had dropped out of Chamberlain's work and been replaced by an interest in the steep roofs, free planning, and more subdued richness of English medieval building. Gables and towers were grouped to yield a varied, romantic outline, and ornamental timberwork was often used in the upper stories. Chamberlain used as much in the way of decorative ironwork, terra-cotta plaques, glazed tiles, and stained-glass windows as the budget could possibly afford.

Each school was carefully planned to provide both sanitation and beauty. The classrooms were spacious and lit by tall windows. The towers, often the most striking architectural features of the school, illustrate Chamberlain's dual interests in sanitation and beauty. In his first school he had used only a simple ventilating turret on the roof and had found it to be excessively heavy, aesthetically unpleasing, and ineffective in removing bad air. In subsequent schools he solved this problem by placing the turret over the staircase. In effect, he heightened the roof of the staircase to form an air chamber. The tower that grows out of this arrangement is a striking confirmation of Chamberlain's view that beauty is based on necessity. Viewed from within, it is a means of ventilation. Viewed from without, and seen amid the long unlovely streets of nineteenth-century row housing, each tower gives picturesque variety and a touch of romance.

Fig. 94. Birmingham Board School, Dixon Road. John Henry Chamberlain. Photo: author.

The 1880s saw increasing complaints against Chamberlain's monopoly of municipal commissions. The practice of the town council was to allow each of the committees instructed by it to choose its own architect. One member of the council complained that, "owing to the power possessed by Mr. J. H. Chamberlain," this system simply amounted to "placing the thing in Mr. J. H. Chamberlain's hands." The mayor blandly replied that "whatever monopoly Messrs. Martin & Chamberlain enjoyed, it was one which had been earned by merit and genius alone."[30] In 1883, a few months before Chamberlain's death, a member of the school board complained that in the thirteen years of its existence, the board had used only one architectural firm: "It was not necesssary for the erection of more schools that they should have the magic wand of Mr. J. H. Chamberlain. The existing schools impressed him with a sense of grim monotony, representing a gloomy craze. The board might build another of the same leaden or he might say clayey aspect, but he did not hope to see it." He went on to complain that among his fellow townspeople the firm of Martin and Chamberlain "was supposed to be almost inspired."[31] Chamberlain was defended by William Kenrick and H. W. Crosskey, who not only praised the appearance of the schools but also pointed out that the firm had accepted very low remuneration and had paid costs out of pocket.

Certainly the schools were highly regarded. Joseph Chamberlain told a graduating class of the school of design that when he first came to Birmingham "the erection of such buildings as their board schools . . . would have been impossible," and he derided those unwilling to spend money on ornament and beauty in public buildings as "almost extinct fossils . . . the megatheria, the great beasts of Birmingham."[32] Liberal organizers used the schools to enhance their party's prestige. A Birmingham Tory, denouncing the electioneering methods of the Liberal caucus in the *National Review*, described its typical methods:

> The working man is "got at." His trading association (such as that of the Carpenters and Joiners) is somehow made subservient to Caucus action. A meeting of the association, *eo nomine*, is called, and emissaries of the Caucus deliver addresses. We were once present at one of these meetings, held, as usual, at a Board School, and it may be taken as a sample of others. Mr. Schnadhorst addressed it. He cleverly identified himself with those he was addressing, pointing out how delightful a thing it was that "we" should have a beautiful building like that as "our" own property, in which to meet and discuss, in a friendly way, matters of public interest. He told them how Lord Randolph Churchill had called them "the mob, the scum, the dregs."[33]

More high-minded critics were equally enthusiastic. J. M. D. Meiclejohn, professor of education at the University of Saint Andrews, praised their beauty, solidity, and efficient arrangement for instruction, adding that "the supply of fresh warmed air, with always new stores of oxygen, seems all that one could wish.[34] The *Pall Mall Gazette* observed in 1894 that "in Birmingham you may generally recognize a board school by its being the best building in the neighbourhood."[35]

The Civic Improvement Scheme requires a more complicated evaluation and suggests some of the limitations of Birmingham Liberalism. In his *Introductory Lecture* of 1858, Chamberlain had complained bitterly about Birmingham's housing for the poor. "Out of the habitual presence of foulness and dirt," he warned, "and the habitual, compulsory disregard of decency, physical and moral debasement has ever sprung and will ever continue to spring." He had urged that "some power [be] authorized to regulate town building that health and life might be in some measure protected."[36]

The Artisans' Dwelling Act of 1875 gave Chamberlain the power he wanted, and the Civic Improvement Scheme was its result. Mayor Joseph Chamberlain worked out the plan among his friends in what he called "the Smokerei-and-Talkerie" before it was ever presented to the town council; it may be assumed that John Henry Chamberlain was a participant in these sessions. Once the plan was approved, it was the firm of Martin and Chamberlain, rather than the borough surveyor, that was asked to lay out the new streets.

The plan was to accomplish several things simultaneously. Most dramatically, it was to beautify the town by tearing down more than forty acres of slums. In addition, it would ventilate the town core by driving a wide new street through the middle of it. The new thoroughfare, eventually known as Corporation Street, would unite the best part of town with the area of cleared rookeries, thus allowing the better sections to expand into the cleared areas. Another feature was that the municipal corporation, instead of at once reselling that portion of the area it had acquired, would retain the freehold and reap a profit when the leases fell due in eighty years. Finally, the scheme would replace approximately five hundred houses containing nine thousand people with an area of multistory housing that would house twice that number. The new homes would be larger and loftier than anything they replaced, with abundant fresh water and the best sanitary devices.

The scheme was in some respects a stunning success, but in providing housing for Birmingham's poor it was very nearly a complete failure. This was a serious matter, for Joseph Chamberlain could never have initiated the plan under the Artisans' Dwelling Act had he not promised to provide artisans' dwellings. Flats had been included in the original plans, but they were never built. In 1885 Joseph Chamberlain found himself explaining this failure to the Royal Commission on the Housing of the Working Classes. His version was that the displaced poor had found little difficulty in locating new dwellings and that there was really no significant overcrowding of population in Birmingham. The members of the commission clearly had trouble believing this, and Chamberlain offered another explanation. Once the land had been cleared for workers' dwellings, the municipal corporation had been unable to find anyone to build them. Asked if he would favor the corporation itself building and managing new housing, he replied that "if we do so, we must at once interfere with private enterprise."[37] It is not surprising that this should mark the outer limit of Joseph Chamberlain's Liberalism. It is sad, however, that John Henry Chamberlain should not have had the opportunity to join Octavia Hill as one of the few to translate Ruskin's moral concern with working-class housing into actual bricks and mortar.

IV

What did Ruskin think of his Birmingham disciple? He certainly knew of his existence for Chamberlain was an early and enthusiastic member of the

Guild of Saint George. Chamberlain's obituary in the *Building News* records that he "delivered many lectures and addresses on its behalf, organizing a local branch of the Guild to advance the principles set forth in *Fors Clavigera.*"[38] In 1871 George Baker, one of John Henry Chamberlain's friends and Joseph Chamberlain's successor as mayor of Birmingham, donated several acres of land to start the guild's work. Chamberlain became one of the cotrustees of the guild. It is a remarkable fact that some leading citizens of a town that owed its prosperity to coal, steam, and iron should have devoted themselves to a utopian organization that would not countenance any source of energy more mechanized than windmills. One would expect that Ruskin would have seized this opportunity and that something noteworthy would have resulted.

The project in which these disparate forces might have combined was the establishment of a Saint George's Museum, which would be a repository for paintings and architectural records as well as an instrument for the regeneration of England. The building was to be designed not by Chamberlain himself but by a Mr. Doubleday, a younger member of the firm. Ruskin saw Doubleday's proposals in 1877 and wrote to Henry Swan: "I have seen Mr. Doubleday's work here—it is sound and good—but won't do for us, unless perhaps in plan of walls. But I am minded to do it all pretty nearly ourselves."[39] This probably means that the plans were too expensive, though it is also possible that Doubleday—whose work at this stage of his career (fig. 95) was close to that of Chamberlain—may have included too much of the terra-cotta, iron, and tile decoration that Ruskin was now referring to as architect's jobbery. That possibility is strengthened by Ruskin's statement on September 11 that he wanted no exhibition, "outside or inside, of any modern ornamental work whatever." Ruskin changed his mind about this, however, when he encountered a young Sheffield grinder named Benjamin Creswick who showed a remarkable talent for carving (and who later became modeling master at the Birmingham School of Art). Ruskin now announced that the museum could be built "St. Mark's way,—brick with marble casing, so I can get my inner walls built and dry at once, and go on at leisure adding panel by panel of decoration." This was Ruskin's plan as he consulted with Doubleday between 1880 and 1882. On May 13, 1882, Ruskin wrote to Swan: "The plans have come safely, and are very pretty, but entirely inadmissable on our present income. The building is to be as I planned it, and in the simplest shell walls faced with marble, and I will see now sternly to getting it drawn out." Doubleday was still the architect at this point, but for reasons probably connected with Chamberlain's death in 1883, Ruskin was soon consulting with E. R. Robson. All we know about Robson's plan is contained in a brief note in the *Architect*. It reported, without apparent irony, that "from

Fig. 95.   Shops and offices, Coffee House Company, Corporation Street, Birming-ham. William Doubleday. Builder, 1883.

the quantity of glass that was to be used in it, [the museum] seemed to re-call the proposals for a new style of architecture that were heard in the eighteen-fifties."[40] It also reported that only one-tenth the necessary funds could be obtained. In the end, Ruskin gratefully accepted the town of Sheffield's offer of an already existing house at Meersbrook Park.

Quite apart from his comments on Doubleday's plan for the museum, other evidence suggests that Ruskin did not especially care for Chamber-lain's version of Ruskinian architecture. Speaking of Wordsworth's simple schoolroom in 1875, Ruskin predicts that the village authorities, in a fit of vanity and folly, will destroy it and all its sacred associations in order to substitute "a grand piece of Birmingham Gothic" (28.435). There is an-other disparaging reference to Chamberlain's schools in letter 80 of *Fors Clavigera*. In it Ruskin complains that he is visiting Birmingham, that it is raining, and that as he gazes out the window a new board school is block-ing his view of the countryside. So much for the law of compensation. Ruskin's only reference to his admirer by name occurs after the architect's death, when Ruskin asks George Thomson to serve as a trustee of the guild—"in lieu of our lost Mr. Chamberlain" (30.304).

All of this makes Ruskin appear grumpy, naïve, and impractical. He was all of these, but he was also capable of acute insights into his contempo-raries. He never appreciated the virtues of the Birmingham Liberals, but he saw their limits quite accurately. In 1877 he visited the town and met with local members of the guild. He approached the midland metropolis with some unease and was both surprised and delighted by his reception. He felt, he said in *Fors Clavigera*, "like one of Napoleon's troops, taken pris-oner by his mortal enemies, and beginning to apprehend that there was indeed some humanity in Englishmen." Then he adds something that he had not found a way to say politely in conversation:

> in all our debate, I was under this disadvantage, that my Birmingham friends could say to me, with full pleasure and frankness, all that was in their minds; but I could not say, without much fear and pause, what was in mine. Of which unspoken regrets this is the quite initial and final one; that all they showed me, and told me, of good, involved yet the main British modern idea that the mas-ter and his men should belong to two entirely different classes; perhaps loyally related to and assisting each other; but yet,—the one, on the whole living in hardship—the other in ease; the one supported in his dishonourable condition by the hope of labouring through it to the higher one,—the other honourably distinguished by their success, and rejoicing in their escape from a life which must nevertheless be always (as they suppose) led by a thousand to one of the British people. (29.172)

This applies to Chamberlain's career in particular as well as to the ethos of the town in general. Chamberlain admired craftsmanship, deplored "excessive" division of labor, and was justly proud of his mediations between employers and workmen, but he did not challenge either the nature of his industrial society or the subcontracting system of the nineteenth-century building trades. A tension remained between Ruskin and Birmingham, one that not even the most inventive disciple could reconcile.

XII

REVALUATION AND A NEW RUSKINISM

THE first phase of Ruskin's influence began in the 1850s with the effort to return to Gothic in its purest, most highly developed form and to continue it as if it had never declined. The second phase began in the early 1870s when the interest in Gothic purity was abruptly abandoned. J. J. Stevenson's Red House (1871) and Norman Shaw's New Zealand Chambers (1872) initiated what was called the Queen Anne Revival. Seddon and Burges campaigned against the new trend, but by 1883 even such a fervent Gothicist as Alfred Waterhouse conceded defeat:

> They [had] hoped that the Gothic revival would be more than a mere revival—that it would turn from a revival into a growth, that they would shortly see the spirit and requirements of the nineteenth century embodied in the dress of the twelfth and thirteenth centuries. But when, as it appeared, they were on the eve of this much to be desired consummation, fickle fashion declared herself tired of medievalism. She called for something else and had it still in what she was pleased to call the style of Queen Anne.[1]

The term itself is unduly restrictive. What it really signifies is a new interest in styles that were once scorned as impure or debased. Models were now found in the vernacular buildings of Kent and Sussex, in the once detestable perpendicular, in "debased" Jacobean, and even in the simple terrace houses of the Georgian period.

The new movement was led by young men who had been trained in the offices of George Gilbert Scott and G. E. Street. When George Cavendish Bentinck assailed Pugin and Ruskin in 1877,[2] demanding a return to the style of Inigo Jones and Christopher Wren, the *Building News* could only observe that: "he is striking the fatal blow when it is too late. Gothicism is already departing from among some of its own adherents."[3] The free classic styles, J. J. Stevenson told the Architectural Association, were "practised by architects who, not long ago, were such exclusive admirers of Gothic art that they could sympathize with Mr. Ruskin's denunciation of these styles as the foul tide of the Renaissance."[4]

Clearly a reaction against the Gothic Revival required a critique of Ruskin. The revaluation that took place in the 1870s and early 1880s can be described in two aspects. In the first, Ruskin's ideas on architecture were discussed and either rejected or reinterpreted. In the second, his ideas on restoration, which had seemed quixotic in the 1850s and 1860s, were given practical application.

I

There were two points on which all the rebels agreed: the chief monuments of the Gothic Revival were vulgar and overblown, and the true poetry of architecture was to be found in England rather than in Italian Gothic. These views found their earliest manifestation in the circle around William Morris and Philip Webb.

It is a fallacy of college surveys to present these men as straightforward disciples who simply carried Ruskin's views into practice. It is easy to see how this overly simplified view should have arisen. Both Morris and Webb were introduced to the Gothic Revival at a time when enthusiasm for rich decoration and Italian Gothic were still new and exciting. Both worked in G. E. Street's office—Morris briefly in 1856 and Webb from 1854 to 1859. Both were in an excellent position to follow the progress of the Oxford Museum, and Morris gained his first practical experience in decorating a building at Woodward's Oxford Union. Morris's prose works of 1856—"The Story of an Unknown Church" and "Shadows of Amiens"—treat architecture almost entirely in terms of ornament and follow Ruskin in assuming that the master mason who carved the portals on a Gothic cathedral would also have been its architect. Webb attended Ruskin's 1857 lecture entitled "The Use of Imagination in Architectural Design" at the Architectural Association. Everything that is known about Morris's and Webb's careers in the 1850s suggests that they would have shared—that their enthusiasm may even have helped inspire—Street's faith that three-quarters of the poetry of architecture lies in its minor details.

Ruskin praised Morris in public, and though his only references to Webb occur in private letters, they are very favorable. In 1867 Ruskin recommended Webb to a potential client as an architect "who will give you perfectly sound and noble work for absolutely just price";[5] a year later Ruskin described Webb as "the only man thoroughly cognizant with Gothic architecture [or] all that is original and beautiful."[6] Morris and Webb responded in kind. W. R. Lethaby, quoting Webb dissenting from one of Ruskin's opinions, added that "like Morris, he would never allow anyone else to make such remarks without protest."[7] There is an ultimate sense in which Morris and Webb were indeed Ruskin's disciples, but they were also, simultaneously, major figures in the late Victorian reinterpretation of Ruskinism.

Unfortunately, the chronology of their changing opinions is obscure. Webb avoided lecturing in public, and Morris did not begin doing so until 1877. Well before that, it would appear, the Morris group had recognized an unresolvable conflict between the spirit of Gothic and that of the age. And it was specifically the Ruskinian architecture of the mid-nineteenth century that they turned against.

Warrington Taylor, the Morris firm's financial manager until his early death in 1870, provides the first indication of their views. A commercial civilization, he wrote, creates "a nervous, unsettled irritability, excessively fatiguing, and, to divert themselves from this, men seek excitement." The architectural response to this craving for sensation is "flash Gothic,"[8] with its showy display of Italian and French details. One might guess from this that Taylor was denouncing the work of such men as Bassett Keeling, but an 1862 letter to E. R. Robson makes it clear that he was really referring to Burges and Seddon.

In place of the self-conscious foreignism of the mid-Victorians, the Morris circle wanted a return to "the poetry at that very insular littleness of English nature."[9] When Morris visited Manchester, he found Waterhouse's Assize Courts to be "a dreary pretentious heap of buildings . . . built in a Gothic which is an insult to the memory of our forefathers."[10] This opinion dates from 1888, but it would have been the same ten or twenty years earlier.

Influential as the Morris group ultimately was, however, they had comparatively little immediate impact on public debate. John T. Emmett, who matters very little to posterity, had a much more dramatic impact on architectural discussion during the early seventies.

Emmett was an unsuccessful architect whose initial enthusiasm for the Gothic Revival gave way to an intense and bitter disillusion.[11] His articles in the *Quarterly Review* contained denunciations of his contemporaries that have never been surpassed. He called Saint James-the-Less a baby house, compared the speckled walls at All Saints', Margaret Street, to a nursery toy, and mocked the childish, half-exotic work at the Oxford Museum. At Scott's Saint Pancras's, then still rising in London, he said: "here the 'public taste' has been exactly suited, and every kind of architectural decoration has been made thoroughly common and unclean."[12] Because the *Quarterly* had great prestige, and because Emmett was rhetorically murderous, the architectural profession reacted with panic. Long extracts from Emmett's articles filled the architectural press; his claims were examined in leading articles; and the RIBA, which usually avoided controversy, devoted not one but two meetings to a refutation of this assault on the proudest achievements of the profession.

J. J. Stevenson was the most prominent of those who answered Emmett's strictures; it is therefore all the more significant that his estimate of the mid-Victorian achievement was nearly as low. And where Emmett only mentions Ruskin once, accusing him of encouraging the profusion of ornament with his lamp of sacrifice, Stevenson was quite firm in blaming Ruskin's influence for at least some of the revival's failures. He opens his book on *House Architecture* (begun in the early 1870s, though not published until 1880) by observing that he lives in a world where "everyone with any pretention to taste knows something about [architecture], has read Ruskin, and considers himself (or herself) a judge." He therefore warns the prospective house builder that Ruskin treats architecture too often from the point of view of Italy rather than of England. "I think some of his views on architecture are open to question," Stevenson says, "and that their practical influence has to some extent been mischievous." Later he records his belief that "confusion and bad art" have been among the results of Ruskin's teachings.[13]

The conviction that Ruskin was in part to blame for the failure of the revival led to a reexamination of some of his key ideas. The one that received the harshest criticism was his identification of architecture with ornament. E. Ingress Bell told members of the Architectural Association that Ruskin was, above all, "the apostle of small things—'details,' in short,"[14] and as proof cited the passage in *The Seven Lamps* about transforming a building into architecture by adding a cable molding. J. J. Stevenson made much the same point when he insisted that a simple arrangement of masses, without any decoration whatever, was enough for architectural beauty. In *House Architecture* he presents a drawing of two towers at Nuremburg (fig. 96) and observes: "Not even such an amount of ornament as a cable moulding is needed, without which Mr. Ruskin thinks a mere utilitarian building, like a fortress, cannot be considered architecture."[15]

This view was soon accepted even by Ruskin's warmest admirers. John Dando Sedding had entered G. E. Street's office in the 1850s when Ruskin's

Fig. 96.   Nuremberg towers. J. J. Stevenson, House Architecture *(1880).*

influence there was at its height. Like many young architectural pupils he was unable to afford *The Seven Lamps* and *The Stones of Venice,* so he borrowed them from Kegan Paul and copied their plates so carefully that Paul said, "he should, in some instances, have scarcely known that they were not the originals."[16] Sedding remained devoted throughout his career to the concept of architecture as a meeting place of all the arts, but by the 1870s he had decisively rejected the idea that the glory of architecture lay in painting and sculpture. "It was Mr. Ruskin," he said, "who first set this fashion of detraction—first launched this theory—since when it has become a perennial platitude that never stales."[17] In an essay entitled "Expression in Architecture," Sedding gives a careful refutation of Ruskin's 1857 lecture "The Use of Imagination in Architectural Design." To the claim that buildings must have figure sculpture to be emotionally expressive, he proposes a simple test: "Knock off all the heads or hurl down all the figures at Amiens and Notre Dame, and how infinitesimal the difference in the general expression of the structure whose lines they enrich!"[18]

Morris and Webb made this an important part of their revision of Ruskinism. Webb wrote to his admirer W. R. Lethaby: "J.R. once held that a building wasn't architecture without sculpture and painting—to me a fallacy on the line of Fergusson. What could have been added to the original N. & S. transept ends of St. Alban's without injury?"[19] Morris told an audience at the Birmingham and Midland Institute in 1884 to "build big and solid and with an eye to strict utility; you will find that will be expressive work enough and will by no means be utilitarian."[20] He maintained on another occasion that the organic life of a building was so interesting and beautiful in itself that it would be a definite pleasure to see a blank wall without any "architectural" features at all so long as it was truly well built. Morris was an ornamentalist, of course, but the products of his craftsmanship appeared inside the building as fabrics, wallpapers, and furniture. "On the outside, one ought to pitch one's note rather low, and try, if one can manage it, to get the houses and buildings to look solid and reasonable, and to impress people with their obvious adaptations to their uses; where they can be made big to make them big, and not to bother about orna-ment."[21] It would become an article of faith among the followers of Morris and Webb that architecture was primarily the art of honest building.

Another basic tenet of the Ruskinian phase of the Gothic Revival was the belief that architectural beauty is an adaptation of the forms com-monest in nature. Attitudes toward this doctrine are more diverse than those toward the theory of ornament. J. J. Stevenson is the harshest critic: "The theory is a total misconception of the whole meaning and use of or-nament in architecture. It is a certain sign of meanness and decay when architectural ornament is a profuse imitation of natural forms."[22] Against Ruskin's emphasis on the curve, Stevenson argues the neoclassical view that straight lines are better suited to the artificial structure of buildings. If this is the case, then Ruskin's complaint that the triglyph has no counter-part in nature is an irrelevancy and his condemnation of the Greek fret becomes equally foolish. Stevenson argues that this pattern actually began in nature as a succession of spirals, but that when the Greeks employed it to ornament buildings they quite rightly reinterpreted their curving proto-type as a series of right angles.

The steady increase in the popularity of cheap, uninspired, and natu-ralistic stone carving added force to Stevenson's views. The protests of Bur-ges and Godwin had carried no weight with the home-buying public, and speculative developers found that they could add a visible touch of distinc-tion to otherwise dull row houses by placing a bit of nature on either side of the front door. In reaction, the condemnations of naturalism in the archi-tectural press became steadily more passionate. Critics often conceded that Ruskin was probably distressed at his own influence, but blamed his doc-trine nonetheless. In 1880 the *Building News* published leaders examin-ing Ruskin's principle that "Art is the expression of man's delight in God's work." By now it probably spoke for the majority of English architects in concluding: "It would not be difficult, in short, to give plausible reasons for reversing Mr. Ruskin's assertion and for avowing that the more closely an architectural style keeps to Nature, the more surely it has arrived at the period of disease and dissolution."[23]

It could be objected that Ruskinian architects quite obviously continued to delight in God's work and that the vines, tendrils, and flowers of Mack-murdo, Voysey, and Baillie Scott are among the glories of architectural decoration. But the key step in the creation of this work was a rejection of the imitative naturalism seen at the Oxford Museum and advocated by George Gilbert Scott.

Once again, Morris is a key figure. Faced with the opposition between

Scott's interpretation of Ruskin and Street's, he chose to develop Street's. Morris fully accepted the need for conventionalization:

> The forms of nature . . . are not used as statements of fact, but as conveying hints of the impressions produced by the facts. And in doing this it is better to sacrifice some of the naturalness of the nature hinted at in detail, in order to get a clearer impression of the idea of the nature. Besides, in most of the surface ornament that we see, the design is repeated mechanically, as in a wall paper, for instance; and this mechanical repetition necessitates a geometrical arrangement of some sort, however skillfully it may be veiled, so that if the designer ties himself to too close an accurate delineation of nature, he will have to limit himself to a small fragment of it repeated over and over again in geometrical order.[24]

In effect, Morris sought a compromise between Ruskin's approach to nature and that of Owen Jones. "Conventionalism," he said, "was compulsory upon the decorator, but the convention must be his own, made so by a thorough understanding of the material worked upon and the subject you are using."[25]

By the end of the 1870s, then, several of Ruskin's admirers had rejected or modified some of his key doctrines. John Dando Sedding went further. He used Ruskinian principles to indict Ruskin's influence.

Like Morris, Sedding was convinced that Gothic required freedom for the craftsman. He maintained that craft traditions survived the change of ornamental vocabulary at the Renaissance and survived, though perhaps in steadily weakening form, right down to the early nineteenth century. Robert Adam, he pointed out, had been able to supply plans and elevations to his workmen with the leading details lightly sketched in and then leave the workmen to do the rest. This was possible because architect and workman shared basic ideas about the nature of good ornament. Robert Adam asked his craftsmen to do something that they knew how to do. The Gothic Revival architect, by contrast, asked his workmen to do something that was altogether strange to them. He thus destroyed the last, weak link in the craft tradition. Not only did the workman have to reach back over several centuries, but he had to imitate the styles of other countries:

> From henceforth you must look no more to the English workshops for the inception of types or evolution of ideas. The old *Téméraire* of English art having been sent to her last home, a bright new Venetian gondola takes her place, and rides proudly out to sea with seven Gothic lamps at her prow, an Oxford graduate and a few able enthusiasts to work the oar, fire off the guns, and take care of the cargo of sketchbooks and romantic literature on board. Naturally the gondola is first attracted to Venice, but as time goes on the taste of the crew changes and you find them flying about in all directions and bringing home

valuable spoils in the shape of numberless new sorts of doors and windows to offer at the feet of a grateful people. And the merit of the new types consists in this, that they are quite unique in England, and that the British workman can-not move a step, as he copies them, without full-sized details of every part.[26]

Sedding is sure than in an ideal state of things "the master builder should be aided by trained craftsmen to whom a symbol, a scratch, a word would be as a seed dropped in fruitful soil."[27] But an architect designing in any of the variants of Ruskinian Gothic would be unable to trust his workman with the smallest detail. Ruskin had inadvertently helped bring about the very enslavement of the craftsmen that he denounced.

Sedding was also one of the several late Victorian architects who pre-ferred to work in the later phases of Gothic. He designed in the style that Ruskin had notoriously denounced as "our detestable perpendicular." Sed-ding was untroubled by this; he simply dismissed it as a crude criticism based on insufficient knowledge. But the fact that so many young men now worked in styles that Ruskin disliked often complicated relations between the critic and his admirers.

Thomas Graham Jackson provides a case in point. He had studied archi-tecture in George Gilbert Scott's office during the 1850s, when Ruskin's in-fluence there was at its height. He took *The Seven Lamps* from the office library, prepared an analysis of it, and looked up the various buildings it referred to in other sources so that he could add his own illustrations. He then studied *The Stones of Venice* with similar care. He had not abandoned his enthusiasm for Ruskin by the time he published *Modern Gothic Archi-tecture* in 1873, but he had certainly come to feel that the Gothic Revival had in some way failed and that its failure was linked to its concept of style.

The crucial turning point in Jackson's career was his design for the Ex-amination Schools at Oxford, where Ruskin was now Slade Professor. The competition was messy even by Victorian standards. It was won by Wood-ward's old partner, Thomas Deane, but the result (fig. 97) was set aside by convocation and a fresh competition was held. G. E. Street, whose work had been highly praised in the first round, considered that Deane had been badly treated and refused to compete in the second. This time the winner was John Oldrid Scott, but once again convocation set aside the result. Jackson entered the picture for the third competition. By now the situation had so changed from the days of the Oxford Museum that the non-Gothic designs were considered heretical. Jackson began by thinking in terms of Gothic, but he soon found the style impractical. Instead of a great hall, such as the other competitors were designing, Jackson began sketching a series of well-lit rooms. That concept of the interior suggested a change on

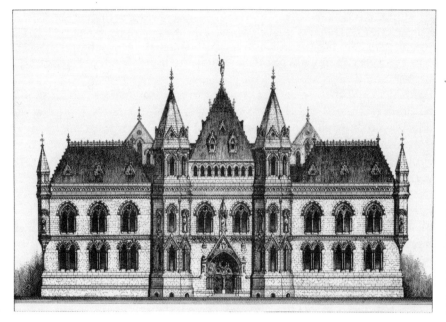

Fig. 97. Proposed Examination Schools, Oxford. Thomas Deane. Building News, *1873.*

the outside. He accordingly abandoned Gothic and began anew in "a sort of Renaissance style." The building finally emerged in Jacobean (fig. 98), which Jackson considered "really Gothic, though it made use of the Classic orders in a way of its own."[28]

Ruskin's opinion was not expressed in print, but it was emphatic nonetheless. He refused even to enter the building for an inspection when Jackson's clerk of the works invited him to do so. Perhaps Ruskin was merely being loyal to the ill-used Deane. It is equally possible that he was being faithful to Victorian Gothic and to Woodward's Anglo-Venetian variant, which Deane was still using at Oxford. That was Jackson's guess. He was sure that Ruskin considered him to be working in a "debased" style. Though both men were in Oxford a good deal during the 1870s, they met only once. Miss Shaw-Lefevre introduced them at Somerville Hall: "he [Ruskin] was standing on the hearthrug surrounded by a group of admiring girl-worshippers such as he liked, and with a shake of the hand our intercourse began and ended."[29]

This incident leaves an impression of estrangement between Ruskin and the young men who were once his admirers. But this is not the whole story, or even the most important part of it. Most of the criticisms of Ruskin made during the 1870s stop short of outright rejection. This frustrated those who were waiting for Ruskin's influence to end. A leader in the *Architect*, probably by Robert Kerr, asked impatiently after one of J. D. Sedding's lectures: "Does Mr. Sedding still cling to the Oxford Graduate or has he flung him aside? Amongst other things, it is not really clear what his attitude is in this respect."[30] At times it may not have been clear to Sedding or his fellows, but eventually they decided what they wished to reject and, more important, what they wished to keep.

One element they wished to preserve was Ruskin's basic concept of style. *Basic* is the key word. We have seen that while Ruskin argued for a single style of the age, he had the effect of encouraging diversity. His young admirers were appalled by the stylistic chaos they saw about them; Sedding declared in dismay that "Darwin's experiment with 6¾ ounces of pond mud, which were found to contain seeds of 537 distinct species," was "a mere trifle" compared to the varieties of Victorian architecture.[31] But this does not in the least prevent them from sharing Ruskin's underlying wish for a common style. This is especially striking in the work of J. J. Steven-

Fig. 98.   *Examination Schools, Oxford. T. G. Jackson. Building News, 1876.*

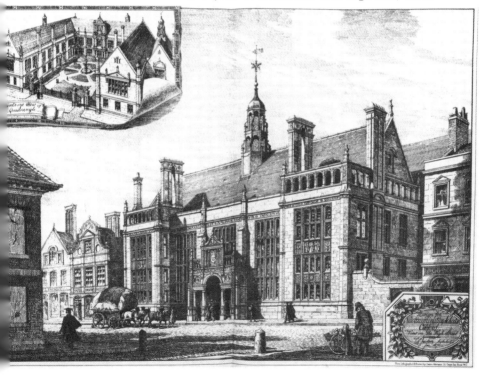

son. He carefully warns readers of *House Architecture* against an uncritical acceptance of Ruskin's ideas, but he ends his book with a page and a half of quotations from "The Lamp of Obedience." He longs for a style that would be, in Ruskin's words which he quotes, like "a code of laws of one kind or another, and that code accepted and enforced from one side of the island to another, and not one code made ground of judgment at York and another in Exeter" (8.253).

How was this to be achieved? The answer lay partly in a skeptical reexamination of what went on in architects' offices and partly in a new look at the contribution of the workmen at the building site.

Jackson, Webb, and Sedding knew that Ruskin shared their discontent with the ways in which Victorian architects did their work, even if his specific complaints were not quite the same as their own. Two passages—one from a public lecture, one from a private letter—show how he pointed toward the arts and crafts synthesis that was now beginning to emerge.

The first passage was part of an 1875 Oxford lecture on Botticelli. A student had shown Ruskin an 1861 paper in the *Ecclesiologist* by William Burges which referred to the cathedral, the baptistry, and the campanile in Florence in terms of less than total admiration. Ruskin answered with an abrupt gesture of dismissal: "You must not be too hard upon him. These are quite the natural impressions of a man who had never been trained to look at sculpture, and had never done anything with his own hand, and had been taught to sell on commission the labour of others" (23.269). Poor Burges! Is it possible that Ruskin was unaware of his admirer's lifelong effort to give meaning to the identification of architecture with sculpture and painting? This seems unlikely. It is much more likely that Burges's efforts were simply not radical enough. He designed sculpture, but he did not execute it. He did not work with his hands.

The private letter is in the same vein. When J. D. Sedding, puzzled as to the direction his career should take, asked for advice, Ruskin answered: "Modern so-called architects are merely employers of workmen on commission, and if you would be a real architect you must always have either pencil or chisel in your hand" (37.199). The pencil was for planning frescoes, not mere elevations. The chisel was for sculpture. Both these statements sound as if Ruskin is merely reiterating the heresy of architecture as decoration, which Sedding has already rejected. But there is something in them that Sedding accepts: the idea of the architect who is something more than an office draftsman. Sedding wants an architect who works with his hands, who is constantly on the building site, who is not easily distinguishable from his craftsmen. Sedding declared Ruskin's view to be that "of a visionary who holds up an impossible standard of perfection, not knowing the requirements and conditions of the age in which we live." Then he added: "Yet I venture to think the theory that underlies Mr. Ruskin's ruling in this matter is unassailable, whether practical or not."[32]

Ruskin's oracular statements were given added force by the discontent of those who had worked in George Gilbert Scott's Spring Garden office. Scott took on so much work and delegated the details so widely that he lost control over the final building. Thomas Graham Jackson recalled:

> I have seen three or four men with drawings awaiting correction or approval grouped outside his door. The door flew open and out he came: "No time to-day;" the cab was at the door and he was whirled away to some cathedral where he would spend a couple of hours and then fly off again to some other great work at the other end of the kingdom. Now and then the only chance of getting instructions was to go with him in the cab to the station.[33]

As a pupil Jackson found this rather fine. Later he found it distasteful. Scott had replaced thought and craftsmanship with division of labor: "One man designs the wall, floors, and roofs, and prepares windows, niches, and panels; another man designs the statues and comes and puts them up in the niches, with the design of which he had nothing to do; another carves the capitals, friezes, and panels, another paints the walls, and designs and executes the coloured decoration; another fills the window with painted glass; each man knows his own branch of art and is ignorant of that of the others."[34] No wonder such architecture failed to achieve unity of style.

J. T. Emmett focused his attention more directly on the workman. He drew attention to the obvious fact that there was no difference between the ways in which Gothic and classic structures were actually built: "The working-man is nowhere seen; he is not even heard of. He is at the 'factory' when the bell rings, and he files and polishes the bit of work that he is set to do; but fancy and volition and artistic thought are wanting; he is but a slave, an incorrect machine."[35] Emmett looks forward to a time when employers will communicate with master builders directly and let architects lapse into their proper roles as students of symbolism.

The claim that the architect should be abolished and his responsibilities returned to the master workmen was Emmett's most explosive contribution to architectural discussion. Its relation to Ruskin is a complicated one. Emmett's language echoes "The Nature of Gothic," but he extends Ruskin's idea of the workman's freedom in a way that finds no warrant in *The Seven Lamps*, *The Stones of Venice*, or even *Fors Clavigera*. His most probable source is James Fergusson, who often ridiculed the pedantry of Gothic Revival architects by comparing them to practical builders. Ruskin has too much respect for hierarchy to propose abolishing architects, and his concern with the craftsman is focused on the carver rather than the builder.

Emmett extends Ruskin's concept of the freedom of the workman in a daring way, but perhaps the most significant aspect of this extension is that few people noticed it. Many, especially those who had not read their Ruskin for some years, assumed that Ruskin's ideas and Emmett's were the same. The *Building News* was typical. It blandly assured its readers that Emmett's ideas "would be more valuable if Mr. Ruskin had not already expressed them twenty years ago."[36]

A number of factors encouraged architects to wonder if they should not abandon their status as gentlemen of the office. One is Ruskin's insistence that they should work with their hands. Another is the growing conviction that Ruskin's distinction between building and architecture is untenable. Still another is Emmett's defense of the craftsman-builder against the scholar-architect. The result is a new claim for the primacy of building. It is possible to trace three responses to this new emphasis, each of which points to one of the dominant attitudes in the late-nineteenth-century debate over Ruskin's ideas.

One is a flat rejection of the idea. J. J. Stevenson was one of the most eloquent of those who replied to Emmett. He argued that the Gothic cathedrals had been designed not by cooperating master workmen but by men who had much the same function as modern architects. He accepted the gulf between design and execution and, assuming that Emmett's claim for the workman was Ruskin's as well, saw no reason why architects needed experience with chisels:

> There may be virtue in working with our hands. The digging and delving to which Mr. Ruskin has set Oxford students may be wholesome moral training. Mr. Gladstone may find benefit in felling trees. Monks, old and modern, have believed in the virtue of manual labour. It might be well for everybody if the old custom still prevailed of apprenticing every lad, however rich, to some hand-working trade. The discipline, however, has been recommended for its moral rather than intellectual benefits, and in architecture especially it is brains, not hands, that are wanted for designing it; and when that talent exists in a workman it is a waste of it to keep him in manual labour.[37]

Stevenson begins the process of rehabilitating the Renaissance conception of the architect that will culminate in the theories of Reginald Blomfield and the later practice of Edwin Lutyens.

A second response was to argue that architectural design ought to be a cooperative process not so much between various workmen as between the architect and his assistants. A series of leaders in the *Building News* transferred Emmett's arguments from the building site to the drafting room:

> We have as yet few workmen capable of enriching a building from the stores of their own invention: could not some of our junior architects supply their place? We no more wish than expect to see the dream of the *Quarterly Review* realized,

and our assistants made the real architects of the present, but where they are competent to design, and capable of designing in harmony with the general scheme of the work they are engaged on, we do not see why some opportunities should not be given them. The architect of a building is, or should be, he who masses out the whole, and influences the work of the subordinate designers. It is a poor ambition for him to be able to boast that everything, great and small, about the building was designed by himself.[38]

This is essentially the plan that was carried into practice in the large and influential office of Norman Shaw.

Ruskin's most ardent admirers were fascinated by a more radical possibility. They sought to break decisively with the professional ideal of the office architect. As J. D. Sedding said:

> The "real" architect of a building is something different to the distant dictator who uses the agency of post and telegram to communicate his wishes, who draws the plans, writes the specifications, and looks in occasionally at the works in progress. He must be his own clerk of the works, his own carver, his own decorator; he must be the familiar spirit of the structure as it rises from the ground, must be ready at hand to meet the passing emergency of site, or crooked wall, or awkward chimney; to suggest the only fit treatment and the only fit detail for a particular place, and generally to make the most of the site and building as applied to it.[39]

Such an architect would obviously have to limit his practice. He would work with a small number of office assistants and be alert for opportunities to employ the craft traditions of his workmen. He would seek to cooperate not only with sculptors and mosaicists but also, and especially, with joiners, plasterers, ironworkers, glaziers, and members of all the other building crafts. The arts and craft guilds that were established in the 1880s and 1890s were an effort to bring this cooperative ideal into being.

The 1870s thus saw a decisive reorientation in the direction of Ruskinism away from the visible features of style and toward a new focus on the nature of work. Perhaps the shift can be described by saying that one set of sacred texts—"The Lamp of Beauty," "The Lamp of Power," the illustrations to *The Stones of Venice*—were replaced by another set consisting of the comments on the workman at the end of "The Lamp of Obedience" and in "The Nature of Gothic." But this omits "The Lamp of Memory." Ruskin's polemic against restoration takes on dramatic new importance in the 1870s, and this happens among architects who were otherwise engaged in a critical reassessment of his influence.

II

Ruskin's views on restoration were first expressed in 1849, but they did not achieve practical effect until the founding of the Society for the Protection of Ancient Buildings in 1877. Since Ruskin's impact was swift in other respects, this time lag requires an explanation. The situation is complicated by the fact that the villains of the struggle over restoration—George Gilbert Scott and G. E. Street—were among the first and most influential of Ruskin's admirers.

We cannot read far in Ruskin without realizing the visceral pain he felt at seeing the monuments of European art and architecture first neglected and then restored with overconfident scholarship. Many churches had suffered terribly. Walls had been demolished and their stones used for gentlemen's houses. Roofs had been neglected and their timbers had rotted. Stone had been permeated by rainwater which, expanding as it froze, destroyed the original surface, and this freeze-thaw cycle was now augmented by industrial pollution. In addition, stylistic changes had been made over the centuries. Wainscotting, high pews, and galleries were intruded into medieval buildings. The growing religious fervor of the nineteenth-century made restorations seem at once a necessity and an act of piety. Decayed stonework was scraped away, and the tool marks of the old masons went with it. Crumbling tracery was replaced by new work in the same style or, if the old work was in the detested perpendicular, by new work in some earlier and more favored style of Gothic. Old stone carving was replaced by modern replicas, the floor was redone in Minton's encaustic tiles, and the bells were recast. All of this was carried out with great enthusiasm, supported by charity bazaars and stirring appeals for funds. In place of a decay that symbolized the religious lethargy of the past, the parish gained a church that was as strong and neat as if it were new—which, according to some, it very nearly was.

Ruskin was the first major author to protest against restoration. Earlier writers had attacked particular blunders, but Ruskin denounced restoration itself. His views are consistent throughout his career and may be briefly summarized. Some architects insisted that though they had scraped away decayed stonework and even rebuilt entire walls, they had carefully maintained the original design. Ruskin flatly refused to accept the distinction between the design, which could be reduplicated, and the execution of it. He insisted that the life of a building was given to it by the hand and eye of the workman, that the touch of each carver and mason contained subtle nuances that were as individual as his handwriting. Because modern restorations replaced the variations of handwork with a machinelike regularity, they entirely destroyed what they claimed to preserve. Restoration was therefore a lie from beginning to end: "a destruction accompanied with false description of the thing destroyed" (8.242). The task of the architect should be preservation: sheets of lead could be used to protect the roof, timber props could support the walls, iron ties could resist lateral pressure. It did not matter if the aid was unsightly; what mattered was preservation of old work. When these means no longer sufficed, there should be no shirking the inevitable: "Look the necessity full in the face, and understand it on its own terms. It is a necessity for destruction. Accept it as such, pull the building down, throw its stones into neglected corners, make ballast of them or mortar, if you will; but do it honestly, and do not set up a lie in their place" (8.244).

Most of the early responses to these views were antagonistic. J. Thomas complained that Ruskin's morbid love of picturesque ruins would prevent architects from sweeping the debris of centuries of classicism out of Gothic cathedrals.[40] The *Ecclesiologist* reminded its readers that "we are not *artists* only" and have a duty to alter churches to meet the needs of worship.[41] The *English Review* agreed with Ruskin that it was absurd to duplicate ancient statues, but thought that no such objection could apply to copying masonry and moldings that were, after all, formed out of geometrical lines that could certainly be duplicated. The important thing was the repairs should "be done as like to the original as is possible."[42] The *Athenaeum* maintained that twenty years of study of Gothic cathedrals must educate architects and that "except in a few instances of peculiarly delicate work, intelligent modern workmen can cut quatrefoils and rosettes sufficiently well for distant parapets and places where time will soon mellow them with a spurious age."[43] One of the very few writers to agree with Ruskin wrote a letter to the *Builder* arguing that as soon as you take away an old piece and make a replica, its interest is gone. Significantly, the editor considered this view sufficiently bizarre that he added a note explaining his decision to publish it: "Although we dissent from the tendency of these remarks, we have given the communication a place, as likely to afford a useful check to some would-be restorers falling away into destructives."[44]

So far we seem to have a standoff: Ruskin expresses his views and right-thinking people reject them. The complicating factor is that the most active restorer in England—George Gilbert Scott—considered Ruskin's views carefully and thought he agreed with most of them. Someday a long and scholarly book will appear showing how much posterity owes Scott, but in the absence of detailed scholarship on his restorations and the choices he faced, it is very difficult to do him justice.[45] At the very least, he was congenitally incapable of heeding Blake's dictum that opposition is true friendship. By co-opting much of Ruskin's argument, Scott confused discussions of restoration for the next twenty-five years.

Scott first read *The Seven Lamps* while preparing a short book entitled *A Plea for the Faithful Restoration of Our Ancient Churches* (1850). In it he argues against reckless, uninformed restoration and in favor of cautious, scholarly restoration. He praises Ruskin's book, even to the point of adopting a passage from "The Lamp of Memory" as his epigraph. Then, with copious quotation from Ruskin, he undercuts Ruskin's argument:

> were it possible by *present* care to nullify the effects of *past* neglect, I would heartily fall in with this advice. I would "watch an old building with an anxious care." I would "guard it as best I might, and at a cost, from the influence of delapidation." I would "count its stones as you would the jewels of a crown; set watches about it as if at the gates of a besieged city; bind it together with iron where it loosens; stay it with timber when it declines." . . . But, alas! the damage is already effected.[46]

It is better to repair the damage ourselves, Scott says, than leave it to the impious hands of others.

Scott defined and practiced his via media for the next twenty-five years. He gave descriptions of the horrors of restoration that surpass anything in Ruskin. He grew rapturous over the tact of the architect who proceeds "with a most tender hand, and with the most scrupulous regard to the original design, the most rigorous determination to preserve every feature, and with the most entire abnegation of self, and devotion to the preservation of the work before us."[47] He urged that a vigilance committee be formed to sound the warning against overzealous restorers, and he warned that restorations should never be left unsupervised lest—as often happened—some overenthusiastic workman decide to tear down all the old work and build it anew. He urged restorers always to preserve the greatest possible amount of old work intact, never to restore carved work or sculpture, and never to add new work except in strict conformity to the evidences of its original form. During the 1850s and 1860s, G. E. Street took much the same path, quoting Ruskin's views with respect and deploring "excessive" restoration.

Ruskin did little to resist the allegedly moderate activities of Scott, Street, and other English restorers. There are two reasons for this. One is that he usually drew his examples from Europe, and the English architects were as appalled as he was by the activities of their Continental counterparts. The other is that he was unable to translate his flamboyant denunciation of restoration into practical advice on buildings that obviously needed care.

Ruskin's remarks to an 1861 meeting of the Ecclesiological Society illustrate his difficulties. Here he was in the lion's den, for the ecclesiologists were among the most fervent Victorian restorers. Their meeting, however, had been called to protest the activities of the presumably destructive restorers in France. The English architectural establishment was present, including Scott, Street, Alexander Beresford Hope, John Henry Parker, Robert Kerr, Benjamin Ferrey, William White, John Pollard Seddon, and George Frederick Bodley. It is safe to guess that most of the younger architects and pupils were there as well. Ruskin's contribution was a high point of the meeting. He was received with cheers and spoke at considerable length. His remarks were potentially explosive in substance, but curiously hesitant in manner.

He began by advising against any formal protest to the French government, partly because it would offend national vanity and partly because the English had not settled their own attitudes toward restoration. The one recommendation he thought they might judiciously make was that when restorations were done, they should be carried out by a sufficient number of men so that they might be completed in a reasonable time. This was not exactly an assault on restoration practices.

Ruskin's next remarks were more passionate, but they expressed more his personal tendency toward despair than his analysis of the objective situation:

> He had desired to know something of thirteenth-century architecture, though not as an artist; because he intended, then, to write an architectural history of the thirteenth century, after the publication of his "Stones of Venice." It was to be a work of many years. He meant to work in those churches for the collection of his materials, but found that all his documents were then in fact destroyed by the operation of the system of restoration which was adopted; and that in five years more they would be completely destroyed; so he gave up the undertaking, and not only that, but he gave up architecture too. He never cared about architecture afterwards. He thought the pursuit of architecture was a hopeless thing if its most important documents were destroyed.[48]

The most obvious effect of these remarks was to make Scott and Street eagerly assure Ruskin that there was indeed enough material left to justify his study of thirteenth-century Gothic.

Ruskin had, however, introduced a metaphor: the building is a document. He then extended this by arguing that the individual touch of the workman is its handwriting.

> Every portion of the work bore the impress of the individual acting with mind and hand,—of the mind and hand of the individual acting upon the stone. All good art was the expression of the whole man: it was the expression of soul and heart, of intellect, and of body. . . . no great art existed which did not carry

with it some expression of the tenderness and of the thoughtfulness of the man,—that was to say, the handwriting of the man on his work; and, unless they had got the handwriting, they had not got the art.[49]

He then went on to refer to the wonderful tenderness of the thirteenth-century workman and briefly digressed into some remarks on Dante and Rossetti.

When he returned to his topic it was for a denunciation of restoration, but not one that would have challenged the most deeply held beliefs of the restorers in his audience. "The necessity of restoration," he told them, "sometimes involved its impossibility."[50] That "sometimes" represented a retreat from the statement in "The Lamp of Memory." He then directed his final remarks to the question of sculpture. He proposed retaining all old sculpture and urged an end to the placing of newly carved, nineteenth-century heads onto thirteenth-century statues. His audience could not have agreed more. The comparison of a building to a document and of the worker's touch to its handwriting would eventually explode mid-Victorian confidence in restoration, but it would take other voices than Ruskin's to make this happen.

Ruskin was more effective in focusing public attention when he refused the RIBA's Gold Medal in 1874, though, as often happened in Ruskin's later career, the shock value of his gesture had to compensate for the vagueness of its content. Ruskin was traveling on the Continent when the institute made its decision. George Gilbert Scott wrote at once to inform him of the honor but officially had to submit a name to the queen before he had actually received Ruskin's acceptance. He had no reason to antici-pate a refusal. Ruskin, after all, had been an honorary member of the insti-tute since 1865. In retrospect, however, it was clear that the RIBA had left itself in an exposed position. The Gold Medal had been created to en-hance the prestige of the entire architectural profession. It was a natural target for anyone who thought that the profession needed blame rather than praise.

Ruskin gave his reasons for the refusal in a letter to Thomas Carlyle:

I cannot accept medals from people who let themselves out to build Gothic Advertisements for Railroads—Greek advertisements for firms in the city— and—whatever Lord Palmerston or Mr. Gladstone chose to order opposite Whitehall—while they allow every beautiful building in France and Italy to be destroyed, for the "job" of its restoration.[51]

Clearly Scott's collapse over the Government Offices had continued to rankle, whatever Ruskin had told Scott privately at the time. There was no reference to this in the public letter to the institute, however. Instead,

Ruskin dwelt entirely on destructive restorations. It was no time to be accepting medals, he said, when the Brancaccio tomb at Naples was used as a lumber room, when the Church of San Miniato in Florence was serving as a common cemetery, when a cross on a spandrel at Santa Maria della Spina could be smashed to pieces and replaced by a modern copy, and when the foundations of Furness Abbey were threatened by vibration from a nearby railroad. In a private letter to Scott, Ruskin added that while he would have gratefully accepted the medal twenty years before, he had now come to doubt the value of such professional bodies as the institute:

> The Primary object of all such Associations is to exalt the power of their own Profession over the mind of the public, power being—in the present century synonymous with Wealth. And the root of all the evil and ruin which this century has seen—(and it has destroyed already more than the French Revolution did, of what *that* had left)—is summed in four words, "Commission on the Cost." Such—from any body of Architects however small, who will bind themselves henceforward to accept a given salary—of (whatever amount according to the standing—they may choose to name)—for their daily work; and to work with their men (or at least with their own hands: on the sculpture of the building)—while they take such salary: from *such* a body, I will take a medal tomorrow.[52]

Scott's explanation to the annual meeting of the institute was careful and fair. He insisted that Ruskin and the RIBA were both laboring to conserve ancient monuments, and he pointed out that the institute had long had a standing committee to deal with the problem. To Ruskin's horror stories he added several of his own, and he denounced the plague of "false and destructive restoration" sweeping over Europe. Then he announced that the Gold Medal would be awarded instead to an architect Ruskin himself admired: George Edmund Street. He concluded by reflecting that "an anathematiser of what is bad claims lesser honours than he who practically carries out what is good."[53]

Yet Ruskin's anathematizing appears to have been one of his most creative gestures. On the surface his action appears quixotic. Of his examples of the mistreatment of monuments, three were Continental, and Furness Abbey was not threatened by architects. Only one of the four actually involved restoration, and there was no reason to think that members of the institute would have disagreed with him on any of them. Ruskin's broader charge that restoration amounted to, as he put it in a private letter three years later, "accursed architects' jobbery" was obviously more explosive. When the *Builder* reprinted the letter containing these words, it did so under the heading "A Shameful Assertion."[54] This charge, however, was made in private, not in public. Rarely can an action have been less precise in its meaning or more successful in its result. Carlyle wrote him from Chelsea: "Your Architect Gold Medal, left stranded on the waste beach, had an immense rumour for some days in London; and I doubt not is still standing like a fateful Sphinx-riddle in the minds of many men. The blame I think was not laid heavily on you, but the astonishment, the mocking pity for the Medal and its authors was large and loud."[55] The refusal of the Gold Medal in 1874 led to the founding of the Society for the Protection of Ancient Buildings three years later. But opponents of restoration needed a more elaborate intellectual framework than Ruskin provided.

We can trace the theoretical underpinnings of the society in speeches given in 1877 by two of its members—J. J. Stevenson and George Aitchison. Stevenson's was much the more shocking of the two. He was chief among those who had "betrayed" the Gothic Revival. He was also one of the several former pupils of George Gilbert Scott who were sharply critical of the way in which Scott conducted his practice. Both these factors must have been present in the minds of the audience when Stevenson stood up at the RIBA to give examples of destructive restoration from the work of Scott and G. E. Street—both of whom were present. The emotion in the discussion following Stevenson's paper was intense, and a second meeting was called to give Scott and Street further opportunity to reply. It is ironic that the full meaning of Ruskin's words on restoration were at last brought home to the architectural profession by a man who was otherwise rather critical of Ruskin's doctrines.

Stevenson began with Ruskin's metaphor: a building is a historical document. But Stevenson's document recorded a much wider range of history than Gothic Revivalists had been accustomed to contemplate. They were transfixed by the notion that Gothic had a high point, followed by a debased period, which was in turn followed by an eighteenth century that was almost beneath contempt. What they rejected as impure—the perpendicular windows put in place of earlier lancets, the post-Reformation pulpit with Corinthian columns—seemed to Stevenson a valuable part of the historical record. He accused the Gothic Revivalists of sweeping away high oak pews, monuments from the time of James I, and galleries with the squire's coat of arms only to embellish the church with "the modern medieval embellishments of restorers, the dreary ranges of long benches covered with sticky-looking varnish, the Minton tile pavements, the new stained glass, hard gaudy purple or dull and colourless, or the gimcrack brasswork in screens and gas-brackets, with their vulgar blue paint, from the eminent firm of Skidmore."[56] In place of an original document that embodied eight hundred years of history, the restorers put a Gothic Revival forgery.

Stevenson did not extend Ruskin's metaphor into a concern with the craftsman's handwriting. That step was taken by Aitchison, who presented a view of the medieval workman that was at once glowing and realistic:

> I do not suppose that every craftsman was an original designer; on the contrary, I suppose this gift was confined to very few, and these usually became the masters; but probably every man knew by rote a certain number of stock patterns and stock shapes. . . . Every craftsman learnt more or less to draw or to model, and there being but one form of ornament in fashion at each particular time and place, the mousetrap man ornamented his trap as well as made it; the master mason carved the stone image as well as cut the stone; the master carpenter carved the wooden image as well as the timber; the master tile-maker designed the tiles as well as made them; the master mosaic-worker found the design as well as put up the work; and this conjunction of artistic and mechanical skill in the same person only died out gradually.[57]

Aitchison assumes, as Stevenson did, the failure of the Gothic Revival. The modern workman, he says, is likely to be an engineer, not a craftsman, and he can never recapture the touch of his medieval counterpart. This argument eliminates the last justification for restoration as practiced by Scott, Street, and the Ecclesiologists. Even if all the archeological skill of the nineteenth century could restore the design of a fourteenth-century church, it could never re-create the handwriting of the original workmen.

It was the founding of the Society for the Protection of Ancient Buildings, under the leadership of Philip Webb and William Morris, that gave practical meaning to Ruskin's broad principles. Its meetings, presided over by Webb and usually adjourning to Gatti's in the Strand for food and more discussion, worked out detailed policies for preservation. In the 1880s and 1890s Webb deliberately set out to train a body of young men in the society's principles and practices. His pupils, as they may be called, included Detmar Blow, Ernest Gimson, William Weir, Sidney and Ernest Barnsley, and William Richard Lethaby. The effect of this education was to strengthen their conviction that architecture was first of all honest building, and thus the society became a primary educational institution for the arts and crafts Ruskinism of the late nineteenth century.

XIII

RUSKIN'S INFLUENCE IN AMERICA

 AMERICAN Ruskinism illuminates its English counterpart by contrast. *Modern Painters* and *The Seven Lamps* were welcomed enthusiastically in Boston and New York, and the *Literary World* gave the common opinion when it observed in 1851 that "it is to the credit of our country and our artists that Ruskin's works have been received so cordially, even enthusiastically, as they have been; and we doubt if the appreciation of them be so general in England as on this side of the Atlantic."[1] Ruskin's ideas quickly began circulating in architects' offices. The diarist George Templeton Strong recorded in 1855 that Richard Upjohn was planning to attempt Venetian Gothic in a proposed new building for Columbia College: "Ruskin has inspired him with the notion."[2] After the Civil War American streets were enlivened with bursts of polychromy, patches of naturalistic carving, and reminiscences of medieval Venice. Yet one major difference between English and American Ruskinism is that one evolves until the end of the century while the other fades after the mid-1870s. It is above all the brevity of Ruskin's influence in America that demands explanation.

I

One of the first results of Ruskin's popularity in America was a periodical titled the *Crayon.* Its editor, a young landscape artist named W. J. Stillman, had met Ruskin while visiting England in 1850 and had returned filled with enthusiasm for the Pre-Raphaelites. He was not alone. He recalled later that "the art-loving public was full of Ruskinian enthusiasm."[3] His magazine soon had a subscription list of over one thousand. It brought American art lovers the latest news about Millais and Holman Hunt, and it directed attention to Giotto, Fra Angelico, and Masaccio. It published Ruskin's *The Poetry of Architecture* and it gave lengthy excerpts from *The Stones of Venice*. It published an admiring description of the Oxford Museum and offered a sympathetic account of Scott's travails with Palmerston.

But although the *Crayon* was a self-consciously Ruskinian periodical, its pages reveal a persistent conflict between Ruskinism on the one hand and a nascent functionalism on the other. At issue is the claim in *The Seven Lamps* that we achieve architecture by adding such an unnecessary feature as a cable molding to an otherwise utilitarian structure. Ruskin's separation of building from architecture does, to be sure, find echoes in the *Crayon*. J. Coleman Hart asserts that "*building* may construct the walls and put openings in them, but *architecture* beautifies and adorns them."[4] Another writer dismisses the view that construction is more important than ornament as "a fearful mistake."[5] The Oxford Museum is praised for a decorative scheme that expresses a meaning of the structure "independent of whatever thought may be bestowed upon the exterior design and details of its plan and construction."[6] Though we might expect these views to be the norm, they are in fact exceptional . This is so because one of the chief architectural contributors to the *Crayon* was a man named Leopold Eidlitz.

Born in Prague in 1823 and educated at the Vienna Polytechnic, Eidlitz arrived in New York City at the age of twenty. He was an exponent of the Romanesque Revival—the *rundbogenstil*—of his native Germany, and he must have been partly responsible for the popularity of the round arch in nineteenth-century New York. He worked skillfully in Gothic as well. He designed banks on Wall Street, a synagogue on Fifth Avenue, a home for P. T. Barnum in Connecticut, and a superb Episcopal church in St. Louis. Many of his buildings, insofar as one can judge from old photographs, had pronounced Ruskinian affinities, including the Venetian Gothic Decker building on Union Square (1870, demolished), the vividly polychromatic Church of the Holy Trinity (1870, demolished), and the Dry Dock Savings Bank (1875, demolished; fig. 99). More than half his output is now destroyed, but characteristic examples that remain in New York City include Saint George's Church (1856, restored 1897) and the addition to the so-called Tweed Courthouse. Eidlitz was an influential figure in American architecture, and he spread his views through his *Crayon* articles, his book *The Nature and Function of Art* (1881), and especially, through vigorous, pungent conversation.

It is not always easy to be sure of Eidlitz's attitude toward Ruskin at each stage of his career. His references in the *Crayon* consist of enthusiastic

Fig. 99.   Dry Dock Savings Bank (demolished). Leopold Eidlitz. New York Sketchbook of Architecture, *1875.*

praise that is only tinged with reservation. Ruskin is "the boldest, most earnest, and most devoted advocate of Art, who, with all his idiosyncracies, has conferred a great boon upon society."[7] Even when he is dismayed to see "Ruskin exalt the Italian Romanesque above every other expression of architecture," Eidlitz still concedes that Ruskin's "ardent and generous nature is too honest to ignore" the northern Gothic.[8] The basic assumptions of his *Crayon* articles, however, are sharply at variance with Ruskin's, and in his 1881 book he criticizes Ruskin explicitly.

"Nature", Eidlitz said in the *Crayon,* is "the only guiding principle for the government of architects."[9] One might expect him, therefore, to share Ruskin's view that "beyond a certain point, and that a very low one, man cannot advance in the invention of beauty, without directly imitating natural forms" (8.139). Eidlitz, however, takes a quite different view of the relation between architecture and nature. Where Ruskin argues that nature conceals construction, Eidlitz assumes that "every natural object shows in its outward form more or less the connection of its component parts."[10] The amount of construction thus revealed, moreover, determines the degrees of expression and beauty. "Nature," he insists, "*constructs* with a single view to the ultimate purpose, and expresses her constructions clearly and boldly in her forms."[11] Eidlitz's understanding of nature led him to insist that in architecture, form and function must be kept in organic relation. He was completely opposed to Ruskin's distinction between building and architecture. He once told H. H. Richardson that "in true Gothic, so long as you find two stones together, you find architecture."[12]

Eidlitz made his differences with Ruskin explicit in his 1881 book, *The Nature and Function of Art*. He quotes the complaint in *The Seven Lamps* that "there is no law, no principle based upon past practice, which may not be overthrown in a moment by the arising of a new condition, or the invention of a new material" (8.21). But laws, Eidlitz objects, are eternal. If one can be overthrown by a new material, it is not a law at all. Ruskin was led into this elementary error because he does not really grasp the fundamental principles of structures: "it is upon forms that his imagination dwells." Even Ruskin's acquaintance with these forms is imperfect: "Some of those he most admires have left on his mind a foggy picture which, had he analyzed it, would have satisfied him less." Eidlitz finds this same lack of steady analysis in Ruskin's illustrations: "they are not representations, but uncertain impressions only, of the things he saw."[13] Finally, Ruskin overestimates the importance of ornament. If the idea of a building is expressed in its structure, as Eidlitz says it ought to be, then the ornament is more a lovely grace than a necessity.

The importance of the *Crayon* for American architecture is thus not quite what it at first appears. The magazine was a primary agent in the spread of Ruskin's prestige, but it also gave a forum to Leopold Eidlitz. And in October 1855 it reprinted (perhaps at Eidlitz's urging?) the previously published views on form and function of Horatio Greenough. The true significance of the *Crayon* is that it gave the first expression to the tension between Ruskinism on the one hand and functionalism on the other.

II

If the architectural Ruskinism of the *Crayon* was wavering, that of the *New Path* was ardent. Among its writers were Peter Bonnett Wight and Russell

Sturgis. They had met while students at New York's Free Academy (later the College of the City of New York) on Twenty-third Street. On their way home from the drawing master's studio each evening they would pass a church under construction at the corner of Twentieth Street and Fourth Avenue. This was the All Souls' Unitarian Church, designed by a young Englishman, Jacob Wrey Mould, who had been trained in Owen Jones's office. Wight and Sturgis made the architect's acquaintance and were soon comparing his working drawings with the progress of the building. They credited their decision to become architects to their fascination with All Souls'. Mould was not a Ruskinian, but his building, clearly based on the polychromatic Romanesque of northern Italy, sent Wight and Sturgis to *The Seven Lamps* and *The Stones of Venice*. On January 27, 1863, they joined with other young admirers of Ruskin in organizing the Society for the Advancement of Truth in Art. Its journal, which appeared from May 1863 to December 1865, was the *New Path*.

Wight and Sturgis used its pages for a brash assault on nearly everything that had been built in New York until their time. Upjohn's Trinity Church was only a good beginning. James Renwick's Grace Church was "a very wretched design in comparison with Trinity, and perfectly worthless in detail."[14] New York University's Tudor building on Washington Square was a sham. Frederick Peterson's Cooper Union was "a splendid advertisement of iron beams, and a monument of architectural folly,"[15] with white Caen stone painted brown where brown stone was too expensive and terra-cotta arches where there could be a savings on Caen stone. Though Wight praised honest log cabins and simple Dutch farm houses, it was clear that the salvation of American architecture would have to come from abroad.

Sturgis, who had traveled in Europe, surveyed possible sources of inspiration in France, Germany, and England. He praised the French school for its "careful and complete *planning*, the accurate adaptation of buildings to their sites," but despised its eclecticism and insisted that the architecture of the future was not to be found in "Rue St. Honoré arcades, Louvre pavilions, the Bibliothèque St. Geneviève and Hôtels of ministers."[16]

Germany offered more attractive possibilities. Sturgis had worked briefly in Leopold Eidlitz's office and had undoubtedly been told which *rundbogenstil* buildings to see. He admired variously colored brick walls and round-arched window heads with radiating colors in the masonry, but he noted that buildings employing these features were in the minority. Civic buildings were designed in a cold, formal classic and churches in a late, inferior Gothic.

In England, Sturgis faced two possibilities. He and Wight already knew the theories of Henry Cole, Owen Jones, Matthew Digby Wyatt, and Christopher Dresser through their acquaintance with Jacob Wrey Mould. The young Americans had clearly learned from this group, and Wight's drawings in particular always tended to resemble plates in the *Grammar of Ornament*. Nevertheless, the Cole group is rejected. Wight and Sturgis knew where their affinities lay. They saw the Gothic Revival as a triumphant progress: "Ruskin had awakened [English architects] to the essential facts they were overlooking; the Pre-Raphaelites appeared, and dragged all England, willing or unwilling, into naturalism, until even the builders of Classic designs were carving stone and hammering iron into leaf forms more or less like mediaeval ornament."[17] Sturgis praised George Gilbert Scott, G. E. Street, John Pollard Seddon, and Richard Norman Shaw (still a Gothicist in the 1860s). He urged American architects to acquire photographs of the capitals at the Oxford Museum.

Wight and Sturgis accepted the distinction between building and architecture. If the men who erected the medieval cathedrals "were only *builders*," said Sturgis, "we shall think Christianity in Europe much less aspiring and purposeful than heathenism in Egypt."[18] He considered the bare structure of a Gothic cathedral to be "only a frame, beautiful as it might be."[19] The glory of architecture was its ornament. Not that the flexibility of Gothic did not permit plain buildings. Sturgis insisted that it was possible to have a fine Gothic design with comparatively simple means; his buildings at Yale fall into this category. But the tendency of his thought was always toward greater richness.

Ornament was to be not only abundant but also specifically naturalistic. This is the basis of Wight's criticism of the interlacing moldings and ultra-conventional carving on Eidlitz's buildings:

> The mind is bewildered with intricacy of moulding, bead and fillet, but the eye is not pleased by faithful images of Nature's forms, for they are not to be found. We are filled with admiration of the designer's fertile invention, but we see no expression of his love for that which is better, greater, more beautiful and lovely than human hands can do, or human mind can conceive.[20]

Sturgis urged capitals that represent "the flowers that you love best, gathered and arranged as your daughters arrange their spring bouquets; or they may perpetuate through the year the foliage of the trees you most regret to see bare of leaves in winter; or they may show birds and squirrels and how they carry themselves among the trees they haunt."[21]

The way to get this ornament was to grant freedom to the men who carved it. In the past such work had always been looked on as only the component part of a whole effect, not as a thing to be made interesting in itself. Moreover, the men who carved it were "degraded by being made the machines to carve other men's designs."[22] This was true even at Mould's All Souls' and his parochial school for Trinity Church. But at Belvedere Terrace in Central Park, necessity had forced a different way of working. The work on the pedestals on either side of the roadway at the top of the stairs

Fig. 100. *National Academy of Design (demolished). P. B. Wight.* National Academy of Design: Photographs of the New Building (1866).

was designed by Jacob Wrey Mould to be produced by others. It was conventionalized and ugly. But as work progressed, according to Wight, the harried architect told his carvers that he had no time to produce detailed drawings and urged them to work on their own. The result could be seen—and despite vandalism still can be—in the bosses on the balustrades on both sides of the stairs leading down to the fountain: "Gothic we call it for want of a better name, but no matter what it be, it is good and beautiful, conventional, but rightly conventional, and as true to nature as it can be made."[23]

The views that Wight and Sturgis expressed in the *New Path* found their physical expression in Wight's National Academy of Design (1863–1865, demolished; figs. 100, 101, and 102). Wight obviously went to Italy for his

Fig. 101. *Capitals from the National Academy of Design.*

Fig. 102. *Capital from the National Academy of Design.*

forms, though he was annoyed when New Yorkers began referring to his building as the Ducal Palace. He insisted that the design, which had originally featured round arches rather than pointed ones, really owed more to Florence and Verona than to Venice. The feature most reminiscent of the Ducal Palace—the blind third floor with its diaper pattern—was actually an example of Gothic flexibility for it covered the studios that needed to be lit from above rather than from the side. Both Wight and Sturgis insisted that the principles expressed in the National Academy were more important than its specific historical echoes. The building's compact shape and bold cornice reflected "The Lamp of Power." The polychromy of gray-and-white Westchester marble with North River bluestone was inspired by "The Lamp of Beauty." The iron railings were wrought rather than cast, and there was provision for mosaic and figure sculpture.

The stone carving was clearly modeled after that of the Oxford Museum. The workmen—all but one of whom were foreign—had to be specially trained. Wight supplied them with both naturalistic drawings and live plants. They began by working on clay models under the close supervision of the architect. Later they were given more freedom, and soon, in spite of three strikes and one Civil War draft call, the building was ornamented by white lilies, narcissus, woodbine, mandrakes, daffodils, trillium, wild bloodroot, jack-in-the-pulpits, arrowheads, cultivated bleeding hearts, azaleas, spiderworts, and other plants. Wight conceded that the degree of naturalism was excessive, but he understood that to be part of the Ruskinian program. Workmen were to begin by selecting nothing and rejecting nothing, but they would then work out for themselves the proper degree of conventionalization.

The National Academy of Design was not a building without progeny. Wight designed important Gothic Revival buildings such as Street Hall at Yale (1864) and the Brooklyn Mercantile Library (1865, demolished; fig. 103). Sturgis designed Farnam, Durfee, and Lawrance halls and Battell Chapel at Yale. But both men saw that their hopes for a Gothic Revival had been too optimistic. Their youthful articles in the New Path and their work for the National Academy represented the high-water mark of their Ruskinism.

Sturgis found his true calling as a critic and scholar. He became an art critic for the Nation, wrote frequently for the North American Review, conducted a regular department for Scribner's, and contributed frequently to the Architectural Record. He served as editor-in-chief of A Dictionary of Architecture and Building (1901–1902). His references to Ruskin grew increasingly critical as his career went on. In 1866 he wrote a warm, sympathetic review of Sesame and Lilies for the North American Review. In 1869 he could still praise Ruskin's illustrations in The Seven Lamps as "absolutely photographic in their accuracy, reproducing every light, shade, and shadow

Fig. 103.   Mercantile Library, Brooklyn, N.Y., P. B. Wight. Builder, 1872.

upon the stone as at the hour when the drawing was made."[24] Eventually, however, he decided that Ruskin appreciated only the picturesque in architecture. In an obituary article in 1900 he concluded that Ruskin "had committed himself, in his youth, and before he or any man could have had time to think anything out, to a variety of statements made so positively, and with such violence of invective showered upon those who disagreed with him, that he wore the fetters of those youthful assertions all his life long."[25] In a 1906 pamphlet titled *Ruskin on Architecture,* he concluded that his one-time master was "a practical draughtsman at the details of form," but "had no notion whatever of the constructor's art" and little sense of the importance of "abstract proportion of part with part."[26] Throughout his career, however, Sturgis maintained a Ruskinian stress on the interdependence of the arts and a warm appreciation for varied surface decoration.

Wight's evolution away from Ruskinism was even more dramatic. He was already dissatisfied with the amount of work he could obtain in New York when he heard a newsboy shouting news of the Chicago Fire of 1871. Realizing that there would be an immense demand for architects, he packed his bags. Between 1871 and the financial panic of 1873, the firm of Carter, Drake, and Wight designed over fifty buildings. Wight later gave up the practice of architecture to become a fireproofing consultant, and in this capacity he was associated with the development of the Chicago skyscraper. He often cast fond backward glances at the *New Path* and the National Academy, but the ideals they expressed seemed sadly irrelevant. "Some of us," he concluded in 1897, "tried to do the impossible."[27] Modern American architecture, he now thought, required a new style based on new materials and advanced technology.

The essential difference between English and American Ruskinism is that one evolves during the 1870s and the other fades. The English abandon their emphasis on style and place new stress on craftsmanship. As a result, we can trace a continuous line from the Ruskinism of G. E. Street to that of Philip Webb to that of W. R. Lethaby. In America we do not find this. There is an arts and crafts movement late in the century, and Wight's furniture designs contributed to it. His later architectural work, by contrast, dealt with the problems posed by mechanization, steel framing, and the tall building. The problem we face in the careers of Wight and Sturgis, therefore, is simply an intensification of the one that confronts us in American architecture as a whole: Why does Ruskinism fade rather than evolve?

There are three answers. One is that Americans quickly gave up the effort to create a tradition of Ruskinian craftsmanship. Wight said in 1866 that with the exception of those he had been able to take to Street Hall in New Haven, the carvers he had trained at the National Academy had reverted to producing Corinthian capitals and egg-and-dart moldings for a Fifth Avenue mansion. If the architect could not rely on those who ornamented his building, neither could he trust those who constructed it. Sturgis commented somewhat mysteriously in 1871 that attempts had been made "in one of our cities" to revolutionize the process of building by employing "an artist to make a design and a superintendent to take this design as a suggestion and guide, and to build from it according to his judgment." But, says Sturgis, "this has resulted disastrously in every case with which the writer is familiar." He concluded that master builders and their foremen were so ignorant of architectural design that the architect's only recourse was "to see that their own brain-work replaces so much handwork as can be spared."[28]

Another reason is that French methods dominated architectural education in the United States from a very early point. Once Richard Morris Hunt came home from the Ecole des Beaux-Arts and set up his own atelier in New York City, it was clear that young Americans, whether they studied architecture in Paris or at MIT, would learn according to the French system. They might be admirers of Ruskin, but their basic design philosophy would be that of the Beaux-Arts.

The third reason might not be as obvious as the first two. In the 1850s, when Ruskin's books were first being read, the English were fascinated by the possibility of a new style growing out of railroad construction and the Crystal Palace. The growth of Ruskin's authority was closely linked with the decline of interest in cast iron. In America, by contrast, that interest did not decline. It grew, and many of the attitudes first formed in response to iron were later transferred to steel. The iron problem was a major factor inhibiting the evolution of Ruskinism, and it therefore requires a section of its own.

III

The iron building is a constantly recurring feature of American architecture in the second half of the nineteenth century. The typical example had an iron facade and, on the interior, iron columns joined by cast- or wrought-iron girders. These buildings were quickly manufactured and could be shipped to remote locations. They made possible large amounts of precast decoration without the expense of hiring carvers. Above all, in a nation whose cities were periodically swept by large-scale fires, they were thought to be fireproof. By 1872 there were said to be two-and-three-quarter miles of iron fronts in lower Manhattan alone.

The overwhelming majority of iron buildings offended against the lamp of truth. Ruskin had forbidden any "direct falsity of assertion respecting the nature of material, or the quantity of labour" (8.59). The typical cast-iron building, by contrast, was painted or "marbleized" to look like stone, and its decoration appeared hand carved. Such buildings were usually designed in Renaissance styles, but Gothic was possible as well. The Grover and Baker Sewing Machine Company used a three-story Gothic window for their Broadway showroom, and in Providence, Rhode Island, William Walker designed an extraordinarily handsome Venetian Gothic building for the corner of Weybosset and Custom House streets. It is a superb example of a certain phase of Ruskinism, and only a magnet gives convincing evidence that it is not stone.

Not surprisingly, iron structures were condemned in the *Crayon*. One contributor assures readers that New York's version of the Crystal Palace was not a success; another warns Thomas U. Walter not to go ahead with the ostentatious display of his cast-iron dome for the U.S. Capitol.

But iron structures would not go away. Merchants demanded them. Some contributors therefore took a more adventuresome attitude. A review of Duncan and Sherman's new bank welcomes iron because it provides "the long-desired, perfect fire-proof construction" and proposes that the material no longer be disguised:

> The coating of iron pillars with scagliola is an absurdity. A true architect would have worked nights in decorating them with gilding and color. . . . What, ashamed of the very merits of the building! and thus attempt to hide the honest iron beams and girders, instead of decorating them truthfully and artistically! When will architects begin to think more, and copy less?[29]

In other words, redeem iron from the charge of deception by treating it truthfully. In that way it should be possible to design an iron building on Ruskinian principles. This solution seems so elegant that for a moment one wonders why Ruskin did not think of it. But Ruskin's instincts were sound. The truthful use of iron subverts Ruskinism.

How this is so may be seen in an 1858 defense of cast iron presented by Henry Van Brunt to the recently founded American Institute of Architects. Twenty-eight years old and a student of Richard Morris Hunt, Van Brunt understood that to meet Ruskin's demand for truth he would have to reject both Ruskin's love of handwork and his hostility to a commercial, industrial civilization:

> The Gothic spirit . . . was a *handicraft spirit,* and, to be expressed in a noble architecture, demanded the sacrifice and thought of a varied ornamentation. Now the age which we are called upon to express is not one of individualities, but of aggregates. It is not one of barbarous sacrifice either of time, labor, money or material, but of wise economy. Science has nearly destroyed personal labor and has substituted the labor of machinery, and almost all the industrial arts are carried on not by hands but by machines.

In an iron age, we will no longer look to architecture for an expression of the thought or aspiration of the workman. Instead, we will find "an architecture of strict mechanical obedience."[30] In place of Ruskin's massiveness and rich variety, Van Brunt calls for lightness, flat metal plates, and reduplicated parts.

Wight did not see the opposition between Ruskinism and iron so clearly. In the *New Path* he condemned New York's iron fronts as "the greatest architectural monstrosities,"[31] and in 1869 he noted that "the best thinkers have doubted whether there can be any such thing as architecture in iron."

Nevertheless, he himself thought there could be. He praised New York's version of the Crystal Palace in the *New Path,* used iron in his National Academy, and advocated the honest use of cast-iron structural elements.

It is clear that Wight's acceptance of iron in the 1860s was motivated by practical concerns. He fully accepted the claim that iron was fireproof. In his 1869 "Remarks on Fire-Proof Construction" he praised Daniel Bogardus's Harper and Brothers building, with its iron front, iron columns, and iron girders, as "the pioneer of the new dispensation."[32] In doing so, he began to slip from Ruskinian social attitudes: only by its honest use, he said, can the fireproof architecture of the nineteenth century be made worthy of a rational and progressive age.

Sturgis was also concerned with the possibility of using iron truthfully. In an 1871 article entitled "Modern Architecture" for the *North American Review,* he defines the falsehood of ordinary iron buildings in a novel way. Their fronts use the forms of traditional post-and-lintel construction. In fact, says Sturgis, the "cross beams" are not really resting on the "columns." The seeming columns are really continuous hollow shafts running from the bottom of the building to the top. The horizontal elements are only attached to the continuous shafts by brackets at each floor level. The architect's task was to find a way of truthfully expressing this revolutionary mode of construction.

In arguing this, Sturgis is developing the Ruskinian standard of truth in a way that will lead it very far from its origins. Ruskin had suggested that a building might be guilty of three types of untruthfulness. Its surfaces might suggest a material other than that of which it was made. Its decoration might suggest that it was made by hand rather than cast. And its supports might suggest a mode of structure or support other than the true one. Clearly iron buildings were guilty on all three counts, but they were guilty on the third count in a way that Ruskin did not foresee. His example of a false assertion concerning support was the comparatively specialized one of the pendants of some late Gothic roofs. Sturgis is extending the idea that a building should truthfully assert its mode of structure by demanding that the facade accurately reflect the network of horizontal and vertical elements behind it. When that is done, the underlying construction comes to control the facade in a way that goes far beyond anything in Ruskin's work. Essentially, Sturgis has stated the problem that functionalists would face in the next decade when they began designing Chicago skyscrapers. Sturgis seems to recognize the direction in which he is going, for he recommends that architects pay less attention to style and more to strict building necessity.

There is another influence besides Ruskin's operating on Wight and Sturgis in the 1860s and 1870s—that of Viollet-le-Duc. Both the Frenchman

and the Englishman were Gothic Revivalists; there is a large overlap between their theories, but they differed in their attitudes toward buildings,
toward iron, and toward the age. The ten volumes of the *Dictionnaire raisonné de l'architecture* (1854–1868) give overwhelming demonstrations of
the ways in which Gothic forms were rational solutions to structural problems. The six volumes of the *Dictionnaire raisonné du mobilier français*
(1858– 1875) enforce the same point. The two volumes of the *Entretiens
sur l'architecture*, which appeared in 1863 and 1872, advocate the truthful
use of iron for vaulting, for floral capitals, for staircases, and for any other
use in which it meets a need. And Viollet-le-Duc, unlike Ruskin, considers the truthful use of iron to be one of the many ways in which medieval
principles of building can lead to a new architecture expressive of a progressive age.

Wight and Sturgis published a page of excerpts from Viollet-le-Duc's
Dictionnaire raisonné du mobilier français in the July 1864 issue of the *New
Path*. By 1868 Wight was reading his translation of Viollet-le-Duc's lectures
at the Ecole des Beaux-Arts to the New York chapter of the American Institute of Architects, and he published them in the November and December 1870 and January 1871 issues of the *Manufacturer and Builder*.
Sturgis reviewed the complete *Dictionnaire raisonné de l'architecture* in the
August 12 and 26, 1869, issues of the *Nation*, and his 1871 article in the
North American Review endorses Viollet-le-Duc's definition of architecture
as "intelligent building."[33] Thereafter references to Viollet-le-Duc tend to
replace those to Ruskin in their writing.

In this shift Wight and Sturgis were representative of advanced architectural taste as a whole. The English read Viollet-le-Duc with care. Burges,
Seddon, and Godwin certainly used his books. Ruskin himself, in spite of
his antipathy toward Viollet-le-Duc's restorations, admired the Frenchman's
sound knowledge of building. He recommended the *Dictionnaire raisonné
de l'architecture* to his Oxford students during the 1870s, and on March 2,
1887, when the young Percy Morley Horder wrote to ask advice about a
possible architectural career, Ruskin answered:

> My dear boy,
>   There is only one book on architecture of any value—and that contains
> everything rightly. M. Viollet le Duc's Dictionary. Every architect must learn
> French, for all the best architecture is in France—and the French workmen are
> in the highest degree skillful. For the rest—you must trust your own feeling and
> observation only. My books are historical or sentimental and very well in their
> way. But you must learn from the things themselves.[34]

This, however, represents Ruskin's personal graciousness rather than any
fundamental change in his theory of architecture. And in general, the En-

glish seem to have been able to admire Viollet-le-Duc without abandoning their more explicit relation to Ruskin. In America, by contrast, Ruskin's influence tends to give way before the French architect's, and the American fascination with the honest use of iron must have been a major reason for this.

After the Chicago Fire of 1871 Wight's attitude toward iron changed in a way that caused a further advance in his architectural evolution. He became persuaded that the fireproofing qualities of iron had been overestimated. It was unreliable at temperatures over 900 degrees Fahrenheit. It tended to soften and lose rigidity. It also expanded, raising floor levels and disrupting structures. And the heated iron members tended to snap when hit with cold water. This did not mean that construction in iron came to an end, for it was not necessarily more hazardous than other building materials, but it was clearly not an answer to the fire problem. Iron—or, before long, steel,—would continue to be used. The problem was to find a way of protecting it from very high temperatures. Wight became interested in the possibility of encasing it first in wood, then in lightweight, terracotta blocks. Eventually this work proved so absorbing that it took him away from the designing of buildings. It left him, however, at the forefront of architectural developments in Chicago during the 1880s. His work was integral to the development of the steel-skeleton skyscraper.

Wight was able to see a connection between the early and late stages of his career. In an 1899 article, "Modern Architecture in Chicago," he observed that the English medieval movement seemed to go in two different directions: in one it led to "the extravagant imitation of Gothic forms by the ignorant architects who did not understand their meaning"; in the other it moved toward a discarding of ornament and "a rational treatment on constructive lines" in which there was little to suggest medievalism.[35] When he listed the key figures in the development of American architecture in 1897, Wight omitted Ruskin but mentioned Viollet-le-Duc, Leopold Eidlitz, Henry Van Brunt, John Wellborn Root, and Louis Sullivan.

IV

A short survey of a few of the leading American architects who felt Ruskin's influence will confirm what the careers of Wight and Sturgis have suggested: iron poses a significant challenge to them, and the Ruskinian element in their thinking gives way to the influence of Viollet-le-Duc.

Harvard's Memorial Hall is a good example of problematic Ruskinism.[36] The chief mover behind it—its Henry Acland, as it were—was Charles Eliot Norton, whose lifelong friendship with Ruskin had begun in Italy in 1856. He had visited the Oxford Museum in 1856 and had praised it in an article for the *Atlantic Monthly* in 1859. It was clearly in his thoughts when he proposed a memorial for the students and alumni of Harvard who had fallen in the Civil War. The building would signal a revolution in taste and exert a moral and aesthetic influence on undergraduates for centuries to come.

Unfortunately, America's Acland failed to secure his Woodward. The competing architects were given less than a month to design a building that would include an academic theater, a dining hall, and a "noble and befitting place for the accumulation of memorials of the dead and the living."[37] Wight declined to enter on the reasonable grounds that he was too busy with other projects. Sturgis did enter, and his proposal (which does not survive) appears to have been Norton's favorite. The winning design, however, was by Henry Van Brunt.

Van Brunt was willing to meet Norton half way, but he was not himself a Ruskinian. His design, in which the three separate uses are clearly expressed in the tripartite division of the building, is a good example of rational French planning. Moreover, Van Brunt was falling under the spell of Viollet-le-Duc even as he was working on Memorial Hall. In April of 1866 he published his review of the first volume of the *Entretiens* in the *Nation*. There he diplomatically referred to Ruskin as an exponent of the "purely literary element" in architecture who, with all his faults, had helped free English architects from prejudice and fashion.[38] By 1875, when his translation of the *Entretiens* appeared, Van Brunt was more explicit. He quoted with evident approval a critic's claim that "since Mr. Ruskin set the example of a literary man erecting himself into a dictator on questions of art, we have been subject to a fearful tyranny in aesthetics."[39] Not surprisingly, Memorial Hall is Ruskinian more in its inspiration than in its execution.

A purer example of the English element can be found in the work of Frederick Clarke Withers.[40] Born in Somerset in 1828 and trained in the office of Thomas Henry Wyatt, Withers came to America to work with Andrew Jackson Downing. He continued to follow developments in his native land, and his American architecture evolved in much the same direction as the English Gothic Revival. His Dutch Reformed Church of 1859 united certain motifs from the Ecclesiologists, such as the central bell cot, with the continuous outline and clifflike banding advocated by Ruskin. His Newburgh Savings Bank of 1866 reproduced many of the features that George Gilbert Scott recommended for urban commercial structures, and the buildings he designed for Washington's Gallaudet College show a similar debt to Scott.

Fig. 104. Courthouse, Third Judicial District, N.Y., Withers and Vaux. New York Sketchbook of Architecture, 1874.

Withers's most spectacular building is surely the Jefferson Market Courthouse (1874; fig. 104) at the corner of Sixth Avenue and Tenth Street in New York's Greenwich Village. It was designed for a triangular site that was to accommodate a market, a jail, a fire lookout station, and a court house. The market and jail have since been removed. Like many American architects, Withers had been impressed by the dramatic tower in William Burges's entry for the 1867 Law Courts competition. He achieved a similar fortresslike effect by placing his fire lookout in the tower at the apex of his triangle. The building is a startling composition in brick and stone banding with naturalistic plant carvings around the fountain and the trial scene from *The Merchant of Venice* carved over the main entrance. There is no doubt some paradox about an American Anglo-Venetian building, but the Jefferson Market Courthouse is a stunning achievement nonetheless.

In the work of Frank Furness we again face a union of English with French elements.[41] Like Van Brunt, Furness studied with Richard Morris Hunt and was well trained in the French philosophy of design. On the other hand, the Ruskinian influence was also strong in his immediate environment. In 1870 his father, a well-known Unitarian minister, addressed the Philadelphia meeting of the American Institute of Architects. The elder Furness endorsed Ruskin's separation of the architect from the mere builder and reminded his audience that a work of architecture is always "a great work of public instruction."[42]

The Reverend Furness also pleaded for a transformation of the Quaker simplicity of Philadelphia's streets, and that is what his son aimed at in his highly decorated, richly polychromatic design for the Pennsylvania Academy of the Fine Arts (1873). The younger Furness clearly gave careful attention to Wight's National Academy of Design and translated some of its characteristics into his own highly original vocabulary. The compact shape of the building may owe much to "The Lamp of Power," but its actual organization is a traditional French plan with an advanced central pavilion. Furness's plant forms may be Ruskinian in inspiration, but their actual design reflects the geometrical, architectural preferences of Owen Jones and Christopher Dresser in England and Viollet-le-Duc in France. The exposed iron within once again reminds us of the *Entretiens*.

The tendency to combine French and English influences can also be seen in the work of Edward Tuckerman Potter and his half brother William Appleton Potter.[43] Edward was born in 1831 and was apprenticed to the office of Richard Upjohn in 1854—at about the time when Ruskin's influence was first felt there. His journals show that he was reading Street's *Brick and Marble* by January of 1857. He visited England in that year and presumably became acquainted with the work of the leading Gothic Revivalists—although, ironically, his only journal reference to a modern building is some praise of London's Crystal Palace. William Appleton was born in 1842 and entered his brother's office as an apprentice in 1867. They set up a joint practice in 1869. Although Edward designed a very striking home for Mark Twain in 1873 and William produced a series of polychromatic courthouses and post offices during nineteen frustrating months as supervising architect to the Treasury Department, their most important Ruskinian works are churches and collegiate buildings. From an embarrassment of riches, it is possible to select three buildings that will show the range of their work: Edward Tuckerman's Nott Memorial at Union College and William Appleton's Chancellor Green Library and Alexander Hall at Princeton University.

The Nott Memorial was once thought to have been the earliest Ruskin-ian building in the United States. In *Architecture: Nineteenth and Twentieth Centuries*, Henry-Russell Hitchcock dated the building to 1858. In his later essay "Ruskin and American Architecture," however, Hitchcock shows that the building in its present form dates from a much later 1872. The campus had been laid out in 1813 by the classicist J. J. Ramée, but funds ran out before the planned central rotunda could be built. The six-teen-sided foundation had been laid, however, so the essential shape of the building had been determined. In 1858 the college decided to complete the structure and asked Edward Tuckerman to provide plans. He prepared a model in which Ramée's classical portico was replaced by a massive Ital-ian Romanesque porch. Once again, there was no money to proceed.

During the 1860s Edward Tuckerman designed a Barryesque bank on Wall Street as well as churches and homes. He shows a Ruskinian devotion to original decorative schemes in which the didactic intent is humorous rather than heavy-handed. At his First Dutch Reformed Church in Sche-nectedy, New York, for example, he designed capitals showing the plants of the Mohawk Valley. He also needed to decorate a wooden screen that would separate the body of the church from the consistory room. For this he designed twelve inventive capitals. The usual religious symbols were expressly forbidden by the canons of the Synod of Dort, so the architect expressed the Victorian delight in nature by designing twelve columns showing the months of the year. He starts with icicle-covered branches of January, follows the arrival, nesting, and eventual departure of the birds, and ends with the hemlocks and cones of December. At a private mansion in Duchess County, New York, he decorated eight black walnut columns with thirty-two different scenes representing the widest possible geographi-cal range of human activity, from eskimos pulling a dog sled in Greenland to a gaucho lassoing a wild bull in Argentina.

Adequate funding finally materialized for the Nott Memorial in 1872. Potter clothed his sixteen-sided, domed structure in a very harmonious polychromy of natural stone and pierced each of sixteen sides with a Gothic arch. On the inside, however, he struck what we now recognize as a persistently non-Ruskinian note in American Ruskinian buildings. He used rolled-iron beams, iron staircases, and galleries with iron beams and corrugated sheet iron.

This combination of a stone exterior with painted iron inside is also found at William Appleton Potter's Chancellor Green Library at Prince-ton. Iron is clearly used for practical reasons—because it has fireproofing qualities and because pierced iron and plate glass permit a maximum amount of light into the interior. But William Appleton, like his brother, was fascinated by the purely aesthetic potentialities of honestly employed iron construction. For both brothers, this open, inventive use of iron indicates that the influence of Ruskin is being modified by that of Viollet-le-Duc. Edward Tuckerman admitted this explicitly. Asked by a client to define the leading characteristics of his style, Edward replied with a pun: "Well, I think perhaps it should be called the English violet order of architecture."[44]

In the work of Withers, Furness, and the Potters, the influence of Ruskin is obvious even after all necessary qualifications have been made. But it may be that some of the most fruitful aspects of Ruskin's influence are subterranean and beyond the reach of documentation.

H. H. Richardson provides an example. Peter Wight, who knew Richardson in his early days in New York and later superintended the construction of his American Merchants Union Express building in Chicago, states quite firmly that Richardson was "not a disciple of Ruskin" but "a studious reader of the works of Viollet-le-Duc."[45] On the other hand, it has long been recognized that in forming his distinctive style Richardson enriched his French design philosophy with a careful study of the English work of Street, Burges, and others. It is hard to believe, though no document exists to clarify the point, that he did not study *The Seven Lamps* for insight into the use of color and the creation of mass. And it is hardly surprising that William Appleton Potter, at such buildings as Princeton's Alexander Hall, should express his Ruskinian concerns with mass, polychromy, and readable sculpture by employing a Richardsonian vocabulary.

The influence of Ruskin is more rarified still in the work of John Wellborn Root. Too little is known of Root's early work when he was in Wight's office, but it is clear that by the 1880s he looked back on the Ruskinian phase of American architecture as a wild extravagance. He called it "the Victorian Cathartic":

> It came upon us in the time of our virgin innocence when architecture seemed the vale of pure Arcadia, and Ruskin was its prophet. Seduced by the blandishments of this new Renaissance, we yielded ourselves easy victims to its sway, and since that fateful day what crimes against Beauty and Truth and Power and the rest of the seven lamps has it not led us to commit.[46]

It will be noticed that though Ruskinian architecture betrayed the lamps of truth, beauty, and power, the lamps themselves are not rejected.

Indeed, they continue to shine in Root's few published essays. In them, he embraces the principle that nature is both a standard and a source for architectural design. "It will always be found," he says in 1885, "that for any given conditions in the decoration of a building, parallel conditions exist in nature, and we have only to differentiate from one to the other."[47] With this assumption, he proceeds to formulate lessons about decoration and color. He agrees with "The Lamp of Beauty" that in nature nothing is colored along the lines of its form. Color is always "entirely distinct" and is "in general characterized in its application by entire absence of definite outline."[48] However, Root then makes the un-Ruskinian observation that in nature only small things are polychromatic and that the greater ones tend toward monochrome. This observation must have been in his mind as he worked on the Monadnock Block. The client, by naming his structure after a mountain in New Hampshire, had invited an architectural analogy with a cliff. This, according to Root's Ruskinian way of thought, required a monochrome rather than the geological banding that Ruskin himself would have employed. The architect therefore chose red brick, but, mindful of the principle that color in nature has no outline and is independent of form, he varied it subtly by making the brick progressively lighter as the building rises. Thus Ruskinian views remain fruitful even for a building that was making the distinction between building and architecture obsolete.

The Ruskinian element is even harder to trace in the work of the critic Montgomery Schuyler, but it is there nonetheless. A friend and protégé of Eidlitz, Schuyler tells readers that Ruskin "has fallen into deep, and largely into deserved discredit as an architecture critic" and complains that Ruskin's "intellectual frivolity" is made even more irritating "by reason of the moral earnestness that attends it." He thought America was plagued by architecture "in the Ruskinian sense," which consisted merely in "the addition of unnecessary features."[49] In 1892 he gave an important statement of his most basic beliefs, entitled "The Point of View," in which he insisted that "the real, radical defect of modern architecture in general, if not of American architecture in particular, is the estrangement between architecture and building." If ever there was a man innocent of Ruskinism, it was surely Schuyler. Yet a critic of "The Point of View" complains: "It seems odd to see the "Lamp of Truth" which burned so brightly for a season a generation ago in the hands of Mr. Ruskin, lighted up once more in this later day, and brandished about by an American critic."[50] Yet the surprise vanished with a moment's thought. The demand for truth, which is what first gave Ruskin his great prestige in America, led to results that Ruskin himself could never have imagined.

Research will undoubtedly discover a great deal more about Ruskin's influence on architecture in the United States during the last three decades of the nineteenth century, but it is not likely to dramatically alter the broad picture given here. Architectural Ruskinism appeared in the late 1850s and 1860s as an English import, part of a broader fascination with the Pre-Raphaelite movement, and it reached its purest expression in the work of Wight and Sturgis. It was from the beginning subject to competition from a functionalist tradition first expressed by Horatio Greenough and persistently reinforced by Leopold Eidlitz. This led to a rejection of

Ruskin's separation of architecture from building. Something similar occurred in England, but there such figures as Philip Webb, William Morris, and J. D. Sedding evolved a new Ruskinism based on craftsmanship, guilds, and the organization of work. American architects, by contrast, were more likely to accept subcontracting, craft unions, and the division of labor. Fascinated with structural innovation and by the honest use first of cast iron, then of structural steel, they replaced Ruskin with Viollet-le-Duc. Yet even after Ruskin was rejected as a fundamental thinker, he remained an important source of individual insights. This is true for H. H. Richardson and John Wellborn Root, and though difficult to trace in detail, it must be true of Louis Sullivan and Frank Lloyd Wright as well. A briefer phenomenon than its English parent, American Ruskinism left a long afterglow.

XIV

THE GUILD MOVEMENT AND
THE DECLINE OF RUSKINISM

 BY the 1880s English Ruskinism had found its new direction. It was now agreed that if a Ruskinian architect was to express any part of his age, it would be its reforming zeal rather than its commercial vigor. Industrialism was now seen as a threat, and Ruskin's comparatively few comments on the modern workman were regarded as the most important of all his writings. Indeed, his quixotic gestures at social reform—sponsoring street sweeping in Seven Dials or a tea shop in Paddington—may now have meant more than all his descriptions of Venetian palaces. Where earlier Ruskinians had been devout churchmen, the new ones were often freethinkers. Some of them were fascinated by labor churches, Tolstoyan communities, homogenic love, and simple life. All of them were united in the belief that the hand of the craftsman gave life, while the accurate finish of mechanical reproduction was a sign of death. Their problem was to find an organizational form for this faith, one that would be an alternative to both the subcontracting of the building sites and the professional isolation of the architect's office.

The form chosen, that of the guild, had deep roots in the nineteenth-century mind. It had appeared in the 1830s and 1840s in the hopes of Joseph Aloysius Hansom, who, inspired by Owenite socialism, sought to combine all builders, from laborers to architects, in a single, self-governing organization.[1] It continued in Alfred Bartholomew's Freemasons of the Church. During the 1850s G. E. Street dreamed of a brotherhood of pious church builders. Ruskin emphasized the importance of guilds in his Oxford lectures of 1873, and Morris lectured on them frequently. Medieval in its origins, vaguely socialist in its implications, at once paternalistic and democratic, the guild idea perfectly matched the complex historical aware-ness of young men who had been nurtured by the Gothic Revival but now sought a freer architecture growing out of new forms of social organization.

I

Arthur Heygate Mackmurdo took a major step toward the organizational form of the arts and crafts movement with his Century Guild.[2] He also provides the best possible introduction to the intellectual setting of the late nineteenth century. We have seen that Ruskinism as a phenomenon is always a union of Ruskin's ideas with elements from other, sometimes quite different, sources. In the 1880s and 1890s the elements combined become ever more disparate, and this was a situation in which a syncretic thinker like Mackmurdo could thrive. He called himself a hero-worshiper and prided himself on the diversity of his heroes. What he said of Christopher Wren applied to his own career: "contending brain tempests were his swad-dling clothes."[3] In his thinking the ideas of Ruskin are modified by the unlikely combination of the ideas of Walter Pater and evolutionary biology.

Mackmurdo's roots reach back to the earliest period of Ruskin's influ-ence. While he was apprenticed to the London architect T. Chatfield Clarke, he would frequently stroll down New Bridge Street, past Wood-ward's Crown Life Assurance building. This was either just before or at about the same time that he read *The Seven Lamps* and *The Stones of Venice:*

> Clearly now do I see how it influenced me in my first work—a house I built in 1873. In Woodward's building, the carving was the design of craftsmen who had adapted their studies of English foliage to the ornamentation of the capitals, string courses, etc. Woodward also commissioned artists to design and execute the internal decorations.[4]

Halcyon House was designed in 1871 or 1872, though its construction was not complete until 1876. During this time, Mackmurdo studied the houses of Philip Webb and Norman Shaw. He also worked for one of the most interesting Gothic church architects, James Brooks. Mackmurdo's first house, with polychromatic brickwork and naturalistic carving of birds and foliage, is a résumé of the enthusiasms of the 1850s and 1860s. He never did anything like it again.

Mackmurdo's association with Ruskin began shortly after he designed

Halcyon House. The two men were psychologically compatible. Ruskin was uncomfortable with equals but extremely generous to those who would submit to his direction. Mackmurdo enjoyed the role of disciple. He attended Ruskin's drawing classes at Oxford and traveled through France and Italy with the master in 1874. He did a drawing of a sepulchral slab in Santa Croce that Ruskin had photographed to illustrate *Mornings in Florence.* He drew the buildings that Ruskin admired, though he also acquired a lifelong enthusiasm for Renaissance architecture. His sketchbooks show that he drew not only buildings but also stones, mountains, insects, and flowers. Some are actually copies of sketches by Ruskin. He read *Fors Clavigera* as it came out in installments. Ruskin's economic doctrines prompted Mackmurdo to write a pamphlet titled *The Immorality of Lending for Payment or Interest* (1878) and led him, after his architecture went out of fashion in the twentieth century, to write on economic reform. He helped promote Ruskin societies in London, Birmingham, and Manchester. When Mackmurdo applied for a post as art professor at Liverpool University, Ruskin declared that

> he has been among my own pupils, distinguished alike by his apprehensive docility, and by great intellectual patience in testing the truth of everything alleged to him. Had he not manifested this resolute independence of character, your acceptance of him as your Professor would be very nearly like electing *me,* with the permission to name my acting substitute.[5]

The Liverpool post failed to materialize, and Mackmurdo, still eager to put his idealism to the test, offered to teach at the Sheffield Museum. Ruskin suggested that he work in London instead, and in 1882 the Century Guild was formed.

Those who were associated with it include Selwyn Image, Heywood Sumner, Herbert Horne, Clement Heaton, and Benjamin Creswick.[6] Image, a key member of the group though he never formally joined, had attended Ruskin's first Slade lecture and had joined Ruskin's first drawing class. Creswick had been sent to Mackmurdo by the master himself.

The purpose of the Century Guild is easily described. Mackmurdo had been impressed by James Brooks's conviction that every detail of his buildings should embody personal feeling as part of a perfectly coordinated conception, but he also saw Brooks's frustrations in attempting to create the architecture he envisioned with the tradesmen who were available. The Century Guild was conceived as an answer to this dilemma. It would enable architects to work alongside craftsmen and to practice the crafts themselves. And it would create an institutional framework for artistic creation that would be a rival to the professional bodies.

In spite of its short life, the Century Guild achieved its goals. Mackmurdo mastered such crafts as repoussé work in brass, and he learned enough cabinetry to design furniture with an awareness of constructive methods. He created very influential designs for wallpapers and fabrics. Selwyn Image designed stained glass, and Herbert Horne did cretonne. Heywood Sumner single-handedly revived the incising process called sgraffito—the results can be seen in his decoration of C. Harrison Townsend's All Saints' Church, Ennismore Gardens. One of the group's most significant achievements was the *Hobby Horse*, an aesthetic journal with contributions by Rossetti, Arnold, Yeats, and Wilde as well as Ruskin.

In all these activities, we can see that Ruskin's influence was modified by the impact of what is broadly termed the aesthetic movement. Mackmurdo and his friend Selwyn Image probably encountered its most influential fig- ure, the reticent don Walter Pater, while they were at Oxford. Mackmurdo met Whistler at Rupert D'Oyly Carte's house in the early 1880s and was soon helping him prepare the decorative scheme for a one-man show.

The aesthetic movement set aside the Gothic Revival's heavy-handed didacticism. Ruskin insisted, sometimes with subtle arguments, sometimes with crude ones, that our moral character was reflected in our responses to color and line. Such men as Pater and Wilde agreed that there was a mo- rality of art, but they did not think it so closely tied to traditional morality as Ruskin imagined. The first appeal of art was to the senses alone. As Wilde said in 1882, this "recognition of the primary importance of the sen- suous element in art, this love of art for art's sake, is the point in which we of the young school have made a departure from the teaching of Mr. Rus- kin—a departure definite and different and decisive."[7] Selwyn Image, writing in the first issue of the *Hobby Horse*, insisted that we are children of the pagan Renaissance as well as of the Christian Middle Ages, and added that "the sooner . . . we see this plainly and confess it to ourselves, and arrange our lives in accordance with the recognition of it, the better."[8] Mackmurdo showed one way to accept the pagan spirit when he urged an audience "more frankly to accept the leading of the senses, as they lean more and more to some refined gratification."[9]

Mackmurdo faced a tension between Ruskin's broad social concerns and Pater's narrower focus on individual temperament. His thinking begins with Pater's. Echoing the famous "Conclusion" to *The Renaissance*, Mack- murdo says that the mission of art is to make more tangible, more nearly permanent, the shifting world of our sensations. This quickening of our emotions is the service of art to life. But Mackmurdo at once gives this definition a broader scope: "To make life less sordid, less dismal, less ugly, less laborious, we make haste to remove the hovels of unhealthiness; we give the people . . . parks, open spaces, free education, increased leisure, libraries, baths, gymnasiums."[10]

Mackmurdo's short book, *Wren's City Churches* (1883), is best understood in terms of his effort to synthesize Ruskin and Pater. The book is most famous for its title page, which is regularly cited as an anticipation of art nouveau, but the text also reveals a new spirit. The immediate purpose of the book was to plead for the preservation of Wren's endangered churches. Regard for these buildings had been low while revived Gothic was in the ascendancy; Ruskin's attack on the deceptive double dome of Saint Paul's had by no means been an isolated phenomenon. Street had proposed rebuilding one of Wren's city churches, Saint Dionis Backchurch, in Ruskinian Gothic, and during the 1870s it was proposed to let William Burges complete the decorations of the interior of Saint Paul's in his distinctive style. Ruskin's own attitude toward Wren was more admiring that his comments in *The Seven Lamps* would suggest, and on March 25, 1872, he instructed his secretary to write a letter opposing plans for the proposed redecoration.[11] Nevertheless, the conventional wisdom of the time held that a love for Gothic was one thing, an appreciation of Wren quite another. When a disciple of Ruskin acccompanies rapturous praise of Wren's art of proportion with savage abuse of Street's Law Courts, he is clearly intending a public declaration of independence from the pieties of the Gothic Revival.

We have seen that Ruskin affects not only the way in which his admirers think about architecture but the way they write about it as well. Mackmurdo is no exception, and his style shows the same mingling of Ruskin and aestheticism as his content. Of one of Wren's spires he says:

> At first glance, who that can at all appreciate its beauty, is not enraptured with the melody of its many mingling notes of form, its dancing buoyancy and splendid balance? . . . And how soft, how grand, are these first notes, so like the opening chords of a Beethoven symphony!—how quiet the transition from square of tower to the octagon of spires![12]

The *Builder* recognized one of the origins of this style when it compared Mackmurdo's prose to "the delirium of a student whose health had failed while cramming for an examination in Ruskinism."[13] But the musical images reflect Pater's essay "The School of Giorgione," and the title of one of Mackmurdo's plates—*Soul Strivings from Struggle into Calm*—sounds dangerously like a cartoon by Du Maurier.

It is characteristic of Mackmurdo's syncretism, however, that the aesthete could also take an informed interest in biology. Mackmurdo attended lectures on evolution by Tyndall and Huxley at London University, and he readily accepted Herbert Spencer as another of his intellectual masters.

Spencer and Ruskin themselves had no doubt that their intellectual systems were incompatible. Spencer recorded his opinion in his autobiography. He had been pleased by *Modern Painters* because it criticized the old masters, and he had therefore opened *The Stones of Venice* with high expectations: "On looking at the illustrations, however, and reading the adjacent text, I presently found myself called upon to admire a piece of work which seemed to be sheer barbarism. My faith in Mr. Ruskin's judgment was at once destroyed."[14] Ruskin, for his part, wrote to Frederick Harrison in 1884: "I was so furious at your praising Herbert Spencer that I couldn't speak" (37.479).

Spencer's comments on architecture are few but suggestive. The most important of them can be found in two early essays, "Use and Beauty" and "The Sources of Architectural Types." Spencer distinguishes, as Ruskin does, between use and beauty. The difference is that Spencer prefers use. He views evolution as a process in which the need for survival creates certain forms. These forms lose their function after the evolutionary process has moved on and survive as mere beauty. Elaborate ornament in architecture is the equivalent of these lovely, useless survivals in nature. Spencer was prepared to enjoy ornament in moderation but not to make it the soul of architecture.

The sharpest difference between Spencer and Ruskin is the former's hostility to revivals. When he visited the aesthetic suburb of Bedford Park with his friend Moncure Conway, Spencer expressed surprise that "a 'progressive' should go far back in matters of architecture."[15] In general, Spencer encourages his admirer to value newness and logical clarity and to delight in ornament without letting it overlay structure.

The visual consequences of Mackmurdo's eclectic hero-worshiping can be seen in the design for a suburban house—an early version of Mackmurdo's Brooklyn House—that appeared in the *Hobby Horse* (fig. 105).

Fig. 105.   *Mackmurdo House.* Hobby Horse, 1887.

Fig. 106.   *Title page of* Wren's City Churches *(1883).*

Mackmurdo defined the essentials of his art as "a systematic design, geometrical proportion of spaces and masses, unity or keeping throughout, so that the whole impresses itself on the mind as one affect; and lastly, the indispensable quality of unexpectedness."[16] All of these can be seen in the house. Its proportions, emphasized by Benjamin Creswick's terra-cotta statues, show Mackmurdo's admiration for the Renaissance. Its shape and color show that he has been impressed by Godwin's White House. Above all, this house shows that the period of visual Ruskinism is over. Few other Ruskinian buildings will break with medieval traditions quite so dramatically, but it is clear that henceforth the Ruskinian nature of architecture must be sought in the cooperation of craftsmen rather than in any specifically visual features.

Mackmurdo's role as a transformer of Ruskinism can also be seen on the title page to *Wren's City Churches* (fig. 106). Instead of the crisp facade of the house, with its ruler-straight lines, we now have lush but beautifully proportioned curves all but crowding the two phoenixes off the page. Clearly Mackmurdo is profiting from the analysis of plant forms that he undertook under Ruskin's tutelage during the 1870s. But he had also, as

Malcolm Haslam points out,[17] attended T. H. Huxley's lectures on marine biology, and he may have read Darwin's *Power of Movement in Plants* (1880) with its analysis of spiral motion in plant growth. Certainly there is a gently flowing, underwater rhythm to Mackmurdo's plants. But of course these forms also represent the flames of the Great Fire of London. Mackmurdo's visual pun looks back to the flame-plant forms of Blake as well as forward to the wit of Aubrey Beardsley.

There is one final aspect of this title page to be noticed. That is the way in which its lush, crowded forms contrast with the rational page layout of the main body of the text. This is a contrast met throughout Mackmurdo's work, and it perhaps reflects Spencer's distinction between use and beauty. Whether designing a chair, a room, or a house, Mackmurdo strives for rational clarity in the structural parts but feels free to create an almost perverse idiosyncrasy in the decorative ones.

II

Mackmurdo's Century Guild was essentially a dress rehearsal for the larger and more successful Art Workers' Guild. The origins of the new organization are found in the early 1880s when two informal discussion groups merged. One, called The Fifteen, was organized at the initiative of the designer Lewis F. Day. Its members, who included Walter Crane, J. D. Sedding, T. M. Rooke, and Hugh Stannus, met at one another's home to give papers and discuss architecture and the decorative arts. The other, called the Saint George's Society after the Bloomsbury church rather than Ruskin's guild, consisted of the extraordinarily talented pupils and assistants in Norman Shaw's office. In January 1884 the two groups came together in the Art Workers' Guild. When the Century Guild disbanded, Selwyn Image, Heywood Sumner, and Clement Heaton all came into the new organization.

The members of the new guild were closer to the tradition of the Gothic Revival than Mackmurdo and his associates. Their buildings were usually clearly related to medieval building traditions, and they were far less willing than Mackmurdo and Selwyn Image to set aside Ruskin's moral reading of architecture. Though he shifted his focus from figure sculpture to the more ordinary aspects of building, C. F. A. Voysey's view in 1895 was essentially the same as that which Ruskin had presented to the Architectural Association in 1857: "Turn a man on to any ordinary house to colour the wood and he will inevitably express, by his work and choice of colour, either unhealthiness or healthiness, sadness or joy. Some expression of thought and feeling there is sure to be. And thus may be imported that human element which adds such immeasurable charm to all noble works of art."[18] Even in making so simple a thing as the handle of a spoon, the craftsman has the power of encouraging "noble pleasures in noble ideas."[19] The words are Voysey's, but they echo Ruskin's characteristic vocabulary, and all members of the Art Workers' Guild would have said something similar.

But if members were united in their ideals of craftsmanship, they were divided on how far they wanted their new organization to be an instrument of social reform. Some favored a club where papers could be read; others wanted an activist society that would campaign for its ideals and sponsor public exhibits and lectures. This crystallized in an internal debate over whether the guild should publically support restrictions on outdoor advertising—a debate that the reformers lost. The energies of the more activist members tended to spin off into other organizations. The Arts and Crafts Exhibition Society organized exhibits and lectures for the public. W. R. Lethaby, Mervyn Macartney, Ernest Gimson, Sidney Barnsley, and Reginald Blomfield organized Kenton and Co., a firm that allowed them to design their own furniture and supervise their own workmen. A Women's Guild of the Arts was formed, and regional Art Workers' Guilds were formed in Liverpool, Birmingham, and Edinburgh.

The Art Workers' Guild membership, which was by election, included many of the best artists and architects of the time. Besides those already mentioned, the rolls included Ernest Newton, W. A. S. Benson, John Belcher, Basil Champneys, Beresford Pite, Detmar Blow, John Brett, C. Harrison Townsend, Edward Prior, Halsey Ricardo, R. W. S. Weir, C. R. Ashbee, and Edwin Lutyens. Since it is impossible to discuss all of them here, I will focus on two who developed Ruskinian themes in especially original ways: W. R. Lethaby and Halsey Ricardo.

Lethaby was born in Barnstaple, the son of a carver and gilder who was a fervent supporter of both Liberal politics and Bible Christianity. He was articled to a local architect and won a prize from the RIBA that enabled him to tour France. He entered Norman Shaw's office in 1879, becoming chief clerk and remaining throughout the 1880s. R. W. S. Weir recalled that "by the time I got to know him he had read everything that Ruskin had ever written and had absorbed his teaching."[20] Reginald Blomfield remembered that Ruskin's books "were to Lethaby as the words of the prophet."[21] Ruskin was withdrawing to Coniston and madness by the time Lethaby arrived in London, but the young man managed to attend one of the storm cloud lectures in 1884.

Lethaby did indeed regard Ruskin as a prophet, but one whose message had to be separated from much that was irrelevant. In 1883, for example, he emphatically set aside Ruskin's view of the Renaissance: "Ruskin's criticism is moral, and he sees in our style corruption and heartlessness; but this can surely have little weight when he admires so profoundly the painting and sculpture of the same age, which is part of the same development as the architecture and practiced by the same men."[22] Lethaby was by no means Ruskin's echo. Quite the contrary, he claims our attention because he was a disciple who showed an alert willingness to modify his master's principles. His changing use of Ruskin's legacy can be traced in two books—his own *Architecture, Mysticism, and Myth* (1891) and a collection of essays edited by Norman Shaw and Thomas Graham Jackson entitled *Architecture, A Profession or an Art?* (1892).

We have seen that Ruskin regarded his distinction between building and architecture as basic to his thought. We have also seen that beginning in the 1870s such admirers as John Henry Chamberlain, Philip Webb, and J. D. Sedding tended to set this distinction aside as a troublesome irrelevancy. The issue did not die, however. Lethaby was still worrying about it in 1891, and his final resolution of the matter shaped the direction of his mature career.

Lethaby seems at first to have accepted Ruskin's distinction. In 1890 he discussed the vexed question with Ernest Gimson. "We decided," he wrote in his diary, "that architecture might bear some such relation to building as religion to morality, and then, borrowing Matthew Arnold's phrase as well as his general idea, we agreed that architecture is building touched with emotion."[23] This view is repeated the following year at the beginning of *Architecture, Mysticism, and Myth:*

> As the pigments are but the vehicles of painting, so is building but the vehicle of architecture, which is the thought behind form, embodied and realised for the purpose of its manifestation and transmission. Architecture, then, interpenetrates building, not for the satisfaction of the simple needs of the body, but the complex ones of the intellect. I do not mean that we can thus distinguish between architecture and building, in those qualities in which they meet and overlap, but that in the sum and polarity of them all; these point to the response to future thought, those to the satisfaction of present need; and so, although no hut or mound, however early or rude, but had something added to it for thought's sake, yet architecture and building are quite clear and distinct as ideas—the soul and the body.[24]

Lethaby tries to escape the harsher implications of Ruskin's duality without quite succeeding. Architecture "interpenetrates" building at the beginning of the paragraph, but is only "added to it" by the end. In fact most of *Ar-*

chitecture, Mysticism, and Myth deals with decoration—the part that is added.

The shift in Lethaby's thought toward a franker acceptance of building as the basis for architecture can be seen the next year in his contribution to *Architecture, A Profession or an Art?* This book, a collection of thirteen essays edited by Norman Shaw and Thomas Graham Jackson, was a protest against the possibility that Parliament would restrict the practice of architecture to those who had passed an appropriate examination. This revived the debate of the 1860s over just what an architect was expected to be. Those favoring registration argued that the architect, like the engineer, should be required to demonstrate his practical knowledge. The older generation of contributors to *Architecture, A Profession or an Art?* denied that this kind of technical knowledge was the essential characteristic of an architect; they insisted, as Ruskin had in 1865, that his natural alignments were with painters and sculptors. Thus Thomas Graham Jackson insisted that architecture's kinship with the sister arts was her glory, but that "her weakness is that her utilitarian side seems to draw her down from the domain of art to that of mere building, into which art need not necessarily enter at all."[25]

So far this is the old debate. Some of the younger men, however, take a new tack and suddenly Lethaby is among them. He has met Philip Webb through the Society for the Protection of Ancient Buildings, and he now accepts Webb's principle that architecture is simply masterful building. He mocks style-mongering and quotes Morris on the pleasures of a large blank wall without any ordinary "architectural" features at all. He concerns himself less with the painter and the sculptor than with the carpenter, the mason, the pasterer, and the plumber. He invites his fellow architects to leave their offices and devote more time to consultation and cooperation with their fellow craftsmen on the building site.

One result of Lethaby's new view is a lively and long-lived debate over the actual activities of medieval architects.[26] We can see how the parties divide in a paper that Lethaby read to the RIBA in 1901 and in the response to it. Lethaby defended his view of architecture as "the whole range of activities associated with the art of building" and insisted that the term *architect* originally meant only "master in building craft." Building was a process of consultation between master craftsmen:

> It was often said that there must have been some coordinating authority, or the carpenter would wish to put the roof upside down; but the reply to that was that the carpenter did not wish to do so, and the employer would have dismissed him if he had. Moreover, the chief master employed, like an officer to-day, would be the general consulting leader. "Instead of vaulting this," the mason would then say to the employer, "we will get Bob to put couples on." There was

no artistic nonsense about it, but it was in the directness of the work that the interest of old buildings lay. It was a matter of true evolution; it was just doing work "as it ought to be done in the craft of masonry." [27]

Lethaby defended this view with all the research he had done as an architectural historian and with all the experience he had gained with the Society for the Protection of Ancient Buildings and as surveyor to the fabric of Westminster Abbey.

His opponents insisted that great buildings were the result of one master design and one supreme authority. Leonard Stokes, commenting on Lethaby's address, was frankly contemptuous:

> The old days were very charming days and one wished one could live in them, when John the mason started by scratching his head, and called in Bob the carpenter, and consulted whether to put a wooden or a stone roof on the top. He joined issue completely with Professor Lethaby there. He did not believe that sort of thing ever existed. [28]

Thomas Blashill denied that a building such as Westminster Abbey could result from a combination of superior craftsmen: "There must have been one master mind who, from the laying of the very first course of stones, had decided and was able, either by drawings or some other way, to teach the workmen what was to be done from the bottom to the top." [29]

It is difficult to know to what extent Lethaby's ideals were actually carried out in the construction of his buildings. In his last work, All Saints' Church, Brockhampton (1901–1902), Lethaby used direct labor rather than subcontracting and he was able to make significant changes in the building (increasing the height of the crossing tower, redesigning the transept windows) as new possibilities disclosed themselves during the process of construction. But the difficulties at All Saints' apparently brought Lethaby to the edge of a breakdown and may have contributed to his decision to give up the practice of architecture. He was extremely interested in the innovative use of new materials (All Saints' featured a mass concrete vault), and he realized that his technical knowledge was becoming obsolete. By 1907 he could write to Sydney Cockerell: "If I were again learning to be a modern architect I'd eschew taste and design and all that stuff and learn engineering with plenty of mathematics and hard building experience." [30] Not surprisingly, his career turned to education. He was principal of the Central School of Arts and Crafts from 1896 to 1911, professor of design at the Royal College of Art from 1900 to 1918, and an important lecturer and writer throughout the 1920s. For that reason, we will return to him in the last chapter to illustrate some of the eventual relations between Ruskinism and the modern movement.

Halsey Ricardo develops Ruskin's interest in architectural color and connects it with the broader theme of social reform. A member of the same banking family that had produced the famous economist, Ricardo was educated at Rugby before becoming articled to a Cheltenham architect. He worked for Basil Champneys, then set off on his own. He cites Ruskin frequently in his writings. In 1898 he reviewed a new edition of *The Art and Pleasures of England* in the *Architectural Review,* praising Ruskin fervently and expressing special admiration for *Fors Clavigera.* In 1900 he reviewed Robert de la Sizeranne's *Ruskin and the Religion of Beauty* for the same magazine. One of his most revealing statements is an 1890 lecture, "On Some of the Conditions of Modern Architecture in Towns."

In this very provocative and wide-ranging talk, Ricardo follows Ruskin in taking the smoke of industrial society as his central concern. All Victorian architects dealt with smoke as a fact. Ricardo goes further and uses it as a symbol:

> We are beginning to recognize that a manufacturing city has an atmosphere of its own, made in greatest measure by the smoke of its own furnaces and its hearths. . . . The reckless and selfish prodigality in the combustion of coal has brought on us what Mr. Ruskin calls 'the storm-cloud of the nineteenth century,' and our days are passed under a sunless canopy of gray smoke. Sunless! that's not the worst of it. Were the sun quite excluded we should pluck up our courage and leave such a doomed city. We are not sunless; a hideous ghastly mockery of a sun, blanched and ghostly, rises and sets to us on what we call our 'fine' days, and while his rays illuminate our gloom, they bleach our colour, destroying gradations of it, making our buildings mere charnel-house skeletons of gray bones in the shadowless dusk.[31]

Though many architects imitated Ruskin's prose or opulent description, few echoed his imagery of disease and death. Ricardo himself usually prefers a more rapturously aesthetic tone; the fact that he here invokes the despairing side of Ruskin's vision shows how passionately he felt about England's condition.

Ricardo's central concern is color, but he uses it as a point of departure for confronting wider social issues. It takes him into a very contemporary-sounding discussion of the effects of energy sources on architecture. He is skeptical about the use of brick, partly because coal is burnt in the making of it, partly because it suffers badly from pollution. He warns against petroleum lamps because of their fumes. He considers electricity more promising, but a great deal of coal must be burnt to produce it. His solution is an increased use of colored tile and glazed brick. It allows the achievement of subtle color harmonies. It is self-cleansing in every rain. Best of all, it makes use of "that best of all heat—the solar heat."[32]

An example of what Ricardo favored can be seen in the very remarkable house that he designed on Addison Road in Kensington.[33] Here glazed surfaces dominate both inside and out. On the exterior, the basement story is faced with blue-gray semivitrified Staffordshire bricks. The structural framework of the upper portion is covered with a creamy terra-cotta. Within this frame are panels of darker glazed brick. Thus the design is defined by color. Ricardo carefully chose only "second best" bricks so that there would be continual variation of hue within the same color. Inside the house, he achieves the Art Workers' Guild ideal of creation by cooperating craftsmen. William de Morgan provided the ceramics, Ernest Gimson the plasterwork, and E. S. Prior the stained glass. The ironwork was created by the Birmingham Guild of Handicraft.

It was obvious that buildings produced by Art Workers' Guild methods would either be homes for wealthy men or institutions paid for by them. Not all members of the guild were troubled by this. After all, their clients were liberal and civilized as well as rich. But those who were most impressed by *Fors Clavigera* sought a new focus for their energies in social reform. They attempted this in a series of 1895 lectures, "The Art and Decoration of Cities," and in the Art Workers' Guild masque of 1899.

The lectures were by Lethaby, Ricardo, Walter Crane, Reginald Blomfield, and T. J. Cobden-Sanderson. Blomfield, already out of step with the others, urged the reformers to emulate Renaissance planning and French formal gardens rather than the wayward fancies of the Middle Ages. The others, however, seemed determined to transform London into a Pre-Raphaelite painting. Lethaby and Cobden-Sanderson proposed to bring form out of chaos by instituting civic pageants to mark important events and seasonal changes. Ricardo wanted to bring coherence to the city by the use of heraldic colors. He observed that mailboxes were already of a uniform color and that omnibuses announced their routes by a color code. This principle could be extended. Each parish could use its own set of symbolic colors from area railings to the town hall. Buildings could have varied colors according to their purposes. Crane wanted all posters banished; instead of being entertained by the vulgar messages of manufacturers, the public would be surrounded by legends and symbols of a new civic mythology.

The fascination with pageantry and heraldic symbolism manifested itself in the Art Workers' Guild masque. Proposed by Walter Crane in 1897, it was finally staged in the city of London's guildhall on June 29, 1899, with the purpose of explaining the arts and crafts philosophy of civic rebirth to city merchants. Among those who designed costume, sets, and lights were Crane, Lethaby, Ricardo, C. H. Townsend, C. R. Ashbee, and Harry Wilson. Arnold Dolmetsch supplied the music. The story was a variant of all the folktales in which a sleeping beauty is woken by a kiss. The beauty is

Fayremonde, who is protected by all seven of Ruskin's lamps of architecture. The hero is Trueheart, who faces a series of monsters ranging from the fashionable world with

> Its conventional ways, its starch and its stays
> Its upholstered plays, its R.I.B.A.'s

to Slumdum who presides over

> Whitechapel horrors the goriest and best of them,
> Blistering profanity fleshing a zest of them,

and culminating in the ubiquitous jerry builder

> Jerry the merry, the artful, the new,
> Jerry the semi-detached, two by two,
> Little Pedlington Mays and District Surveyors,
> Microbe tanks, drain-pipes, and typhoid purveyors[34]

Fayremond's dreams are enlivened by visions of the world's great cities as they appeared before industrialism, and when she is awakened London is renewed as an arts and crafts paradise. It perhaps goes without saying that as an act of propaganda the masque was a failure. The audience was suspicious of the evening's implied socialism, and the costumes and props, which had looked quite beautiful in the workshops, appeared dull and shapeless on the stage. The drive toward urban reform among Ruskin's late-century admirers was momentarily stalled.

III

Charles Robert Ashbee's Guild of Handicraft was a more radical attempt than the Art Workers' Guild to change the nature of work and to establish a new relation between art and life.[35] It began in the east end of London and then moved to Chipping Camden in the Cotswolds where it established itself as a community of craftsmen. The guild eventually failed, and Ashbee, who had been a persuasive apologist for his ideals while it was growing, proved a clear-sighted analyst of what had gone wrong. He provides a clear example of the collision between Ruskinian morals and aesthetics on the one hand and the demands of a competitive industrial economy on the other.

Ashbee was born in 1863, the son of a wealthy, philistine merchant who achieved posthumous fame for his large collection of pornography.[36] The son set out to be everything that the father was not. He attended Cambridge, where self-culture and social reform had replaced religion as guiding passions for talented undergraduates. Years later he recalled that his papers in the examinations for the history schools were torn up and his marks canceled because he had followed Ruskin in defining value as "the strength or availing of anything towards the sustaining of life."[37] As a young man in London he, along with his college friends Lowes Dickinson and Edward Carpenter, traveled to Hammersmith to hear Morris lecture on private property. They went afterward to Morris's home where Ashbee, sensitive to its furnishings and its harmony of colors, felt as though he had stepped into Millais's portrait of Isabella. It seemed clear to the young man that he was to be part of a many-sided movement aimed at the transformation of industrial England.

After Cambridge he articled himself to the architect George Frederick Bodley and took up residence in Toynbee Hall, the settlement founded in the east end so that university men might aid in solving the problems of the slums. Ashbee formed a small reading group for the study of Ruskin's work. They first concentrated on such texts as *The Crown of Wild Olives* (containing "Traffic") and *Fors Clavigera,* then moved from doctrine to application by setting up a class for the study of design. This attracted thirty members and proved to be the nucleus of the Guild of Handicraft, which was inaugurated on June 23, 1888, on the top floor of a warehouse in Commercial Street. It had talent, ideals, and a working capital of fifty pounds.

Ashbee explained the rationale for his guild many times, but perhaps the most useful account for our purposes was that given to the Architectural Association in May of 1892. In the 1860s, the AA had been a hotbed of Ruskinian influence. With the new movements of the 1870s, however, and especially with the withdrawal of the arts and crafts men from the professional organizations, it had taken on a very different color. It was now becoming home to young men who were fascinated by classicism. Ashbee was in the lions' den and chose his words carefully.

As always in Victorian architectural discussion, Ashbee's focus is on style. It is not, however, the concept of historic style that would have been familiar in the 1860s. Sedding and others had redefined style as the coherence that results from a certain kind of work process. Ashbee continues in this tradition, but makes his definition even broader:

> The origin of style lies in the social relations of men to men, in their state of society, in their habitude to one another, in the leisure they may have for the thinking out of problems and the creation of forms. In short, the origin of style is a social, not an artistic question. The question of style, therefore, is solving

itself for the young architect, and will do so more and more as he grasps his relationship to the workman and the body social.[38]

Ashbee sees the guild ideal emerging all about him in the close collaboration between architects and painters, metalworkers, carvers, and cabinetmakers. Style emerges when architects educate workmen in their principles and themselves in relation to the crafts.

The audience was almost wholly unmoved. They ignored the broad reach of Ashbee's social idealism and concentrated on his disparagement of the office architect. E. W. Mountford thought it was unnecessary for an architect to gain any of the skills of a craftsmen when he could show what was wanted by a drawing. Sydney Vacher was sure that "if the drawings and specifications were clear and explicit, the result would be more satisfactory than if each workman was consulted in turn."[39] These men were not just solid in their opposition, they were robust and confident. They had good reason to think that they, rather than Ashbee, represented the future. They certainly represented the present: they were successful practitioners who were beginning to take on the kind of major commissions that George Gilbert Scott would have handled at midcentury. Ashbee's practice, by contrast, must have seemed to them marginal and unexciting.

Yet Ashbee's guild was for some years a remarkable success. From the beginning it combined workshops and schoolrooms so that students could be taught by craftsmen and drafted into the workshop as need and opportunity arose. By the first anniversary there were eight guildsmen and seventy pupils. During the 1890s the guild had eight different workshops employing a total of between sixty and seventy workmen and apprentices. It was patronized by the leading arts and crafts architects, and its work was exhibited in London, Vienna, Turin, Paris, Berlin, Munich, and Frankfurt.

The guild's success was more than just commercial. It did indeed, as Ashbee had hoped it would do, make craftsmen out of men whose talents would otherwise have been wasted. John Pearson was unusual in that he had previous experience as a potter for William de Morgan, but he was unemployed and in bad health when Ashbee found him. William Hardiman, who eventually became the guild's chief modeler in silver, had been trundling a catmeat barrow in Whitechapel for fifteen shillings a week. William White had been working as an assistant in a cheap London bookshop, and Arthur Cameron had been an office boy.

Ashbee mastered a mode of production, but was defeated by the market place. His predicament was accentuated by the guild's move to Chipping Camden in 1902. On the one hand, the members were able to live and work on a utopian, arts and crafts basis. They opened workshops, repaired cottages, cultivated garden plots, staged plays, remodeled a disused malt house into a school, and for a time approached the ideal of a self-sufficient community. On the other hand, they had to judge their success by ordinary standards of double entry bookkeeping. The need to move goods to and from the country and to keep a large supply of materials always on hand ensured that costs would remain high even when sales fell. The fact that the guild pursued several different crafts meant that it required more overhead in terms of secretarial work than would have been necessary in a single trade. The guild's obligations as a limited liability company also necessitated complicated bookkeeping and required the employment of a special clerk. This was when times were good. When they turned bad in the trade depression of 1906–1907, the guild was paralyzed. It could not simply sack part of its community, and it could not, as it had in London, send its highly skilled workmen off to find employment elsewhere until trade picked up again.

While the contradictions in the guild's commercial position were becoming troublesome, Ashbee found himself troubled by a different kind of challenge from an unexpected quarter. Shortly before his move to the countryside, Ashbee toured the United States to help set up an American version of England's National Trust. He visited Chicago and met Frank Lloyd Wright. Like Ruskin and Ashbee, Wright saw architecture as an integration of the arts. The fact that he and Ashbee shared so many basic beliefs made their differences more dramatic.

The date of their meeting is significant. Nine months before, Wright had presented a major address—it is almost a dithyramb—entitled "The Art and Craft of the Machine" to the Western Society of Engineers. In it he proposed that while Ruskin and Morris had once been correct in opposing the machine, their attitude must now be abandoned. The machine was the hope of democracy, the liberator of the spirit, and, surprisingly, the salvation in disguise for the arts and crafts movement. The machine had already created an architectural form in the tall modern office building, and it was now requiring the simplicity and process of elimination for which Morris had pleaded. The best modern arts and crafts shop, Wright maintained, would be an experimental station where industrial processes might be explored before large-scale manufacture was begun.

Ashbee put the issue between them in these terms:

> [Wright] threw down the glove to me in characteristic Chicagoan manner when we discussed the Arts and Crafts. "My God," he said, "is Machinery, and the art of the future will be the expression of the individual artist through the thousand powers of the machine,—the machine doing all those things that the individual workman cannot do. The creative artist is the man who controls all this and understands it."

He was surprised to find out how much I concurred, but I added the rider that the individuality of the average had to be considered in addition to that of the 'artistic creator' himself.[40]

The origins of this debate go back to "The Nature of Gothic." Wright and Ashbee are pitting the Renassance mastermind against the free Gothic workman.

Ashbee's dilemma is that he sees the attractions of the machine but is unwilling to sacrifice the individuality of the average man. He grapples with the problems, and there is a steady evolution in his attitude. In 1901 he could say of Ruskin's diatribes against machinery: "We find a truth in the husk of rhetoric, and how great a truth, any direct labour in the industrial arts reveals."[41] By 1906, however, he could see only the husks of rhetoric: "The Luddite for sure was dead, and so was the intellectual Luddite of the type of John Ruskin, who condemned all machines."[42] By 1911 he stated bluntly that "modern civilization rests on the machine, and no system for the endowment, or the encouragement, or the teaching of art can be sound that does not recognize this."[43] In *Where the Great City Stands* (1917), Ashbee almost adopts Wright's position, praising him for thinking out each part of a building with reference to the machine that would make it and for eliminating all ornament except that which he could, through the machine, control.

Unfortunately, this evolution in Ashbee's thought comes at the same time as both the financial collapse of the Guild of Handicraft and a massive shift in taste toward the Georgian Revival. Ashbee therefore could not achieve a practical solution of the problem of the machine within his guild. His career moved toward city planning, and that, as we shall see, was a common development among Ruskin's admirers in the twentieth century.

IV

Ashbee's Guild of Handicraft pushed its ideals to the limit and therefore could no longer evade the contradictions in its position. But even had Ashbee not done this, he would have faced a declining demand for the kind of architecture and crafts that he wanted to supply. Most of the architects who can in any sense be called Ruskinian found their careers fading during the first decade of the new century. The contrast between the dates of their last major buildings and their deaths tells the story. Lethaby died in

1931 but had retired from practice in 1902. C. H. Townsend and Halsey Ricardo both died in 1928, but their last major buildings date from 1912 and 1914 respectively. Edward Prior died in 1932, but his career as an architect was finished in 1912. Mackmurdo died in 1942, four decades after the conclusion of his work as an architect.

The decline of arts and crafts architecture can be traced to two broad causes. The first is that the nation wanted architects who could enhance a mood of imperial grandeur. It wanted pomp and rhetoric on the scale of Scott's Government Offices or Street's Law Courts, though not in the same Gothic style. The last generation of Ruskinian architects, however, had retreated from this kind of work. Rejecting division of labor and the cash nexus, they were in no position to express the official values of their society. So they designed houses and churches, while public buildings were built in some variant of a classical style. The movement that began modestly with John Brydon's Chelsea Vestry Hall (1885), continued with A. Burmwell Thomas's Belfast City Hall (1897), John Belcher's Colchester Town Hall (1897), Stewart and Richards's Cardiff City Hall (1897), John Brydon's government buildings in Westminster (1898), William Young's War Office in Whitehall (1898), Aston Webb's Royal Naval College (1899), Edward Mountford's Old Bailey Criminal Courts (1900), Burmwell Thomas's Stockport Town Hall (1904), and Edward Mountford's Lancaster Town Hall (1906–1907).

The other factor is that the arts and crafts men failed to create an educational system. The Art Workers' Guild provided a forum for the exchange of ideas and encouraged cooperation among architects, artists, and craftsmen, but after a few early efforts it did not concern itself with the training of architectural students. The classicists, on the other hand, devoted a great deal of time and thought to architectural education. When England's first university course in architecture was established at Liverpool, it was based on classic doctrines.

The decline in Ruskin's influence accelerated among architects during the two decades before his death. In 1882 we find a writer complaining that "people generally know too little of Ruskin."[44] References to his work become vague and inaccurate. "Above all," Hugh Roumieu Gough told the Society of Architects in 1885, "take as your motto the wisest words I believe that were ever uttered by our friend John Ruskin and 'ornament your construction but do not construct your ornament!'"[45] Once someone would have quickly pointed out that the words belonged to Owen Jones. Now no one noticed. "Do younger artists read Ruskin now?" asked the *Studio* in 1897. "One doubts if they read him as an earlier generation did."[46]

When Ruskin died in 1900, the *Builder's* obituary called him "a voice of the past rather than of the present."[47] The *Architect and Contract Reporter* accepted his loss with perfect calm:

> The long period which has elapsed since John Ruskin ceased to wound the susceptibilities of practicing architects by his words has produced something which is akin to forgiveness for his attacks and we can join in the general, if placid, regret for his loss and pity his disappointment at the scanty results which such intense and continuous labour has produced.[48]

Occasionally, and especially behind the scenes, the response was much livelier. Henry Wilson recalled: "There came a sudden clamour outside, the door burst open and another well-known artist rushed in dancing and frantically waving an evening paper. 'Ruskin's dead! Ruskin's dead!' he cried; then, sinking into a chair, 'Thank God, Ruskin's dead! Give me a cigarette.'"[49] Many must have felt this way. Ruskin's presence had been a heavy one for a long time, and his moralizing—any moralizing—was now felt as a burden. Yet what is truly surprising is how reluctant many artists and architects were to let him go. "Every word I believe to be fallacious," Norman Shaw said of Ruskin's work, "but I read it with pleasure and lay it down with regret."[50] If only a single quotation could be used to sum up the combined disagreement and nostalgia with which Ruskin was now regarded, it would be this one from the 1907 *Architectural Review:*

> One wonders a little how much real influence he has on the architectural student of today. Probably very little, which is easily understood, but unfortunate. The present writer was once a devout Ruskinian, and abjured Wren and all his works as savouring of the Pit. Pure bigotry of course, and easy to laugh at twenty years later. It may be doubted, however, whether an ultimate wide appreciation of the best in all architecture is not in fact fostered by earlier extravagances based on Ruskin taken neat. Ruskin's teachings may be *démodés*, but his spirit remains and will remain.[51]

XV

SUMMARY AND AFTERMATH

 By the first decades of the twentieth century it was widely agreed that Ruskinism had run its course. It remained only to describe the phenomenon historically and to decide which—if any—of its elements remained of value. Reginald Blomfield, Geoffrey Scott, and W. R. Lethaby pursued the second of these tasks in forceful polemics, but the more modest work of historical description was rarely attempted.

The most obvious reason for this was the violent reaction against Victorian architecture that afflicted early-twentieth-century taste. Those who wrote on the subject at all were more eager to maintain their ironic tone than to do detailed research. In such a situation, half-truths flourished.

Great as Ruskin's influence was, for example, it was exaggerated still further until Ruskin was considered almost the sole creator of the Gothic Revival. Credit or blame was sometimes shared with Pugin, but rarely with any understanding of the differences between Pugin's understanding of architecture and Ruskin's.

There was also a widespread tendency to judge Ruskinian architecture by standards alien to it. Those who admired the classical tradition accused Ruskin of replacing sane critical standards with Anglo-Venetian chaos. Those who admired the International Style blamed Ruskin for not seeing the promise of the Crystal Palace.

The academic study of Victorian architecture began very late, and it has still not settled Ruskin's place. One difficulty is that Nikolaus Pevsner, one of the greatest of architectural historians, seems to have been exasperated with Ruskin and impatient at the sheer mass of his verbiage. Pevsner tended to be attracted to Victorians to the extent that they were, to use the title of his influential book, *Pioneers of Modern Architecture*. It is quite hopeless to try fitting Ruskin into this role. More than most Victorians, he saw the outlines of the twentieth century and hated it.

A more promising step was taken in the last chapter of Henry-Russell-Hitchcock's *Early Victorian Architecture in Britain* (1954). It was titled "Ruskin or Butterfield?" and it asked how many of the "Ruskinian" characteristics of Victorian architecture were due to other sources. This shifted attention from Ruskin's relation to the moderns to the interplay between Ruskin and his contemporaries.

Victorian architecture now received the academic attention it required, and the early 1970s show the publication of John Summerson's *Victorian Architecture* (1970), Paul Thompson's *William Butterfield* (1971), Robert Macleod's *Style and Society* (1971), Steven Muthesius's *The High Victorian Movement in Architecture* (1972), and George L. Hersey's *High Victorian Gothic* (1972). Each of these books had something valuable to say about Ruskinism, but none dealt with it as a whole. Eve Marion Blau's *Ruskinian Gothic* (1982) approached its subject directly but dealt only with the work of Deane and Woodward.

Meanwhile a major revival of interest in Ruskin had occurred among literary critics. On the whole, this did not contribute a great deal to an understanding of Ruskinism in architecture. There were, however, two very striking exceptions. Kristine Ottesen Garrigan's *Ruskin on Architecture* (1973) and John Unrau's *Looking at Architecture with Ruskin* (1978) illuminate the complexities of Ruskin's views and Unrau's *Ruskin and St. Mark's* gives important insight into controversies over restoration. Two important essays have appeared in a volume titled *The Ruskin Polygon*, edited by John Dixon Hunt and Faith M. Holland. They are J. Mordaunt Crook's "Ruskinian Gothic" and Edward N. Kaufman's "'The Weight and Vigour of Their Masses': Mid-Victorian Country Churches and 'The Lamp of Power.'"

This volume is the first to treat architectural Ruskinism as a continuously evolving phenomenon. Accordingly, it is useful to pause on the edge of its last phase and summarize what has been said thus far.

I

Two assumptions should govern the study of Ruskin's influence on Victorian architecture. The first is that any instance of Ruskinism is always the creation of at least two men. Ruskinism never results simply from the impact of a great thinker on his passive disciples. Victorian architects had problems that Ruskin did not fully appreciate, and they often designed buildings to serve functions that he did not admire. We should expect, therefore, that the elements of a Ruskinian building will exist in a state of tension and sometimes of contradiction.

The second is that Ruskinism is a phenomenon that continually evolves. This is so for several reasons. One is that there are ambiguities and shifts of emphasis within Ruskin's books. His view on the degree to which ornament should be naturalistic is rather different in *The Seven Lamps* than in the first volume of *The Stones of Venice*. His insistence that the hand of the workman gives life is hard to reconcile with his sharp distinction between building and architecture. Another reason for the evolution of Ruskinism is that Ruskin himself continued to alter his views on architecture after he had published his most famous books on the subject. The new stress on sculpture and painting in the 1855 preface to *The Seven Lamps* is one example. His preference in the late 1850s for French over Italian styles of Gothic is another. A result of these shifts is that the Ruskin who fascinated G. E. Street is not quite the same figure who commanded the attention of C. R. Ashbee. Complicating the situation still further is the fact that both Ruskin and his admirers were apt to interpret the same doctrine—that of the liberty of the workman, for example—rather differently in the 1850s and 1880s. Ruskinism constantly changes, but, at least in retrospect, the causes and direction of that change can be determined.

One factor conditioning Ruskin's influence is the fact that he came to architecture from the outside. He first studied buildings by sketching them in picturesque scenes or by thrilling to their rich associations in the poetry of Byron and Scott. Though Ruskin outgrew many of the limitations of this early education, it left its mark in two of the most salient aspects of his understanding of architecture. First, he was intensely responsive to the visual facts of a building—the weathering of a surface, the hue of an arch—but less sensitive to more abstract aspects such as proportional systems and structural relations. Second, he expected architecture to convey a depth and range of emotion that is normally associated with painting, sculpture, or lyric poetry.

Young architects, trained in what seemed to them the cold disciplines of classical masters, welcomed his books with delight. They imitated his prose, copied his illustrations, and set off for Europe to see the buildings that he held up for admiration. Many must have muttered at their drawing tables, as George Frederick Bodley is said to have done, "I wonder what Ruskin would make of that."[1] The architects shared their enthusiasm with a large segment of the educated public, and the first phase of Ruskinism is part of a general upswelling of interest in architecture that took place in mid-Victorian England. Many a potential client must have imitated the paint manufacturer in Wolverhampton who, deciding to build a country house, first bought a copy of *The Seven Lamps of Architecture.*[2]

Ruskin's views were never without significant opposition. Pugin offered a different approach to the relation between structure and decoration; Owen Jones put forward an alternative system of polychromy; Christopher Dresser showed different ways of using natural forms in decoration; and some writers, with Robert Kerr at their head, made opposition to Ruskin a lifelong crusade.

But ultimately the opposition froim Ruskin's critics is of less importance than the revisions of his ideas carried out by his admirers. The most obvious of these is in the area of religion. Ruskin was an Evangelical when he wrote *The Seven Lamps* and *The Stones of Venice.* Those who welcomed his work were usually associated with the Ecclesiological Society, and they accepted the Tractarian theology that underlay the new reforms in church architecture. Such matters were explosive in the 1850s, and this difference might have severely limited his popularity among architects. That it did not do so may be credited to a careful decision on the part of leading Ecclesiologists to welcome Ruskin's architectural opinions while ignoring his religious views. By the end of the 1850s Ruskin had himself abandoned his early Evangelicalism, and while sectarian tensions played a large part in forming his views and in conditioning the responses of his earliest readers, they do not play a major role in the evolution of his influence.

The case is quite different with the other major point of contention between Ruskin and his early admirers—that of the choice of a style. This large problem may be divided into two aspects. In one, style is conceived as a visual formula that guides a designer and lends harmony to the buildings of a given period. In the other, style is regarded as a medium for the expression of aspirations and values. Both aspects were problematic for those who hoped to revive Gothic as a universal style in a commercial and industrial age.

The Gothic Revivalists certainly needed to evolve a visual concept of style that would be appropriate not only to churches but also to banks, clubhouses, hospitals, hotels, commercial buildings, and pumping stations. Ruskin helped them by drawing attention to the value of Italian and French styles of Gothic and by advancing particular doctrines of mass, ornament, polychromy, and workmanship. In another sense, however, he fell short of his young admirers' deepest needs. Ruskin feared architectural eclecticism. Though he had explained the charms of Italian Romanesque and Gothic at considerable length, he urged architects to confine themselves to Early English Decorated with perhaps some slight admixture of French Decorated. His admirers took a different attitude. Where Ruskin stopped at the verge of eclecticism, they hoped to go through it and emerge at the other end with a single unified style of the age. And where Ruskin in *The Seven Lamps* was hesitant about prospects for a noble architecture in the nineteenth century, his young admirers were enthusiastic. The last chapter of *The Stones of Venice*, the Edinburgh lectures, and Ruskin's various statements during the 1850s show that the architects made a convert of the critic. During the 1850s and early 1860s, Ruskin was an active figure in the world of Victorian architecture and a public advocate of the Gothic Revival.

There was, however, a tension in the Ruskinism of the 1850s and 1860s that Ruskin at first tried to ignore. It centered on whether Gothic could be a modern style, expressive of the aspirations of the nineteenth century. There are two answers to this question, both Ruskinian.

In the first, Ruskin helps show what the content of modern Gothic should be. He shows such architects as George Gilbert Scott, G. E. Street, and John Pollard Seddon that it is still possible to design buildings that will breathe the spirits of sacrifice, truth, power, beauty, life, memory, and obedience. He proves that it is possible to create profoundly urban buildings that will still convey the truths that God first revealed in nature.

In the second answer, however, Ruskin shows himself to be a more radical critic of the age than he at first appeared. From the mid-1860s on, he engages in relentless assaults on the faithlessness of the society that pays for Gothic Revival buildings and the division of labor by which they are built. He is now convinced that the ideal of a lovely modern Gothic is an absurdity, appropriately symbolized by a transplanted bit of Venetian grace befouled by a thick layer of English soot.

This second aspect of Ruskin's thought, however, was not immediately visible to his admirers of the late 1850s and early 1860s. They did not see Ruskin the social critic emerging in the later volumes of *Modern Painters* or in *Unto This Last*. Perhaps they did not feel it necessary to read Ruskin when he was writing on topics apparently unrelated to architecture. Perhaps their now very busy careers left little time for speculation about the relation between art and society. Whatever the cause, John Henry Chamberlain was nearly alone among the Gothic Revivalists in eagerly welcoming Ruskin's social criticism.

The 1860s therefore saw not only the continued popularity of Ruskin among architects but an explosion of possible Ruskinisms. Some designers stressed Ruskin's effects of mass; others explored his ideas on polychromy; still others exploited every opportunity for naturalistic figure carving. Certain architects designed buildings that looked like transplants from medieval Italy, and others created a new, Victorian style that looked like nothing ever seen before. Lowbrow architects employed Ruskinian mannerisms for public houses and music halls, while highbrows, such as Burges and Godwin, sought to follow Ruskin's post-1855 stress on figure sculpture. For all its variety, however, the Ruskinism of the 1860s could usually be defined in terms of visual features recommended somewhere in Ruskin's work.

But during the 1870s the value of this visual Ruskinism was brought into question. Suddenly the massiveness of Gothic modernism appeared merely heavy, its color schemes seemed vulgar, and its abundant provision of ornament looked like an effort to detract attention from feebleness of form. Above all, the fascination with French and Italian versions of Gothic looked like a betrayal of native traditions of workmanship.

In the normal course of things Ruskin's influence as an architectural thinker would have declined during the 1870s—as indeed it did in the United States. In England, however, there was a shift in interest from one side of Ruskin's work to another. Suddenly Ruskin's most important ideas concerned the liberty of the workman, the nature of the architect's responsibilities, and the tension between architecture and the society that produced it. But the new Ruskinism was no more monolithic than the old one. It is possible to find in it four points of controversy, and each of these would continue to promote change.

One is the old question of what constitutes a style. Ruskin's admirers now no longer think of style as a mixture of certain kinds of visual features, and they no longer seek a style that will express the ideals of their commercial and industrial society. Instead, they conceive of architectural style as the inevitable result of a healthy way of building, and they know that traditional craft methods are imperiled in the Victorian age.

A second point of controversy is Ruskin's distinction between building and architecture. To Philip Webb, to W. R. Lethaby, to all members of the arts and crafts movement, this was an absurdity that would have to be abandoned. Architecture was above all the art of honest building. By asserting this, Ruskin's second generation of admirers freed themselves from their elders' undue fascination with the carver and the art-workman. They showed new interest in the traditional building crafts of the stonemason, the bricklayer, and the plasterer. The stress on building was especially important in the effort to give practical application to Ruskin's attack on restoration. If the essence of Gothic lay in the hand of the worker, and if the worker was not just the sculptor but the ordinary laborer, it followed that no modern workman, crippled by the division of labor, could ever hope to restore the glory of a medieval building. Preservation, not restoration, was the task of confronting architects.

Finally, Ruskin's comments on the nature of the architect were capable of varied interpretation. Ruskin himself rejected both the effort to make the architect one with the engineer and the considerably more successful attempt to make him a professional man, separated by social gentility from the handworker and by specialized training from the artist and sculptor. Some of Ruskin's admirers in the 1880s and 1890s went even further, arguing that buildings did not require a single designing mind but could result from the cooperation of master craftsmen. This led to experiments with guilds in the 1880s and 1890s and efforts to create buildings by direct labor.

But the closer the guilds came to challenging the division of labor and the subcontracting system, the more they tended to fail. By the end of the century there is a sense that the arts and crafts men were beating against the limits imposed by their society. Their mode of building was time-consuming and expensive, and the mood that their buildings expressed was ill suited to the national boisterousness of imperial England. Although many of Ruskin's admirers were at the highpoint of their personal creativity, there was less and less call for their services.

At the same time, Ruskin's original rejection of modern technology began to haunt his followers. At a time when it was absolutely necessary to decide what laws should govern steel frames and reinforced concrete, such books as *The Seven Lamps* and *The Stones of Venice* seemed merely old-fashioned.

By the first decade of the twentieth century, then, Ruskinism was very nearly a thing of the past. One might expect that it would simply fade away and be replaced by the new functionalism of modern architecture.

Instead, a surprising thing happens. The force that replaced Ruskinism has a very close kinship with the classicism that Ruskinism had replaced in the 1850s. With the Georgian Revival, English architecture gives the appearance of going full circle. The transition between Ruskinism and functionalism, on the other hand, was tenuous but real.

II

One of the most influential figures urging a return to classical principles was H. H. Statham, who became editor of the *Builder* in 1884 and remained there until 1910. Believing that a right understanding of architecture was based on the orders, he set out to show that Ruskin's denigration of them was wrong. As he put it in a 1900 article entitled "The Truth about Ruskin," "an order is not merely a form of capital; it is essentially the whole relation and proportion of column and superstructure, and that is the reason why the study of the Classic Orders is still the best training for architectural students, as it means the study of proportion and relative character in all the details of the design."[3] We are back, it will be noticed, with the same charges that unfriendly critics made against Ruskin's views when they first appeared. The difference is that now these charges are made not just against Ruskin but against the whole tradition that he helped initiate. Lethaby, for example, is "one of the reactionary spirits, who want to hunt down the orders, and precedent, and tradition, and all that."[4]

Statham's attacks were unrelenting. In 1888 he denounced *The Stones of Venice* as "an immense rhetorical rhapsody, of exaggerated and unwieldy dimensions," "the product of a remarkably impressionable mind, intoxicated with the associations and suggestions of the place" but written with "no sort of logic or sequence."[5] In 1897 he dismissed Robert de la Sizeranne's *Ruskin et la religion de la beauté* as representing "a phase of thinking which a good many of us have been through and come out of again."[6] In 1898, when *The Stones of Venice* emerged in yet another edition, Statham could only shake his head in incredulity and quote the judgment he had rendered ten years earlier: "if there are second-hand booksellers in the twentieth century, they will probably have a good many copies on sale of an aesthetic treatise in three volumes, which will be 'bad stock' only saleable for the beautiful execution of many of the illustrations."[7] His obituary article of January 27, 1900, proclaimed that Ruskin did "not really appear to have had any fixed principles in regard to art; his only principle was that of saying the most effective and picturesque thing that occurred to him at the moment."[8] Three months later he denounced the first issue of the *Ruskin Union Journal* as "one of the symbols of the childish worship of Ruskin, which seems to have received a fresh impulse by the event of his decease."[9] Ruskin's drawings won Statham's admiration, but his praise of them was accompanied by the suggestion that "Ruskin would have been a greater man, and would have left a more incontestable reputation behind him, had he devoted his powers to producing art instead of writing so much about it."[10]

The attitude—more accurately, the change of attitude—of the *Architectural Review* toward Ruskin was even more significant than that of the *Builder*. The *Review* was founded in 1896 by men associated with the Art Workers' Guild, and its attitude toward Ruskin was close to reverential. It reproduced one of his drawings in its 1897 Christmas issue and was soon able to report that a copy had been put into the hands of the ailing Ruskin and that he had been so pleased by the quality of reproduction that other drawings would soon follow. When Ruskin died in 1900, the magazine responded by placing a full-page portrait at the head of its next issue. The change came in 1905. Mervyn Macartney replaced Henry Wilson as editor, and the magazine suddenly emerged as the major vehicle for the Georgian Revival. Its articles now were on Decimus Burton and C. R. Cockerell.

A similar shift took place in the career of Edwin Lutyens. A close friend of Detmar Blow, who had toured French cathedrals with Ruskin, Lutyens had an intimate acquaintance with the ideas he was now rejecting. Writing to Herbert Baker of his design for the interior of Heathcote, he says: "I want something persisting and dominating, with horizontal lines, to stratify the diarhetic conditions produced by the promiscuous villadom: in fact an architectural bismuth." [11] The casual reference shows how well Lutyens and Baker knew *The Seven Lamps*. In "The Lamp of Beauty" Ruskin cites the crystal form of the bismuth as one that the architect should not imitate because it occurs so rarely in nature. Designing an architectural bismuth, Lutyens rejects the argument that an architect ought to choose forms commonest in nature.

Lutyens embraces the order as Statham understood it—a system of subtle mathematical relationships that unifies the entire building inside and out. This view necessarily magnifies the designing architect and subordinates the craftsman: "The thought and design, in that they are specialized, should become super-thought; and, in that they are specialized, they must be in advance of and distinctly beyond the conceptions of their fellow men." [12] Architecture once again becomes the achievement of a few dominating geniuses:

> In architecture Palladio is the game!! It is so big—few appreciate it now, and it required training to value and realize it. The way Wren handled it was marvellous. Shaw had the gift. To the average man it is dry bones, but under the hand of a Wren it glows and the stiff materials became as plastic clay.
>
> I feel sure that if Ruskin had seen that point of view he would have raved as beautifully as he raved for the Gothic, and I think he did have some insight before he died: his later writings were much more gentle toward the Italian Renaissance.

"It is a big game," Lutyens concludes, "a high game, one not beyond the mind of a Ruskin, for he is a big man, but quite outside his preference." [13]

Lutyens was too self-conscious of his lack of formal education to risk much on writing and lecturing. Reginald Blomfield, by contrast, was a university man who combined intellectual bluntness with robust self-confidence. He was extremely influential. An early member of the Art Workers' Guild, he resigned in 1903 when the battle of the styles began again in earnest. He wrote, he lectured at the Royal Academy, and his views formed the basis of the curriculum when the first university course in architecture was established at Liverpool.

For Blomfield, as for Lutyens, discussions of architectural theory tended to revolve around Ruskin's name even when Ruskin's ideas were being rejected:

> I used always to differ from Lethaby when we talked about Ruskin. As an undergraduate at Oxford I had attended Ruskin's lectures, and my suspicions were aroused when he advised the undergraduates to go and dig at Hinksey instead of "wasting their time" on the river, or at games. Some of them did go, and made a horrible mess of the road, which of course had to be done all over again. Ruskin attracted the amateurs and sentimentalists of his time by treating art and morals as interchangeable terms.[14]

Arguing with Ruskin's admirers became a lifelong activity for Blomfield. In 1902 he expressed dismay at the influence of "fifty years of unchallenged dogmatism on the part of an eloquent writer."[15] In 1913 an author named March Phillipps presented a vigorous restatement of the arts and crafts philosophy in the *Morning Post*. Blomfield replied in his capacity as president of the RIBA and, dismissing Phillipps's defense of guilds and the workman as "only a repetition of the outcries of Ruskin,"[16] was generally felt to have won the encounter. In 1931, when he wrote a memorial article on Lethaby for the *RIBA Journal*, Blomfield's passions were still sufficiently aroused that he used it for an assault on Ruskin's allegedly baneful influence.

Throughout his career, Blomfield made three basic charges against Ruskin. First, he attacked the distinction between building and architecture. Second, he accused Ruskin of emphasizing detail at the expense of plans and sections. Finally, he insisted that Ruskin failed to perceive the autonomy of the aesthetic emotions and muddled his judgments with a fusty moralism.

But Ruskin's faults are not merely his own. Blomfield presents a version of architectural history in which the manly art of Wren and Chambers perishes beneath a flood of moralism, sentimentality, and undisciplined ornament. The appropriate institutionalization of this disaster was the Architectural Museum:

> Here the student—I am drawing upon the somewhat uncertain memory of twenty years ago—might find models of half the famous Gothic capitals of England hung up to nails on the wall. . . . The whole idea of such a museum was the faithful reflex of the amateur preciosity that controlled English architecture thirty to forty years ago. The amateur was on safe ground with ornament.[17]

The recovery was to consist of a return to the architecture of precedent and proportion.

Blomfield's views were both assumed and extended in Geoffrey Scott's *The Architecture of Humanism* (1914). This volume represents the final step in the decline of Ruskin's reputation as an architectural thinker. Scott was in the happy position of justifying a revolution that had already occurred. His love of the Baroque still raised eyebrows, but in practice the success of the Georgian Revival meant that there was an audience waiting for a consistent theory. Blomfield, whom Scott called the most philosophical of our critics, had not quite provided one, so Scott stepped forward as a new Lessing to separate the arts. Knowing that the dragon was half dead, Scott anxiously assured his readers that a death blow was still necessary: "although few serious students of architecture would now confess themselves Ruskinian, and none would endorse those grand anathemas without reserve, the phrases of Ruskin's currency are not extinct." [18]

Like Bernard Berenson, with whom he was closely associated, Scott unites formalism and psychology. Architecture presents a combination of spaces, masses, and lines, which we unconsciously interpret in terms of human functions: "through these spaces we can conceive ourselves to move; these masses are capable, like ourselves, of pressure and resistance; these lines, should we follow or describe them, might be our path and our gesture." [19] This was true of all great architecture, but it was understood best in the Renaissance.

Actually, very little of Scott's book is given over to a defense of his theory. Most is devoted to an assault on all approaches to architecture that stress something other than plastic form. Rival ideas are sorted into four fallacies: romantic, mechanical, ethical, and biological. Two of these are illustrated with extensive citations from Ruskin. The romantic fallacy, which finds in architecture qualities more appropriate to literature, leads to overemphasis on symbolism and exalts small bits of decoration, usually taken from nature, at the expense of order and proportion. The ethical fallacy is found lurking behind nearly all of Ruskin's views. Scott does not directly quote Ruskin for his mechanical or biological fallacies, but "The Lamp of Truth" and the attack on the double dome of Saint Paul's would surely exemplify the first; Ruskin's assumption, which he shares with nearly all his contemporaries, that styles grow and decay is an instance of the second.

Clearly anyone who agrees that these fallacies are indeed fallacious can leave Ruskin unread. For the next three decades Scott's book was essential reading for anyone who cared about architecture. One of its most significant victories came from its impact on an Oxford undergraduate named Kenneth Clark. "*The Architecture of Humanism* had made a profound impression on me," Clark said later in the 1949 edition of his 1928 book, *The Gothic Revival*, "and Scott's powers of lucid exposition had blinded me to the fundamental unreality of his position." [20] Scott's assumptions permeated Clark's book, which immediately replaced Charles Eastlake's 1872 volume as the standard account of its subject. Geoffrey Scott had not only assailed Ruskin but had also gotten the history of Ruskin's influence rewritten from his own point of view.

III

If English architectural theory comes full circle, if Ruskinism is defeated by the Georgian Revival, then what is the relation between Ruskin and the struggling modern movement. One would expect a straightforward antagonism. Ruskin criticized the increasing dependence on the machine; the modernist accepted it. Ruskin stressed craftsmanship; the modernist explored the standardization of parts. The Futurist Marinetti urged Englishmen to "disencumber yourselves of the lymphatic ideology of your deplorable Ruskin,"[21] and many young men must have been willing to do so. But there are definite, if sometimes thin, lines of connection between Ruskin and modern architects and planners.

Frank Lloyd Wright accurately predicted one direction of Ruskinian influence when he urged architects who would not embrace the machine to "wait and work sociologically where great work may still be done by them."[22] Ruskin had spoken in *Sesame and Lilies* of achieving "through sanitary and remedial action in the houses that we have; and then the building of more, strongly beautiful, and in groups of limited extent, kept in proportion to their streams and walled round, so that there may be no festering and wretched suburb anywhere, but clean and busy street within the open country without, with a belt of beautiful garden and orchard round the walls" (18.138). The detailed procedures for achieving this goal are not to be found in Ruskin's works, and this means that his influence on town planning is more likely to be found in moral impetus than in day-to-day methods. It was considerable nonetheless.

Both Raymond Unwin and Patrick Geddes began their careers as something very close to disciples of Ruskin. Geddes, in fact, credited Ruskin's prose with bringing him out of a period of personal depression. He wrote a pamphlet on Ruskin's economics in 1884, an article titled "Political Economy and Fine Art" in the *Scottish Art Review* for 1889, and an article titled "John Ruskin as Economist" in the *International Monthly* for 1900. Both men became advisors on garden cities and town redevelopment. Unwin was associated with the planning of New Earswick near York, Letchworth Garden City, and Hampstead Garden Suburb. Geddes's *City Development*

(1904) was one of the most influential volumes in the history of town planning. It was of immediate benefit to C. R. Ashbee as he sought to preserve his Ruskinian idealism when the arts and crafts movement declined. Ashbee's *Where the Great City Stands* (1917) shows him turning to garden cities, town planning, and civic amenities.

But of all Ruskin's admirers, it was W. R. Lethaby who did most to establish lines of continuity between arts and crafts ideals and the new movements of the twentieth century. In 1896 he made the acquaintance of a young German named Hermann Muthesius, who had been sent to London for the express purpose of bringing back the best ideas of English architecture, crafts, and industry. The two men became friends, and Lethaby looked on with keen interest when Muthesius returned to Germany and joined such men as Walter Gropius and Peter Behrens in forming the Deutsche Werkbund. In this organization the conflicting claims of craftsmanship and mechanization were debated more thoroughly than in England, and the issue was resolved in favor of standardization, prefabrication, mass production, and clear expression of function. Lethaby followed these German developments closely. His reactions must have been complicated, for there was a gulf between the architecture he loved, with its emotional warmth and rich historical associations, and the much more impersonal buildings that the young Germans were creating. "I would rather be dealing with rubble and thatch than with concrete and steel,"[23] he said on one occasion. Even in the middle of a talk recommending modern German architecture he could suddenly declare, "I hate it, but it was not made for me."[24] Nevertheless, he became a pioneering figure in introducing the new architecture into England. When the Design and Industries Association was founded as a near equivalent of the Deutsche Werkbund, Lethaby was a leading member. Hamilton Temple Smith, one of its organizers, later recalled him as "the elder statesman—or, more aptly, perhaps the godfather of the DIA" and added that "his philosophy of life was the touchstone by which we continually tested the soundness of our own ideas."[25]

The question to ask is how much of Ruskin Lethaby communicated to the modern movement. He himself had no doubt as to his position. He speaks of Ruskin as the master and presents himself as a disciple. The actual state of the case is more complicated.

We have seen that among the areas of tension in Ruskinism, three are especially likely to lead to shifting emphases and new formulations: the choice of a style, the relation of architecture to nature, and the distinction between building and architecture. Lethaby resolves all three of these questions and does so in ways that tend to leave a large portion of the Ruskinian tradition behind.

Most dramatically, he brings us to the point where Ruskin's antifunctionalism is transformed into its opposite. He took the first step toward this in the 1890s when he embraced Philip Webb's idea that architecture is primarily the art of honest building. But the term *building* still implies the traditional materials of wood and stone. By the first decade of the twentieth century, however, Lethaby is concerning himself with concrete and steel. This leads him to shift his emphasis from practical building craft to elegant engineering and to reinterpret the relation between architecture and nature in Darwinian terms. "Design," he now tells us, "is properly adaptation, selection, variation."[26] This, in turn, leads him to reject the kind of naturalistic ornament that is added on. Though he still recommends thought-provoking sculpture and murals in appropriate places, the decoration he now admires is simply the appropriate finish to a work of engineering. His example is the "fresh and gay" painting of automobiles.[27]

Lethaby now rejects the historic styles altogether. Ruskin had argued in "Traffic" that style was only a form of millinery when divorced from faith, but he had not abandoned style. Lethaby now argues that the textbook styles can never be more than millinery under any circumstances. "The midrib of architecture, or rather its very body, throughout the ages has been a developing construction, the rest is of the nature of clothing and embroidery—often very delightful but not essential architecture."[28] We can see the distance he has traveled when we see him momentarily enmeshed in an old Victorian controversy. In 1919 Lethaby told his readers:

> Go to such remarkable make-believe buildings as Inigo Jones's Whitehall Palace and Street's Law Courts, and make up your minds once and for all. The skills of these things are indeed amazing; but they are the skills of play actors grimacing without a language. They do not speak to our affection, nor to our intelligence, but only to a sort of amazement that these things should be so.[29]

In the 1860s many voices would have denied that Street's Gothic was a sham. Now a reader wrote to defend Whitehall as "most easily adaptable to modern requirements." This whole controversy had lost its zest for Lethaby. "Please," he said, "I am tired."[30] Geoffrey Scott's version of the Renaissance inspired in him a similar weariness. Style, he now said, meant only "mastery and competence."[31] All great buildings, he said on another occasion, "have been erected in the structural style."[32]

Lethaby resolves some of the conflicts of the Ruskinian tradition and abandons many of its surface features. He preserves what he regards as its basic principles but reinterprets them in terms of his new, functionalist premises.

He continues, for example, to place great stress on the doctrine of work. In "The Lamp of Life" Ruskin had written: "I believe the right question to ask, respecting all ornament, is simply this: Was it done with enjoyment—

was the carver happy while he was about it?" (8.218). Lethaby rephrases this rule, dropping the emphasis on ornament and carvers but preserving the essential emphasis: "What I elect to call beautiful is my reading in work of evidence that the people producing it were healthy all round and noble."[33]

Above all, Lethaby preserves Ruskin's ethical imperatives and his conviction that to have great architecture we must also have green spaces, unpolluted streams, and smokeless skies. Or as he put it at the conclusion of a summary of Ruskin's leading ideas: "Quality of life is the end of all rational activity."[34]

Lethaby preserves the vigor of Ruskin's general ideas, but at the cost of detaching them from their specifics. One can imagine the young men of the Design and Industries Association agreeing with all that he said and wishing to give it practical application, but feeling no need to go back to *The Seven Lamps* or *The Stones of Venice*. In the middle decades of the twentieth century, Ruskin's direct impact reaches the vanishing point, while the influence of Raymond Unwin, Patrick Geddes, and Lethaby continues. It is everywhere, for example, in Lewis Mumford. Lethaby was surely right when he wrote: "Ruskin, having been defeated while he lived, has perhaps his greatest reward in being forgotten. His was not a business for showy recognition, but his thought saturates this generation through and through."[35]

NOTES

PREFACE

1. Candidus [W. H. Leeds], "Ruskinism," *Civil Engineer and Architect's Journal* 17 (February 1854):74. Leeds wrote widely under this pseudonym, and its appearance can safely be taken to identify his authorship. See, for example, Nikolaus Pevsner, *Some Architectural Writers of the Nineteenth Century* (Oxford: Clarendon Press, 1972), 86.
2. "The Political Economy of Art,"
   Building News 4 (January 8, 1858): 29.
3. "Mr. Ruskin's Lecture," *Architect* 4 (October 15, 1870):213.
4. "The Mutation and Cultivation of the Popular Taste: Mr. Ruskin; Mr. Gladstone; Mr. Beresford-Hope," *British Architect* 2 (October 16, 1874):241.
5. "The Late Mr. Ruskin," *Builder* 77 (January 27, 1900):77.

CHAPTER I. AN ARCHITECTURAL EDUCATION

1. Maria Edgeworth, *Works* (Boston: S. H. Parker, 1826), 10:294.
2. Treatments of Ruskin's changing attitudes toward the sublime, the beautiful, and the picturesque can be found in George P. Landow, *The Aesthetic and Critical Theories of John Ruskin* (Princeton: Princeton University Press, 1971); and in John Dixon Hunt, *Ut Pictura Poesis*, the Picturesque, and John Ruskin," *Modern Language Notes* 93 (December 1978):794–818.
3. *The Prose Works of William Wordsworth*, ed. Alexander B. Grosart (London: E. Moxon, 1876), 2:233.
4. The best account of Ruskin's training in watercolor is found in Paul Walton, *The Drawings of John Ruskin* (Oxford: Clarendon, 1972).
5. *The Works of John Ruskin*, ed. E. T. Cook and Alexander Wedderburn (London: George Allen, 1903–1912), 8:313. Unless otherwise
   noted, all further references to Ruskin's work will be to this edition; most will be incorporated in the text.
6. George L. Hersey discusses Ruskin's debt to Loudon in *High Victorian Gothic* (Baltimore: Johns Hopkins University Press, 1972). See also John Gloag, *Mr. Loudon's England* (London: Oriel, 1970).
7. John Claudius Loudon, "Progress of Architecture in Britain in 1938," *Architectural Magazine* 2 (June 1938): 532–533.
8. Verus [pseud.], "Remarks on Forsyth's Architectural Opinions," *Architectural Magazine* 2 (June 1835): 245.
9. John Claudius Loudon, *Encyclopedia of Cottage, Farm, and Villa Architecture* (London: Longman, 1836), 1122.
10. *The Diaries of John Ruskin*, ed. Joan Evan and John Howard White-

house (Oxford: Clarendon, 1956), 1:85–86.

11. Ibid., 111.
12. Ibid., 142.
13. Ibid., 118.
14. *Ruskin in Italy: Letters to His Parents, 1845*, ed. Harold I. Shapiro (Oxford: Clarendon, 1972), 51.
15. Ibid., 54.
16. Ibid., 187.
17. B.S. [pseud.], "Christian Architectures," *Anglo-Saxon* 2 (April 1850): 330.
18. The most sophisticated presentation of this view can be found in

Kristine Ottesen Garrigan, *Ruskin on Architecture* (Madison: University of Wisconsin Press, 1973). Her account of Ruskin's limitations is vigorously contested in John Unrau, *Looking at Architecture with Ruskin* (Toronto: University of Toronto Press, 1978). My approach is closer to Dr. Garrigan's. Ruskin's understanding of architecture is brilliant but partial and it is very difficult to follow the dynamics of his influence unless his gaps are clearly seen.

CHAPTER II. JOHN RUSKIN, C. R. COCKERELL, AND THE PROPORTIONS OF ARCHITECTURE

1. Zeta [pseud.], "Our 'Rotten Rags,'" *Builder* 11 (October 22, 1853):654.
2. There is a possible exception to this. Ruskin declares in an appendix to the first volume of *The Stones of Venice* that "my good friend Mr. Cockerell wonders, in one of his lectures, why I give so much praise to this 'crazy front of Lucca'" (9.430). E. T. Cook and Alexander Wedderburn cannot track down this reference, however, and neither can I. It was presumably suppressed before the lecture appeared in print.
3. A. W. N. Pugin, *An Apology for the Revival of Christian Architecture* (London: John Weale, 1843), 33.
4. *Ruskin's Letters from Venice, 1851–1852*, ed. J. L. Bradley (New Haven: Yale University Press, 1955), 185.
5. "Mr. Ruskin at the South Kensington Museum," *Building News* 4 (January 22, 1858):91.
6. Rudolph Wittkower, *Palladio and Palladianism* (New York: Braziller, 1974), 59.
7. C. R. Cockerell, *Builder* 7 (February 16, 1850):77.
8. Ibid., 3 (February 8, 1845):63.
9. Ibid., 9 (February 8, 1851):85.
10. Ibid.
11. David Watkin, *The Life and Work of*

C. R. Cockerell (London: A. Zwemmer, 1974), 92.
12. The historical background to the nineteenth-century controversy can be found in P. H. Scholfield, *The Theory of Proportion in Architecture* (Cambridge: Cambridge University Press, 1958).
13. C. R. Cockerell, *Builder* 4 (January 17, 1846):25.
14. Ibid., 6 (February 12, 1848):75.
15. Samuel Huggins, "Classical Columnar Architecture and the 'Stones of Venice,'" *Builder* 11 (December 3, 1853):723.
16. "Ruskin on Architecture," *Illustrated London News* 22 (December 17, 1853):514.
17. An Architect [pseud.], *Something on Ruskinism with a Vestibule in Rhyme* (London: R. Hastings, 1851), 37.
18. Edward Lacy Garbett, *Rudimentary Treatise on the Principles of Design in Architecture* (London: John Weale, 1850), 2.
19. Candidus [W. H. Leeds], "Candidus's Notebook," *Civil Engineer and Architect's Journal* 12 (July 1849):195.
20. [W. H. Leeds], "Fine Arts," *Athenaeum*, March 22, 1851, p. 330. Leeds is identified as the author in

Leslie A. Marchand, *The Athenaeum: A Mirror of Victorian Culture* (Chapel Hill: University of North Carolina Press, 1941). Subsequent attributions of material in the *Athenaeum* are based on this source.

21. W. H. Leeds, *Rudimentary Architecture for the Use of Beginners and Students*, 2d ed. (London: John Weale, 1851), 94–95.

22. John Ruskin, "Use of Imagination in Modern Architectural Design," *Building News* 3 (January 30, 1857): 119.

23. Ibid., 120.

24. "Chips of Criticism," *Building News* 3 (February 27, 1857): 208.

25. Samuel Huggins, "Pre-Raphaelite Definition of Architecture," *Civil Engineer and Architect's Journal* 20 (July 1857): 213.

26. Ruskin, "Use of Imagination," 120.

27. Huggins, "Columnar Architecture and the 'Stones of Venice,'" 744.

28. T. L. Donaldson, "Modern Theories of Architectural Taste," *Builder* 12 (December 30, 1854): 508.

29. White is discussed in Paul Thompson, "The Writings of William White," in *Concerning Architecture; Essays on Architectural Writers and Writing*, ed. John Summerson (London: Penguin Press, 1968), 226–237.

30. William White, "Systematic Proportion in Architecture," *Civil Engineer and Architect's Journal* 31 (January 1868): 2.

31. Ibid.

32. Ibid., 2–3.

33. Ibid., 3.

34. Ibid.

CHAPTER III. CHAPEL AND CHURCH: THE RELIGIOUS BACKGROUND TO ARCHITECTURAL THEORY

1. Richard Hurrell Froude, *Literary Remains*, ed. John Keble and John Henry Newman (London: Rivington, 1838–1839), 1:433.

2. Quoted in William Blanch, *Ye Parish of Camberwell* (London: E. W. Allen, 1875), 209.

3. *The Journals of the Rev. John Wesley*, ed. Nehemiah Curnock (New York: Eaton and Mains, 1910–1916), 5:176.

4. "New Churches in and near London," *Ecclesiologist* 20, n.s. 17 (October 1859): 324–325.

5. George Gilbert Scott, *Personal and Professional Recollections* (London: S. Low, 1879), 88.

6. Thomas Mozley, *Reminiscences* (London: Longmans, Green, 1882), 2:131.

7. "On the Transitional Churches Built of Late Years in and about London," *Ecclesiologist* 4, n.s. 1 (March 1845): 59.

8. The most thorough attempt to decipher the subjects of Ruskin's windows can be found in Stephen Bridges, "John Ruskin's Window in St. Giles' Church, Camberwell," *Journal of the British Society of Master Glass Painters* 16, no. 3 (1974–1975): 34–38.

9. I am grateful to Harold I. Shapiro for calling this reference to my attention.

10. "New Churches," *Ecclesiologist* 4, n.s. 1 (March 1845): 89.

11. Henry Melvill, *Sermons Preached on Public Occasions* (New York: Stanford and Swords, 1847), 59.

12. A. W. N. Pugin, *Contrasts* (London: Dolman, 1841), 4.

13. "Mr. E. A. Freeman, in Reply to the *Ecclesiologist*," *Ecclesiologist* 5, n.s. 2 (May 1846): 181.

14. *Ruskin in Italy*, ed. Harold I. Shapiro (Oxford: Clarendon Press, 1972), 206. I am grateful to Harold Shapiro for drawing this passage to my attention.

15. John Ruskin to Rev. Edward Clayton, February 16, 1848, in the col-

lection of the Ruskin Galleries, Bembridge School.

16. Quoted in Ruskin, *Works*, 9:438.

17. Quoted in "Ruskin Unmasked," *Building News* 3 (November 20, 1857):1214. This is a review of a paper that Howard first gave in 1852 and subsequently reprinted. Howard asserts that Pugin was preparing a defense of himself against Ruskin's attack at the time of his death.

18. The disparity between Ruskin's statements was first noted by John Unrau in "A Note on Ruskin's Reading of Pugin," *English Studies* 48 (1967):20–22. Ruskin's notes are reprinted in Patrick R. M. Conner, "Pugin and Ruskin," *Journal of the Warburg and Courtauld Institutes* 41 (1978):344–350.

19. "Mr. Ruskin's Stones of Venice," *Fraser's* 49 (February 1854):128.

20. [J. B. Atkinson,] "Classic or Gothic: The Battle of the Styles," *Blackwood's* 91 (March 1862):295. This article is attributed to Atkinson in *The Wellesley Index to Victorian Periodicals* (Toronto: University of Toronto Press, 1966–). Further attributions from this source are cited simply as Wellesley Index.

21. [George Walter Thornbury,] "Review," *Athenaeum*, May 20, 1854, p. 612. Marchand.

22. B.S. [pseud.], "Christian Architecture," *Anglo-Saxon* 2 (April 1850):326.

23. [Coventry Patmore,] "The Stones of Venice," *British Quarterly Review* 18 (November 1853):467. This and all subsequent attributions to Patmore are based on J. D. Reid, *The Mind and Art of Coventry Patmore* (New York: Macmillan, 1957).

24. [Henry Morley,] "Contemporary Literature," *Westminster Review* 60, n.s. 4 (October 1853):590. Wellesley Index.

25. [Coventry Patmore,] "Ruskin's Stones of Venice," *British Quarterly Review* 13 (May 1851):478. Reid.

26. "Ruskin's Stones of Venice," *Gentleman's Magazine*, n.s. 36 (August 1851):135.

27. J. M. Capes,] "Ruskin's Seven Lamps of Architecture," *Rambler* 4 (July 1849), 193–194. Wellesley Index.

28. "Ruskin's Stones of Venice," *Christian Observer* 50 (August 1851):545.

29. "The Stones of Venice," *Tait's Edinburgh Magazine* 18 (May 1851):291.

30. "Ruskin's Stones of Venice," *Dublin University Magazine* 38 (September 1851):261.

31. Matthew Digby Wyatt, "Fine Arts," *Athenaeum*, September 1, 1849, p. 890.

32. "Reviews," *Civil Engineer and Architect's Journal* 17 (June 1854):230.

33. Candidus [W. H. Leeds], "Ruskinism," *Civil Engineer and Architect's Journal* 17 (February 1854):75.

34. "The Stones of Venice, Vol. II," *Ecclesiastic* 15 (October 1853):470.

35. "Mr. Ruskin's Seven Lamps of Architecture," *Ecclesiologist* 10, n.s. 7 (October 1849):112.

36. "Mr. Ruskin's Stones of Venice," *Ecclesiologist* 7, n.s. 9 (August 1851):275.

37. Ibid., 275–276.

38. John Guille Millais, *The Life and Letters of John Everett Millais* (London: Methuen, 1899), 1:204.

39. Quoted in Mary Lutyens, *Millais and the Ruskins* (New York: Vanguard Press, 1967), 40.

40. John Everett Millais to Charles Collins, August 1853, in the Pierpont Morgan Library (Bowerswell Papers—S 1853, letter 12).

41. "Architectural College," *Builder* 1 (February 1843):24.

42. John James Ruskin to his son, in the collection of the Ruskin Gallery, Bembridge School.

43. John Ruskin to Daniel Moore, No-

vember 21, 1853, in the Pierpont Morgan Library (MA2186, no. 1).

44. Ibid.

45. John James Ruskin to his son, December 1853, Ruskin Gallery.

46. John James Ruskin to his son, December 12, 1853, Ruskin Gallery.

47. John James Ruskin to his son, December 1853, Ruskin Gallery.

48. Quoted in Lutyens, *Millais and the Ruskins*, 247.

49. John Ruskin to Daniel Moore, un-

dated, Pierpont Morgan Library (MA2186, no. 11).

50. John Ruskin to Daniel Moore, undated, Pierpont Morgan Library (MA2186, no. 12).

51. John Ruskin to Daniel Moore, undated, Pierpont Morgan Library (MA2186, no. 13).

52. Virginia Surtees, *Reflections of a Friendship: John Ruskin's Letter to Pauline Trevelyan* (London: George Allen, 1979), 76.

CHAPTER IV. DESCRIBING BUILDINGS: RUSKIN AND NINETEENTH-CENTURY ARCHITECTURAL PROSE

1. George Gilbert Scott, *A Plea for the Faithful Restoration of Our Ancient Churches* (London: John Henry Parker, 1850), 12.

2. Joseph Woods (1776–1864) was an architect who was obliged by poor health to give up his profession. He lived in Europe for many years and wrote on botany as well as architecture. Devoted to Greek and Roman architecture, he counted among his friends such men as Sir John Soane, George Basevi, and T. L. Donaldson. See "The Late Mr. Joseph Woods, Architect," *Builder* 22 (January 23, 1864): 56.

3. George Wightwick (1802–1872) practiced in Plymouth and wrote extensively on architecture. He was a fervent admirer of Sir John Soane and in 1846 dedicated his *Hints to Young Architects* to C. R. Cockerell. Details of his life are given in Arthur T. Bolton, "George Wightwick, Architect," *Architect* 99 (January 24, 1919): 63. Wightwick's position in associationist thought is examined in George L. Hersey, *High Victorian Gothic* (Baltimore and London: Johns Hopkins University Press, 1972), 34–38.

4. Joseph Woods, *Letters of an Architect from France, Italy, and Greece* (Lon-

don: John and Arthur Arch, 1828), 1:5.

5. Ibid., 6–7.

6. George Wightwick, *The Palace of Architecture: A Romance of Art and History* (London: James Fraser, 1840), 123–124.

7. [J. M. Capes], "Ruskin's Seven Lamps of Architecture," *Rambler* 4 (July 1849): 193–194. Wellesley Index.

8. George Wightwick, "Comments on Ruskin's 'Seven Lamps of Architecture,'" *Architect and Building Operative* 1 (1849): 483.

9. Woods, *Letters*, 256, 259.

10. Candidus [W. H. Leeds], "Candidus's Notebook," *Civil Engineer and Architect's Journal*, 12 (June 1849): 161.

11. "Ruskinism," *Civil Engineer and Architect's Journal* 14 (May 24, 1851): 291.

12. "Reviews," *Civil Engineer and Architect's Journal* 14 (May 10, 1851): 266.

13. [Coventry Patmore,] "Gothic Architecture—Present and Future," *North British Review* 27 (May 1858): 189. Reid.

14. George Edmund Street, *Brick and Marble in the Middle Ages; Notes of a Tour in the North of Italy* (London: John Murray, 1855), 123.

15. Ibid., 125.
16. Ibid., 126–127.
17. John Pollard Seddon, "The Relation of Architecture to Painting and Sculpture," *Builder* 9 (March 22, 1851):180. Seddon was so fond of this paragraph that he used it fifteen years later at the conclusion of a paper, "Art in Relation to Architecture," *Civil Engineer and Architect's*

Journal 39 (April 1, 1866):91.
18. John Henry Chamberlain, "The Range of Gothic Art," *American Architect and Builder's Monthly* 1 (June 1870):52.
19. *Recollections of Thomas Graham Jackson,* ed. Basil H. Jackson (London: Oxford University Press, 1950), 199.

CHAPTER V. RUSKINISM: ITS VISUAL CONTENT

1. "Ruskin's 'Stones of Venice,'" *Christian Observer* 50 (August 1851):55.
2. "Review," *Civil Engineer and Architect's Journal* 14 (July 19, 1851): 385, 387.
3. [Coventry Patmore,] "Ruskin's 'Stones of Venice,'" *British Quarterly Review* 13 (May 1851):487. Reid.
4. "Ruskin's 'Stones of Venice,'" *Christian Observer,* 542.
5. Sir Walter James, "On the Influence of Some Contemporary Writers on the Architecture of the Day," *Builder* 25 (July 6, 1867):483.
6. [Matthew Digby Wyatt,] "Fine Arts," *Athenaeum,* September 1, 1849, p. 890. Marchand.
7. [W. E. Ayton,] "Ruskin on Architecture and Painting," *Blackwood's Edinburgh Magazine* 75 (June 1854):743. Wellesley Index.
8. "Mr. Ruskin's Seven Lamps of Architecture," *Ecclesiologist* 11, n.s. 8 (October 1849):114.
9. "Ruskin's Stones of Venice," *Church of England Quarterly Review* 30 (July 1851):141.
10. E. L. Garbett, *Rudimentary Treatise on the Principles of Design in Architecture* (London: John Weale, 1850), 101.
11. [Coventy Patmore,] "Character in Architecture," *North British Review* 10 (August 1851):253. Reid.
12. "Discussion on Polychromatic Embellishments in Greek Architec-

ture," *Builder* 10 (February 21, 1852):114.
13. Ibid., 115.
14. "Discussion on Polychromatic Embellishments," *Builder* 10 (February 14, 1852):98.
15. "Review," *Guardian* (London), August 24, 1853, p. 567.
16. "Discussion on Polychromatic Embellishments in Greek Architecture," p. 114.
17. Owen Jones, "Plan for Decorating the Building of the Exhibition of 1851," *Journal of Design and Manufactures* 4 (January 1851):132.
18. [Matthew Digby Wyatt,] "Fine Arts," *Athenaeum,* September 1, 1849, p. 890. Marchand.
19. The Lambeth Wood Carving Works is described in the *Builder* 18 (September 1, 1860):553.
20. Candidus [W. H. Leeds], "Candidus's Notebook," *Civil Engineer and Architect's Journal* 12 (June 1849): 162.
21. *Edinburgh Advertiser,* November 22, 1853, p. 1.
22. Christopher Dresser, *The Art of Decorative Design* (London: Day and Son, 1862), 149.
23. "Iron Architecture," *Building News* 3 (January 9, 1857):34.
24. J. L. Roget, "Tesserae," *Architect* 41 (March 27, 1889):179–180.
25. Garbett, *Rudimentary Treatise,* 74.
26. [Coventry Patmore,] "The Aesthetics of Gothic Architecture," *British*

Quarterly Review 10 (August 1849): 64. Reid.

27. Patmore, "Ruskin's 'Stones of Venice,'" 490.

28. A. W. N. Pugin, *The True Principles of Pointed or Christian Architecture* (London: Henry G. Bohn, 1853), 1.

29. Owen Jones, *The Grammar of Ornament,* (London: Day and Son, 1856), 5.

CHAPTER VI. RUSKINISM AND THE SPIRIT OF THE AGE

1. Anti-Copyism [pseud.], "The Army and Navy Club Competition," *Builder* 5 (August 14, 1847): 385.

2. A. Welby Pugin, "How Shall We Build Our Churches?" *Builder* 8 (March 23, 1850): 135.

3. Robert Kerr, *The Newleafe Discourses on the Fine Art Architecture* (London: John Weale, 1846), 76, 152.

4. [W. E. Ayton,] "Ruskin on Architecture and Painting," *Blackwood's Edinburgh Magazine* 75 (June 1854): 746. Wellesley Index.

5. "Fine Arts," *Athenaeum*, August 12, 1854, p. 998.

6. "The Seven Lamps of Architecture," *Sharpe's London Journal* 10 (November 1849): 256.

7. [Matthew Digby Wyatt,] "Fine Arts," *Athenaeum*, September 1, 1849, p. 889. Marchand.

8. Matthew Digby Wyatt, "Books," *Journal of Design and Manufactures* 2 (October 1849): 72.

9. "Conversazione at the Architectural Exhibition," *Builder* 16 (January 9, 1858): 21–22.

10. I have attempted to trace this process in "John Ruskin, Coventry Patmore, and the Nature of Gothic," *Victorian Periodicals Review* 12 (Winter 1979): 130–140.

11. [Coventry Patmore,] "Modern Painters," *Douglas Jerrold's Shilling Magazine* 4 (July 1846): 11. Reid.

12. [Coventry Patmore,] "Ruskin and Architecture," *North British Review* 12 (February 1854): 89. Reid.

13. Ibid., 90.

14. John Ruskin, "Architectural Association," *Building News* 3 (January 30, 1857): 119.

15. John Pollard Seddon, *Progress in Art and Architecture* (London: D. Bogue, 1852), 119.

16. Ibid., 11–12.

17. Ibid.

18. Ibid., 12.

19. Henry-Russell Hitchcock, *Early Victorian Architecture* (New Haven: Yale University Press, 1954), 606.

20. Alexander Beresford Hope, "Mr. Hope's Essay on the Present State of Ecclesiological Science in England," *Ecclesiologist* 7, n.s. 4 (March 1847): 88.

21. Hitchcock, *Early Victorian Architecture*, 587.

22. George L. Hersey, *High Victorian Gothic* (Baltimore: Johns Hopkins University Press, 1972), 183.

23. Paul Thompson, "All Saints' Church, Margaret Street, Reconsidered," *Architectural History* 8 (1965): 73–94. Thompson also discusses the church in *William Butterfield* (Cambridge: MIT Press, 1971).

24. Quoted in Thompson, "All Saints' Church Reconsidered," 76.

25. "New Churches, *Ecclesiologist* 10, n.s. 7 (April 1850): 432–433.

26. "Mr. Ruskin's Seven Lamps of Architecture," *Ecclesiologist* 10, n.s. 7 (October 1849): 119.

CHAPTER VII. BENJAMIN WOODWARD AND THE FORMATION OF RUSKINIAN GOTHIC

1. Woodward's career is described in Eve Marion Blau, *Ruskinian Gothic: The Architecture of Deane and Woodward, 1845–61* (Princeton: Prince-

ton University Press, 1982).

2. Quoted in ibid., 32.

3. "New Museums, &c. Trinity College, Dublin," Builder 12 (August 12, 1854):425.

4. "Workmen's Capitals," Builder 14 (March 29, 1856):171.

5. Quoted in Letters of Dante Gabriel Rossetti to William Allingham, 1854–1870, ed. George Birkbeck Hill (New York: Frederick A. Stokes, 1897), 146.

6. Much of the information in this section is derived from Ellen Krathen Morris, "The Mid-Victorian Competition: Style, Type, and Image in Architectural Evaluation," Ph.D. diss., Princeton, 1977.

7. "The Designs for the Oxford Museum and Library," Builder 12 (November 18, 1854):590–591.

8. "The Architectural Exhibition," Civil Engineer and Architect's Journal 19 (January 1856):2.

9. "Designs for Oxford Museum and Library," 591.

10. "The New Museum at Oxford," Athenaeum, November 11, 1854, p. 1372.

11. J.F. [James Fergusson], Builder 12 (November 18, 1854):591.

12. "The Oxford New Museum," Civil Engineer and Architect's Journal 25 (August 1862):225.

13. "Report of the Oxford Museum Delegacy," Athenaeum, December 16, 1854, p. 1531.

14. F.G.S. [pseud.], "The Oxford University Museum," Macmillan's Magazine 5 (April 1862):532.

15. "The Oxford New Museum," Building News 5 (January 14, 1859):29.

16. Athenaeum, February 3, 1855, p. 152.

17. Quoted in J. B. Atlay, Sir Henry Wentworth Acland (London: Smith, Elder, and Co., 1903), 207.

18. "Oxford New Museum," 29.

19. Quoted in Morris, "Mid-Victorian Competition," 413.

20. Quoted in Blau, Ruskinian Gothic, 65.

21. Reflections of a Lifetime; John Ruskin's Letters to Pauline Trevelyan, 1848–1866, ed. Virginia Surtees (London: George Allen and Unwin, 1979), 98.

22. Quoted in Blau, Ruskinian Gothic, 66.

23. Ibid.

24. Reflections of a Lifetime, 74–75.

25. William Tuckwell, Reminiscences of Oxford (London: Cassell, 1900), 49.

26. Reflections of a Lifetime, 95.

27. Quoted in Blau, Ruskinian Gothic, 242.

28. Reflections of a Lifetime, 134.

29. John Ruskin to his father, March 6, 1859, in the Yale University Library.

30. Sublime and Instructive; Letters from John Ruskin to Louisa, Marchioness of Waterford, Anna Blunden and Ellen Heaton, ed. Virginia Surtees (London: Michael Joseph, 1972), 220.

31. Jay Wood Claiborne, "Two Secretaries: The Letters of John Ruskin to Charles Augustus Howell and the Rev. Richard St. John Tyrwhitt," Ph.D. diss., University of Texas at Austin, 1969, pp. 345–346.

32. Quoted in Peter Ferriday, "The Oxford Museum," Architectural Review, December 1962, p. 415.

33. Ibid.

34. "Baptist Chapel," Builder 15 (December 5, 1857):706.

35. "The Oxford Museum," Builder 17 (June 18, 1859):401.

36. The extent to which the Oxford Museum carving follows Ruskin's doctrines is discussed in John Unrau, Looking at Architecture with Ruskin (Toronto: University of Toronto Press, 1978), 130ff.

37. "The University Museum, Oxford," Builder 13 (June 23, 1855):292.

38. Jennifer Sherwood and Nikolaus Pevsner, Oxfordshire (Harmondsworth: Penguin Books, 1966), 135.

39. "Oxford New Museum," 5 (Febru-

ary 18, 1859):161.

40. Ibid., 6 (April 6, 1860):173.

41. "The Offices of the Crown Life Assurance Company, Bridge Street, Blackfriars, London," *Building News* 4 (July 16, 1858), 725; and "Architecture of Our Day," *Builder* 16 (December 18, 1858):842.

42. "Architecture of Our Day," December 4, 1858, p. 810.

43. Ibid., December 18, 1858, p. 842.

44. Reason in All Things [pseud.], "Letters to the Editor," *Building News* 3 (June 12, 1857):615.

45. "The Competition Designs in Westminster," *Building News* 3 (May 22, 1857):501.

46. *Builder* 15 (May 16, 1857):270.

47. "Lecture on the Government Buildings Competition," *Building News* 3

(June 12, 1857):614.

48. *Builder* 15 (May 16, 1857):271.

49. John Ruskin, "Use of Imagination in Modern Architectural Design," *Building News* 3 (January 30, 1857).

50. "Prizes for Wrought Iron-Work and Stone Carving," *Builder* 14 (April 5, 1856):193.

51. "Mr. Ruskin at the South Kensington Museum," *Building News* 4 (January 22, 1858):93.

52. Quoted in Blau, *Ruskinian Gothic*, 134.

53. James Fergusson, *A History of Modern Architecture* (London: J. Murray, 1891), 2:114.

54. "Oxford New Museum," 5 (January 14, 1859):29.

55. "University Museum, Oxford," p. 292.

CHAPTER VIII. THE 1850S: THE STRUGGLE FOR A VICTORIAN GOTHIC

1. "Oxford Architectural Society," *Ecclesiologist* 6, n.s. 3 (December 1846):228.

2. George Gilbert Scott, "On the Present Position and Future Prospects of the Revival of Gothic Architecture," *Builder* 15 (October 10, 1857):572.

3. George Gilbert Scott, *Personal and Professional Recollections* (London: S. Low, 1879), 158.

4. Ibid., 210.

5. George Gilbert Scott, *Remarks on Secular and Domestic Architecture, Present and Future* (London: John Murray, 1857), 191.

6. Ibid., 34–35.

7. "Art in Architecture—A Dialogue," *Builder* 15 (November 28, 1857):688.

8. *Builder* 16 (January 2, 1858):1.

9. Leslie Sutton, "Eclectic Gothic," *Building News* 4 (January 29, 1858):99.

10. "Gothic Architecture," *Times*, January 16, 1858, p. 12.

11. Charles Boutell, "Some Remarks on the Progress and Development

of Gothic Architecture," *Building News* 4 (January 29, 1858):113.

12. George Gilbert Scott, "On the Formation of a Medieval Museum," *Builder* 9 (February 15, 1851):104.

13. "Architectural Museum," *Builder* 11 (January 8, 1853):20.

14. *Athenaeum*, October 21, 1854, p. 1251.

15. "Premiums for Carving at the Architectural Museum," *Builder* 14 (January 12, 1856):21.

16. "The Architectural Museum," *Times*, January 16, 1858, p. 5.

17. "The Exhibition of Competition Designs for the Government Offices," *Builder* 15 (May 9, 1857):261.

18. "The Competition Designs in Westminster Hall," *Building News* 3 (May 22, 1857):501.

19. "Glances Backward," *Building News* 6 (January 6, 1860):2.

20. Cited in Ruskin, *Works*, 16:xxxii.

21. Scott, *Personal and Professional Recollections*, 178.

22. "Oxford Architectural Society," *Ecclesiologist* 18, n.s. 15 (August 1857):247.

23. Scott, *Personal and Professional Recollections*, 192–193.

24. "Classic or Gothic: The Battle of the Styles," *Blackwood's Edinburgh Magazine* 91 (March 1862):287.

25. William Tite, "The Present Condition and Future Prospects of Architecture," *Builder* 13 (November 17, 1855):550.

26. "Gothic or Classic?" *Builder* 14 (March 1, 1856):115.

27. *Building News* 5 (November 11, 1859):1020.

28. "Parliamentary Intelligence," *Times*, July 9, 1861, p. 7.

29. "Competition and the Foreign Office," *Building News* 5 (February 25, 1859):19.

30. "The New Foreign Office," *Building News* 5 (February 25, 1859):175.

31. "Mr. Ruskin on Venice," *Builder* 17 (February 19, 1859):126.

32. E.A.F. [E. A. Freeman], "Gothic or Classic?" *Times*, October 19, 1859, p. 9.

33. The incident is recounted in *The Recollections of Thomas Graham Jackson* (London: Oxford University Press, 1950), 141.

34. E. A. Freeman, "The Foreign Office—Gothic or Classic? *National Review* 10 (January 1860):48.

35. E. A. Freeman, "Architecture at Oxford," *Architect* 38 (December 16, 1887):363.

36. James Bryce, *Studies in Contemporary Biography* (London: MacMillan, 1903), 269.

37. The letter is quoted by permission of the trustees of the Pierpoint Morgan Library and of the Ruskin estate.

38. Scott, *Personal and Professional Recollections*, 201.

39. A Correspondent [pseud.], "George Edmund Street," *Architect* 39 (May 25, 1888):295.

40. Steven Muthesius, *The High Victorian Movement in Architecture* (London: Routledge and Kegan Paul, 1972), 42, 189.

41. "The Architectural Exhibition," *Builder* 13 (December 15, 1855): 599.

42. G. E. Street, *Brick and Marble in the Middle Ages* (London: John Murray, 1855), 4–5.

43. Ibid., 81.

44. Ibid., 165.

45. Ibid., 258.

46. Ibid., 253.

47. G. E. Street, "On the Future of Art in England," *Ecclesiologist* 19, n.s. 16 (August 1858):238.

48. G. E. Street, "A Plea for the Revival of True Principles of Architecture in the Public Buildings of Oxford," *Builder* 11 (June 25, 1853):404.

49. *RIBA Transactions*, 1864–1865, p. 148.

50. "Architectural Museum: To Art-Workmen," *Builder* 16 (March 6, 1858):156.

51. G. E. Street, "The Right Use of Ancient Examples," *Builder* 16 (March 6, 1858): 156.

52. Ibid.

53. George Gilbert Scott, "On the Selection of Objects for Study in the Architectural Museum," *Builder* 16 (April 3, 1858):227.

54. G. E. Street, "The Right Use of Ancient Examples—'Conventional' and 'Naturalistic,'" *Builder* 16 (April 3, 1858):229.

55. G. E. Street, "The Right Use of Ancient Examples," *Building News* 4 (February 26, 1858):221. This passage was omitted from the *Builder's* transcript.

56. Street, "Right Use of Ancient Examples—'Conventional' and 'Naturalistic,'" 228.

57. John Unrau, *Looking at Architecture with Ruskin* (Toronto: University of Toronto Press, 1978), 146.

58. Henry-Russell Hitchcock, "G. E.

Street in the 1850s," *Journal of the Society of Architectural Historians* 19 (December 1960):165. There is a discussion of the foreign sources of the design in Neil Jackson, "The Un-Englishness of G. E. Street's Church of St. James-the-Less," *Architectural History* 23 (1980):86–93.

59. "The Law Courts and the Commons," *Architect* 7 (March 30, 1872):75. The controversy is discussed in David B. Brownlee, *The Law Courts: The Architecture of George Edmund Street* (Cambridge: MIT Press, 1984).

60. Seddon's work is illustrated in Michael Darby, *John Pollard Seddon* (London: Victoria and Albert Museum, 1983).

61. Quoted in Nikolaus Pevsner, *Studies in Art, Architecture and Design* (New York: Walker and Co., 1968), 12.

62. J. Neville Warren, "Schools for Workmen," *Builder* 9 (September 27, 1851):613.

63. John Pollard Seddon, *Memoir and Letters of the Late Thomas Seddon* (London: J. Nisbet, 1858), 6.

64. The building is discussed in Geoffrey Tyack, "A Victorian Architectural Correspondence," *Architectural History* 22 (1979):78–87.

65. Ibid., 79.

66. Benjamin Disraeli, *Lothair* (London: Longmans, Green, 1870), 230.

67. "The Oxford Museum," *Guardian* (London), December 29, 1858, p. 1040.

68. "Gothic Art at the International Exhibition," *Building News* 8 (May 9, 1862):320.

69. Coventry Patmore, "Ruskin's Seven Lamps of Architecture," *North Brit-*
ish Review 12 (February 1850):191.

70. *Builder* 11 (August 6, 1853):498.

71. Thomas James, "On the Prospects of Architectural Development," *Ecclesiologist* 15, n.s. 12 (December 1854):410.

72. "Decorative Designs in Brickwork," *Building News* 7 (April 12, 1861): 299.

73. Dr. Barclay, "Modern Leicester," *Building News* 11 (March 4, 1864): 166.

74. *Builder* 14 (May 3, 1856):237.

75. "Gothic Art in the International Exhibition," *Building News* 8 (May 9, 1862):320.

76. Ibid.

77. This section draws on Xenia Norman, "The Life and Work of Alfred Waterhouse, R.A., in and around Manchester," thesis in the Manchester Central Reference Library; and Stuart Allen Smith, "Alfred Waterhouse: Civic Grandeur," in *Seven Victorian Architects*, ed. Jane Fawcett (University Park: Pennsylvania State University Press, 1972):102–121.

78. "Mr. Waterhouse, A.R.A., on the Study of Architecture," *Architect* 29 (March 3, 1883):46.

79. Asa Briggs, *Victorian Cities* (New York: Harper and Row, 1970), 56.

80. "Parliamentary Intelligence," *Times*, August 5, 1859, p. 4.

81. Alfred Waterhouse, "A Short Description of the Manchester Assize Courts," *RIBA Transactions*, 1865, p. 174.

82. "Mr. Waterhouse on Colour Decoration," *Building News* 60 (January 23, 1891):123.

83. Ibid., 124.

CHAPTER IX. THE 1860S: TRIUMPH AND DISPERSAL

1. R. P. Pullan, "Lectures at the Architectural Exhibition," *Building News* 8 (June 14, 1861):504.

2. This work is both discussed and illustrated in Andor Gomme, Michael Jenner, and Bryan Little,

Bristol: An Architectural History (London: Lund Humphries, 1979), 335–385.

3. "The New East and West India Dock-House," *Building News* 24 (September 21, 1877):278.

4. This aspect of Ruskin's influence is discussed in Henry-Russell Hitchcock, "Victorian Monuments of Commerce," *Architectural Review* 105 (February 1949):61–74.

5. Leslie Sutton, "Eclectic Gothic," *Building News* 4 (January 29, 1858):99.

6. "A Design for the Chelsea Vestry Hall," *Builder* 16 (December 18, 1858):849.

7. "Building Progress—Metropolitan Works," *Building News* 3 (September 18, 1861):218.

8. "The Victorian Architecture Craze," *Building News* 7 (March 5, 1861):218.

9. Quoted in Priscilla Metcalf, *James Knowles: Victorian Editor and Architect* (Oxford: Clarendon Press, 1980), 100. Metcalf discusses the Grosvenor style on pages 129–155.

10. "Grosvenor Hotel, Pimlico," *Building News* 10 (March 20, 1863):210.

11. Burges's career is discussed and illustrated in J. Mordaunt Crook, *William Burges and the High Victorian Dream* (Chicago: University of Chicago Press, 1981).

12. Information on this period is given in Margaret Richardson, "George Aitcheson," *RIBA Journal* 87 (January 1980):38–40.

13. M. M. Didron and William Burges, "Iconographie du palais ducal de Venise," *Annales archéologiques* 17 (1857):71.

14. Godwin's work is discussed in Dudley Harbron, *The Conscious Stone* (New York: Benjamin Blom, 1971), 176.

15. E. W. Godwin, "Gothic or Classic," *Builder* 15 (March 28, 1857):176.

16. Ibid.

17. Quoted in Harbron, *Conscious Stone,* 151.

18. William Burges, "Sketches vs. Measured Drawings," *Building News* 11 (September 1, 1865):605–606.

19. William Burges, "The Modern Development of Medieval Art," *Builder* 22 (June 18, 1864):450.

20. "Brick Architecture," *Building News* 11 (August 12, 1864):609.

21. E. W. Godwin, "Art Cliques," *Building News* 12 (October 13, 1865):707.

22. Ibid., November 3, 1856, p. 767.

23. The building and contemporary responses to it are discussed in James Stevens Curl and John Stambrook, "E. Bassett Keeling, Architect," *Architectural History* 16 (1973):60–69.

24. Quoted in ibid., 64–65.

25. "Strand Music Hall," *Building News* 11 (November 18, 1864):864.

26. *Building News* 10 (November 20, 1863):368.

27. John Pollard Seddon, "Oyster-Culture, Architecturally Considered," *Building News* 14 (February 8, 1867):98.

28. John Pollard Seddon, "Acrobatic Gothic," *Building News* 11 (October 21, 1864):780.

29. Burges, "Modern Development of Medieval Architecture," 449.

30. "Ecclesiological Society," *Building News* 4 (June 4, 1858):582.

31. William Burges, "The Late Exhibition," *Ecclesiologist* 23, n.s. 20 (October 1862):336.

32. Ibid.

33. E. W. Godwin, "On Some Buildings I Have Designed," *British Architect* 10 (November 29, 1878):210.

34. E. W. Godwin, "The Sister Arts in Relation to Architecture," *Builder* 20 (March 29, 1862):220.

35. Ibid., 221.

36. Godwin, "On Some Buildings I Have Designed," 221.

37. William Burges, *Art Applied to Industry* (Oxford: John Henry and

James Parker, 1865), 7–8.

38. E. W. Godwin, "The Architectural Exhibition, 1867," *Building News* 14 (May 17, 1867):337.

39. William Burges, "Art and Religion," in *The Church and the World*, ed. Orby Shipley (London: Long-

mans, Green, 1868), 575.

40. Godwin, "Architectural Exhibition, 1867," 337.

41. Godwin, "On Some Buildings I Have Designed," 211.

42. Ibid.

CHAPTER X. RUSKIN VERSUS THE PROFESSION

1. *Builder* 14 (April 19, 1856):214.

2. "The Architectural Association," *Builder* 15 (October 10, 1857):577.

3. Ibid.

4. "St. Martin's School of Art," *Building News* 4 (April 23, 1858):430.

5. Ibid.

6. Ibid.

7. C.B.A. [pseud.], "The Education of Artist Workmen, Their Proper Work, and The Way to It," *Building News* 9 (January 2, 1863):3.

8. William White, "On Iron-work— Its Legitimate Use and Proper Treatment," *RIBA Transactions*, 1865–1866, p. 22.

9. William Kenrick, "Technical Education as Applied to Art Industry," *Transactions of the National Association for the Advancement of Art* (1891):226.

10. "Architects and Carvers," *Building News* 11 (March 31, 1865):231.

11. *RIBA Transactions*, 1865–1866, p. 28.

12. "Human and Animal Forms As Employed in Art," *Building News* 11 (January 5, 1865):2.

13. "Architectural Association," *Building News* 5 (June 3, 1859):524.

14. Ibid., November 11, 1859, p. 1021.

15. Ibid., 6 (January 14, 1860):281.

16. George Gilbert Scott, "Thoughts and Suggestions on the Artistic Education of Architects," *Builder* 22 (May 12, 1864):184.

17. "The Figural Class of the Architectural Association," *Building News* 11 (March 16, 1865):175.

18. "A Discussion upon the Report of the Artistic Architectural Educa-

tion Committee," *RIBA Transactions*, 1864–1865, p. 17.

19. Information on the circumstances surrounding "Traffic" is drawn from Andrew Saint, *Richard Norman Shaw* (New Haven: Yale University Press, 1976); and from Igor Webb, "The Bradford Wool Exchange: Industrial Capitalism and the Popularity of Gothic," *Victorian Studies* 20 (Autumn 1976):45–68.

20. Quoted in Webb, "Bradford Wool Exchange," 60.

21. G.H.G. [pseud.], "Paraphrased Notes, Original & Selected," *Building News* 10 (May 13, 1864):459.

22. E. W. Godwin, "The New Bradford Exchange," *Builder* 22 (June 18, 1864):459.

23. A. W. Blomfield, "Architectural Study and Architectural Progress," *Builder* 19 (November 2, 1861): 750.

24. "Gatherings at Manchester—Architectural and Sanitary," *Builder* 17 (January 29, 1859):75.

25. "Building Stones Used in Manchester" *Building* 18 (January 14, 1860):27.

26. R. W. Billings, "A Lecture on Many Subjects," *Building News* 7 (January 11, 1861):34.

27. "London Architecture and the City," *Builder* 22 (September 17, 1864):678–680.

28. *RIBA Transactions*, 1864–1865, pp. 147–148.

29. Ibid., 152.

30. Robert Kerr, "The Battle of the Styles," *Builder* 18 (May 12, 1860):294.

31. John Summerson, *Victorian Architecture: Four Studies in Evaluation* (New York: Columbia University Press, 1970), 9.

32. *RIBA Transactions*, 1864–1865, p. 150.

33. Robert Kerr, "Conversazione of the Architectural Association," *Builder* 23 (November 4, 1865):781.

34. "Professor Kerr on the Architecturesque," *Builder* 27 (January 23, 1869):61.

35. *Architect* 4 (October 22, 1870), 226. *The Dictionary of National Biography* records the fact that Kerr wrote leaders for the *Architect*.

36. Robert Kerr, "English Architecture Thirty Years Hence," *RIBA Transactions*, 1883–1884, p. 221.

37. Robert Kerr, "Ruskin and Emotional Architecture," *RIBA Journal*, 3d series, 7, no. 9 (1900):181.

38. *RIBA Transactions*, 1864–1865, p. 149.

39. Ibid., 152.

40. Ibid., 154–155.

41. Ibid., 1869–1870, pp. 102–103.

42. "Mr. Ruskin at the Working Men's College," *Builder* 22 (February 13, 1864):119.

43. Ruskin's letters to Henry Swan are quoted by permission of the trustees of the Rosenbach Museum and Library and of the Ruskin Estate.

CHAPTER XI. JOHN RUSKIN, JOHN HENRY CHAMBERLAIN, AND THE CIVIC GOSPEL

1. Quoted in B. I. Coleman, ed., *The Idea of the City in Nineteenth Century Britain* (London: Routledge and Kegan Paul, 1973), 166.

2. "Mr. Joseph Chamberlain, M.P., on Art," *British Architect* 6 (December 15, 1876):372.

3. "Northampton," *Building News* 12 (July 14, 1865):495.

4. Quoted in "Art in Birmingham—From Our Own Correspondant," *Building News* 11 (February 10, 1865):94.

5. "Birmingham and Its Progress," *Builder* 13 (December 8, 1855):587.

6. J. H. Chamberlain, "On the Introduction of Colour, including painting in Fresco, to promote or heighten the effect of Architectural Composition generally." This manuscript is in the library of the Royal Institute of British Architects.

7. These details are reported in J. A. Langford, *Modern Birmingham and Its Institutions* (Birmingham: W. Downing, 1871), 1:240.

8. "Notes and Comment," *Architect* 30 (October 27, 1883):256.

9. "The Late Mr. J. H. Chamberlain," *Times*, October 29, 1883, p. 5.

10. Quoted in Asa Briggs, *Victorian Cities* (New York: Harper and Row, 1970), 196.

11. Quoted in ibid., 199.

12. A. W. Dale, *The Life of R. W. Dale* (New York: Dodd, Mead, 1899), 634–635.

13. J. H. Chamberlain, *An Introductory Lecture on the Offices and Duties of Architecture* (Birmingham: Cornish Brothers, 1858), 10.

14. J. H. Chamberlain, "Truth and Falsehood in Architecture," *Building News* 4 (September 10, 1858):921.

15. M.A. [pseud.], "Naturalistic Architecture and Natural Architects," *Building News* 4 (October 1, 1858):979.

16. J. H. Chamberlain, "On the 'Seven Lamps of Architecture,'" *British Architect* 9 (October 24, 1879):164.

17. Chamberlain, *Introductory Lecture*, 8–9.

18. J. H. Chamberlain, "The Range of Gothic Art," *American Architect and Builder's Monthly* 1 (June 1870):50–51.

19. Quoted in Briggs, *Victorian Cities,* 206.
20. Chamberlain, *Introductory Lecture,* 5.
21. Ibid., 6–7.
22. J. H. Chamberlain, "Sculpture and Gothic Architecture," *Builder* 18 (August 18, 1860):533.
23. J. H. Chamberlain, "The Progress of Design," *Building News* 9 (June 12, 1863):446.
24. J. H. Chamberlain, "The Law of Necessity," *American Architect and Builder's Monthly* 1 (July 1870):67.
25. Chamberlain, "On the 'Seven Lamps of Architecture,'" October 17, 1879, p. 151.
26. Chamberlain, "Law of Necessity," 67.
27. Ibid.
28. Ibid.
29. Quoted in Asa Briggs, "Introduction," in *History of the Elementary School Contest in England,* by Francis Adams (Brighton: Harvester Press, 1972).
30. "The Birmingham Corporation and Employment of Architects," *Builder* 40 (January 22, 1881):107.
31. "The Architectural Commissions of the Birmingham School Board," *Architect* 29 (June 16, 1883):402–403.

32. "Mr. Joseph Chamberlain, M.P., on Art," *British Architect* 6 (December 15, 1876):323.
33. A Birmingham Tory [pseud.], "The Local Working of the Birmingham Caucus," *National Review* 6 (March 27, 1877):177.
34. Quoted in "Education and How It Is Lodged in Birmingham," *British Architect* 7 (March 27, 1877):177.
35. Quoted in Francis Greenacre and Peter Clark, "Where 'Beacons of the Future' Fade into the Past," *Times Educational Supplement* 2809 (March 21, 1969):918.
36. Chamberlain, *Introductory Lecture,* 8–9.
37. Testimony of Joseph Chamberlain, June 17, 1884, before the Royal Commission on the Housing of the Working Classes. *Irish University Press Series of Parliamentary Papers:* vol. 2, *Urban Areas: Housing* (Dublin: Irish University Press, 1977), 549.
38. "The Late Mr. John Henry Chamberlain," *Building News* 45 (October 26, 1883):637.
39. The Ruskin-Swan correspondance is in the Rosenbach Museum and Library.
40. "Notes and Comments," *Architect* 44 (September 26, 1890):190.

CHAPTER XII. REVALUATION AND A NEW RUSKINISM

1. "Mr. Waterhouse, A.R.A., on the Study of Architecture," *Architect* 29 (March 3, 1883):46.
2. George Cavendish Bentinck, "The Decline and Fall of English Architecture," *Building News* 32 (February 23, 1877):205–206.
3. "Mr. Bentinck on the Present State of English Architecture," *Building News* 32 (March 2, 1877):211.
4. J. J. Stevenson, "Queen Anne and Other Forms of Free Classic Architecture," *Architect* 33 (February 27, 1875):125.
5. Quoted in W. R. Lethaby, *Philip*

Webb and His Work (London: Raven Oak Press, 1979), 30.
6. Quoted in Jay Wood Claiborne, "Two Secretaries: The Letters of John Ruskin to Charles Augustus Howell and the Rev. Richard St. John Tyrwhitt," Ph.D. diss., University of Texas, 1969, p. 113.
7. Lethaby, *Philip Webb and His Work,* 247.
8. Warrington Taylor, "Of Certain Contrasts between French and English Gothic," *Building News* 12 (January 6, 1865):17.
9. Quoted in Mark Girouard, *Sweet-*

ness and Light (Oxford: Clarendon Press, 1977):15.

10. *The Letters of William Morris to His Family and Friends,* ed. Philip Henderson (London: Longmans, Green, 1950), 303.

11. Emmett's life is described in J. Mordaunt Crook, "Introduction," in *Six Essays,* by John T. Emmett (New York: Johnson Reprint Corporation, 1972).

12. Ibid., 9.

13. J. J. Stevenson, *House Architecture* (London: Macmillan, 1880), 1:5, 105.

14. E. Ingress Bell, "Unrest in Architecture," *Builder* 38 (May 1, 1880): 537.

15. Stevenson, *House Architecture,* 1: 45.

16. H. H. Wilson, "The Late J. D. Sedding and His Work," *Building News* 61 (December 4, 1891):784.

17. John Dando Sedding, "Expression in Architecture," *Transactions of the National Association for the Advancement of Art* (1889):184.

18. Ibid., 158.

19. Lethaby, *Philip Webb and His Work,* 132.

20. William Morris, "The Gothic Revival II," in *The Unpublished Lectures of William Morris,* ed. Eugene LeMire (Detroit: Wayne State University Press, 1969), 82–83.

21. *The Collected Works of William Morris* (New York: Russell and Russell, 1966), 397.

22. Stevenson, *House Architecture,* 1: 48.

23. "Art the Imitation of Nature?" *Building News* 39 (November 19, 1880):519. Another leader on the same subject, "The 'Nature Theory' at the Bar of Fact," appeared on December 3, 1880.

24. "Mr. Morris on Decorative Design," *Building News* 48 (April 17, 1885): 602.

25. "Mr. William Morris on Popular Ar-

tistic Culture," *Building News* 44 (March 9, 1883):582.

26. J. D. Sedding, "The Modern Architect and His Art," *Architect* 32 (November 15, 1884):314.

27. Quoted in H. H. Wilson, "Concerning Drawing," *Architectural Review* 5 (1898):184.

28. *The Recollections of Thomas Graham Jackson* (London: Oxford University Press, 1950):141.

29. Ibid., 199.

30. *Architect* 29 (March 24, 1883):187.

31. J. D. Sedding, "About Modern Design," *Architect* 29 (March 10, 1883):162.

32. J. D. Sedding, "Architecture: Old and New," *British Architect* 15 (June 17, 1881):299.

33. *Recollections of Thomas Graham Jackson,* 58–59.

34. Thomas Graham Jackson, *Modern Gothic Architecture* (London: H. S. King, 1873), 203–204.

35. J. T. Emmett, *Six Essays,* with an introduction by J. Mordaunt Crook (New York: Johnson Reprint Corp., 1972), 31.

36. "Architecture and the Quarterly Review," *Building News* 22 (May 10, 1872):369.

37. J. J. Stevenson, "The Architectural Profession," *British Architect* 11 (January 16, 1875):32.

38. "Assistants and Office Management," *Building News* 22 (May 17, 1872):389.

39. Sedding, "Architecture: Old and New," 299.

40. J. Thomas, "The Movement against Church Restoration," *Builder* 8 (January 19, 1850):29.

41. "Mr. Ruskin's Seven Lamps of Architecture," *Ecclesiologist* 10, n.s. 7 (October 1849):118.

42. "Ruskin's Lamps of Architecture," *English Review* 15 (March 1851):75.

43. "Fine Arts," *Athenaeum,* August 12, 1854, p. 998.

44. "The Restoration Question,"

Builder 8 (August 31, 1850):413.

45. The most useful discussions of the subject can be found in Jane Fawcett, "A Restoration Tragedy: Cathedrals in the Eighteenth and Nineteenth Centuries," in *The Future of the Past,* ed. Jane Fawcett (New York: Watson-Guptill, 1976); and Gavin Stamp, "Sir Gilbert Scott and the 'Restoration' of Mediaeval Buildings," *AA Files* 1 (Winter 1981–1982):89–97.

46. George Gilbert Scott, *A Plea for the Faithful Restoration of Our Ancient Churches* (London: John Henry Parker, 1850):121–122.

47. George Gilbert Scott, *Remarks on Secular and Domestic Architecture, Present and Future* (London: John Murray, 1857):225.

48. "On the Destructive Character of Modern French Restoration," *Builder* 19 (June 22, 1861):423.

49. Ibid.

50. Ibid.

51. *The Correspondence of Thomas Carlyle and John Ruskin,* ed. George Allen Cate (Stanford: Stanford University Press, 1982), 180.

52. John Harris, "The Ruskin Gold Medal Controversy" *RIBA Journal* 70 (April 1963):166.

53. Ibid.

54. "A Shameful Assertion," *Builder* 35 (June 23, 1877):642.

55. *Correspondence of Thomas Carlyle and John Ruskin,* 190.

56. J. J. Stevenson, "Architectural Restoration: Its Principles and Practice," *RIBA Transactions,* 1876–1877, p. 225.

57. George Aitchison, "Ancient Buildings: What Principles Should Govern Their Restoration or Their Preservation," *Builder* 35 (September 29, 1877):983.

CHAPTER XIII. RUSKIN'S INFLUENCE IN AMERICA

1. Quoted in Francis G. Townsend, "The American Estimate of Ruskin, 1847–1860," *Philological Quarterly* 32 (January 1953):75. The American response to Ruskin is discussed in Roger B. Stein, *John Ruskin and Aesthetic Thought in America* (Cambridge: Harvard University Press, 1967). Ruskin's specifically architectural influence is discussed in Henry-Russell Hitchcock, "Ruskin and American Architecture, or Regeneration Long Delayed," in *Concerning Architecture,* ed. John Summerson (London: Penguin Press, 1968).

2. Quoted in Sarah Bradford Landau, *Edward T. and William A. Potter* (New York: Garland, 1979), 100.

3. W. J. Stillman, *Autobiography of a Journalist* (Boston: Houghton, Mifflin, 1901), 1:222.

4. J. Coleman Hart, "Unity in Architecture," *Crayon* 6 (March 1859):85.

5. "Book Notices," *Crayon* 1 (January 24, 1855):58.

6. "The Oxford Museum," *Crayon* 6 (August 1859):251.

7. Leopold Eidlitz, "Cast Iron and Architecture," *Crayon* 5 (January 1859):22.

8. Leopold Eidlitz, "On Style," *Crayon* 5 (May 1858):141.

9. Ibid., 140.

10. Leopold Eidlitz, "On Aesthetics in Architecture," *Crayon* 8 (April 1861):112.

11. Leopold Eidlitz, "Christian Architecture," *Crayon* 5 (February 1858):53.

12. Quoted in Montgomery Schuyler, "A Great American Architect: Leopold Eidlitz," in *American Architecture,* ed. William H. Jordy and Ralph Coe (Cambridge: Harvard University Press, 1961), 1:143.

13. Leopold Eidlitz, *The Nature and Function of Art* (New York: A. C. Armstrong, 1881), 38.

14. Russell Sturgis, "Our 'Architects' Examined," New Path 1 (May 1863):33.
15. P. B. Wight, "What Has Been Done and What Can Be Done," New Path 1 (September 1863):53.
16. Russell Sturgis, "An Important Gothic Building," New Path 2 (May 1864):21.
17. Russell Sturgis, "Our 'Articles' Examined," New Path 1 (July 1863):36.
18. Ibid., 20.
19. Ibid., 21.
20. Wight, "What Has Been Done and What Can Be Done," 58.
21. Sturgis, "Our 'Articles' Examined," June 1863, p. 46.
22. Wight, "What Has Been Done and What Can Be Done," October 1863, p. 74.
23. Ibid.
24. [Russell Sturgis,] "Viollet-le-Duc's French Mediaeval Architecture," Nation 9 (August 26, 1869):173. Sturgis is identified as the author in Poole's Index to Periodical Literature.
25. Russell Sturgis, "Art Criticism and Ruskin's Writing on Art," Scribner's 27 (April 1900):512.
26. Russell Sturgis, Ruskin on Architecture (New York: D. Appleton, 1906), v.
27. P. B. Wight, "The Possibilities of American Architecture," Inland Architect 29 (July 1897):55.
28. Russell Sturgis, "Modern Architecture," North American Review 112 (April 1871):379, 391.
29. "Architecture," Crayon 3 (July 1856):215.
30. Henry Van Brunt, "Cast Iron in Decorative Architecture," Crayon 6 (January 1859):17.
31. Wight, "What Has Been Done and What Can Be Done," September 1863, p. 55.
32. P. B. Wight, "Remarks on Fire-Proof Construction," Committee on Library and Publications, American

Institute of Architecture, New York, 1869, p. 59.
33. Russell Sturgis, "Modern Architecture," North American Review 71 (January 1871):161.
34. Percy Morley Horder to John Ruskin, March 2, 1887, in the British Architectural Library, RIBA, London, Manuscripts and Archives Collection, P. R. Mornley Horder Papers, HoPR/1/1/1. Kristine Ottesen Garrigan comments on Ruskin's attitude toward Viollet-le-Duc in Ruskin on Architecture, 86–88.
35. P. B. Wight, "Modern Architecture in Chicago," Pall Mall Magazine 18 (July 1899):299.
36. The building is discussed in Robert B. Shaffer, "Ruskin, Norton, and Memorial Hall," Harvard Library Bulletin 3 (Spring 1949):213–231.
37. Ibid., 216.
38. Henry Van Brunt, "Architectural Reform," in Architecture and Society, ed. William A. Coles (Cambridge: Harvard University Press, 1969), 91.
39. Henry Van Brunt, "Introduction to Viollet-le-Duc's Discourses," in Coles, Architecture and Society, 101.
40. Withers's career is explored in detail in Francis R. Kowsky, The Architecture of Frederick Clark Withers (Middletown, Conn.: Wesleyan University Press, 1980).
41. Furness's work is discussed in James F. O'Gorman, The Architecture of Frank Furness (Philadelphia: Philadelphia Museum of Art, 1973).
42. William H. Furness, "The Architect An Artist," Penn Monthly 2 (June 1871):304.
43. The Potters' works are discussed in Sarah Bradford Landau, Edward T. and William A. Potter (New York: Garland, 1979).
44. Ibid., 171.
45. P. B. Wight, "H. H. Richardson," Inland Architect 7 (May 1886):60.
46. John Wellborn Root, "Architectural

Freedom," *Inland Architect* 8 (December 1886):65.

47. John Wellborn Root, "Architectural Ornamentation," *Inland Architect* 5 (April 1885):54.

48. Ibid., 55.

49. Montgomery Schuyler, "Glimpses of Western Architecture," in Jordy and Coe, *American Architecture*, 265, 183.

50. "American Architecture," *Architectural Record* 2 (July–September 1892):105.

CHAPTER XIV. THE GUILD MOVEMENT AND THE DECLINE OF RUSKINISM

1. Hansom's early Owenite socialism is discussed in my article, "The *Builder* in the 1840's: The Making of a Magazine, The Shaping of a Profession," *Victorian Periodicals Review* 14 (Fall 1981):87–93.

2. I am indebted to Malcolm Haslam's account of Mackmurdo's career in "A Pioneer of Art Nouveau," *Country Life* 157 (February 27, 1975; March 6, 1975):504–506, 574–579. The Century Guild, as well as the Art Workers' Guild, is described in Peter Stansky, *Redesigning the World* (Princeton: Princeton University Press, 1985).

3. Arthur Mackmurdo, "A History of the Arts and Crafts Movement," manuscript in the William Morris Gallery, Walthamstow, 88–89. Quoted by permission of the trustees of the William Morris Gallery.

4. Ibid.

5. "Two Letters of John Ruskin," *Ceylon Causerie,* June 1938, pp. 18–19.

6. Work by associates of Mackmurdo is discussed and illustrated in Gleeson White, "The Work of Heywood Sumner," *Studio* 4 (May 1898): 153–163; and in "The Work of Mr. Selwyn Image," *Studio* 5 (June 1898):3–10.

7. Oscar Wilde, "*L'envoi,*" in *The Complete Works of Oscar Wilde* (New York: National Library Company, 1909), 6:31.

8. Selwyn Image, "The Representation of the Nude," *Hobby Horse* 1 (1886):80.

9. Arthur Mackmurdo, "The Presidential Address," *Transactions of the National Association for the Advancement of Art, 1891,* 170.

10. Ibid., 165.

11. Jay Wood Claiborne, "Two Secretaries: The Letters of John Ruskin to Charles Augustus Howell and the Rev. Richard St. John Tyrwhitt," Ph.D. diss., University of Texas, 1969, p. 295.

12. Arthur Mackmurdo, *Wren's City Churches* (Orpington: George Allen, 1883), 48–59.

13. "Wren's City Churches," *Builder* 46 (April 16, 1884):567.

14. Herbert Spencer, *Autobiography* (New York: Appleton, 1904), 1: 403–404.

15. Moncure Conway, *Autobiography* (New York: Houghton Mifflin, 1905), 2:373.

16. "Liverpool Art Club," *Architect* 42 (December 6, 1889):332.

17. "Haslam, "A Pioneer of Art Nouveau," 506.

18. C. F. A. Voysey, "The Aims and Conditions of the Modern Decorator," *Journal Of Decorative Art* 15 (1895):85–86.

19. "On Craftsmanship," *Architectural Association Notes* 19 (1904):72.

20. R. W. S. Weir, *William Richard Lethaby* (London: Central School of Arts and Crafts, 1938), 7.

21. Reginald Blomfield, "W. R. Lethaby," *RIBA Journal* 39 (1932): 5–6.

22. W. R. Lethaby, "English and French Renaissance," *Architect* 29 (June 30, 1883):434.

23. W. R. Lethaby, "Ernest Gimson's London Days," in *Ernest Gimson: His Life and Work* (Stratford-upon-Avon: Shakespeare Head Press, 1924), 2.

24. W. R. Lethaby, *Architecture, Mysticism, and Myth* (New York: Braziller, 1975), 1–2.

25. Thomas Graham Jackson, "Introduction," in *Architecture, A Profession or an Art?* ed. R. Norman Shaw and T. G. Jackson (London: John Murray, 1892), 12.

26. The consequences of this debate are described in Andrew Saint, *The Image of the Architect* (New Haven: Yale University Press, 1983), 19–51.

27. W. R. Lethaby, "Education in Building," *Builder* 80 (June 22, 1901): 603.

28. Ibid., 605.

29. Ibid.

30. Quoted in *Friends of a Lifetime: Letters to Sydney Carlyle Cockerell,* ed. Viola Meynell (London: Jonathan Cape, 1940), 130.

31. Halsey Ricardo, "On Some of the Conditions of Modern Architecture in Towns," *Architect* 43 (February 28, 1890): 132.

32. Ibid., March 7, 1890, p. 154.

33. This house is discussed and extensively illustrated in "An Essay in Colour Architecture," *Architectural Review* 21 (1907): 159–173.

34. *Beauty's Awakening: A Masque of Winter and Spring* (London, Printed for the Art Workers' Guild by the Guild of Handicraft, 1899): 26, 29.

35. Information on Ashbee can be found in Alan Crawford, *C. R. Ashbee* (New Haven: Yale University Press, 1985); Gilian Naylor, *The Arts and Crafts Movement* (Cambridge: MIT Press, 1971); and in Shirley Bury, "An Arts and Crafts Experiment: The Silverwork of C. R. Ashbee," *Victoria and Albert Museum Bulletin* 3 (January 1967): 18–25.

36. See Steven Marcus, *The Other Victorians* (New York: Basic Books, 1966), 34–76.

37. C. R. Ashbee, *Socialism and Politics* (Camden: Essex House Press, 1906), 4.

38. C. R. Ashbee, "The Relation of the Architect to the Workmen," *Building News* 43 (June 3, 1892): 759.

39. Ibid.

40. Quoted in Alan Crawford, "Ten Letters from Frank Lloyd Wright to Charles Robert Ashbee," *Architectural History* 13 (1970): 64.

41. C. R. Ashbee, *An Endeavour toward the Teaching of John Ruskin and William Morris* (Camden: Essex House Press, 1901), 29.

42. C. R. Ashbee, *A Book of Cottages and Little Houses* (London: Batsford, 1906), 107.

43. C. R. Ashbee, *Should We Stop Teaching Art* (London: Batsford, 1911).

44. "Books," *Building News* 43 (August 25, 1882): 227.

45. Hugh Rouimeu Gough, "Royal Institute of British Architects—Presidential Address," *Building News* 49 (November 6, 1885): 719.

46. "Reviews of Recent Publications," *Studio* 2 (July 1897): 65.

47. "Ruskin's Influence on Architecture," *Builder* 78 (January 27, 1900): 73.

48. "John Ruskin," *Architect and Contract Reporter* 115 (January 26, 1900): 58.

49. Henry Wilson, "The Education of the Architect," *RIBA Journal* 24 (September 1917): 255.

50. Quoted in Andrew Saint, *Richard Norman Shaw* (New Haven: Yale University Press, 1976), 321.

51. "Notes," *Architectural Review* 21 (1907): 71.

CHAPTER XV. SUMMARY AND AFTERMATH

1. Quoted by David Verey in "George Frederick Bodley," in *Seven Victorian Architects*, ed. Jane Fawcett (University Park: Pennsylvania State University Press, 1977), 84.

2. Mark Girouard, *The Victorian Country House* (Oxford: Clarendon Press, 1971), 165.

3. H. H. Statham, "The Truth about Ruskin," *Fortnightly* 73 (March 1900):424.

4. H. H. Statham, "The Order in Modern Architecture," *Builder* 85 (November 7, 1903):458.

5. "The New Edition of 'The Stones of Venice,'" *Builder* 78 (January 27, 1900):73.

6. "A French Exposition of Ruskin," *Builder* 73 (July 3, 1897):1.

7. "Books," *Builder* 75 (July 15, 1899):59.

8. "Ruskin's Influence on Architecture," *Builder* 78 (January 27, 1900):73.

9. *Builder* 78 (April 21, 1900):396.

10. "The Ruskin Exhibition," *Builder* 80 (February 9, 1901):128.

11. Quoted in Christopher Hussey, *The Life of Sir Edwin Lutyens* (New York: Scribner, 1950), 128.

12. Quoted in ibid., 120.

13. Quoted in ibid., 112.

14. Reginald Blomfield, "W. R. Lethaby: An Impression and a Tribute," *RIBA Journal* 39 (1932):296.

15. Reginald Blomfield, "Municipal Bodies and Architecture," *Architectural Review* 2 (1902):112.

16. Reginald Blomfield, "The Criticism of Architecture," *Builder* 54 (November 7, 1913):483.

17. Reginald Blomfield, "On Architectural Education," *RIBA Journal* 12 (1905):240.

18. Geoffrey Scott, *The Architecture of Humanism* (Garden City, N.J.: Doubleday, 1956):98.

19. Ibid., 157.

20. Kenneth Clark, *The Gothic Revival* (Harmondsworth: Penguin Books, 1964), xiv.

21. Quoted in Reyner Banham, *Theory and Design in the First Machine Age* (London: Architectural Press, 1960), 123.

22. *Frank Lloyd Wright: Writings and Buildings*, ed. Edgar Kaufman and Ben Raeburn (New York: Meridian Books, 1960), 64.

23. W. R. Lethaby, "A National Architecture—IV," *Builder* 115 (October 25, 1918):261.

24. W. R. Lethaby, *Form in Civilization* (London: Oxford University Press, 1957), 197.

25. Quoted in Fiona MacCarthy, *All Things Bright and Beautiful: Design in Britain 1830 to Today* (London: George Allen and Unwin, 1972), 78–79.

26. W. R. Lethaby, "A National Architecture—IX," *Builder* 115 (November 29, 1918):405.

27. W. R. Lethaby, "Observations and Suggestions—VII," *Builder* 117 (August 1, 1919):115.

28. W. R. Lethaby, "A National Architecture—II," *Builder* 115 (October 11, 1918):229.

29. W. R. Lethaby, "Observations and Suggestions—VIII," *Builder* 117 (September 5, 1919):239.

30. W. R. Lethaby, "The Beauty of Structures and Make-Believe Styles," *Builder* 117 (September 19, 1919):287.

31. W. R. Lethaby, "A National Architecture—I," *Builder* 115 (October 4, 1918):213.

32. W. R. Lethaby, "A National Architecture—III," *Builder* 115 (October 18, 1918):243.

33. Lethaby, *Form in Civilization*, 164.

34. Ibid., 146.

35. Ibid., 184.

INDEX

(Figures in italic are illustration numbers.)